For You in Full Blossom

19

story and art by
HISAYA NAKAJO

HANA-KIMI
For You in Full Blossom
VOLUME 19

STORY & ART BY HISAYA NAKAJO

Translation & English Adaptation/David Ury
Touch-Up Art & Lettering/Primary Graphix
Design/Izumi Evers
Editor/Jason Thompson

Editor in Chief, Books/Alvin Lu
Editor in Chief, Magazines/Marc Weidenbaum
VP of Publishing Licensing/Rika Inouye
VP of Sales/Gonzalo Ferreyra
Sr. VP of Marketing/Liza Coppola
Publisher/Hyoe Narita

Printed in the U.S.A.

Published by VIZ Media, LLC, P.O. Box 77010, San Francisco, CA 94107

Shôjo Edition
10 9 8 7 6 5 4 3 2

First printing, August 2007
Second printing, August 2007

www.viz.com
store.viz.com

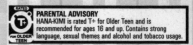

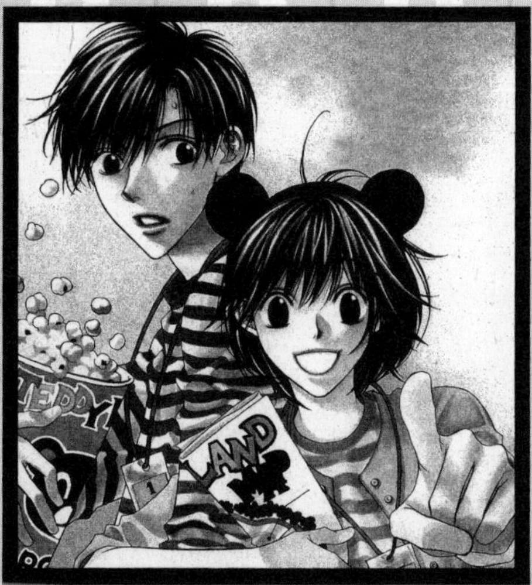
LAND

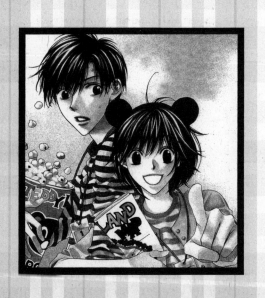

CONTENTS

Hana-Kimi Chapter 105 5

Hana-Kimi Chapter 106 27

Hana-Kimi Chapter 107 57

Hana-Kimi Chapter 108 89

Hana-Kimi Chapter 109 119

Hana-Kimi Chapter 110 143

Hana-Kimi Chapter 111 169

About the Author...191

Previews 192

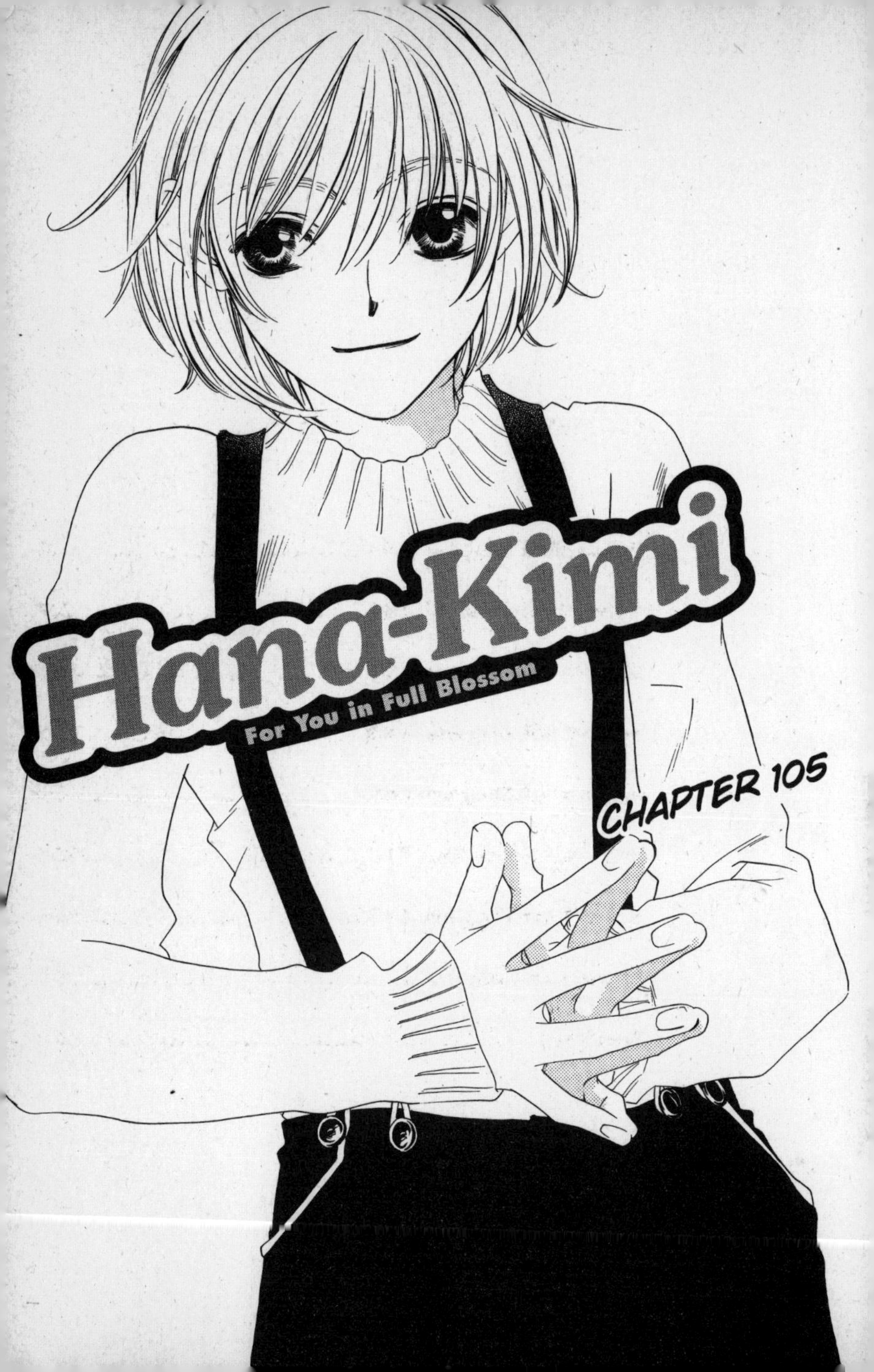
Hana-Kimi
For You in Full Blossom
CHAPTER 105

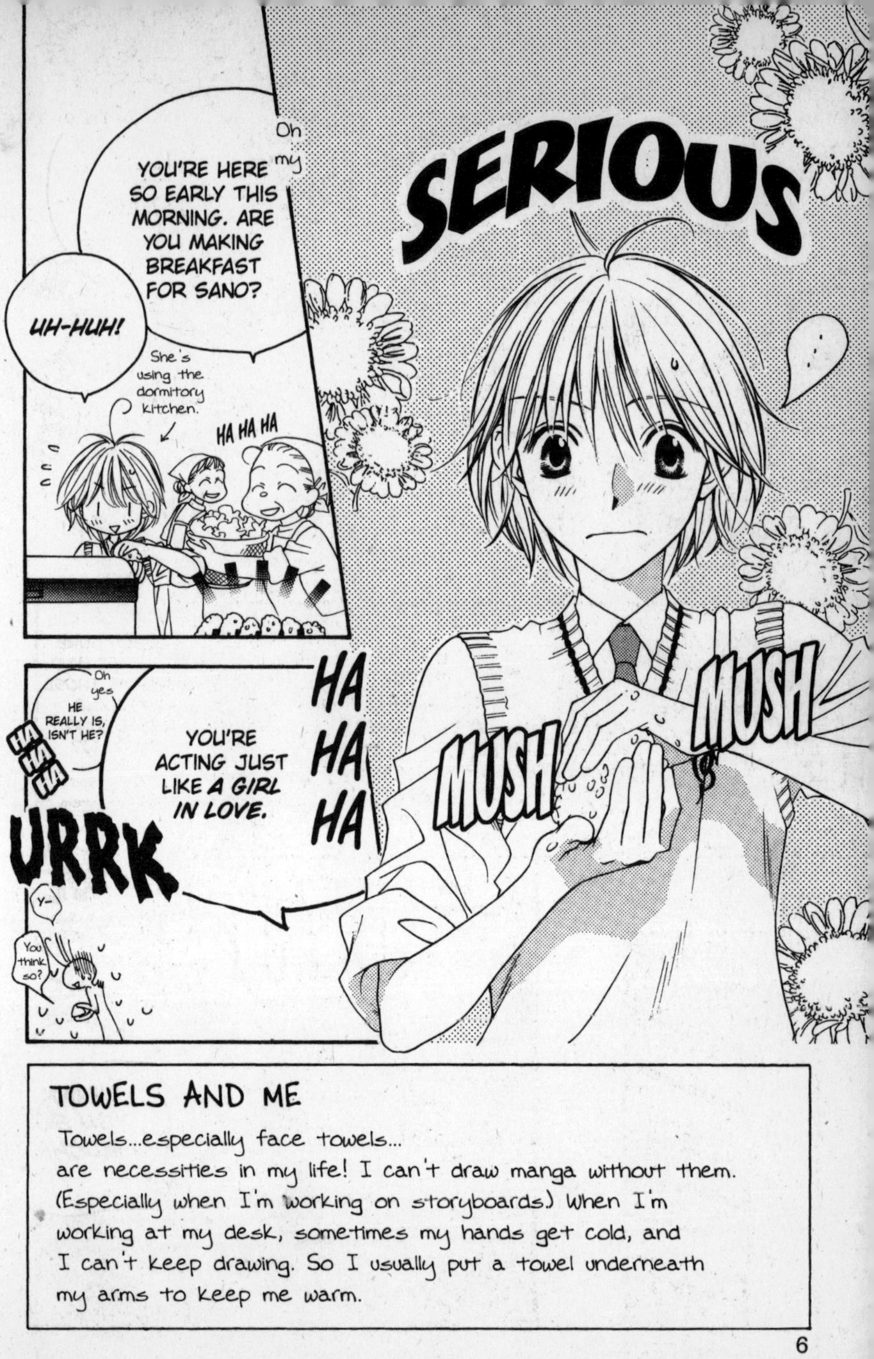
SERIOUS
MUSH
MUSH
Oh my
YOU'RE HERE SO EARLY THIS MORNING. ARE YOU MAKING BREAKFAST FOR SANO?
UH-HUH!
She's using the dormitory kitchen.
HA HA HA
HA HA HA
YOU'RE ACTING JUST LIKE A GIRL IN LOVE.
Oh yes
HE REALLY IS, ISN'T HE?
HA HA HA
URRK
Y-
You think so?

TOWELS AND ME

Towels...especially face towels...
are necessities in my life! I can't draw manga without them. (Especially when I'm working on storyboards.) When I'm working at my desk, sometimes my hands get cold, and I can't keep drawing. So I usually put a towel underneath my arms to keep me warm.

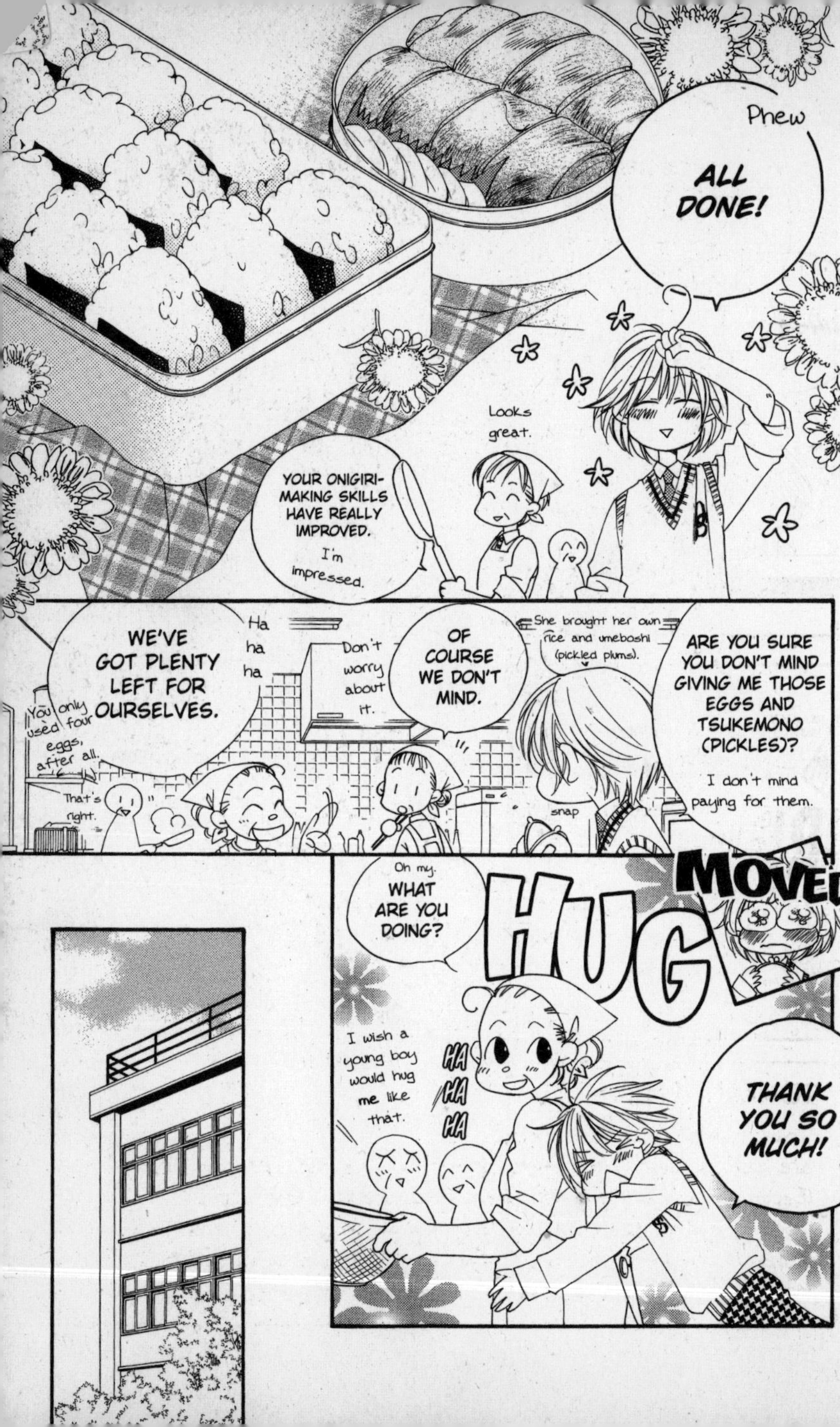
Phew
ALL DONE!
Looks great.
YOUR ONIGIRI-MAKING SKILLS HAVE REALLY IMPROVED.
I'm impressed.
ARE YOU SURE YOU DON'T MIND GIVING ME THOSE EGGS AND TSUKEMONO (PICKLES)?
I don't mind paying for them.
She brought her own rice and umeboshi (pickled plums).
snap
OF COURSE WE DON'T MIND.
Don't worry about it.
Ha ha ha
WE'VE GOT PLENTY LEFT FOR OURSELVES.
You only used four eggs, after all.
That's right.
MOVED
HUG
Oh my. WHAT ARE YOU DOING?
THANK YOU SO MUCH!
HA HA HA
I wish a young boy would hug me like that.

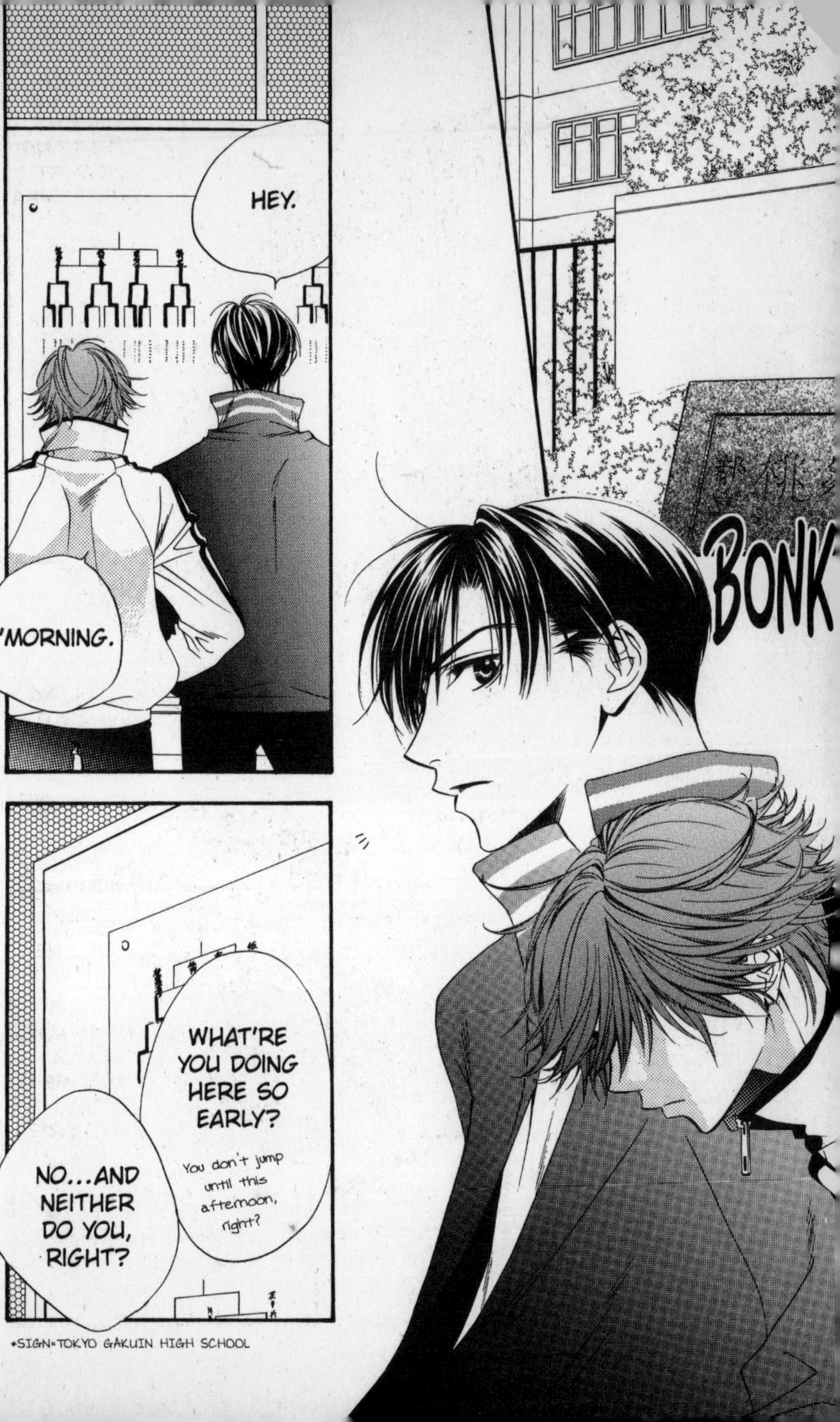
BONK
HEY.
'MORNING.
WHAT'RE YOU DOING HERE SO EARLY?
You don't jump until this afternoon, right?
NO...AND NEITHER DO YOU, RIGHT?

*SIGN=TOKYO GAKUIN HIGH SCHOOL

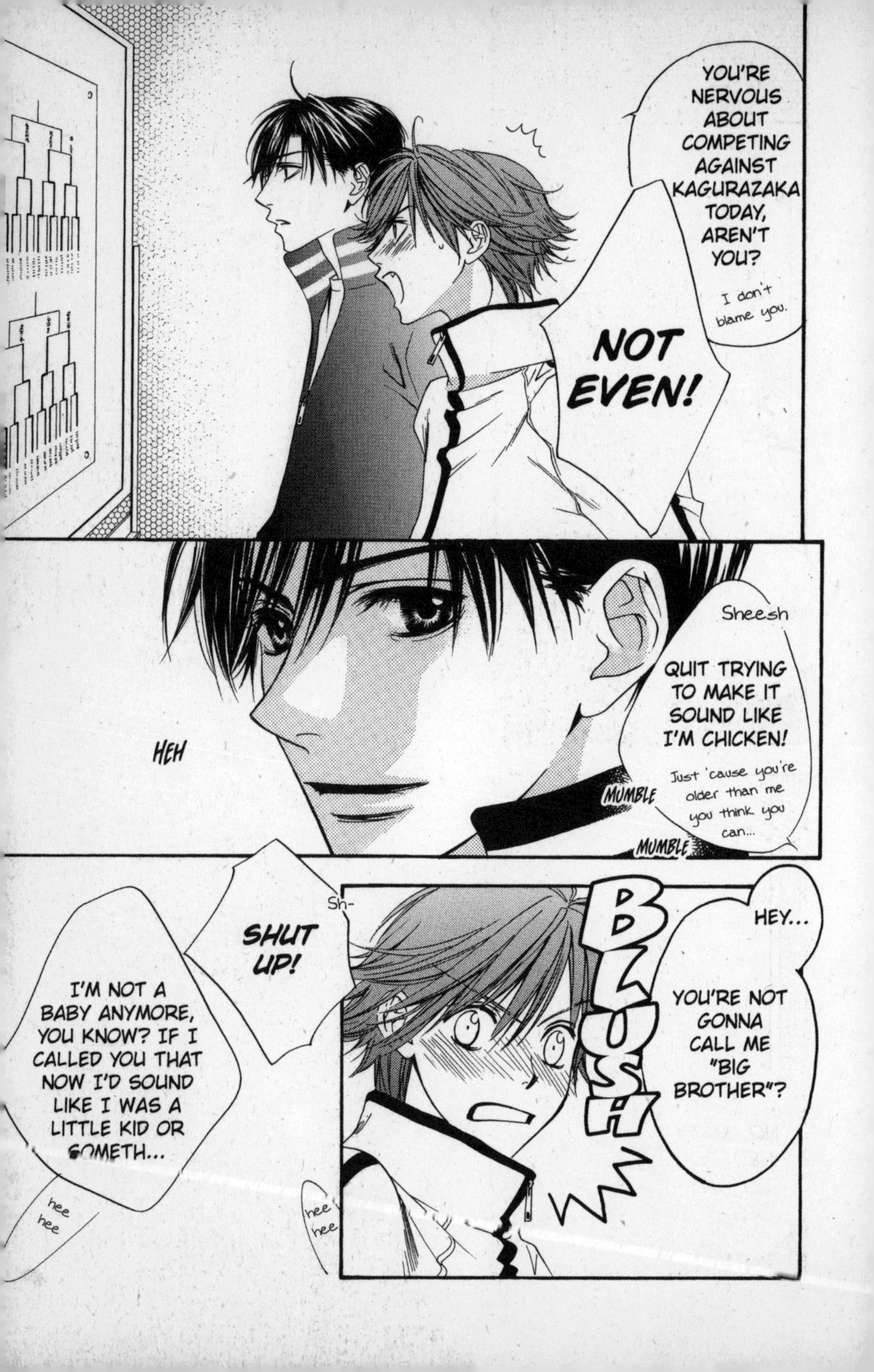
YOU'RE NERVOUS ABOUT COMPETING AGAINST KAGURAZAKA TODAY, AREN'T YOU?
I don't blame you.
NOT EVEN!
Sheesh
QUIT TRYING TO MAKE IT SOUND LIKE I'M CHICKEN!
Just 'cause you're older than me you think you can...
MUMBLE
MUMBLE
HEH
HEY...
YOU'RE NOT GONNA CALL ME "BIG BROTHER"?
BLUSH
Sh-
SHUT UP!
I'M NOT A BABY ANYMORE, YOU KNOW? IF I CALLED YOU THAT NOW I'D SOUND LIKE I WAS A LITTLE KID OR SOMETH...
hee hee
hee hee

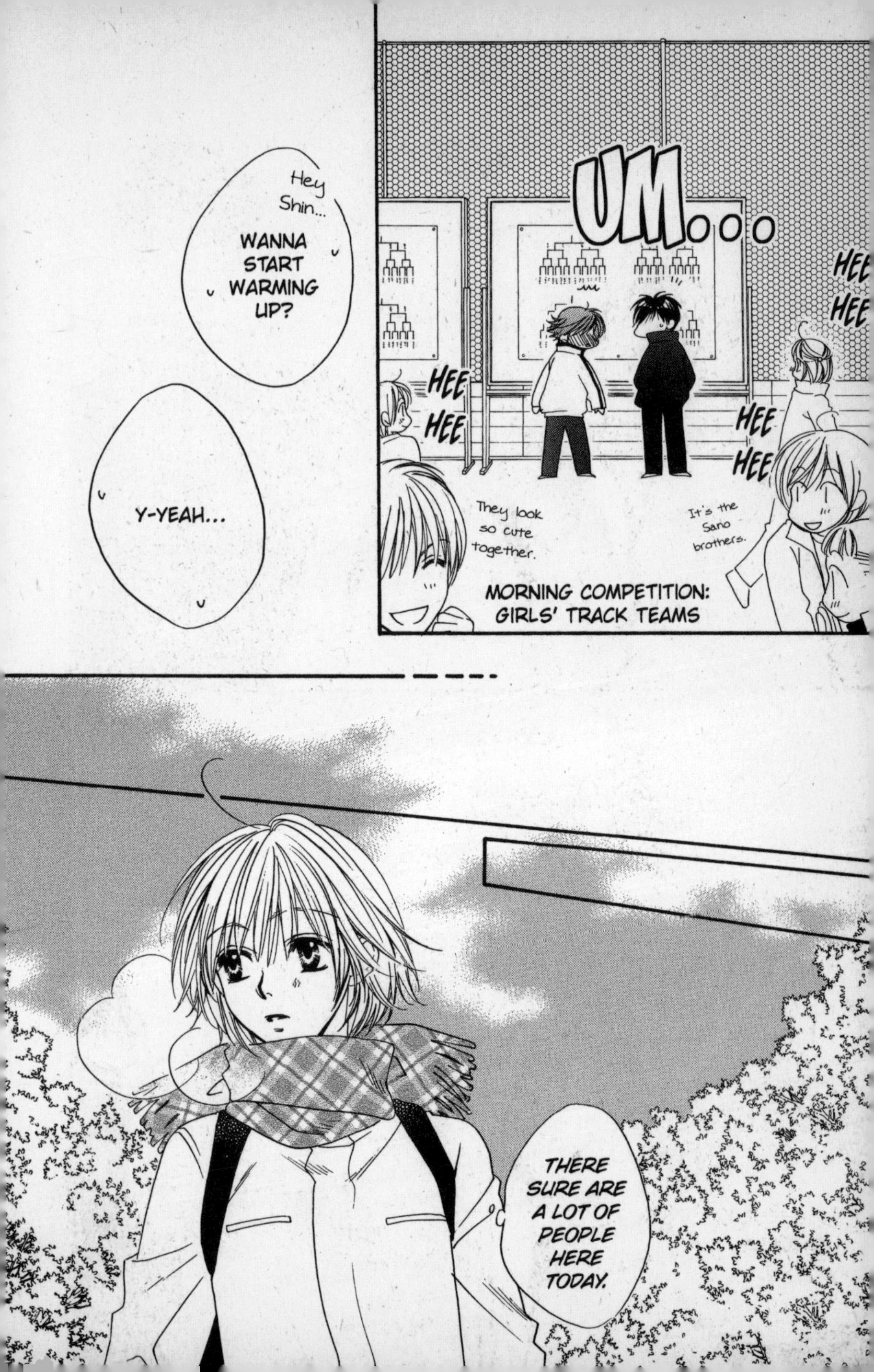
HEE HEE
UMooo
HEE HEE
HEE HEE
It's the Sano brothers.
They look so cute together.
MORNING COMPETITION: GIRLS' TRACK TEAMS
Hey Shin... WANNA START WARMING UP?
Y-YEAH...
THERE SURE ARE A LOT OF PEOPLE HERE TODAY.

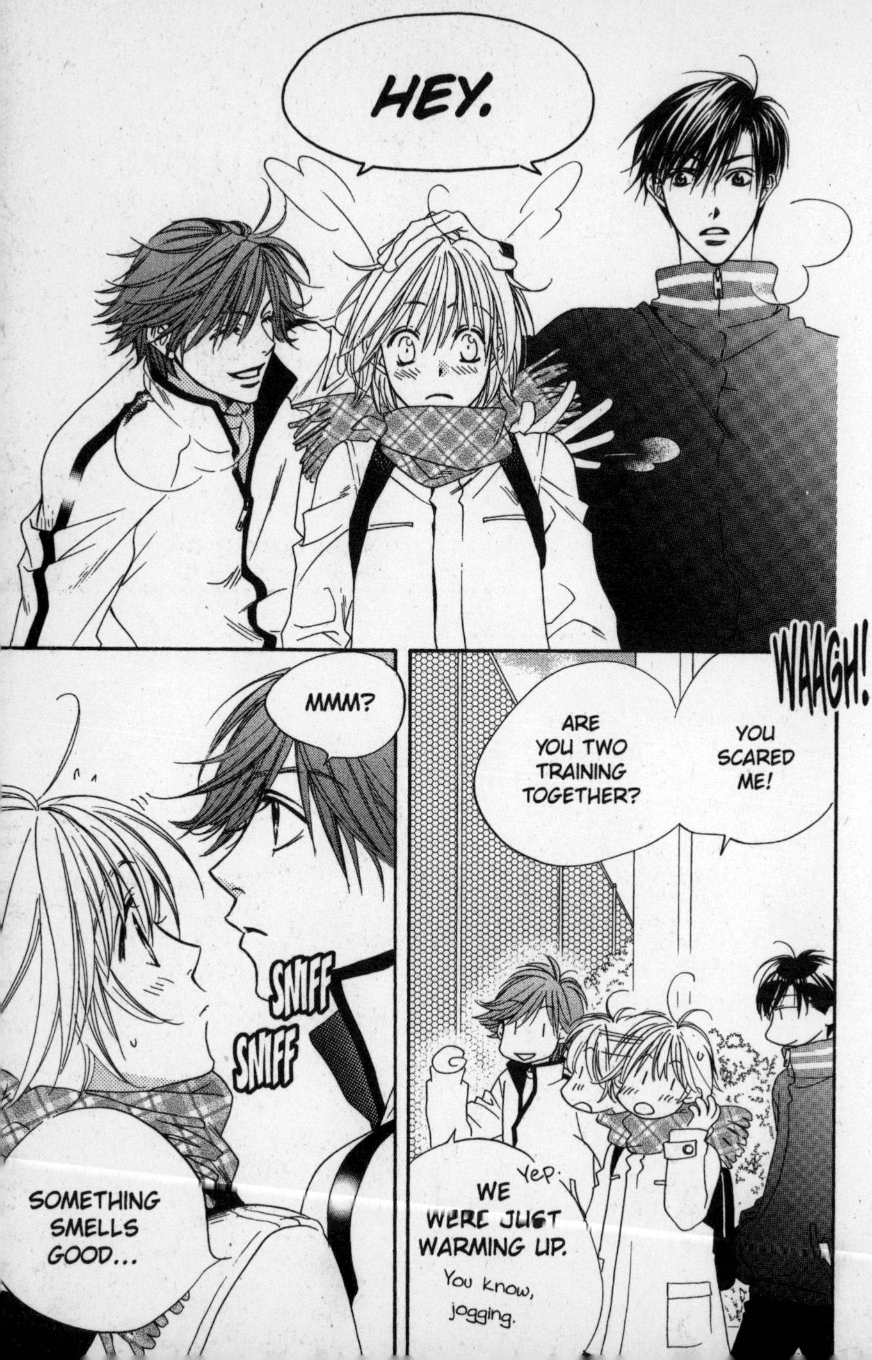
HEY.
WAAGH!
YOU SCARED ME!
ARE YOU TWO TRAINING TOGETHER?
Yep.
WE WERE JUST WARMING UP.
You know, jogging.
MMM?
SNIFF
SNIFF
SOMETHING SMELLS GOOD...

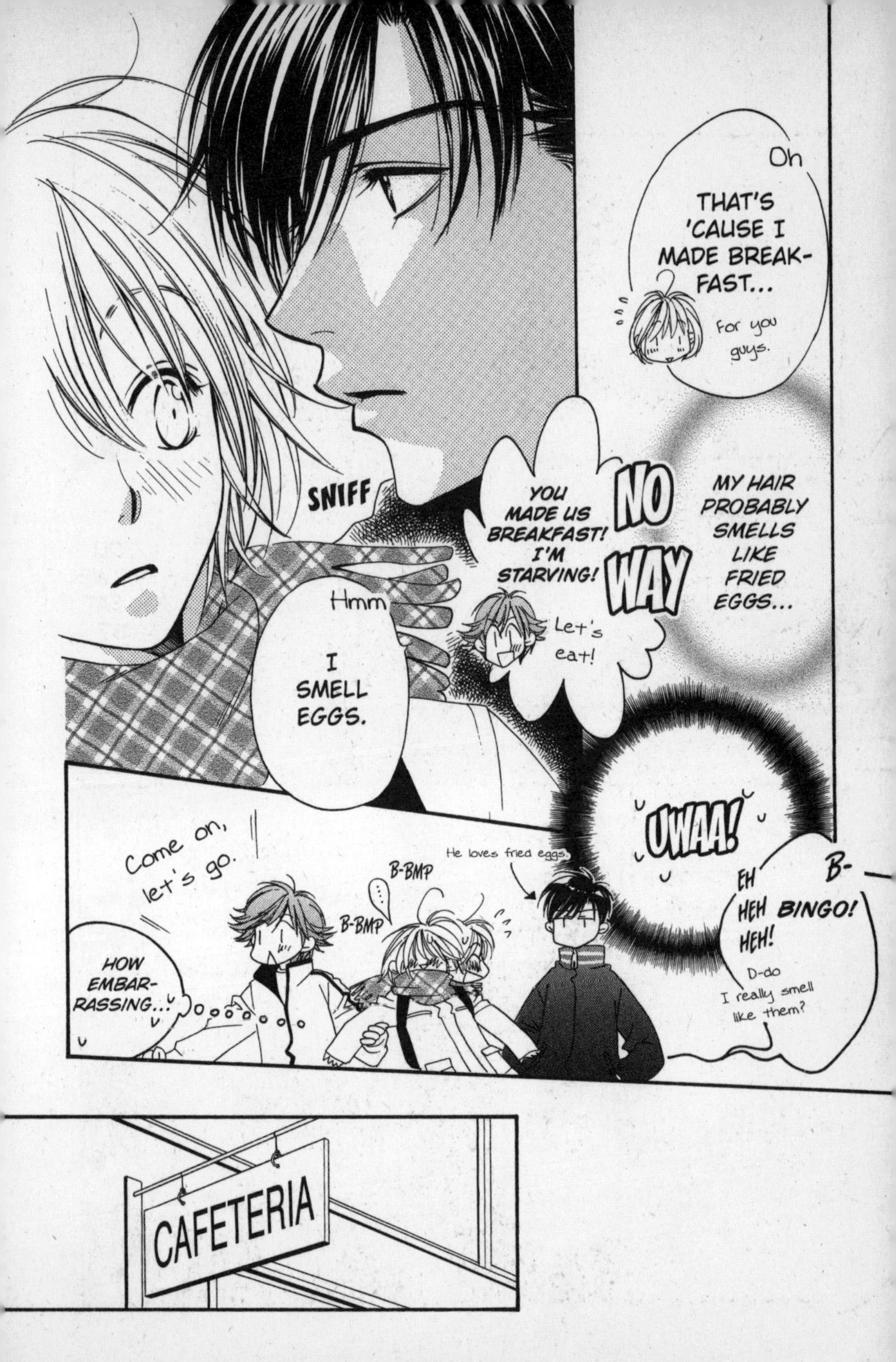
Oh
THAT'S 'CAUSE I MADE BREAK-FAST...
For you guys.
MY HAIR PROBABLY SMELLS LIKE FRIED EGGS...
NO WAY
YOU MADE US BREAKFAST! I'M STARVING!
Let's eat!
SNIFF
Hmm
I SMELL EGGS.
UWAA!
B-BINGO!
EH HEH HEH!
D-do I really smell like them?
He loves fried eggs.
B-BMP
...
B-BMP
Come on, let's go.
HOW EMBARRASSING...
CAFETERIA

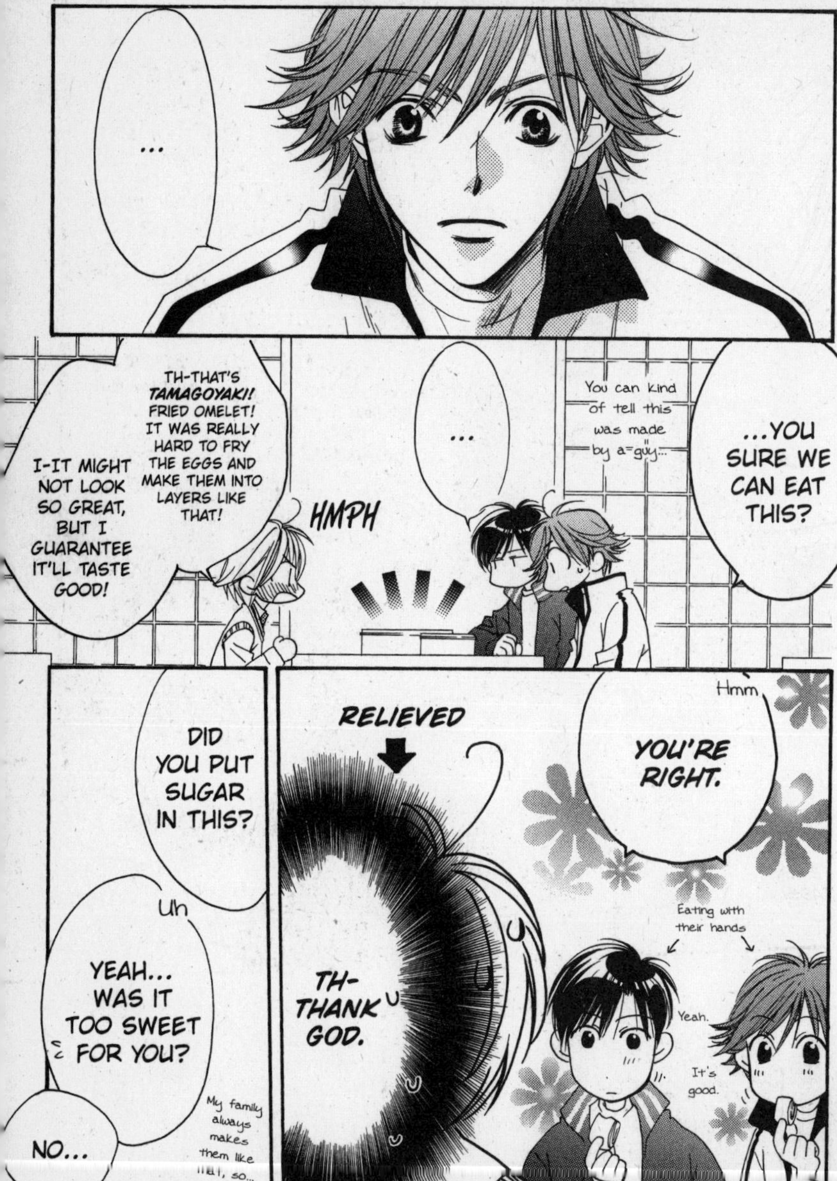
...
...YOU SURE WE CAN EAT THIS?
You can kind of tell this was made by a guy...
...
HMPH
TH-THAT'S TAMAGOYAKI! FRIED OMELET! IT WAS REALLY HARD TO FRY THE EGGS AND MAKE THEM INTO LAYERS LIKE THAT!
I-IT MIGHT NOT LOOK SO GREAT, BUT I GUARANTEE IT'LL TASTE GOOD!
Hmm
YOU'RE RIGHT.
RELIEVED
TH-THANK GOD.
Eating with their hands
Yeah.
It's good.
DID YOU PUT SUGAR IN THIS?
Uh
YEAH... WAS IT TOO SWEET FOR YOU?
NO...
My family always makes them like that, so...

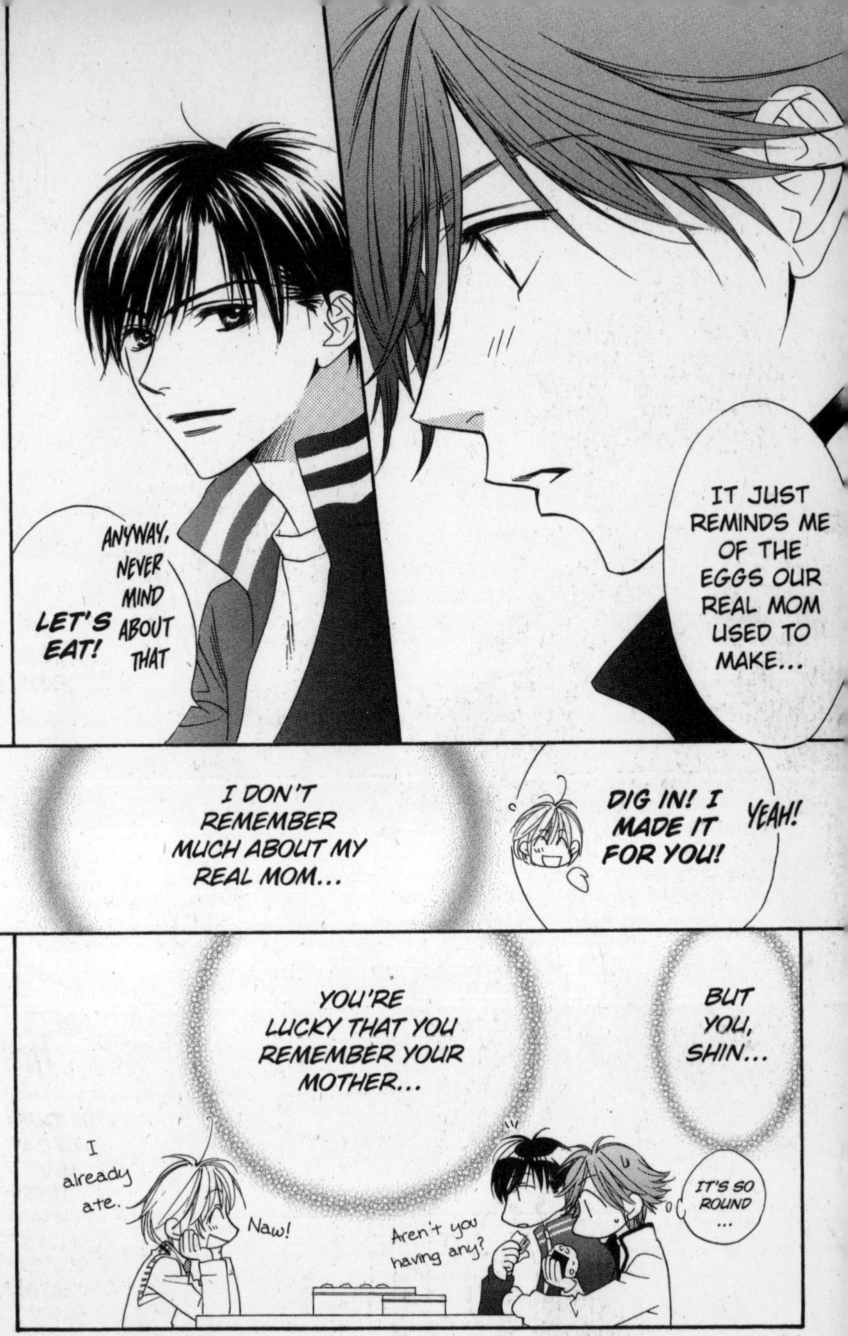
IT JUST REMINDS ME OF THE EGGS OUR REAL MOM USED TO MAKE...
ANYWAY, NEVER MIND ABOUT THAT
LET'S EAT!
DIG IN! I MADE IT FOR YOU!
YEAH!
I DON'T REMEMBER MUCH ABOUT MY REAL MOM...
BUT YOU, SHIN...
YOU'RE LUCKY THAT YOU REMEMBER YOUR MOTHER...
IT'S SO ROUND...
Aren't you having any?
Naw!
I already ate.

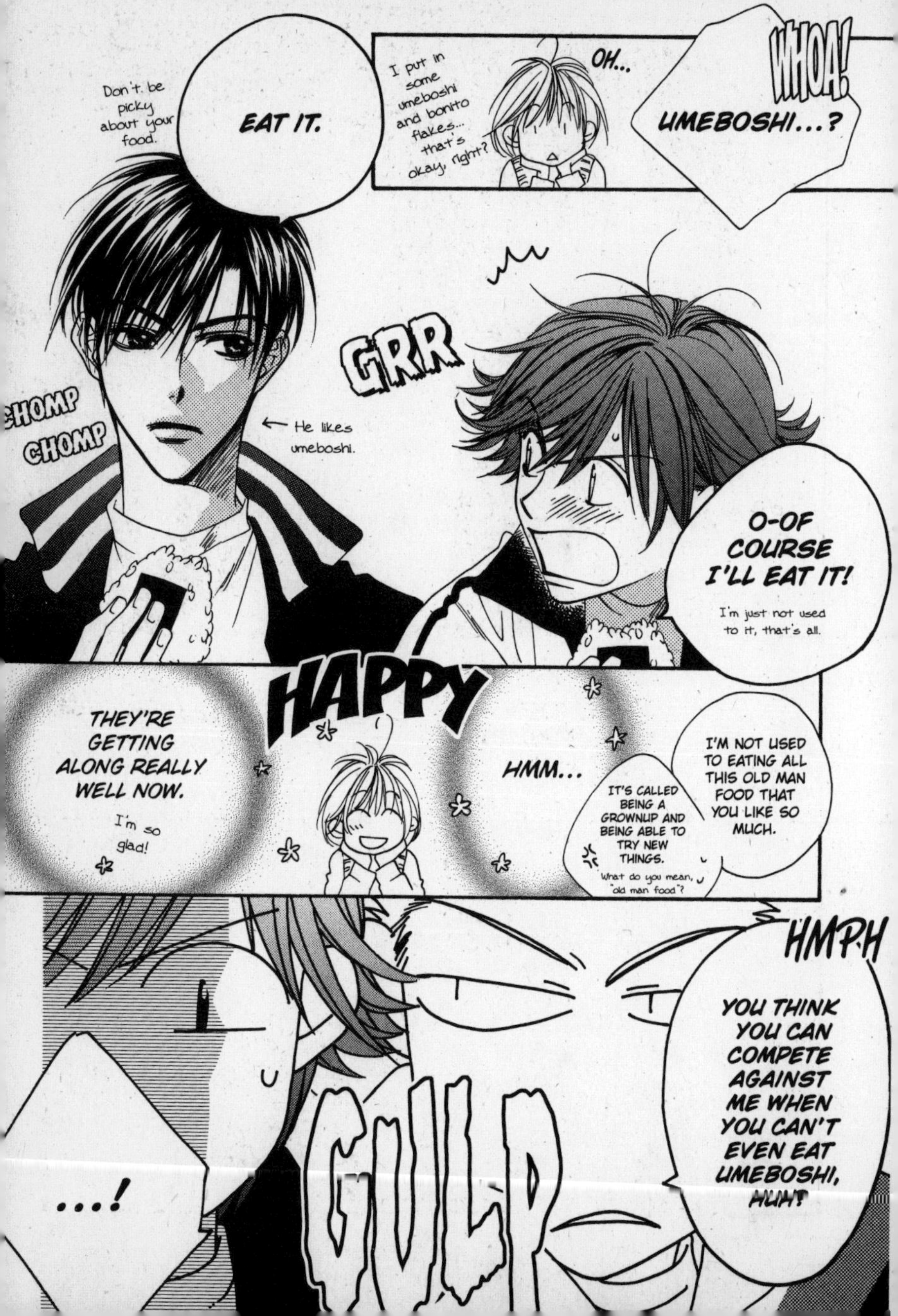
WHOA!
UMEBOSHI...?
OH...
I put in some umeboshi and bonito flakes... that's okay, right?
EAT IT.
Don't be picky about your food.
GRR
O-OF COURSE I'LL EAT IT!
I'm just not used to it, that's all.
CHOMP CHOMP
He likes umeboshi.
I'M NOT USED TO EATING ALL THIS OLD MAN FOOD THAT YOU LIKE SO MUCH.
IT'S CALLED BEING A GROWNUP AND BEING ABLE TO TRY NEW THINGS.
What do you mean, "old man food"?
HMM...
HAPPY
THEY'RE GETTING ALONG REALLY WELL NOW.
I'm so glad!
HMPH
YOU THINK YOU CAN COMPETE AGAINST ME WHEN YOU CAN'T EVEN EAT UMEBOSHI, HUH?
GULP
...!

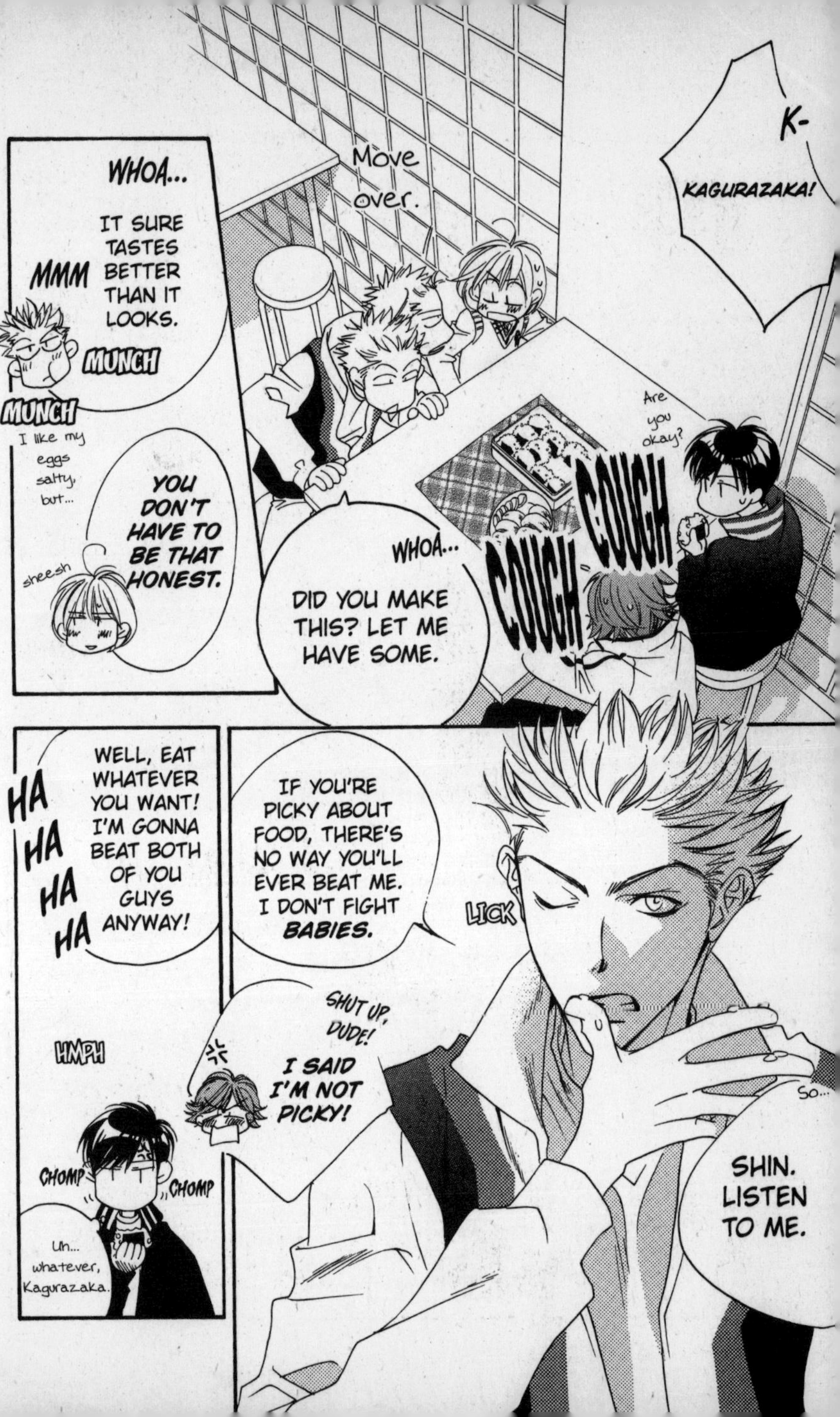
K-
KAGURAZAKA!
Move over.
Are you okay?
COUGH COUGH
WHOA...
DID YOU MAKE THIS? LET ME HAVE SOME.
WHOA...
IT SURE TASTES BETTER THAN IT LOOKS.
MMM
MUNCH
MUNCH
I like my eggs salty, but...
YOU DON'T HAVE TO BE THAT HONEST.
sheesh
So...
SHIN. LISTEN TO ME.
LICK
IF YOU'RE PICKY ABOUT FOOD, THERE'S NO WAY YOU'LL EVER BEAT ME. I DON'T FIGHT BABIES.
SHUT UP, DUDE!
I SAID I'M NOT PICKY!
HMPH
WELL, EAT WHATEVER YOU WANT! I'M GONNA BEAT BOTH OF YOU GUYS ANYWAY!
HA HA HA HA
CHOMP
CHOMP
Uh... whatever, Kagurazaka.

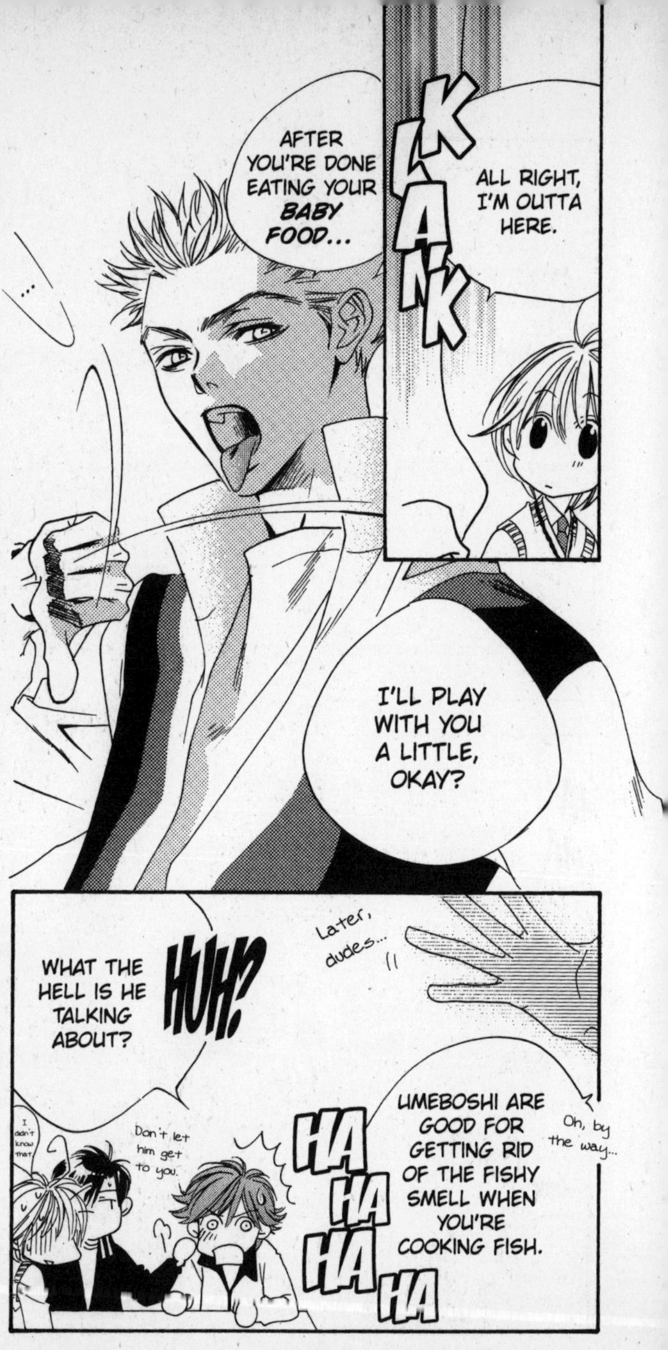
KLANK
ALL RIGHT, I'M OUTTA HERE.
AFTER YOU'RE DONE EATING YOUR *BABY FOOD*...
I'LL PLAY WITH YOU A LITTLE, OKAY?
...
Later, dudes...
Oh, by the way...
UMEBOSHI ARE GOOD FOR GETTING RID OF THE FISHY SMELL WHEN YOU'RE COOKING FISH.
HA HA HA HA
HUH?
WHAT THE HELL IS HE TALKING ABOUT?
Don't let him get to you.
I didn't know that.

19

It's **Hana-Kimi** volume 19! Mizuki and Nakatsu are on the cover in Chinese outfits. Nakatsu's popularity is growing (ha ha)! That's not really why I put him on the cover, though. Nakatsu is my favorite character to draw in color. Drawing Sano isn't nearly as fun. I like drawing Mizuki and Nakatsu together, so I really enjoyed working on this volume's cover illustration.

Sorry, Sano...

19

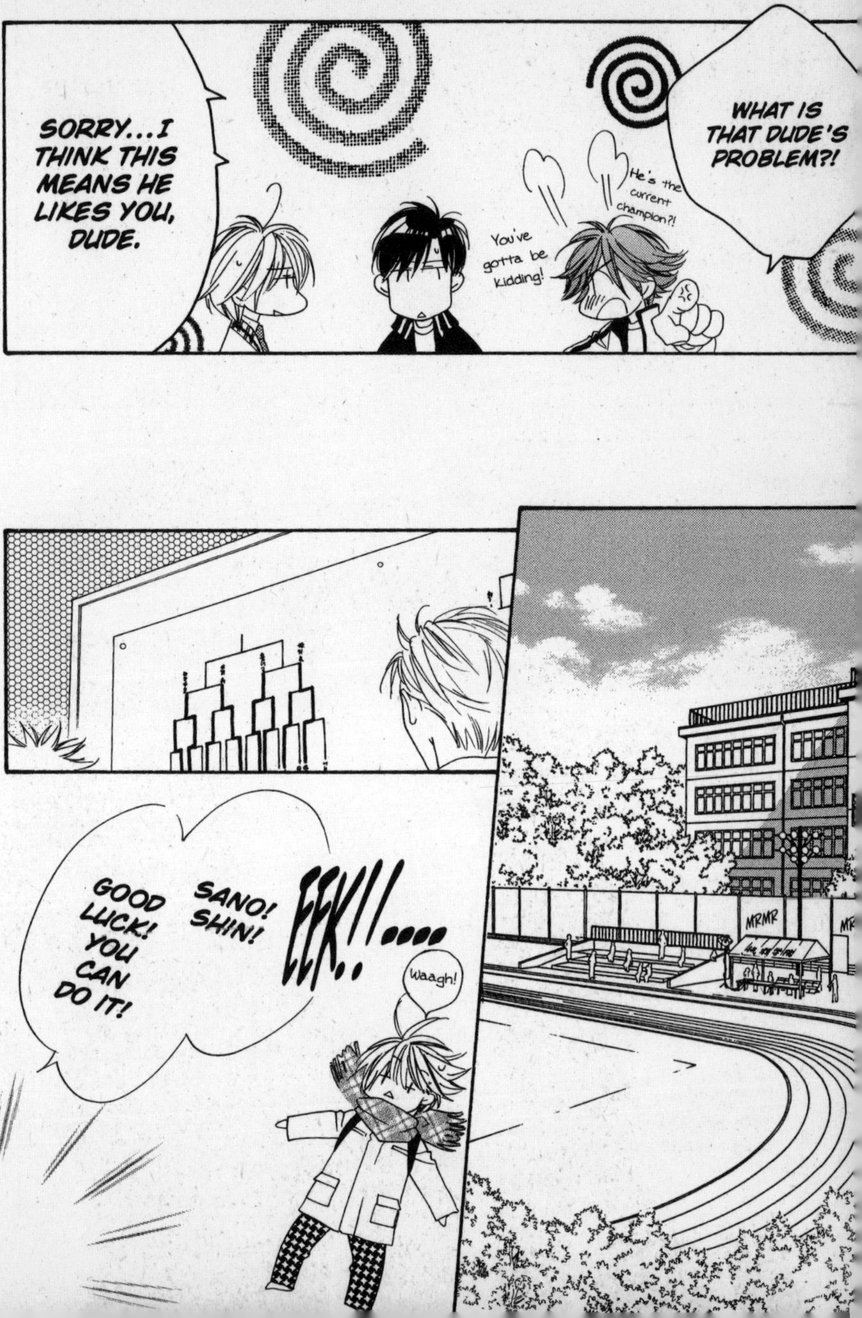
WHAT IS THAT DUDE'S PROBLEM?!
He's the current champion?!
You've gotta be kidding!
SORRY...I THINK THIS MEANS HE LIKES YOU, DUDE.
EEK!!....
SANO! SHIN!
GOOD LUCK! YOU CAN DO IT!
Waagh!

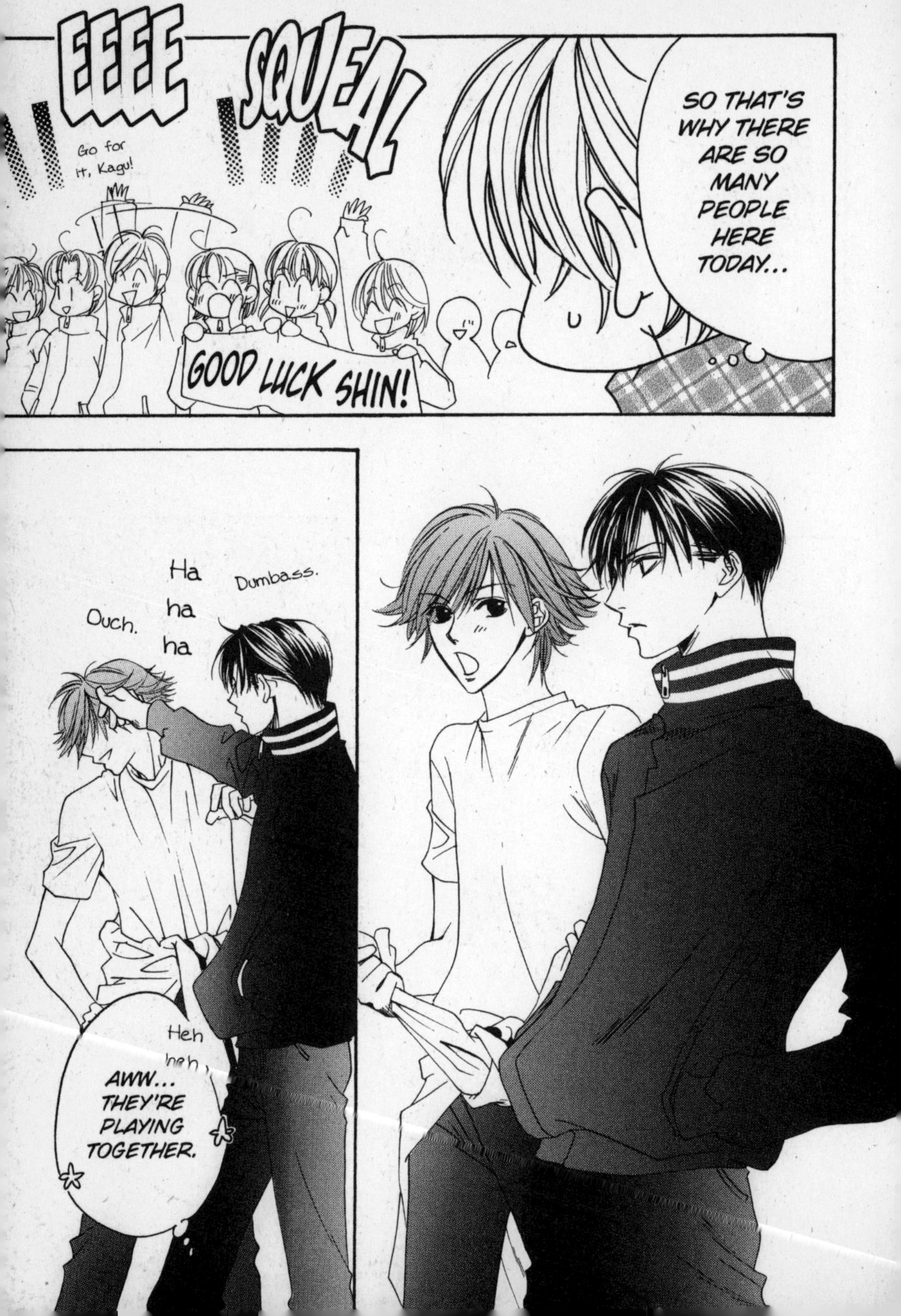
SO THAT'S WHY THERE ARE SO MANY PEOPLE HERE TODAY...
SQUEAL
EEEE
Go for it, Kagu!
GOOD LUCK SHIN!
Dumbass.
Ha ha ha
Ouch.
Heh heh
AWW... THEY'RE PLAYING TOGETHER.

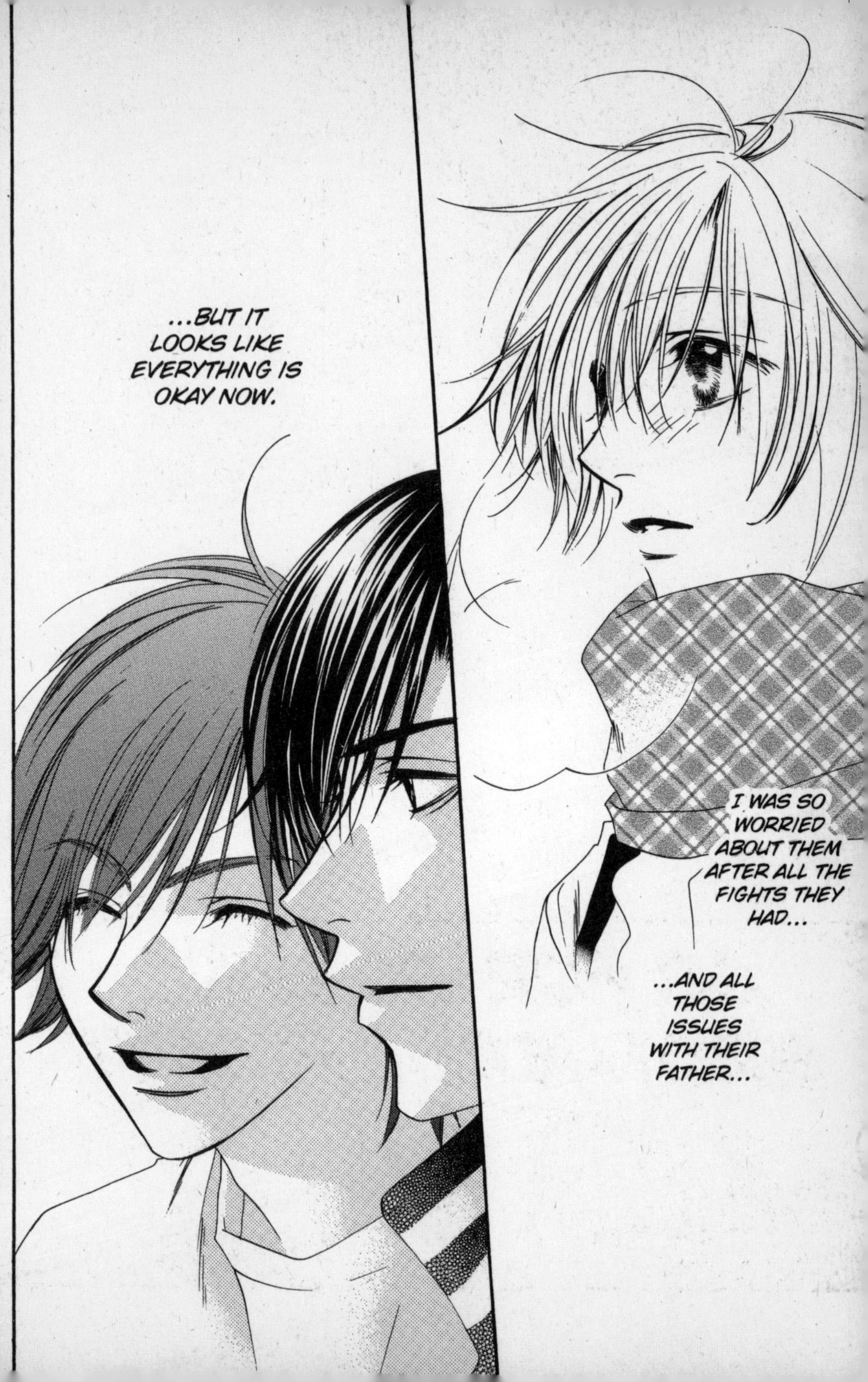
I WAS SO WORRIED ABOUT THEM AFTER ALL THE FIGHTS THEY HAD...
...AND ALL THOSE ISSUES WITH THEIR FATHER...
...BUT IT LOOKS LIKE EVERYTHING IS OKAY NOW.

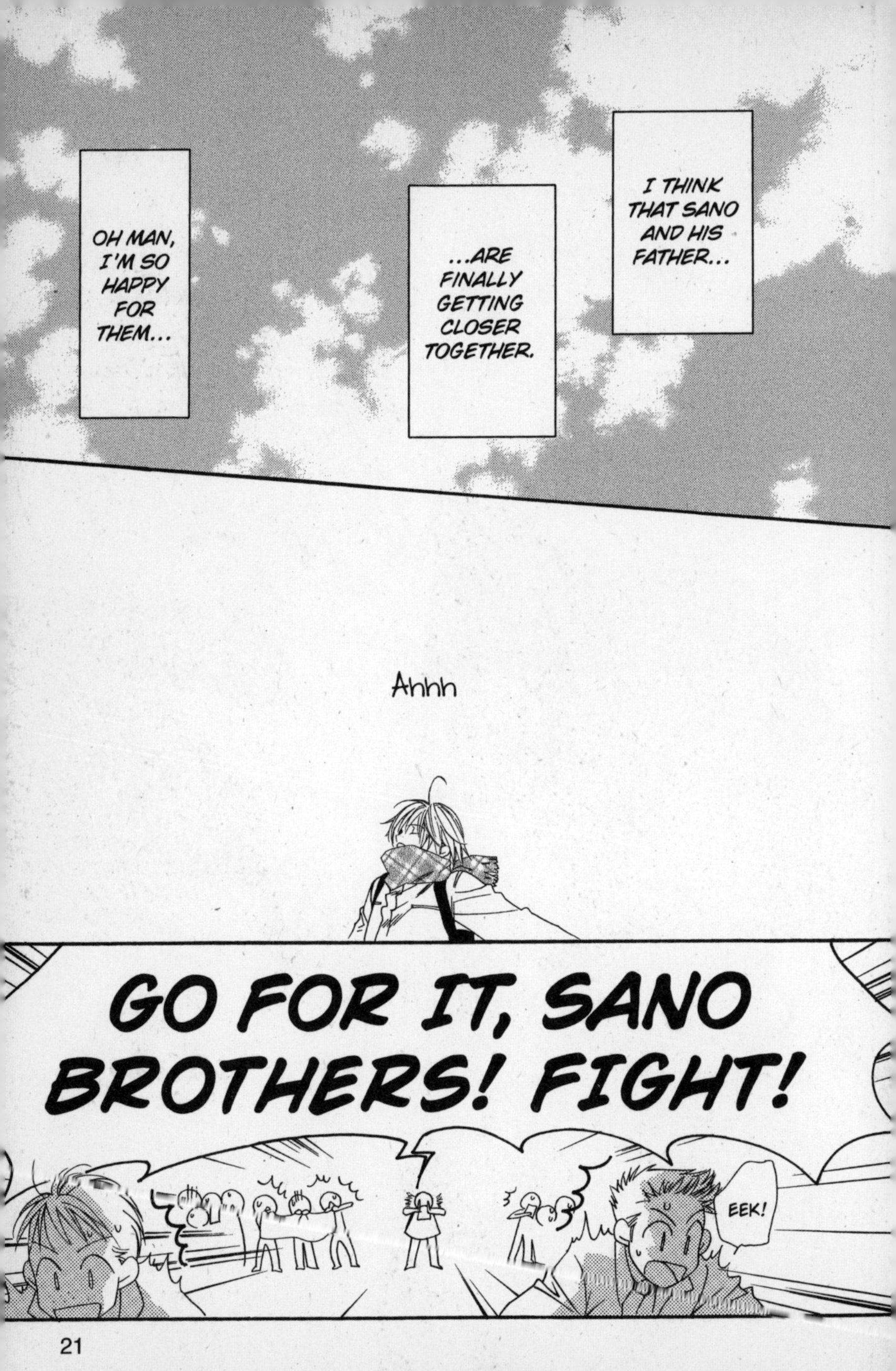
I THINK THAT SANO AND HIS FATHER...
...ARE FINALLY GETTING CLOSER TOGETHER.
OH MAN, I'M SO HAPPY FOR THEM...
Ahhh
GO FOR IT, SANO BROTHERS! FIGHT!
EEK!

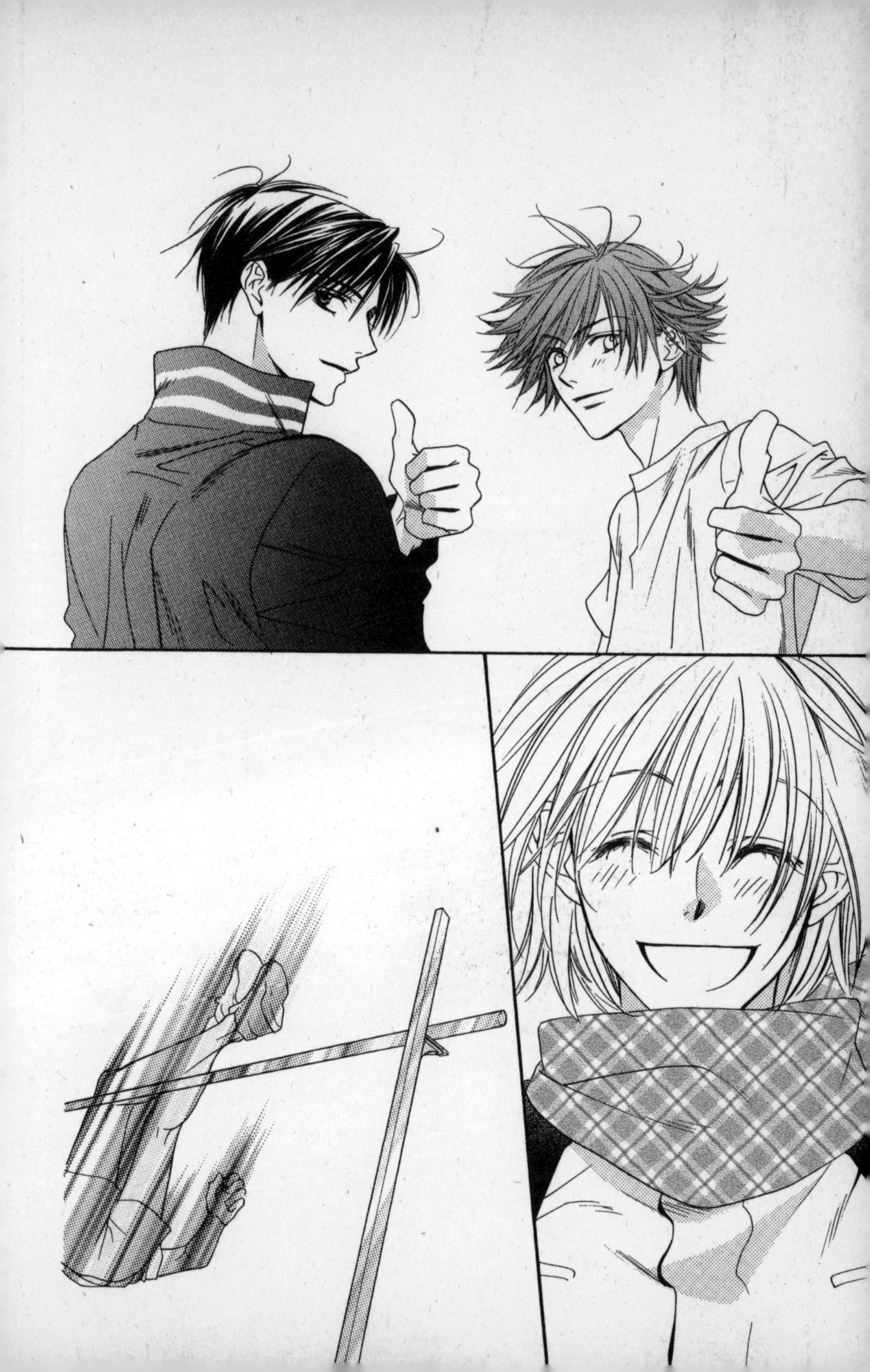

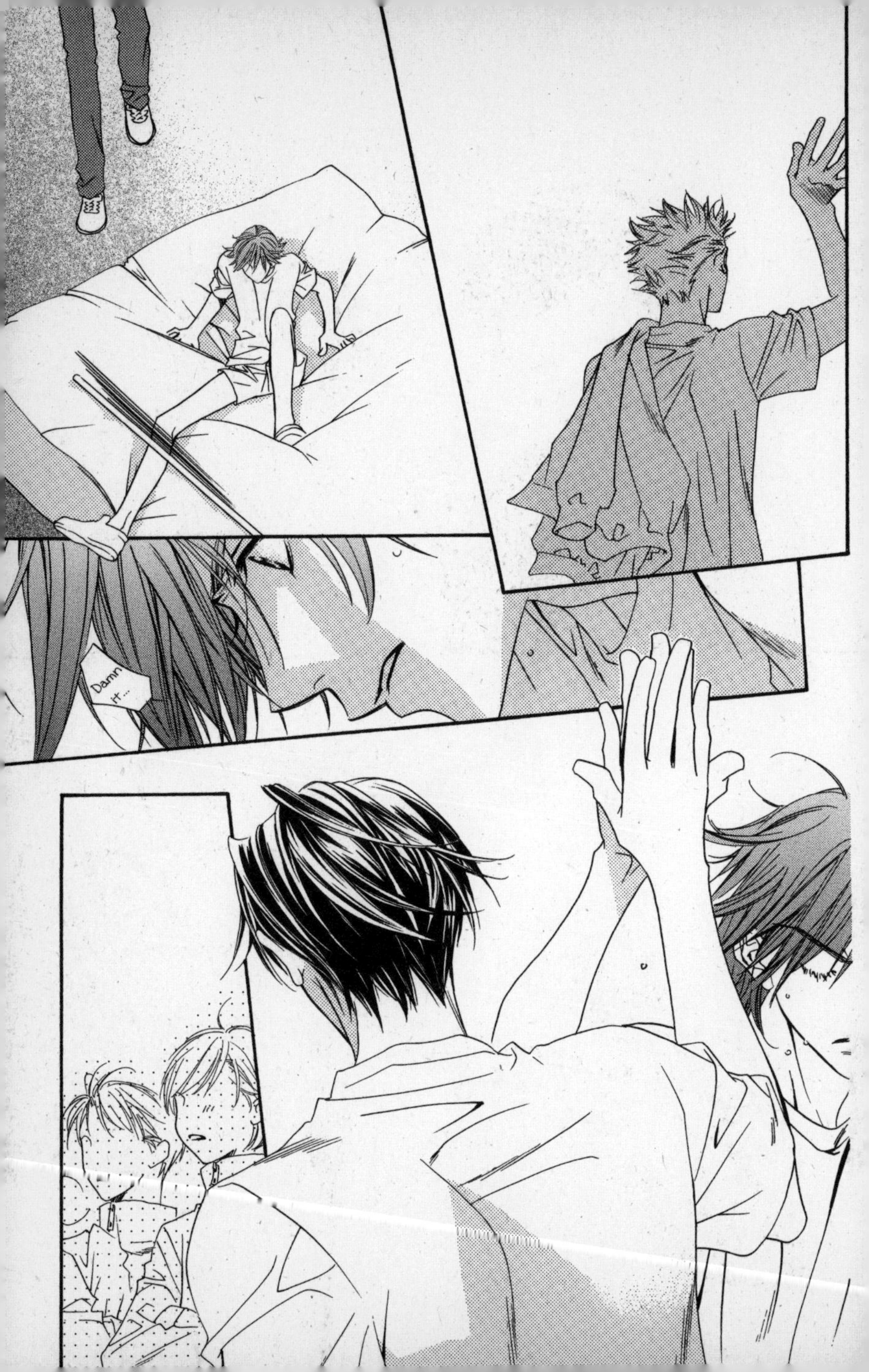
Damn it...

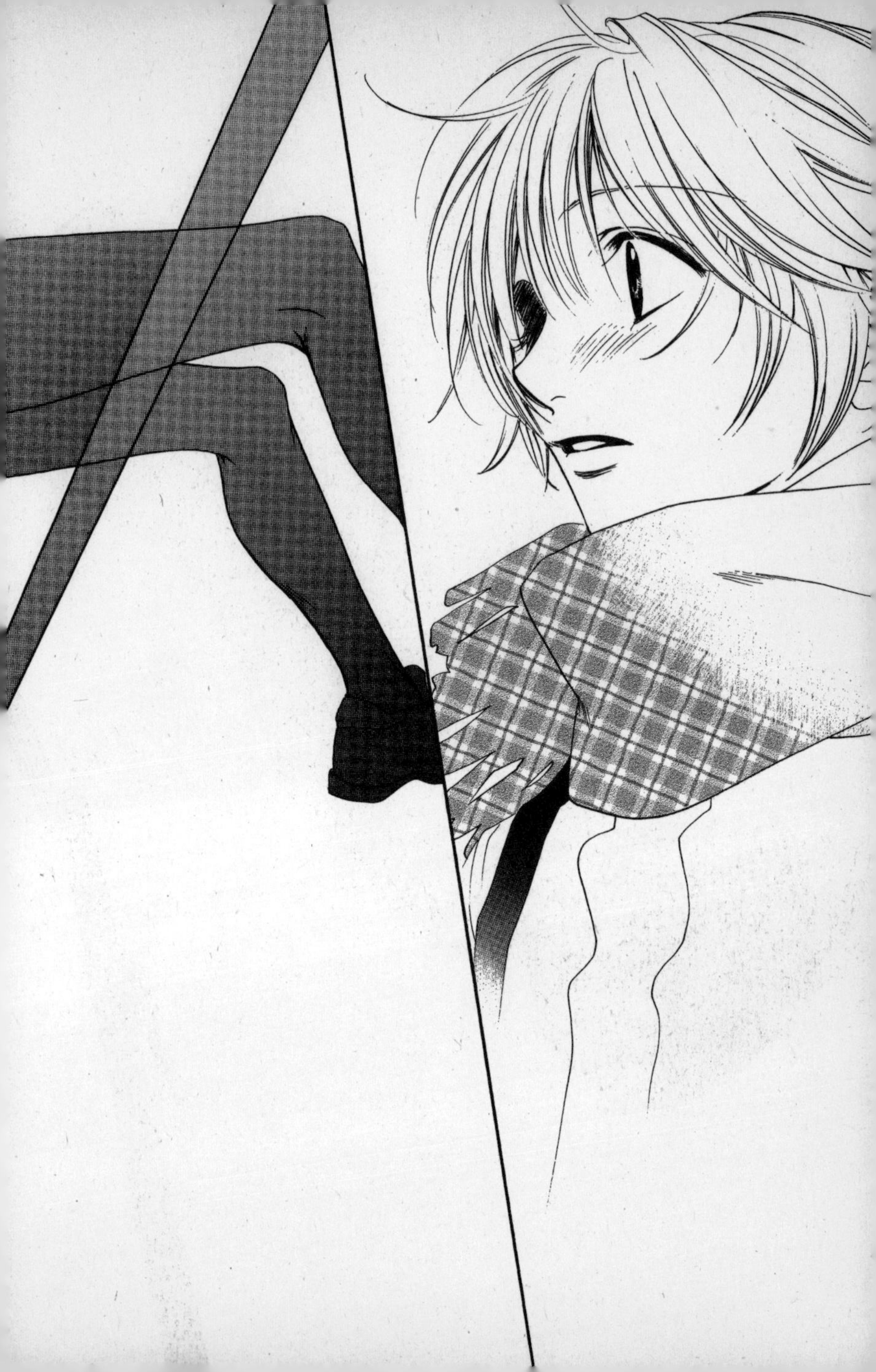

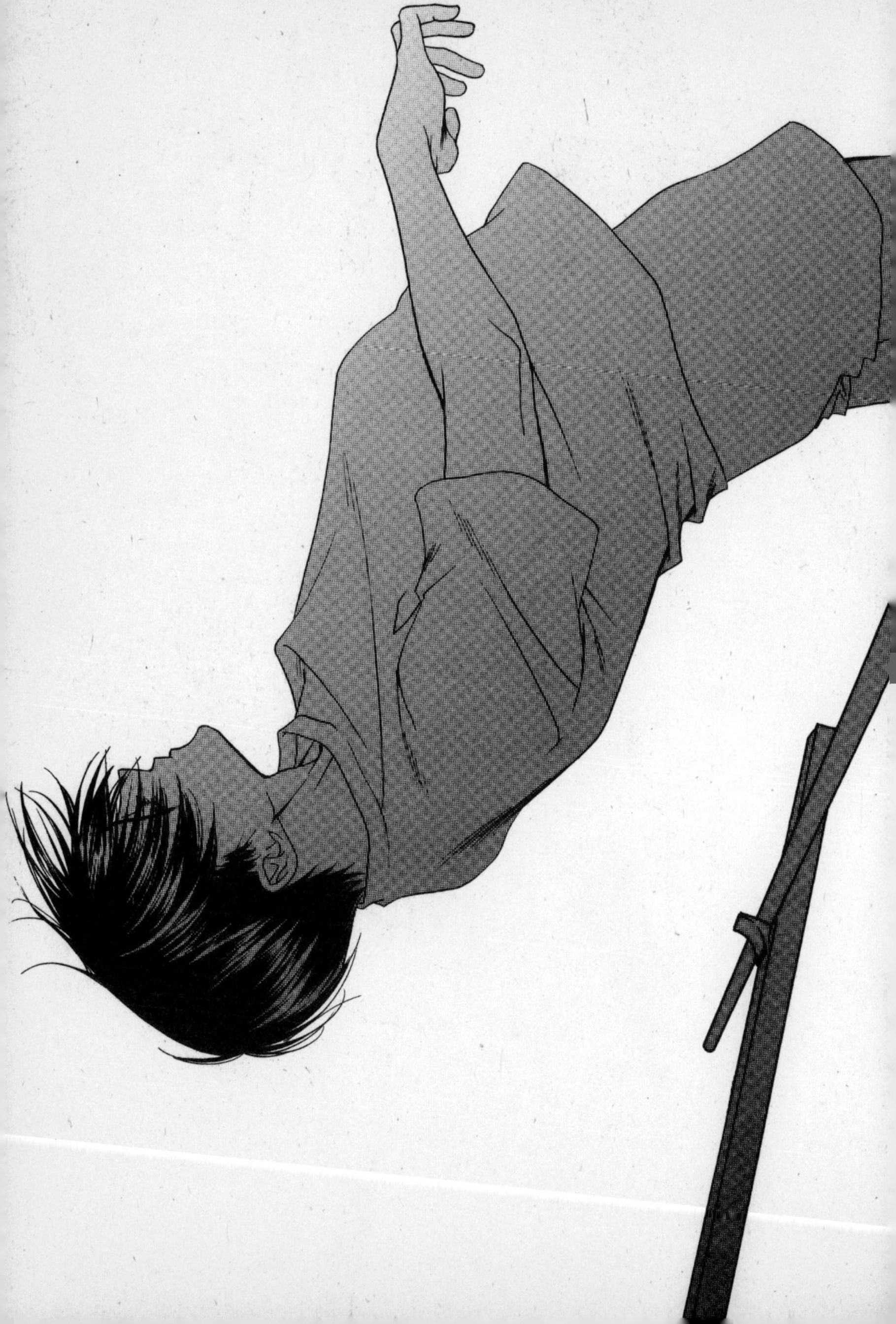

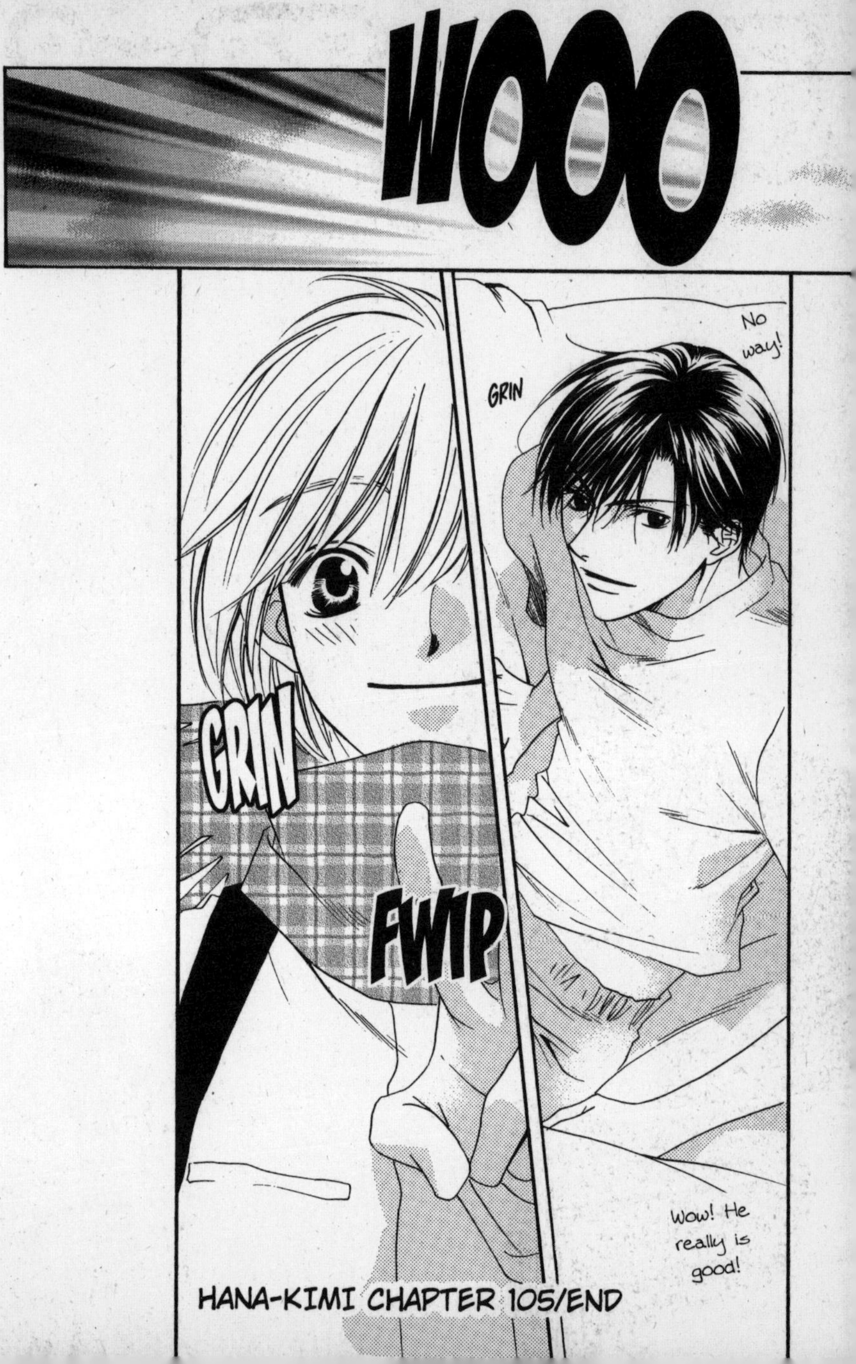
WOOO
No way!
GRIN
GRIN
FWIP
Wow! He really is good!

HANA-KIMI CHAPTER 105/END

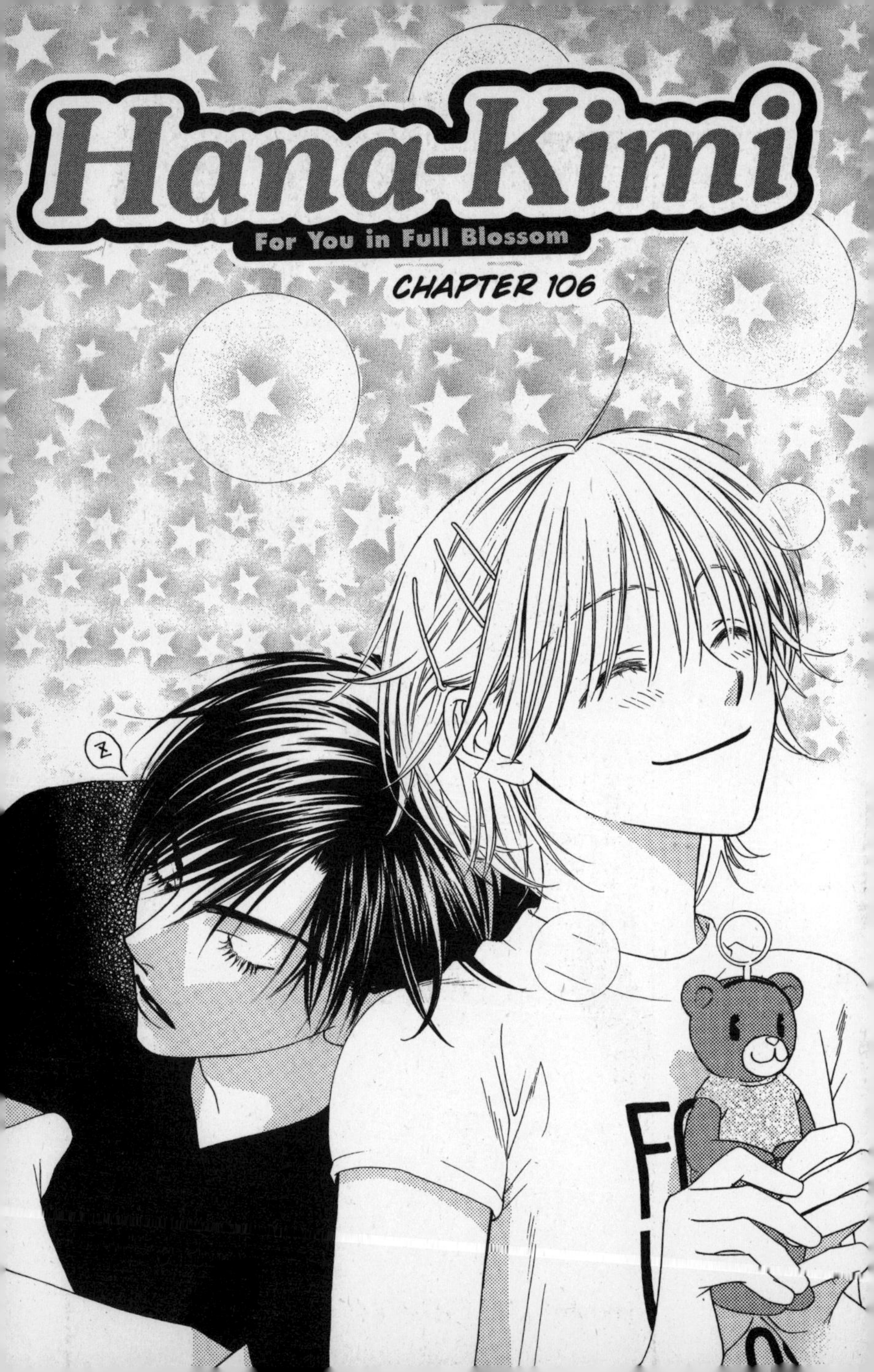
Hana-Kimi
For You in Full Blossom
CHAPTER 106

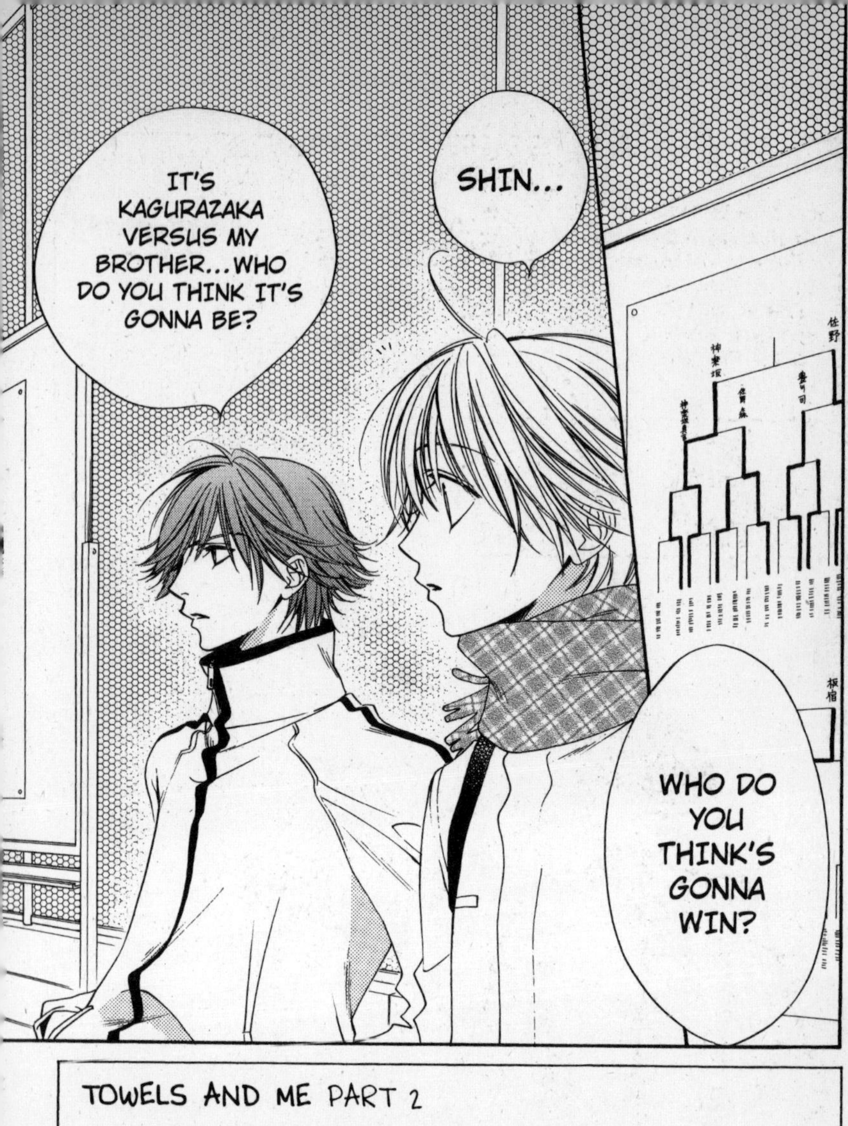
SHIN...
IT'S KAGURAZAKA VERSUS MY BROTHER...WHO DO YOU THINK IT'S GONNA BE?
WHO DO YOU THINK'S GONNA WIN?

TOWELS AND ME PART 2

The surface of a towel is so soft and warm. I use them all the time when I'm working, but... I keep staining my towels with ink, so they end up looking like rags. But I can't stop using them...

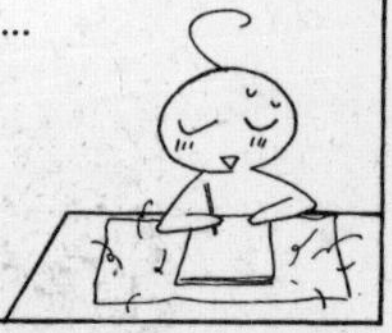

I use a soft towel now.

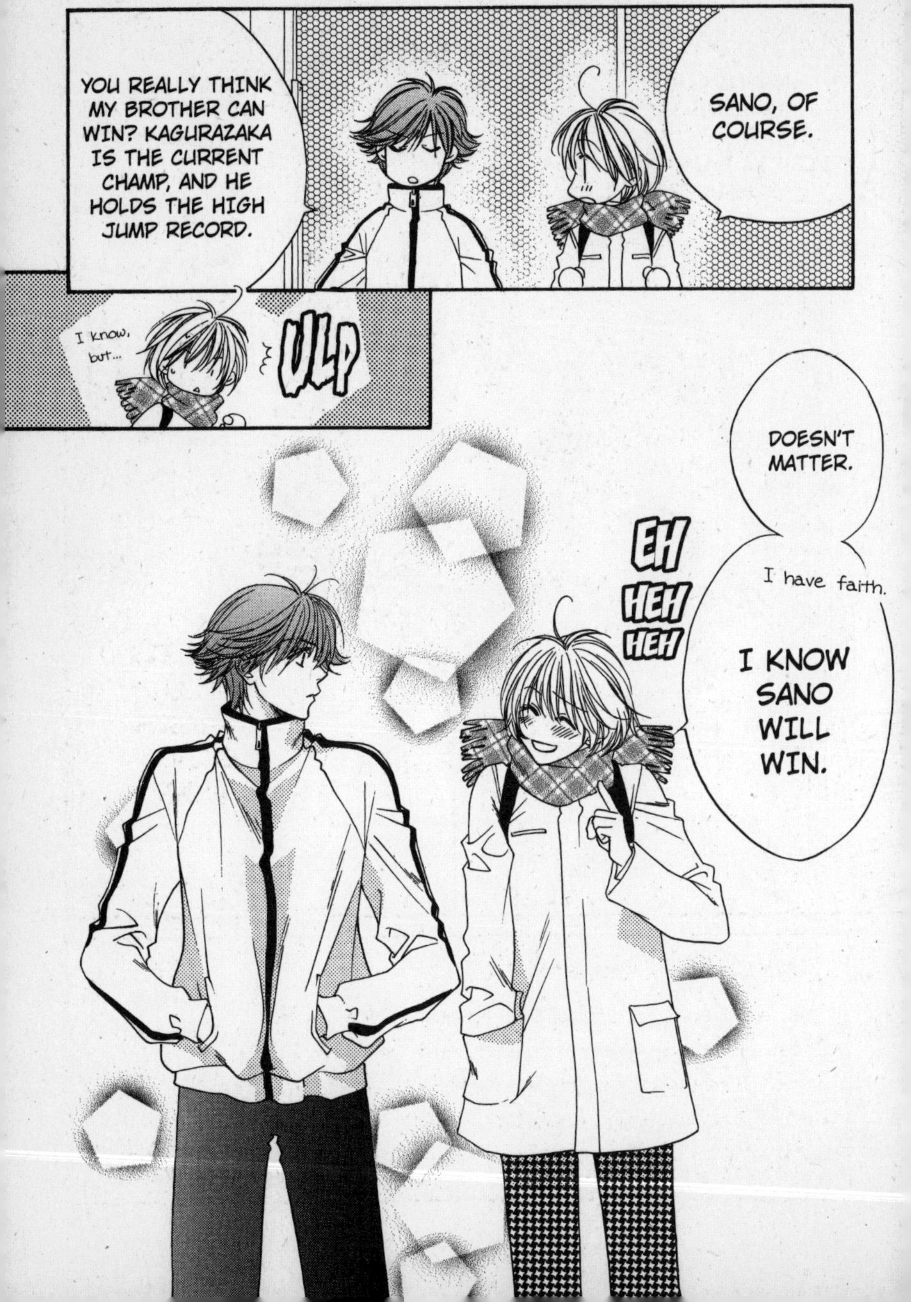
SANO, OF COURSE.
YOU REALLY THINK MY BROTHER CAN WIN? KAGURAZAKA IS THE CURRENT CHAMP, AND HE HOLDS THE HIGH JUMP RECORD.
ULP
I know, but...
DOESN'T MATTER.
I have faith.
I KNOW SANO WILL WIN.
EH HEH HEH

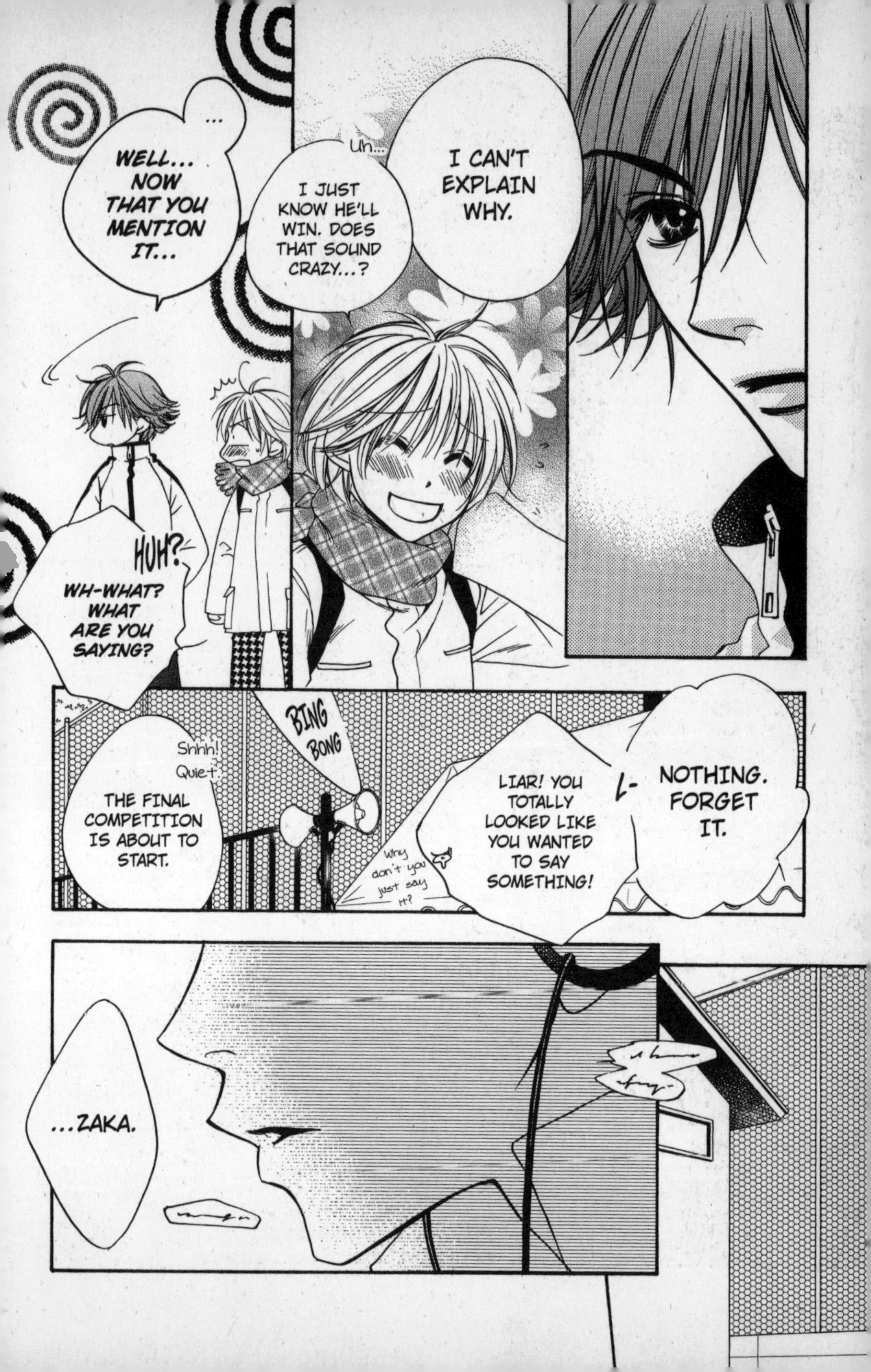
I CAN'T EXPLAIN WHY.
Uh...
I JUST KNOW HE'LL WIN. DOES THAT SOUND CRAZY...?
...
WELL... NOW THAT YOU MENTION IT...
HUH?
WH-WHAT? WHAT ARE YOU SAYING?
NOTHING. FORGET IT.
I-
LIAR! YOU TOTALLY LOOKED LIKE YOU WANTED TO SAY SOMETHING!
Why don't you just say it?
BING BONG
Shhh! Quiet.
THE FINAL COMPETITION IS ABOUT TO START.
...ZAKA.

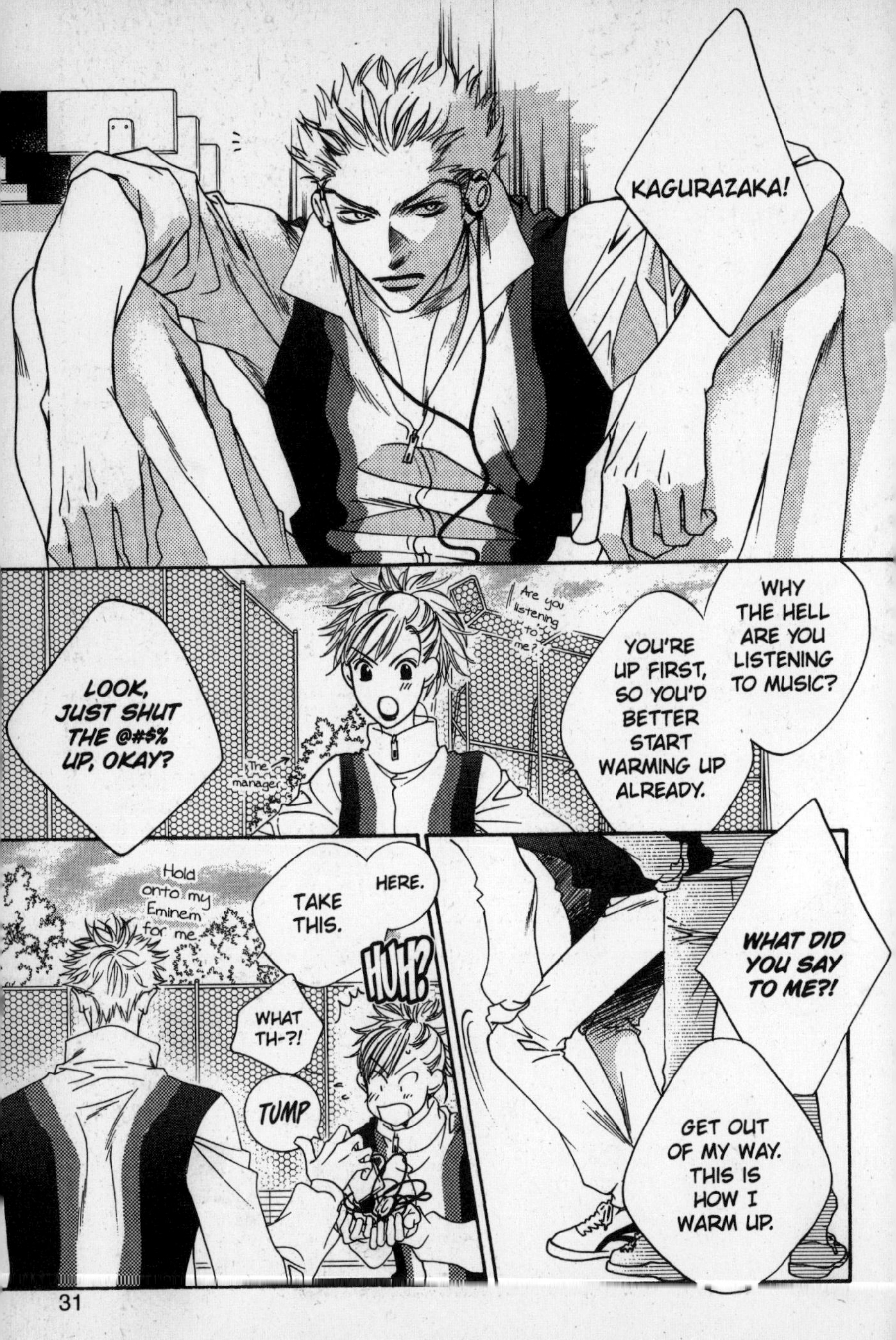
KAGURAZAKA!
WHY THE HELL ARE YOU LISTENING TO MUSIC?
YOU'RE UP FIRST, SO YOU'D BETTER START WARMING UP ALREADY.
Are you listening to me?
The manager
LOOK, JUST SHUT THE @#$% UP, OKAY?
WHAT DID YOU SAY TO ME?!
GET OUT OF MY WAY. THIS IS HOW I WARM UP.
HERE.
TAKE THIS.
Hold onto my Eminem for me.
HUH?
WHAT TH-?!
TUMP

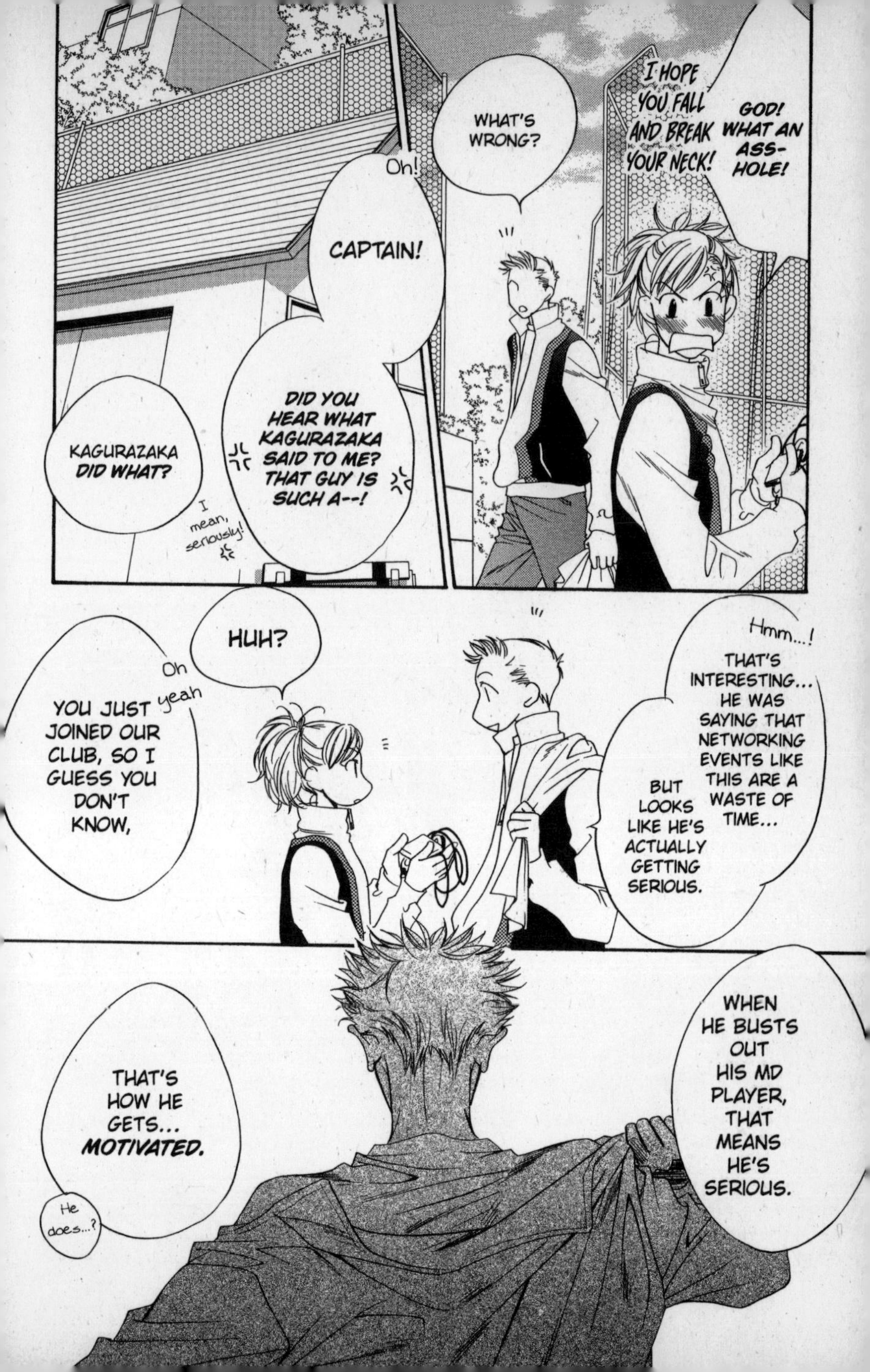
GOD! WHAT AN ASS-HOLE!
I HOPE YOU FALL AND BREAK YOUR NECK!
WHAT'S WRONG?
Oh!
CAPTAIN!
DID YOU HEAR WHAT KAGURAZAKA SAID TO ME? THAT GUY IS SUCH A--!
KAGURAZAKA DID WHAT?
I mean, seriously!
Hmm...!
THAT'S INTERESTING... HE WAS SAYING THAT NETWORKING EVENTS LIKE THIS ARE A WASTE OF TIME...
BUT LOOKS LIKE HE'S ACTUALLY GETTING SERIOUS.
HUH?
Oh yeah
YOU JUST JOINED OUR CLUB, SO I GUESS YOU DON'T KNOW,
WHEN HE BUSTS OUT HIS MD PLAYER, THAT MEANS HE'S SERIOUS.
THAT'S HOW HE GETS... MOTIVATED.
He does...?

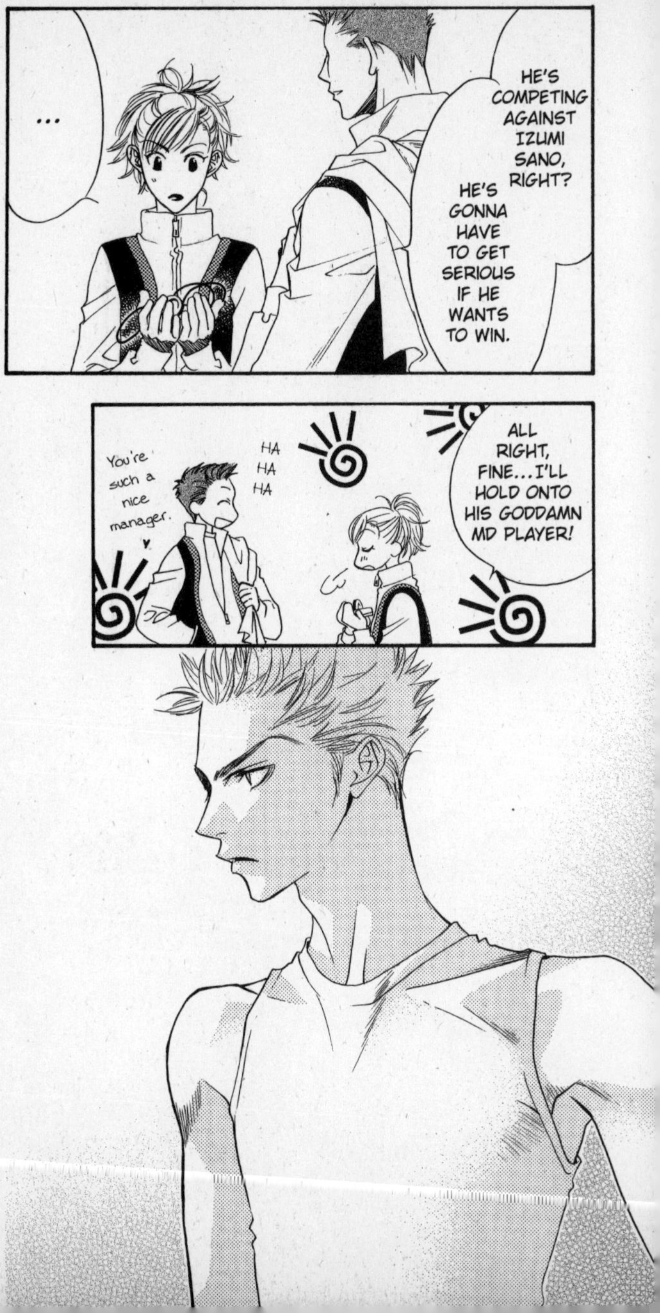
HE'S COMPETING AGAINST IZUMI SANO, RIGHT?
HE'S GONNA HAVE TO GET SERIOUS IF HE WANTS TO WIN.
...
ALL RIGHT, FINE...I'LL HOLD ONTO HIS GODDAMN MD PLAYER!
HA HA HA
You're such a nice manager.

FINALE

The networking event is almost over. It's been a long time...if you count the days in the manga, the event has been going on for 10 days! (The Sano family went back home after the final day) Geez, enough already... While I was working on this episode, I must admit that I was worried that it was getting too long. Heh heh...Oh well. I guess Osaka High School is unlike any other school in existence! By the way, it seems like my own high school was kind of strange compared to some other schools. I notice that a lot when I hear my assistants talking about their high schools.

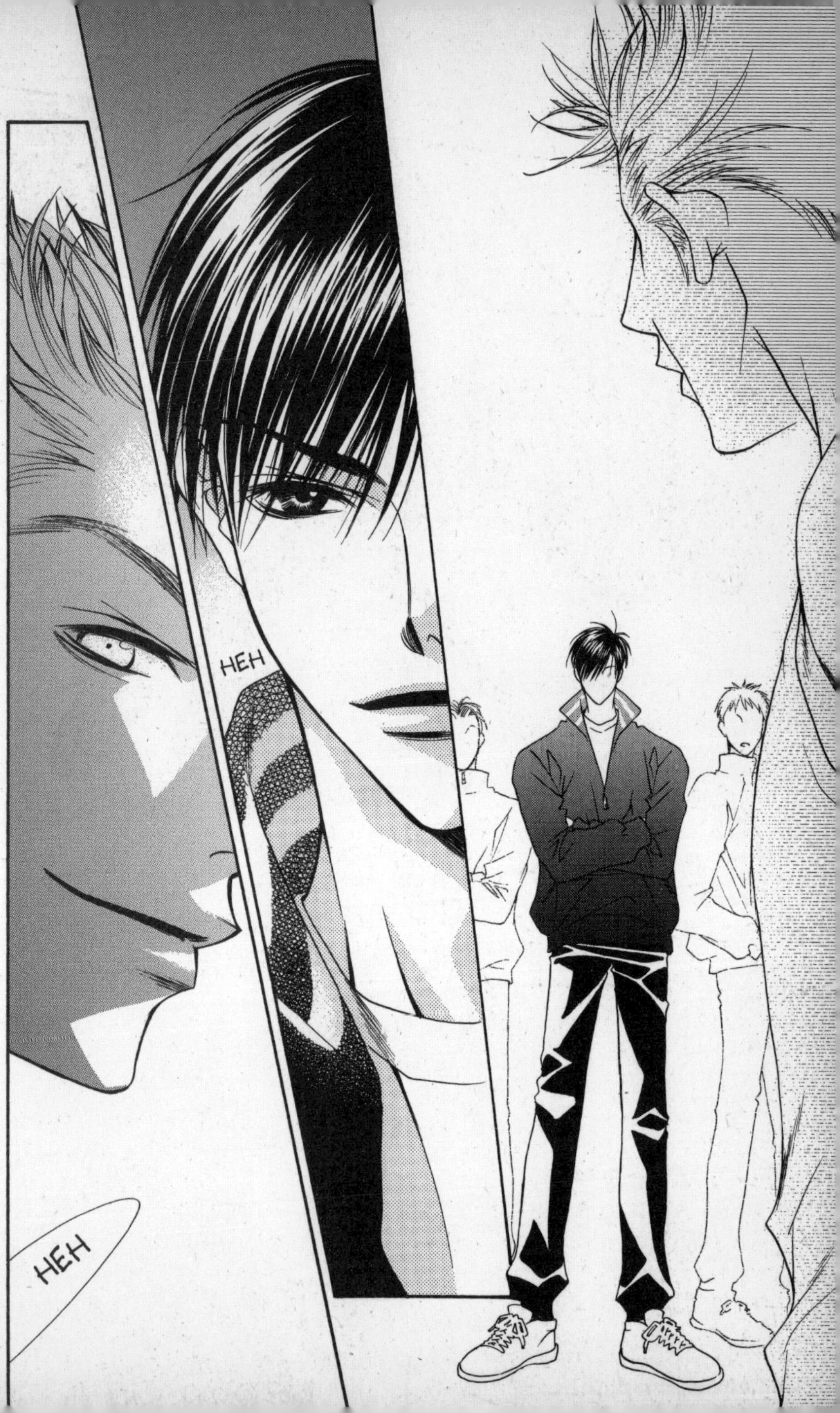
HEH
HEH

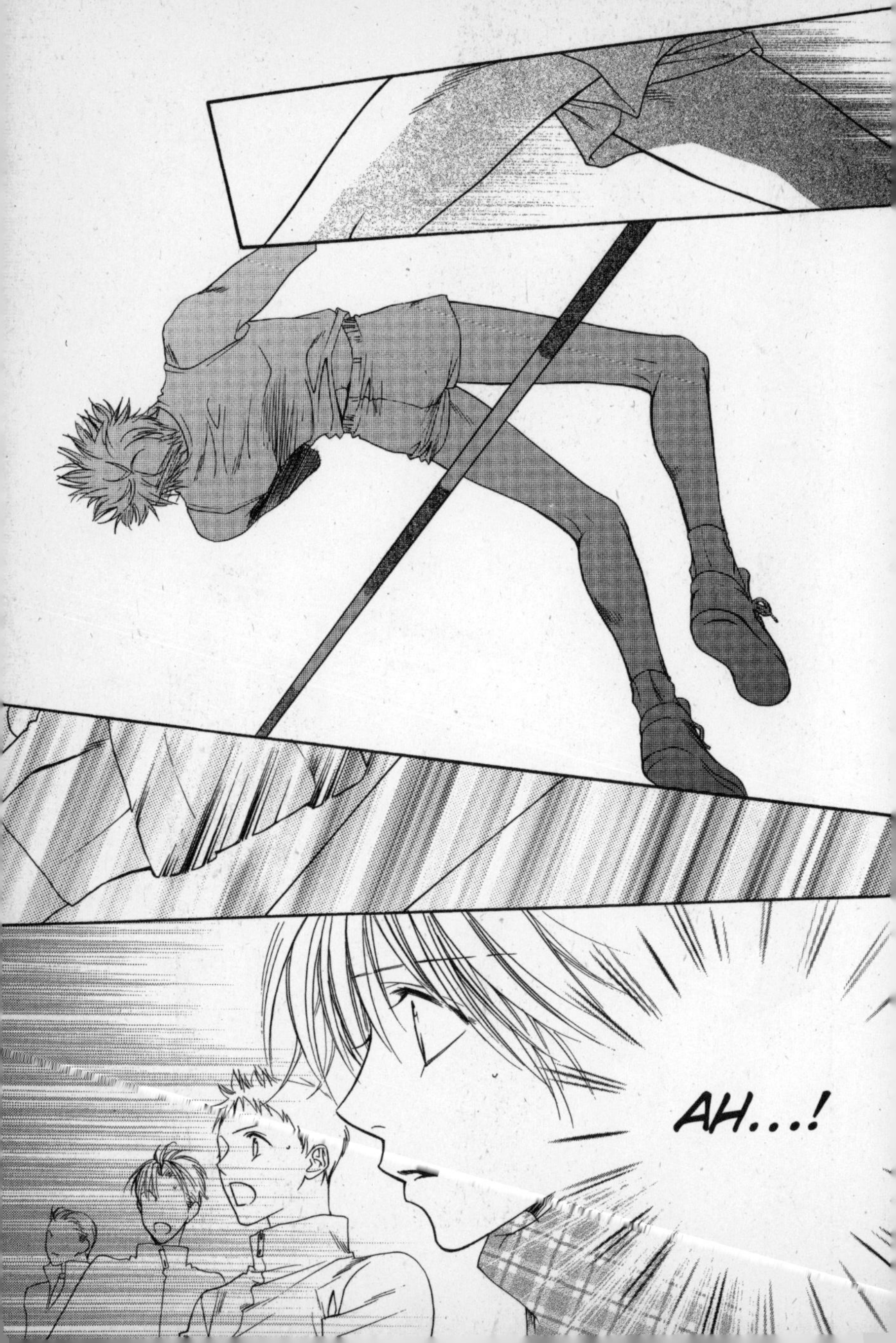
AH...!

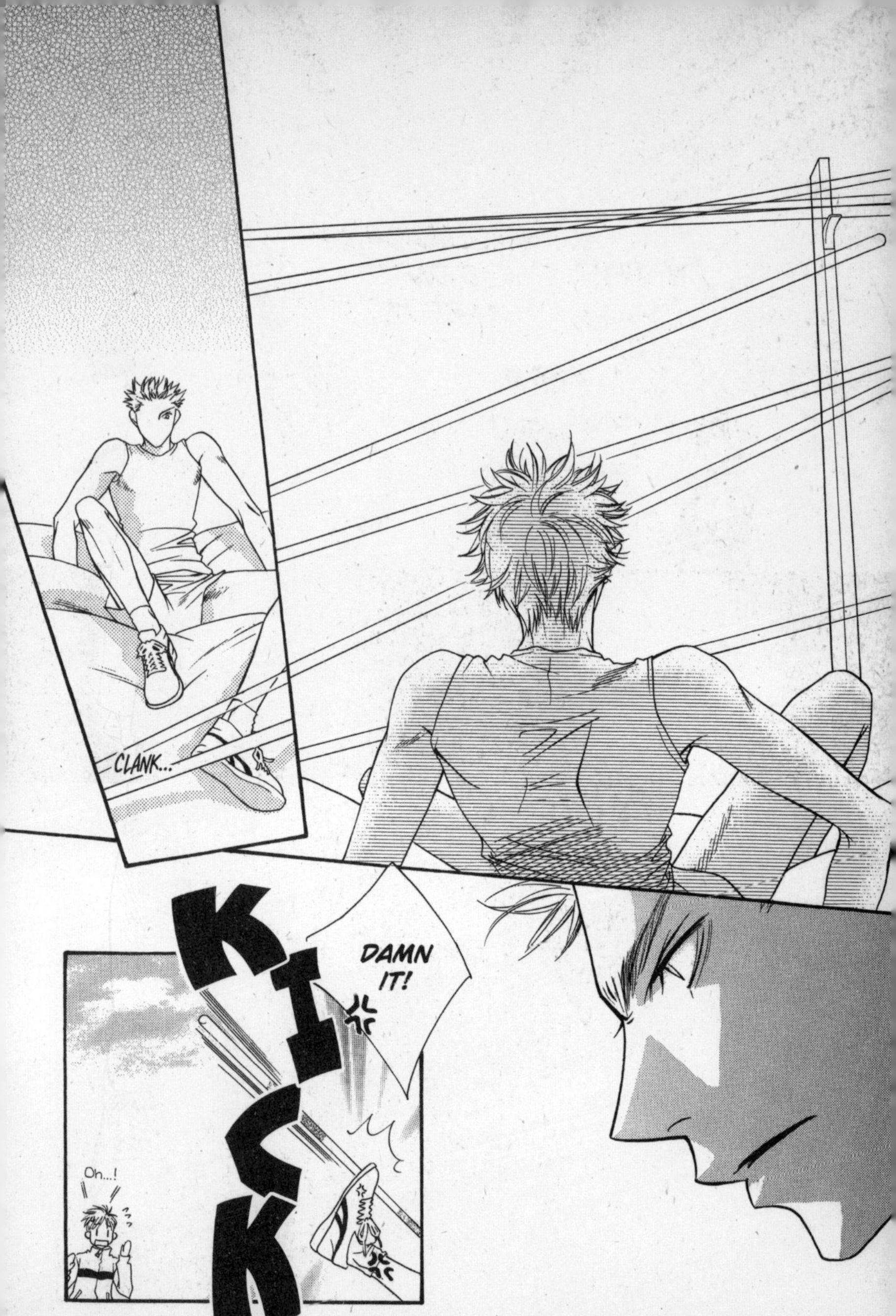
CLANK...
DAMN IT!
KICK
Oh...!

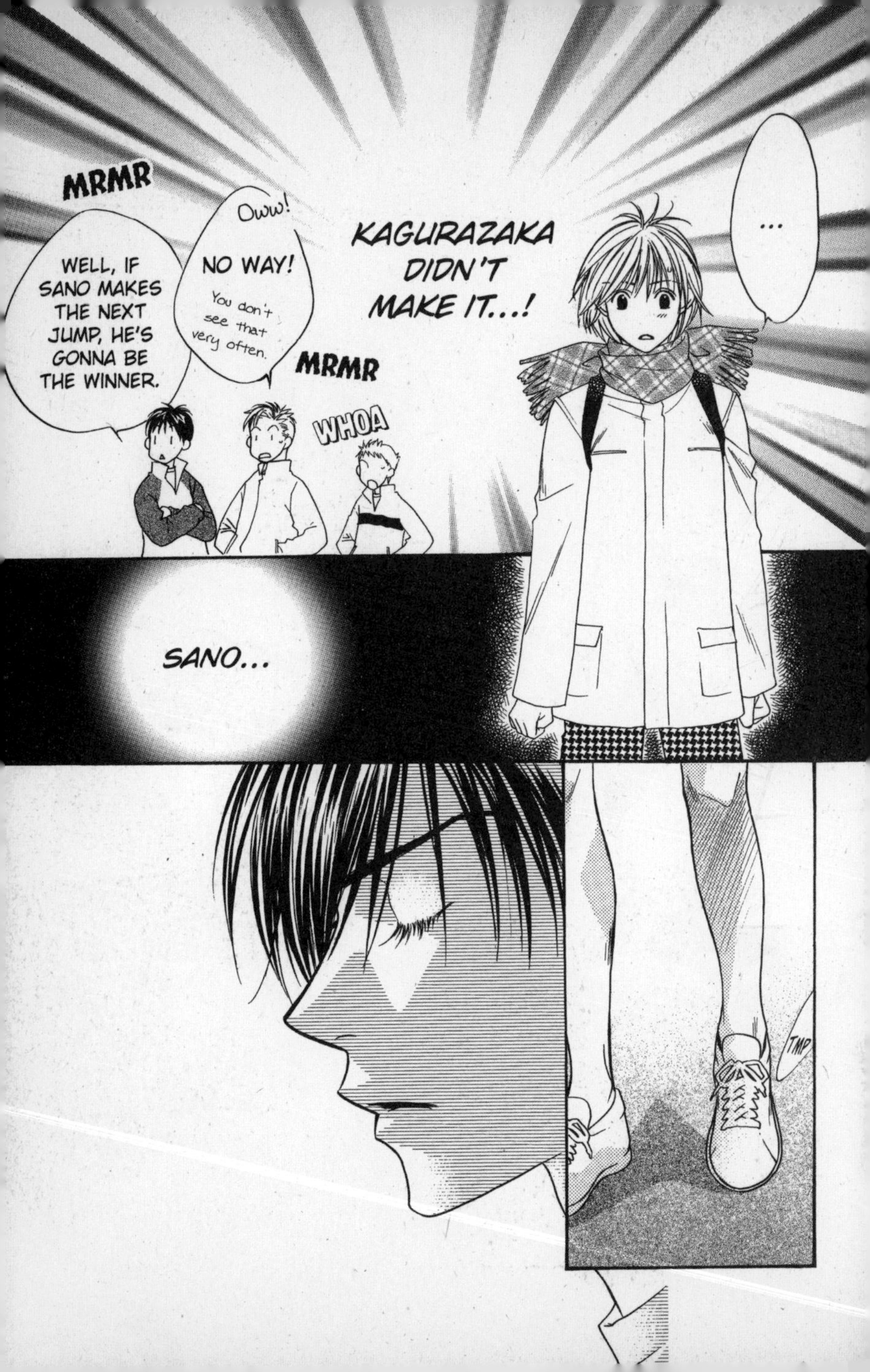
...
KAGURAZAKA DIDN'T MAKE IT...!
Oww!
NO WAY!
You don't see that very often.
MRMR
WHOA
WELL, IF SANO MAKES THE NEXT JUMP, HE'S GONNA BE THE WINNER.
MRMR
SANO...
TMP

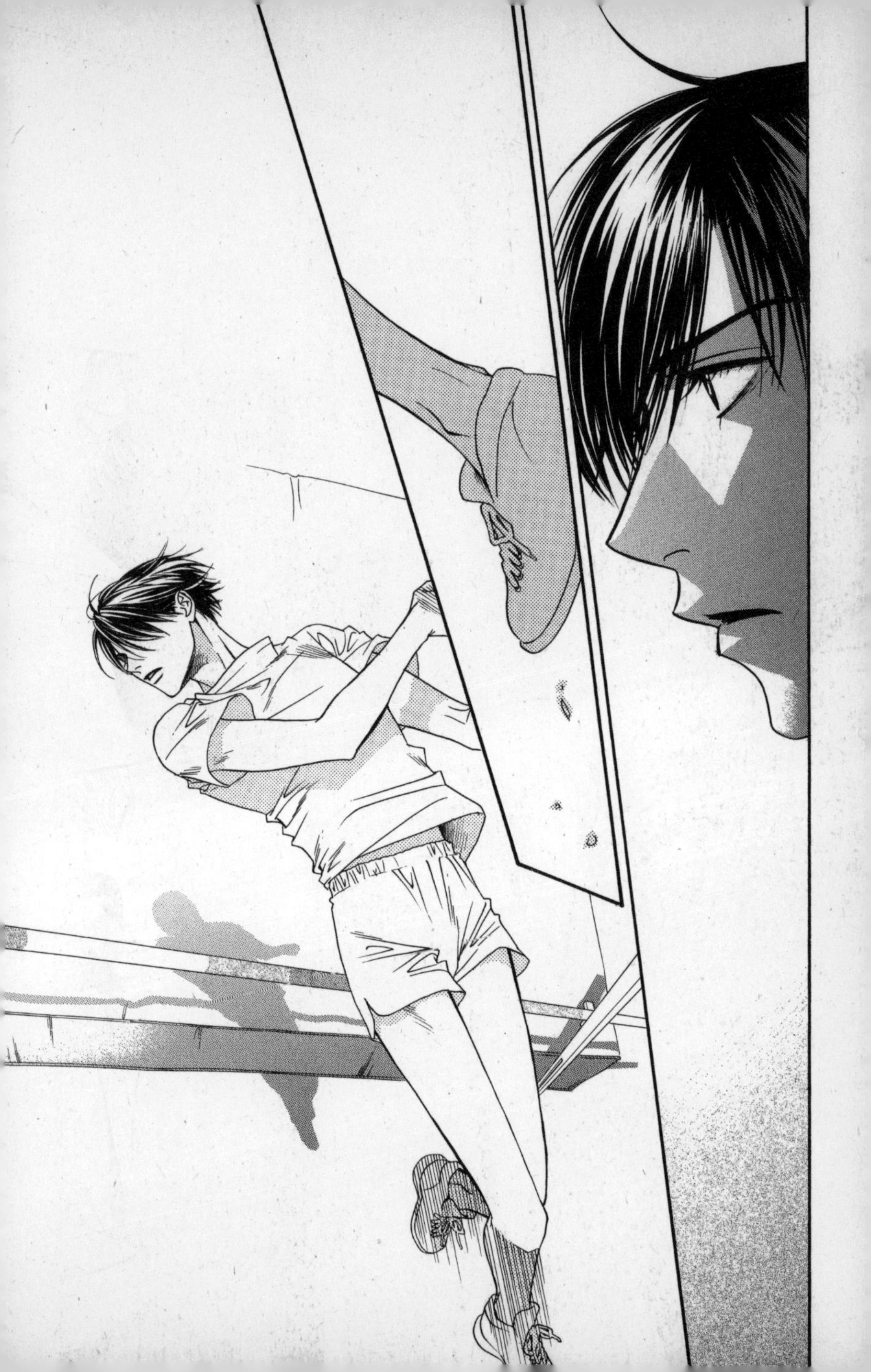

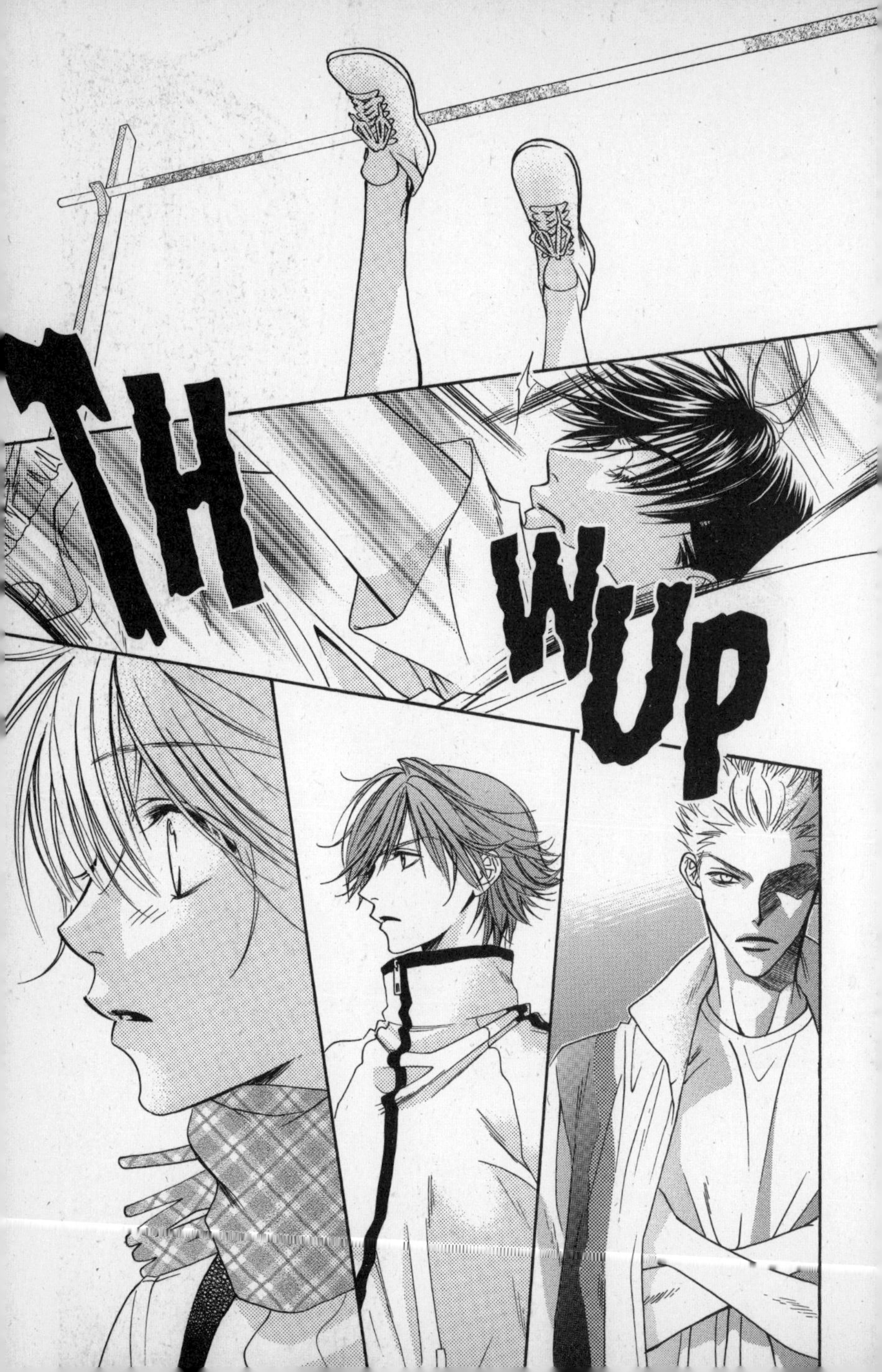
THWUP

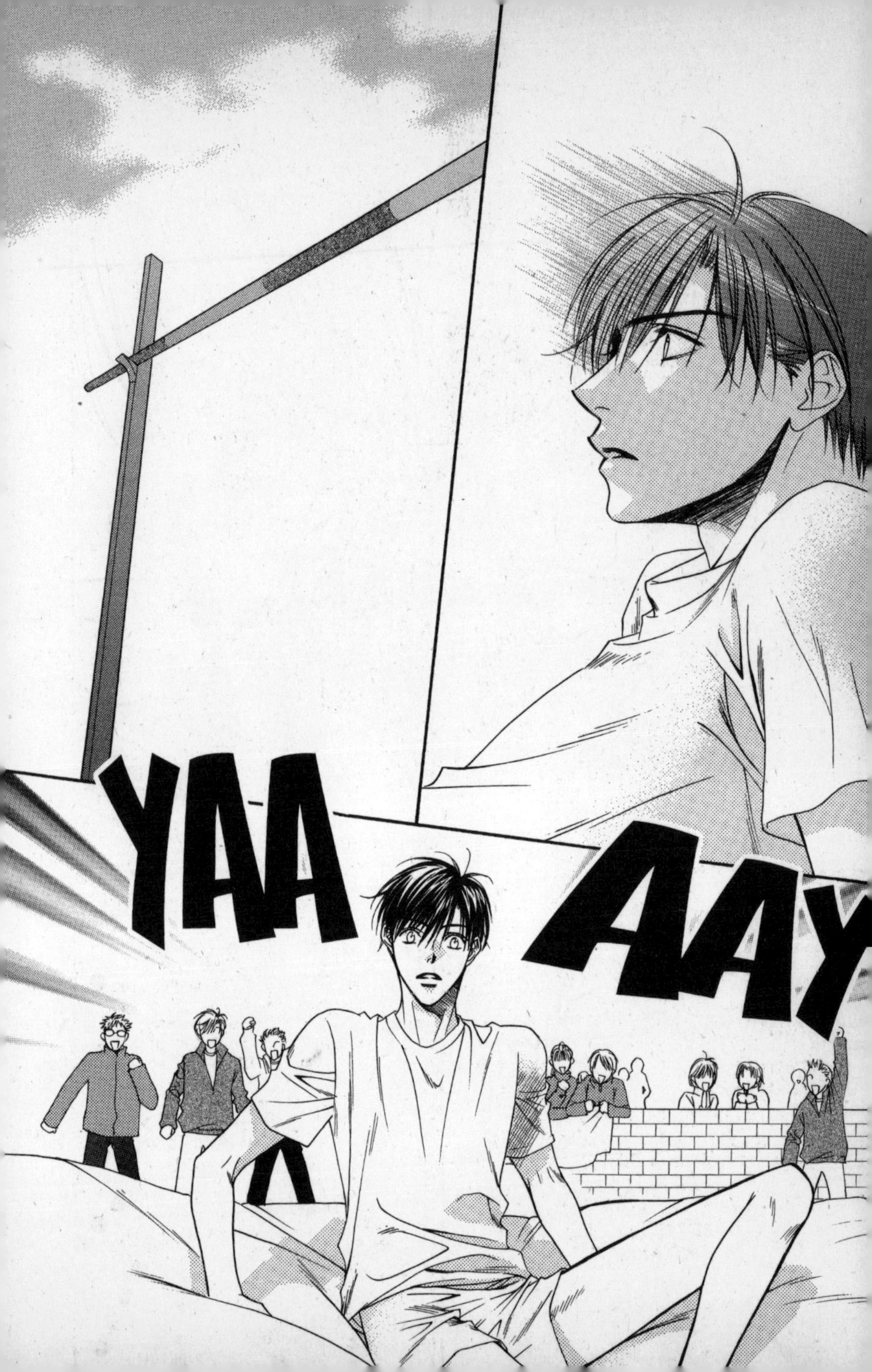
YAAAAY

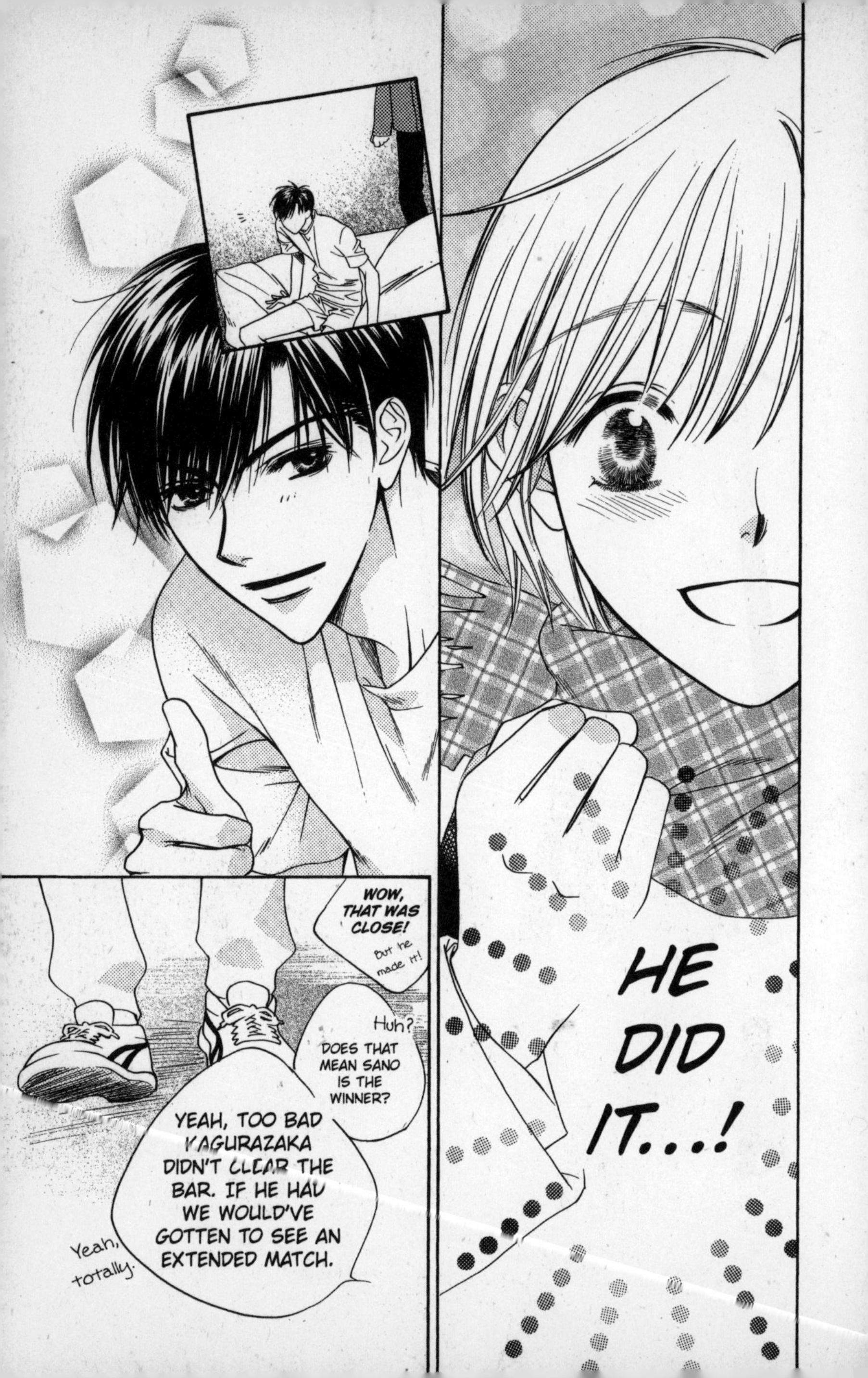
HE DID IT...!
WOW, THAT WAS CLOSE!
But he made it!
Huh?
DOES THAT MEAN SANO IS THE WINNER?
YEAH, TOO BAD KAGURAZAKA DIDN'T CLEAR THE BAR. IF HE HAD WE WOULD'VE GOTTEN TO SEE AN EXTENDED MATCH.
Yeah, totally.

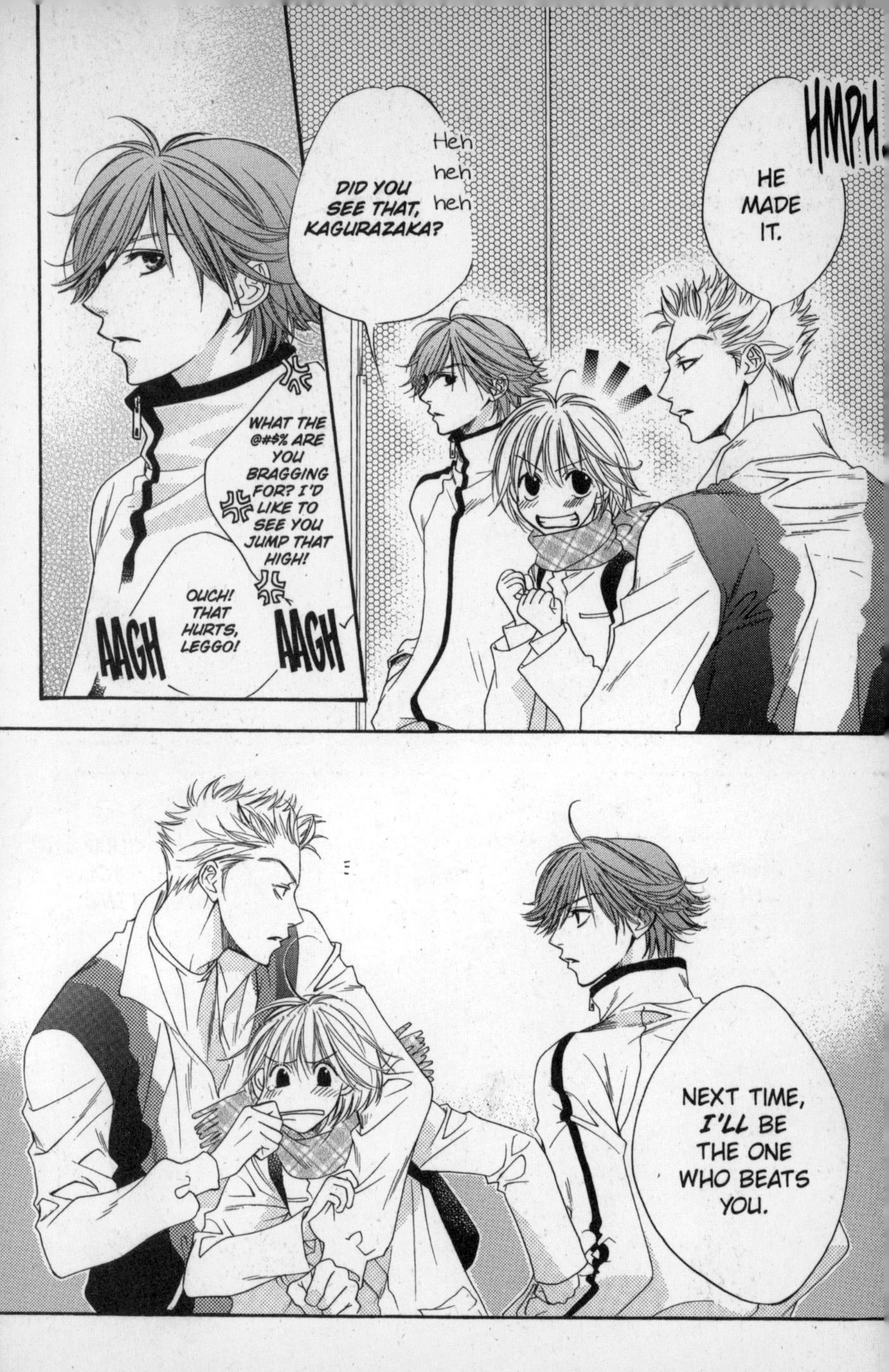
HMPH
HE MADE IT.
Heh heh heh
DID YOU SEE THAT, KAGURAZAKA?
WHAT THE @#$% ARE YOU BRAGGING FOR? I'D LIKE TO SEE YOU JUMP THAT HIGH!
AAGH
OUCH! THAT HURTS, LEGGO!
AAGH
NEXT TIME, *I'LL* BE THE ONE WHO BEATS YOU.

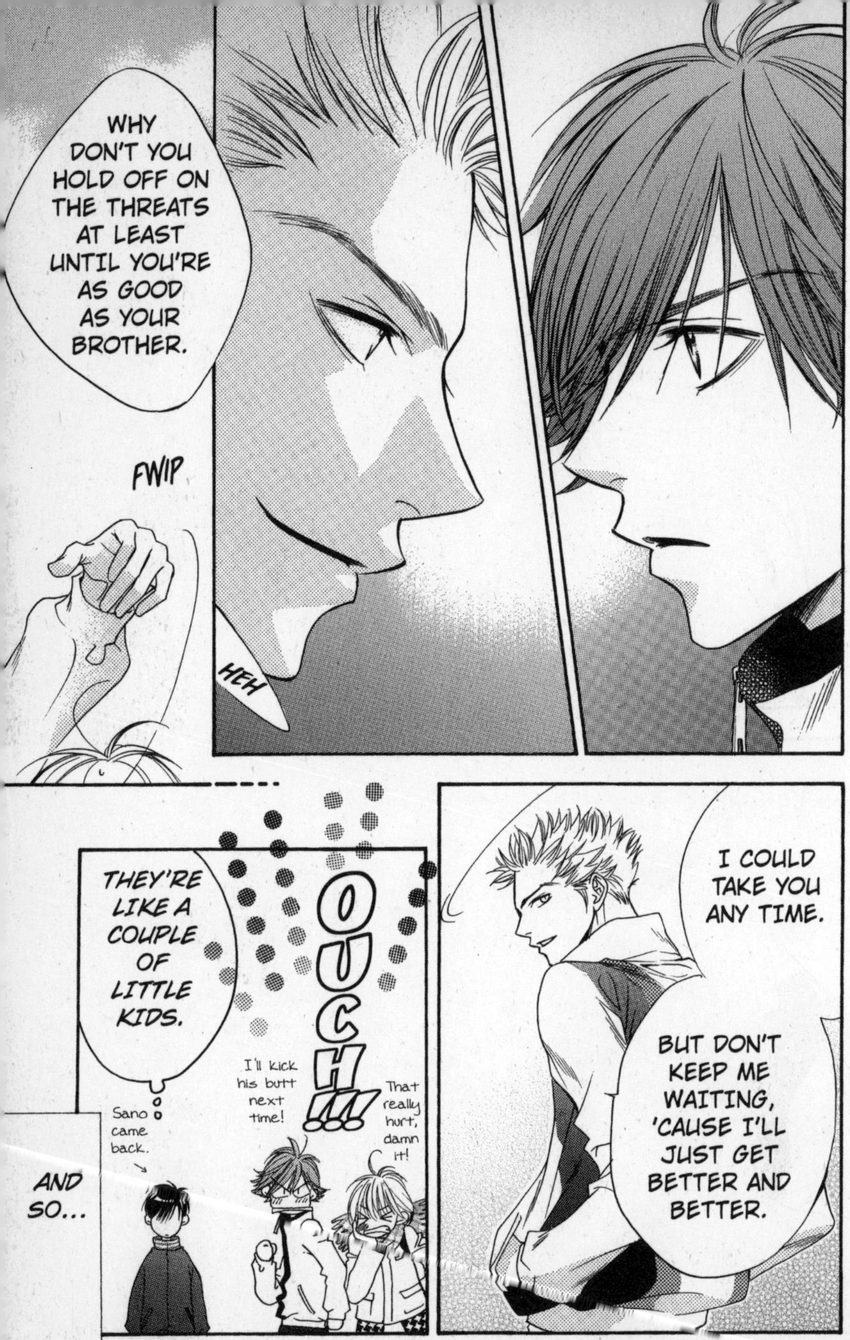
WHY DON'T YOU HOLD OFF ON THE THREATS AT LEAST UNTIL YOU'RE AS GOOD AS YOUR BROTHER.
HEH
FWIP
I COULD TAKE YOU ANY TIME.
BUT DON'T KEEP ME WAITING, 'CAUSE I'LL JUST GET BETTER AND BETTER.
OUCH!!!
That really hurt, damn it!
I'll kick his butt next time!
THEY'RE LIKE A COUPLE OF LITTLE KIDS.
Sano came back.
AND SO...

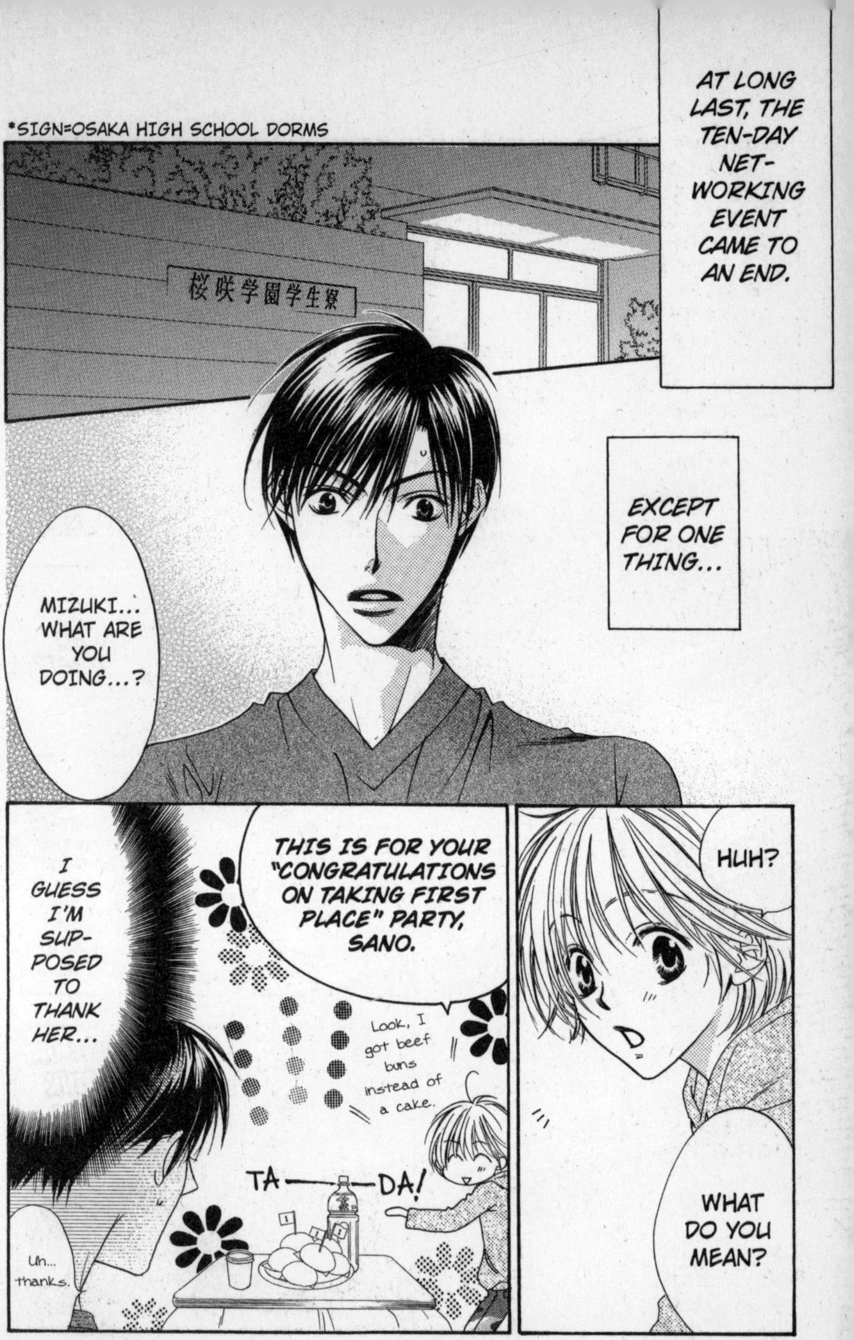
AT LONG LAST, THE TEN-DAY NET-WORKING EVENT CAME TO AN END.
*SIGN=OSAKA HIGH SCHOOL DORMS
桜咲学園学生寮
EXCEPT FOR ONE THING...
MIZUKI... WHAT ARE YOU DOING...?
HUH?
WHAT DO YOU MEAN?
THIS IS FOR YOUR "CONGRATULATIONS ON TAKING FIRST PLACE" PARTY, SANO.
I GUESS I'M SUP-POSED TO THANK HER...
Look, I got beef buns instead of a cake.
TA——DA!
Uh... thanks.

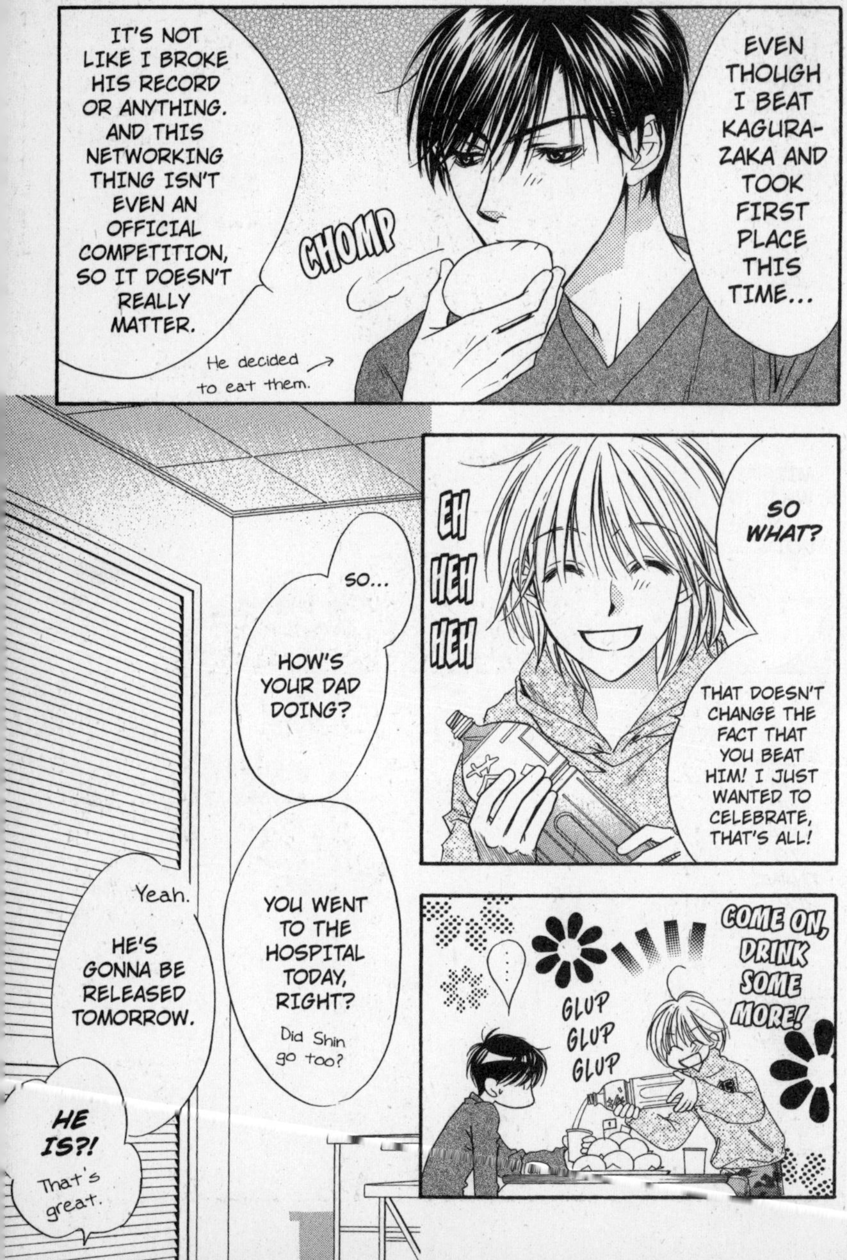
EVEN THOUGH I BEAT KAGURA-ZAKA AND TOOK FIRST PLACE THIS TIME...
CHOMP
IT'S NOT LIKE I BROKE HIS RECORD OR ANYTHING. AND THIS NETWORKING THING ISN'T EVEN AN OFFICIAL COMPETITION, SO IT DOESN'T REALLY MATTER.
He decided to eat them.
SO WHAT?
EH HEH HEH
THAT DOESN'T CHANGE THE FACT THAT YOU BEAT HIM! I JUST WANTED TO CELEBRATE, THAT'S ALL!
COME ON, DRINK SOME MORE!
GLUP GLUP GLUP
...
SO...
HOW'S YOUR DAD DOING?
YOU WENT TO THE HOSPITAL TODAY, RIGHT?
Did Shin go too?
Yeah.
HE'S GONNA BE RELEASED TOMORROW.
HE IS?!
That's great.

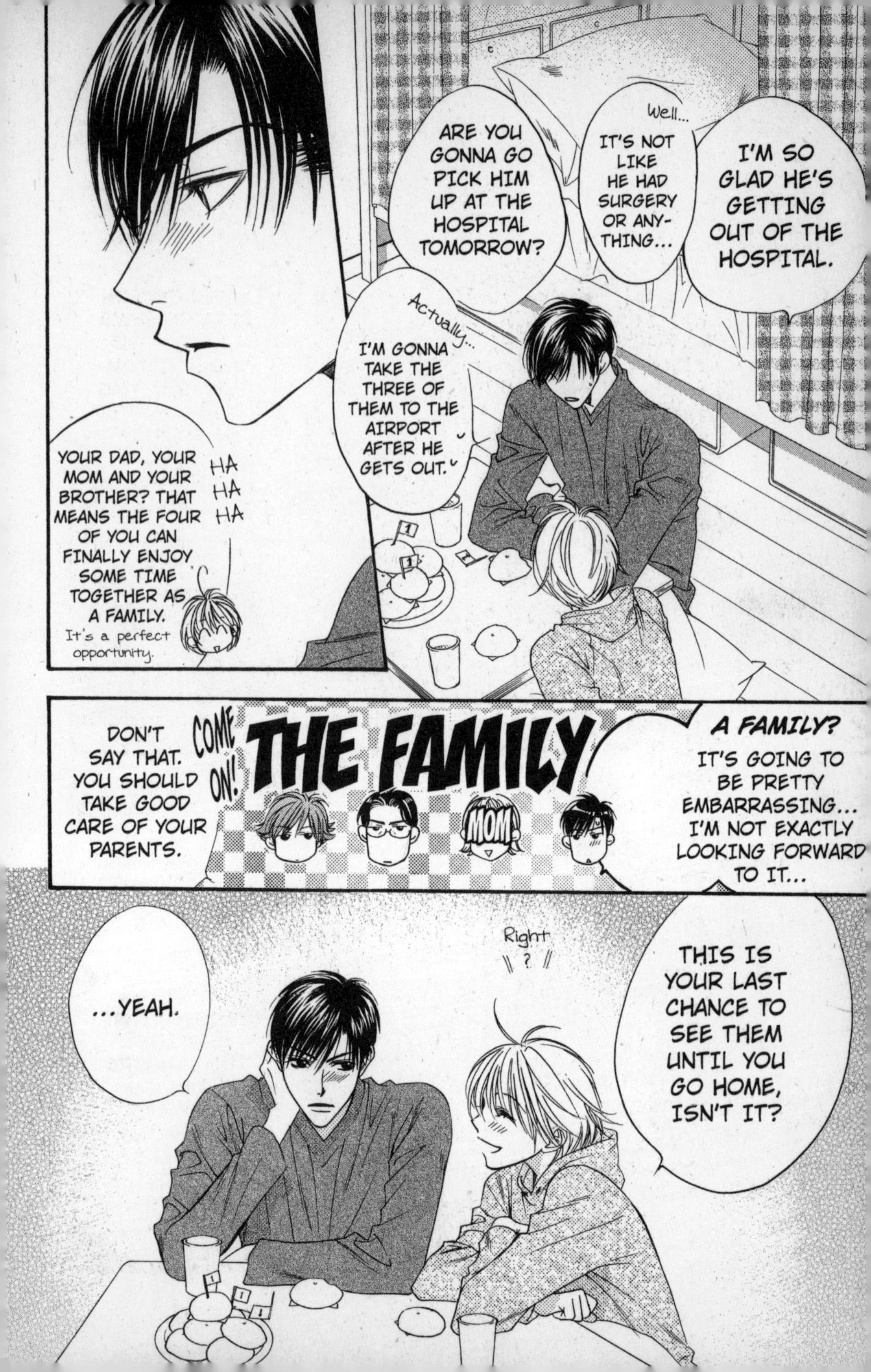
I'M SO GLAD HE'S GETTING OUT OF THE HOSPITAL.
Well...
IT'S NOT LIKE HE HAD SURGERY OR ANY-THING...
ARE YOU GONNA GO PICK HIM UP AT THE HOSPITAL TOMORROW?
Actually...
I'M GONNA TAKE THE THREE OF THEM TO THE AIRPORT AFTER HE GETS OUT.
YOUR DAD, YOUR MOM AND YOUR BROTHER? THAT MEANS THE FOUR OF YOU CAN FINALLY ENJOY SOME TIME TOGETHER AS A FAMILY.
HA HA HA
It's a perfect opportunity.
A FAMILY?
IT'S GOING TO BE PRETTY EMBARRASSING... I'M NOT EXACTLY LOOKING FORWARD TO IT...
THE FAMILY
MOM
COME ON!
DON'T SAY THAT. YOU SHOULD TAKE GOOD CARE OF YOUR PARENTS.
THIS IS YOUR LAST CHANCE TO SEE THEM UNTIL YOU GO HOME, ISN'T IT?
Right?
...YEAH.

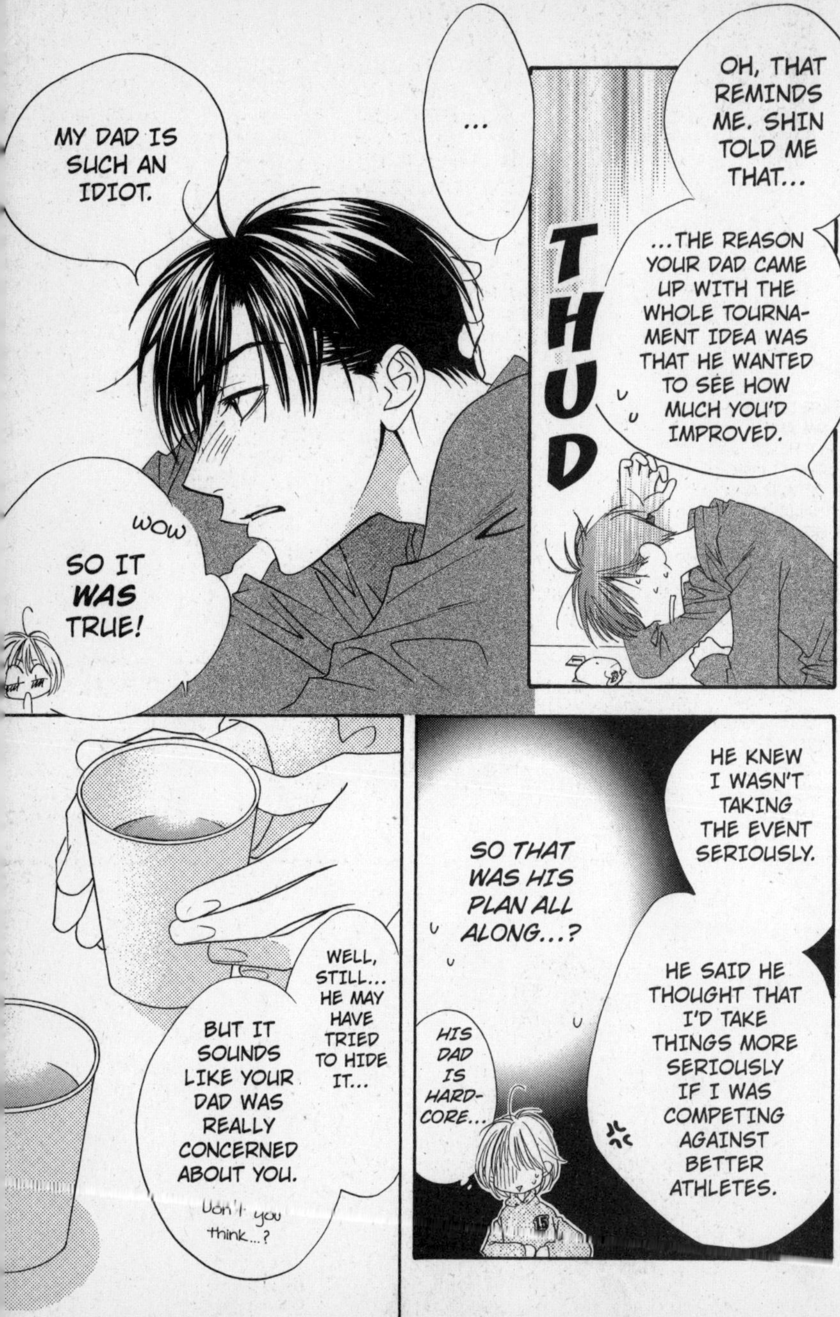
OH, THAT REMINDS ME. SHIN TOLD ME THAT...
...THE REASON YOUR DAD CAME UP WITH THE WHOLE TOURNAMENT IDEA WAS THAT HE WANTED TO SEE HOW MUCH YOU'D IMPROVED.
THUD
...
MY DAD IS SUCH AN IDIOT.
WOW
SO IT WAS TRUE!
HE KNEW I WASN'T TAKING THE EVENT SERIOUSLY.
SO THAT WAS HIS PLAN ALL ALONG...?
HE SAID HE THOUGHT THAT I'D TAKE THINGS MORE SERIOUSLY IF I WAS COMPETING AGAINST BETTER ATHLETES.
HIS DAD IS HARD-CORE...
WELL, STILL... HE MAY HAVE TRIED TO HIDE IT...
BUT IT SOUNDS LIKE YOUR DAD WAS REALLY CONCERNED ABOUT YOU.
Don't you think...?

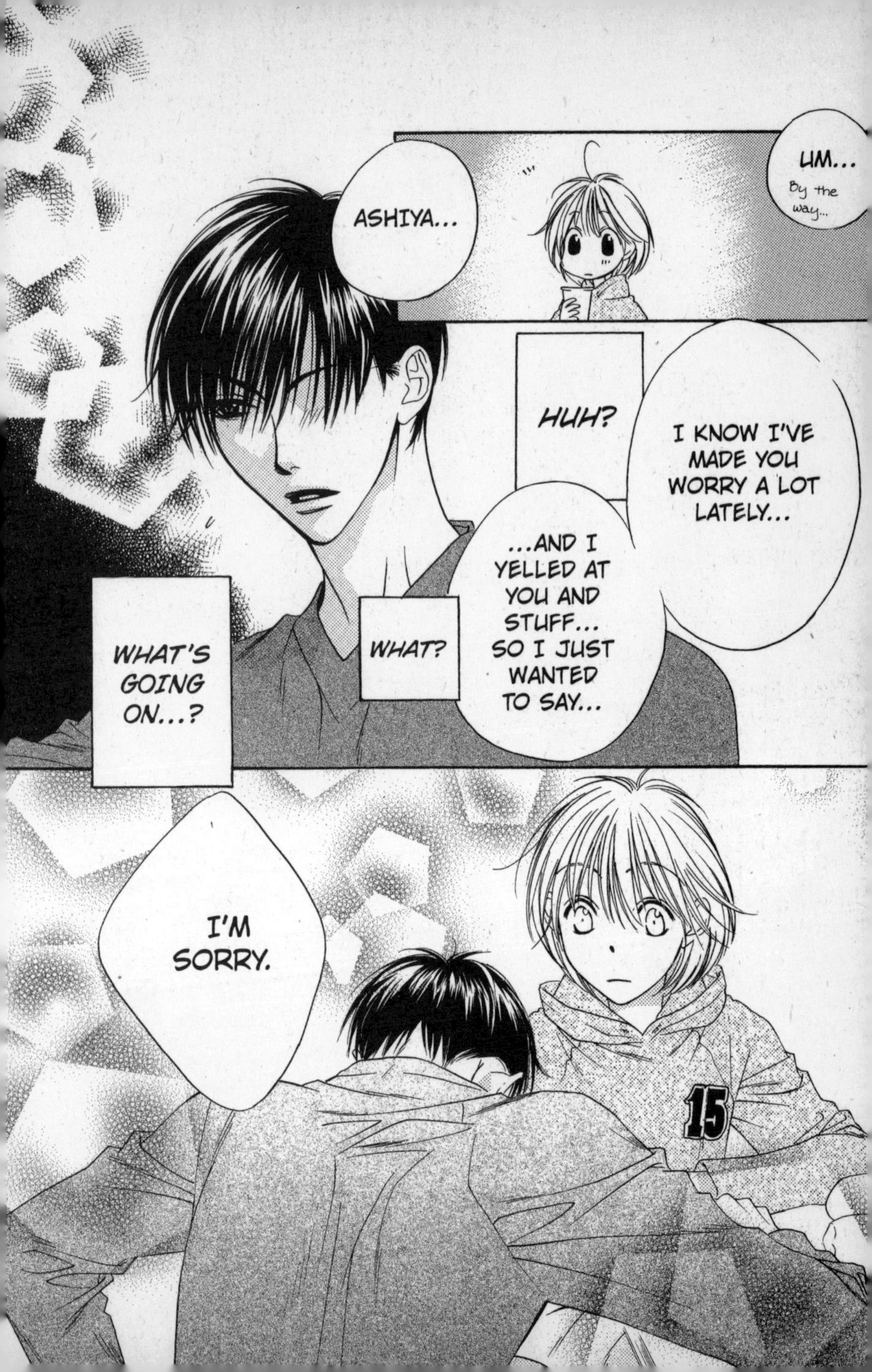
UM...
By the way...
ASHIYA...
HUH?
I KNOW I'VE MADE YOU WORRY A LOT LATELY...
...AND I YELLED AT YOU AND STUFF... SO I JUST WANTED TO SAY...
WHAT?
WHAT'S GOING ON...?
I'M SORRY.
15

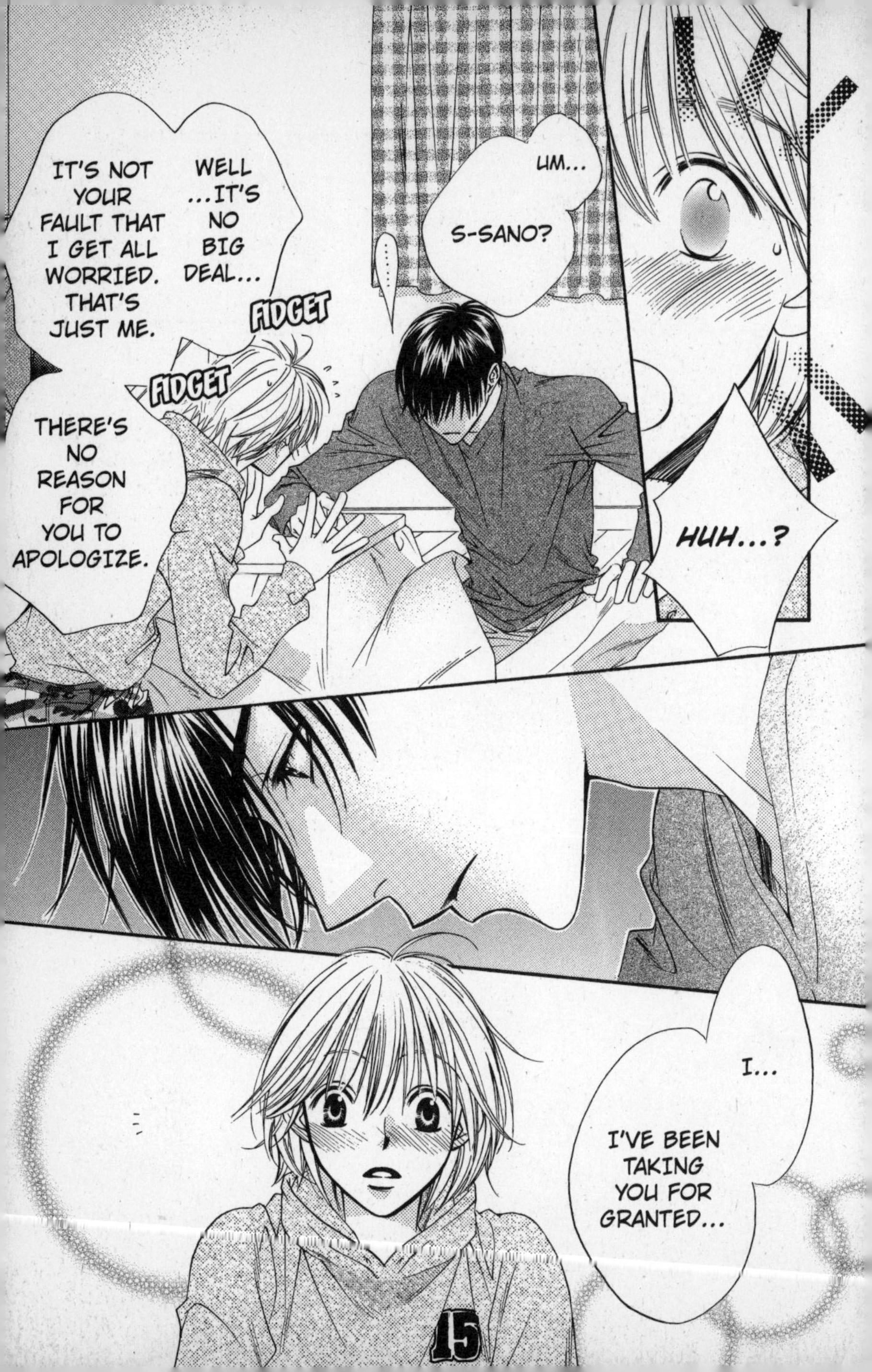
HUH...?
UM...
S-SANO?
...
WELL ...IT'S NO BIG DEAL...
IT'S NOT YOUR FAULT THAT I GET ALL WORRIED. THAT'S JUST ME.
FIDGET
FIDGET
THERE'S NO REASON FOR YOU TO APOLOGIZE.
I...
I'VE BEEN TAKING YOU FOR GRANTED...

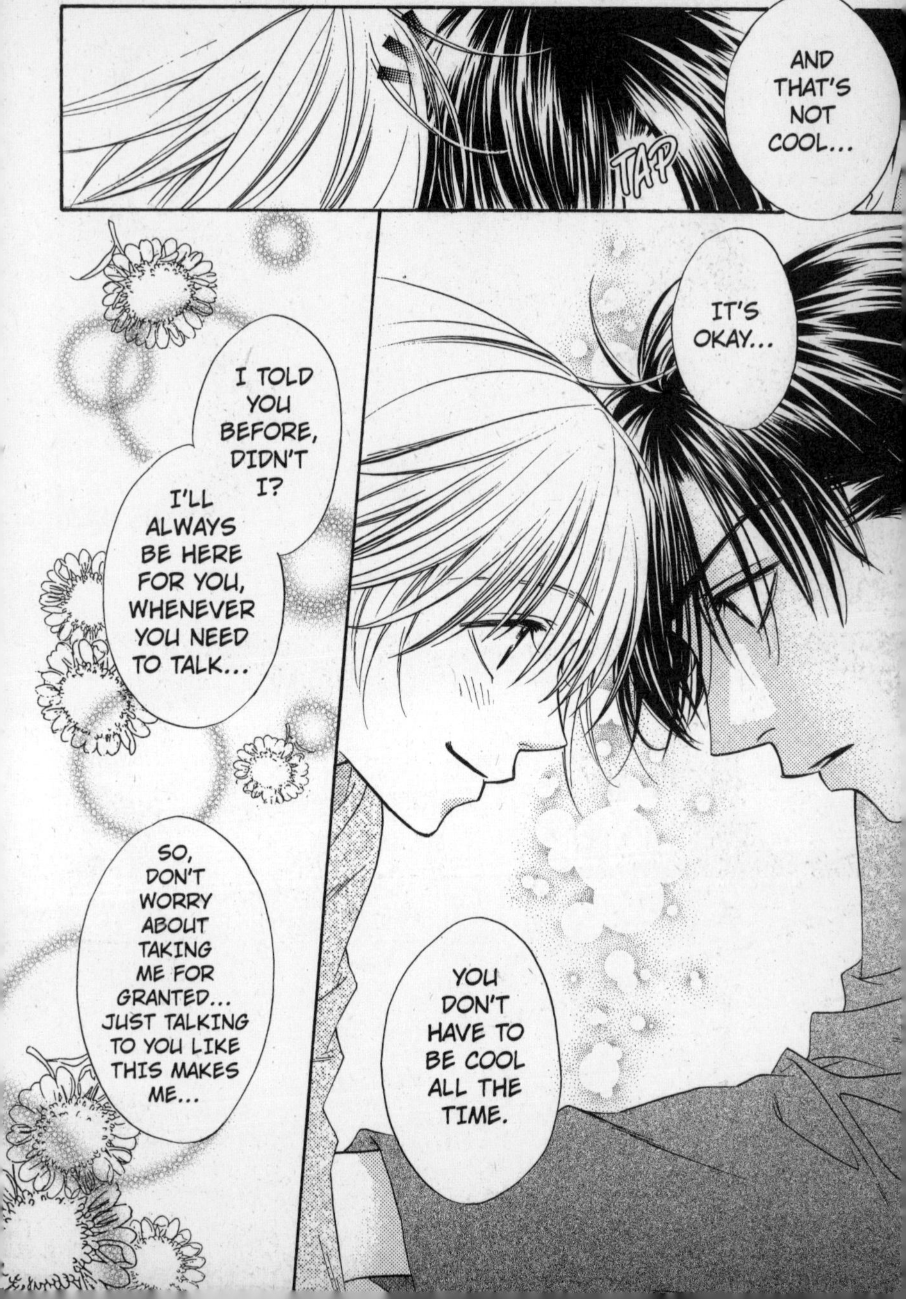
AND THAT'S NOT COOL...
TAP
IT'S OKAY...
YOU DON'T HAVE TO BE COOL ALL THE TIME.
I TOLD YOU BEFORE, DIDN'T I?
I'LL ALWAYS BE HERE FOR YOU, WHENEVER YOU NEED TO TALK...
SO, DON'T WORRY ABOUT TAKING ME FOR GRANTED... JUST TALKING TO YOU LIKE THIS MAKES ME...

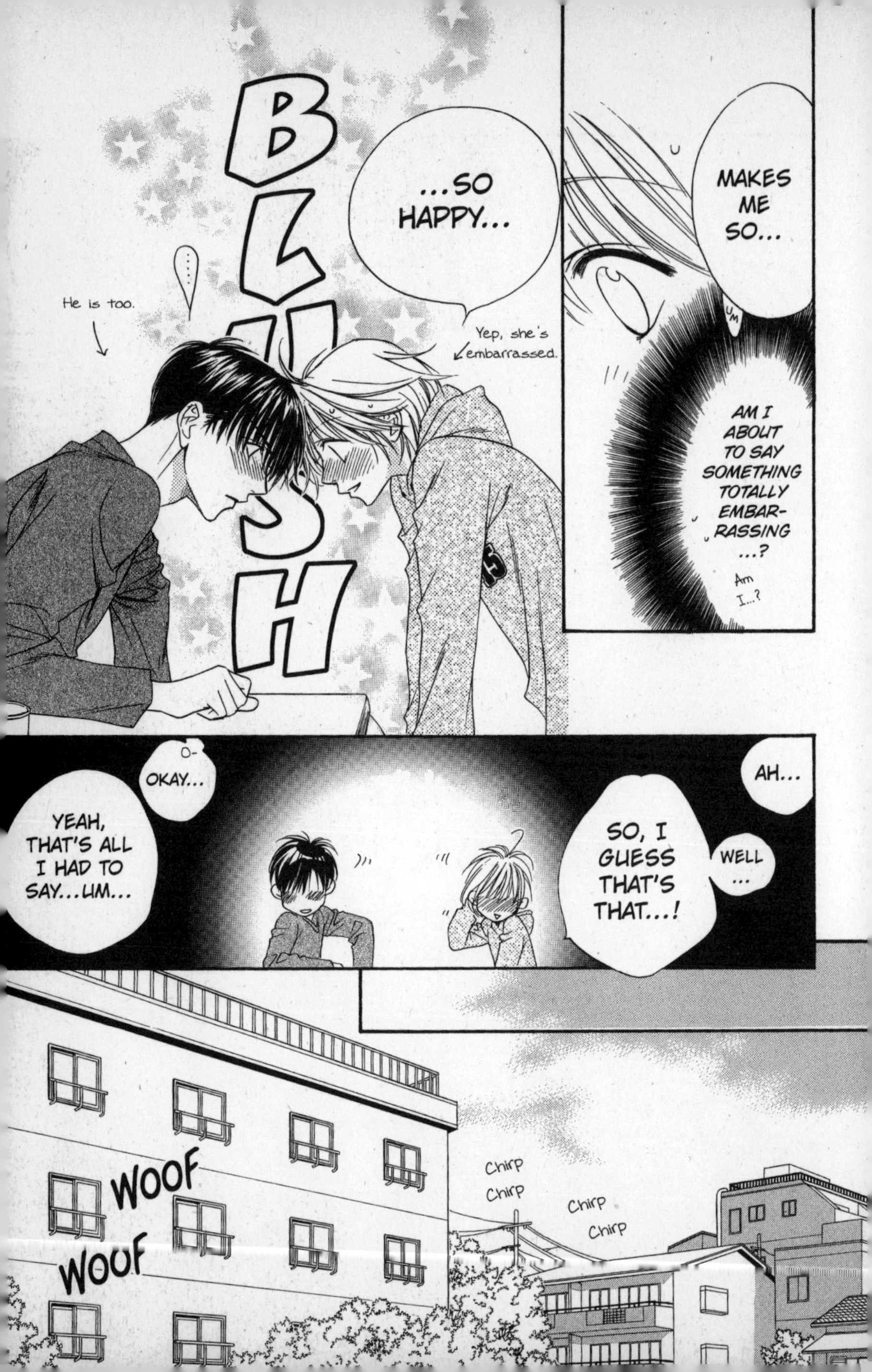
MAKES ME SO...
UM
AM I ABOUT TO SAY SOMETHING TOTALLY EMBARRASSING ...?
Am I...?
...SO HAPPY...
Yep, she's embarrassed.
BLUSH
...
He is too.
AH...
WELL ...
SO, I GUESS THAT'S THAT...!
O-OKAY...
YEAH, THAT'S ALL I HAD TO SAY...UM...
Chirp
Chirp
Chirp
Chirp
WOOF
WOOF

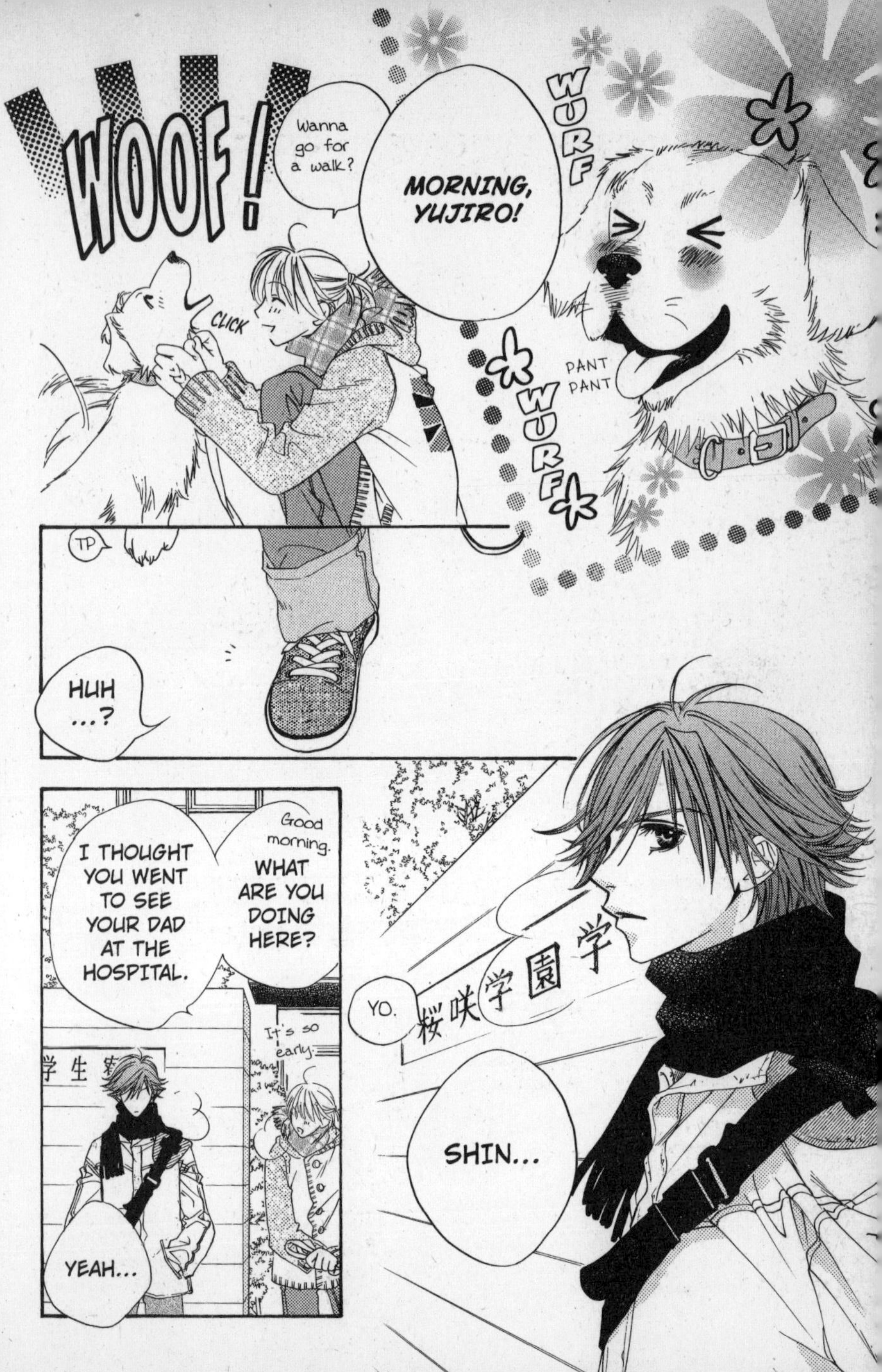
WURF
MORNING, YUJIRO!
Wanna go for a walk?
WOOF!
CLICK
PANT PANT
WURF
TP
HUH ...?
YO.
桜咲学園
SHIN...
Good morning.
WHAT ARE YOU DOING HERE?
I THOUGHT YOU WENT TO SEE YOUR DAD AT THE HOSPITAL.
It's so early.
YEAH...

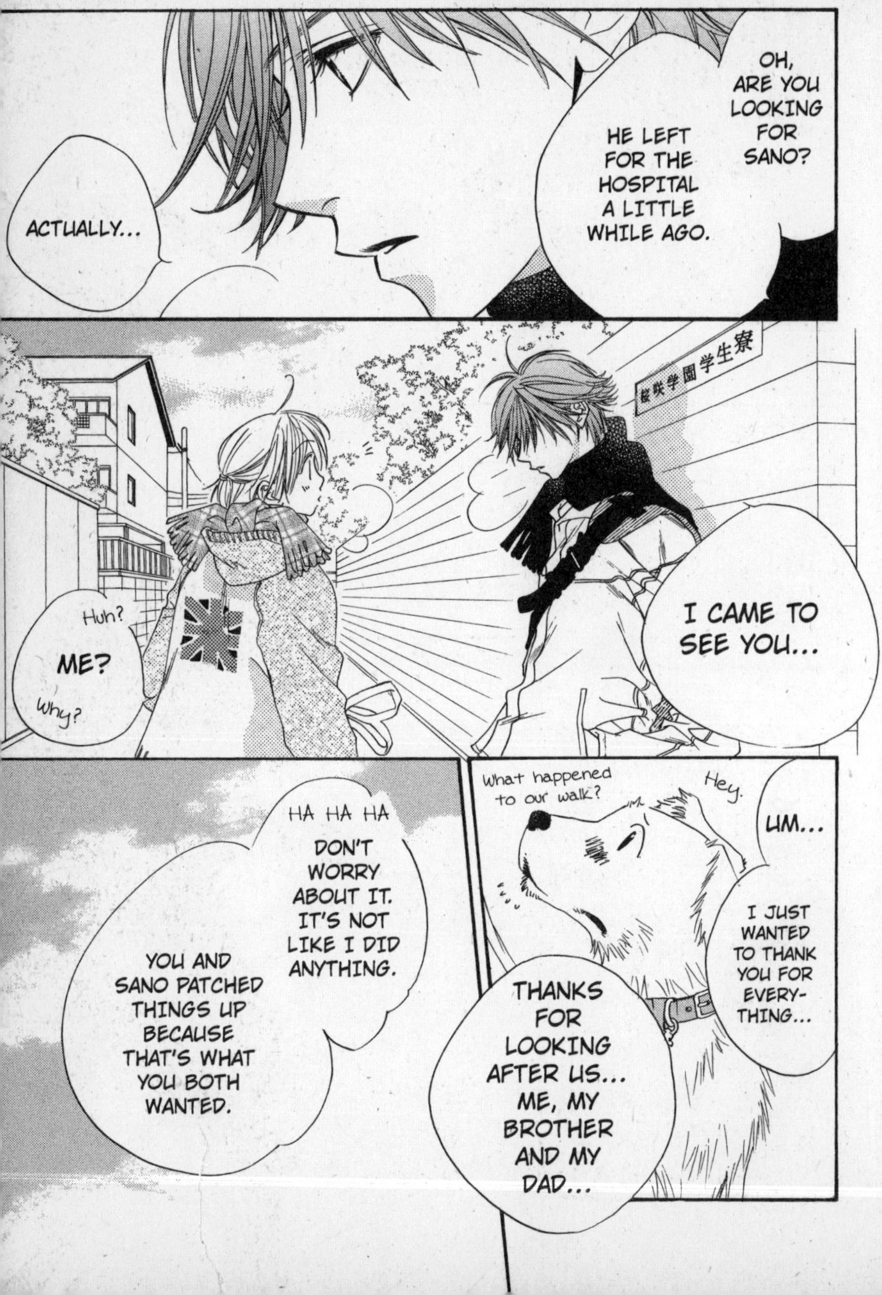
OH, ARE YOU LOOKING FOR SANO?
HE LEFT FOR THE HOSPITAL A LITTLE WHILE AGO.
ACTUALLY...
桜咲学園学生寮
I CAME TO SEE YOU...
Huh?
ME?
Why?
Hey.
What happened to our walk?
UM...
I JUST WANTED TO THANK YOU FOR EVERY-THING...
THANKS FOR LOOKING AFTER US... ME, MY BROTHER AND MY DAD...
HA HA HA
DON'T WORRY ABOUT IT. IT'S NOT LIKE I DID ANYTHING.
YOU AND SANO PATCHED THINGS UP BECAUSE THAT'S WHAT YOU BOTH WANTED.

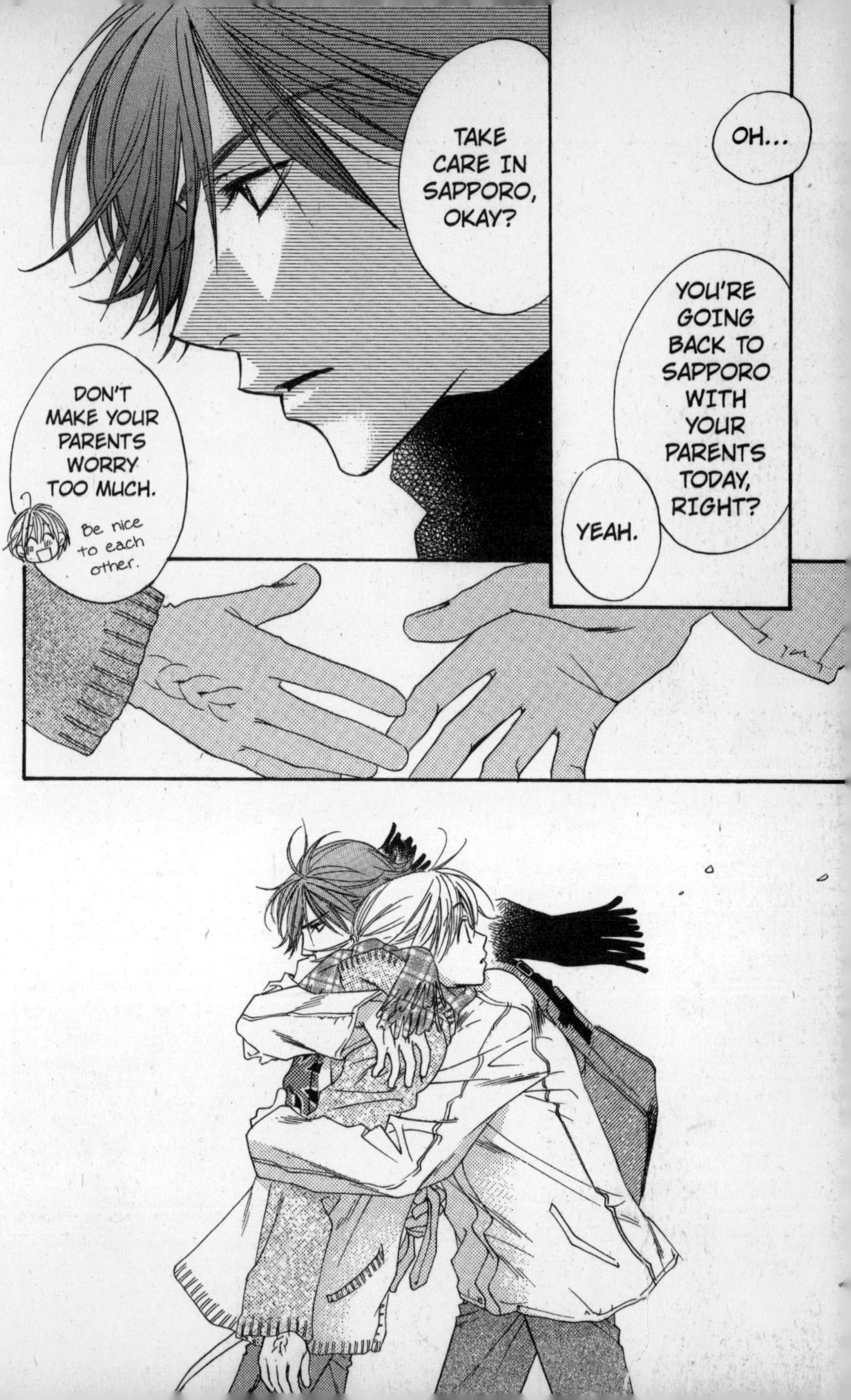
OH...
YOU'RE GOING BACK TO SAPPORO WITH YOUR PARENTS TODAY, RIGHT?
YEAH.
TAKE CARE IN SAPPORO, OKAY?
DON'T MAKE YOUR PARENTS WORRY TOO MUCH.
Be nice to each other.

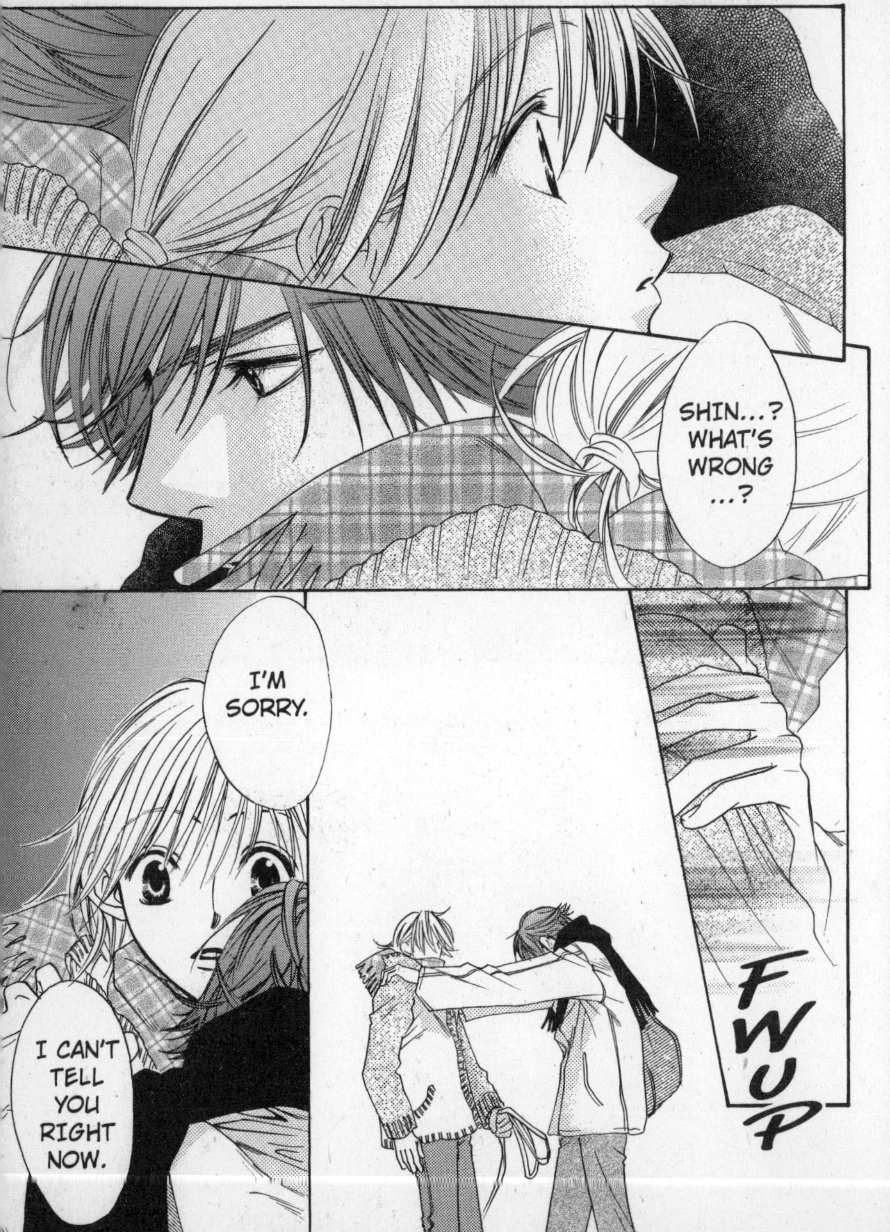
SHIN...? WHAT'S WRONG ...?
FWUP
I'M SORRY.
I CAN'T TELL YOU RIGHT NOW.

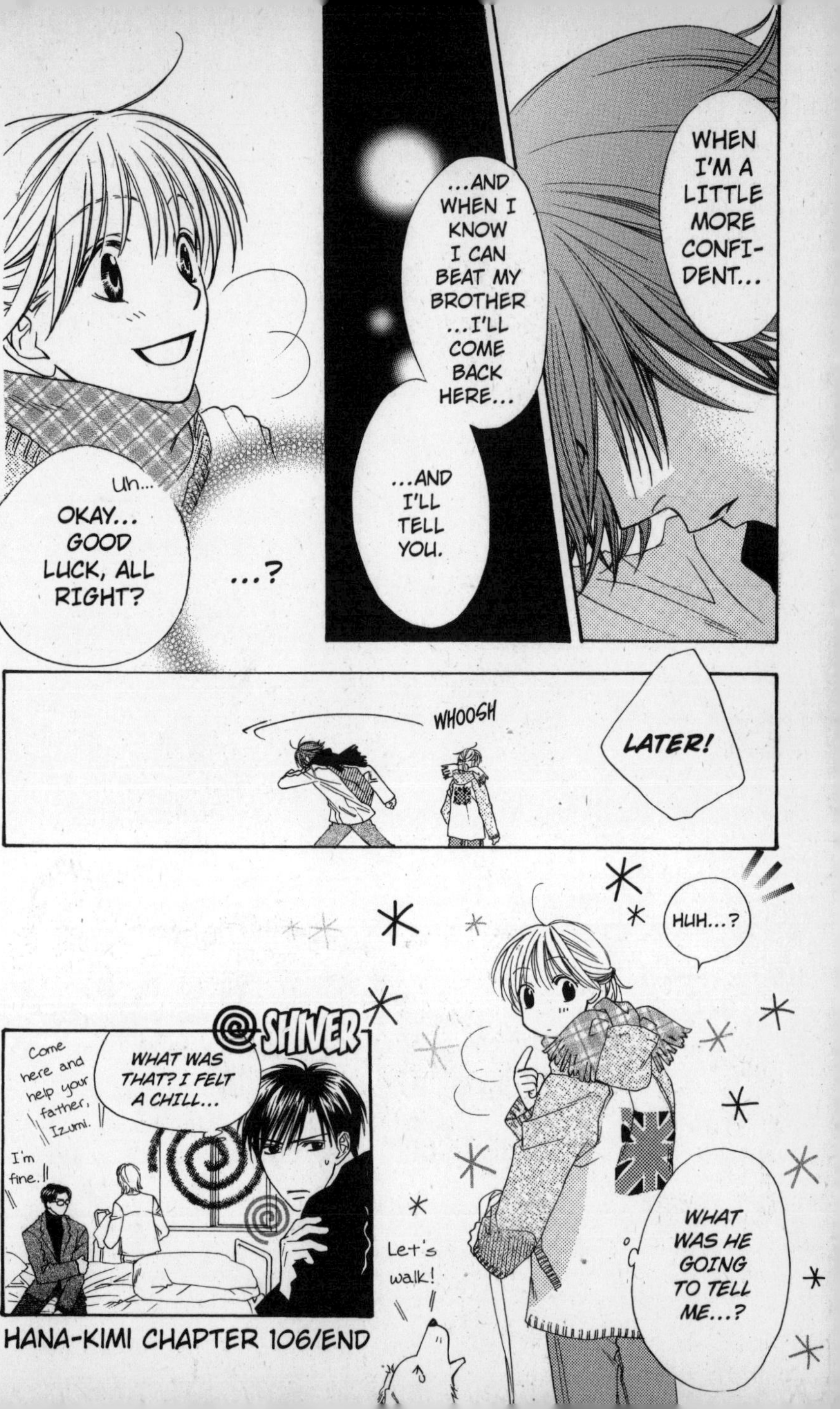
WHEN I'M A LITTLE MORE CONFIDENT...
...AND WHEN I KNOW I CAN BEAT MY BROTHER ...I'LL COME BACK HERE...
...AND I'LL TELL YOU.
Uh...
OKAY... GOOD LUCK, ALL RIGHT?
...?
LATER!
WHOOSH
HUH...?
WHAT WAS HE GOING TO TELL ME...?
Let's walk!
SHIVER
WHAT WAS THAT? I FELT A CHILL...
Come here and help your father, Izumi.
I'm fine.

HANA-KIMI CHAPTER 106/END

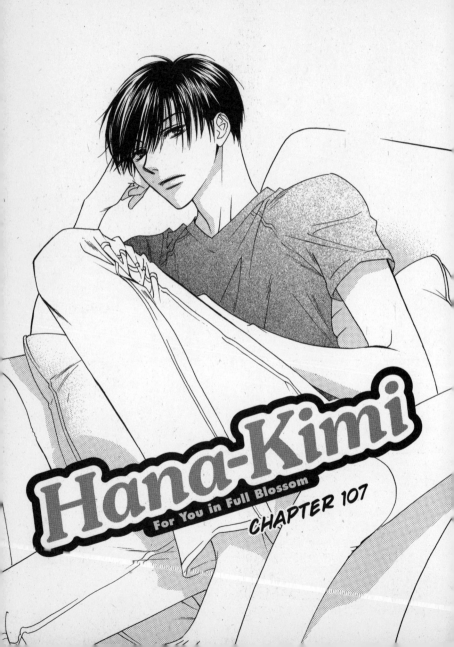

Hana-Kimi
For You in Full Blossom
CHAPTER 107

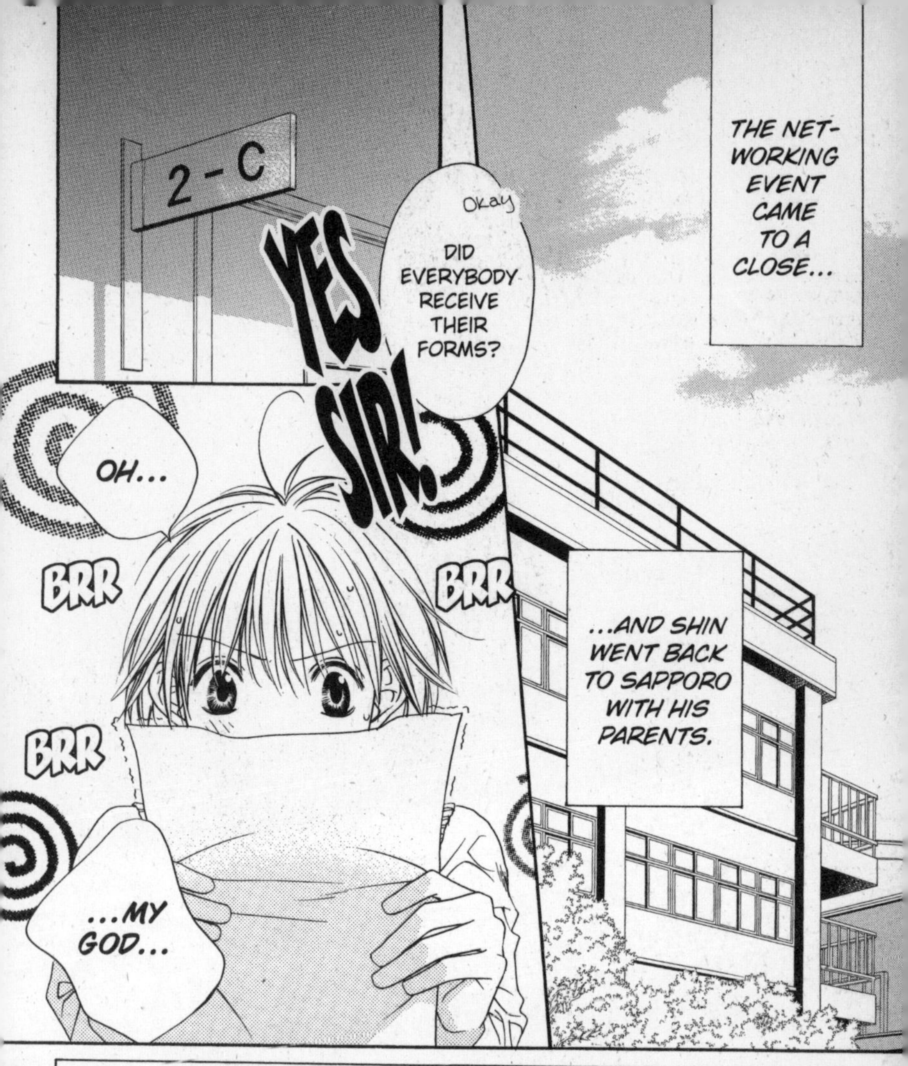
THE NET-WORKING EVENT CAME TO A CLOSE...
...AND SHIN WENT BACK TO SAPPORO WITH HIS PARENTS.
2-C
Okay
DID EVERYBODY RECEIVE THEIR FORMS?
YES SIR!
OH...
BRR
BRR
BRR
...MY GOD...

CHEEKY AND ME

There are many different kinds of teddy bears out there from brands like Stife and Merry Thought, but I've finally found my favorite bear! It's perfect! It's called the Cheeky Bear and it's made by Merry Thought. Apparently, when Queen Elizabeth saw this teddy bear for the first time, she said, "What a cheeky face!"

Size 10 is my favorite.

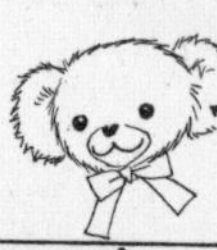
There's a tiny bell inside his ear.

I've got ten of these at home.

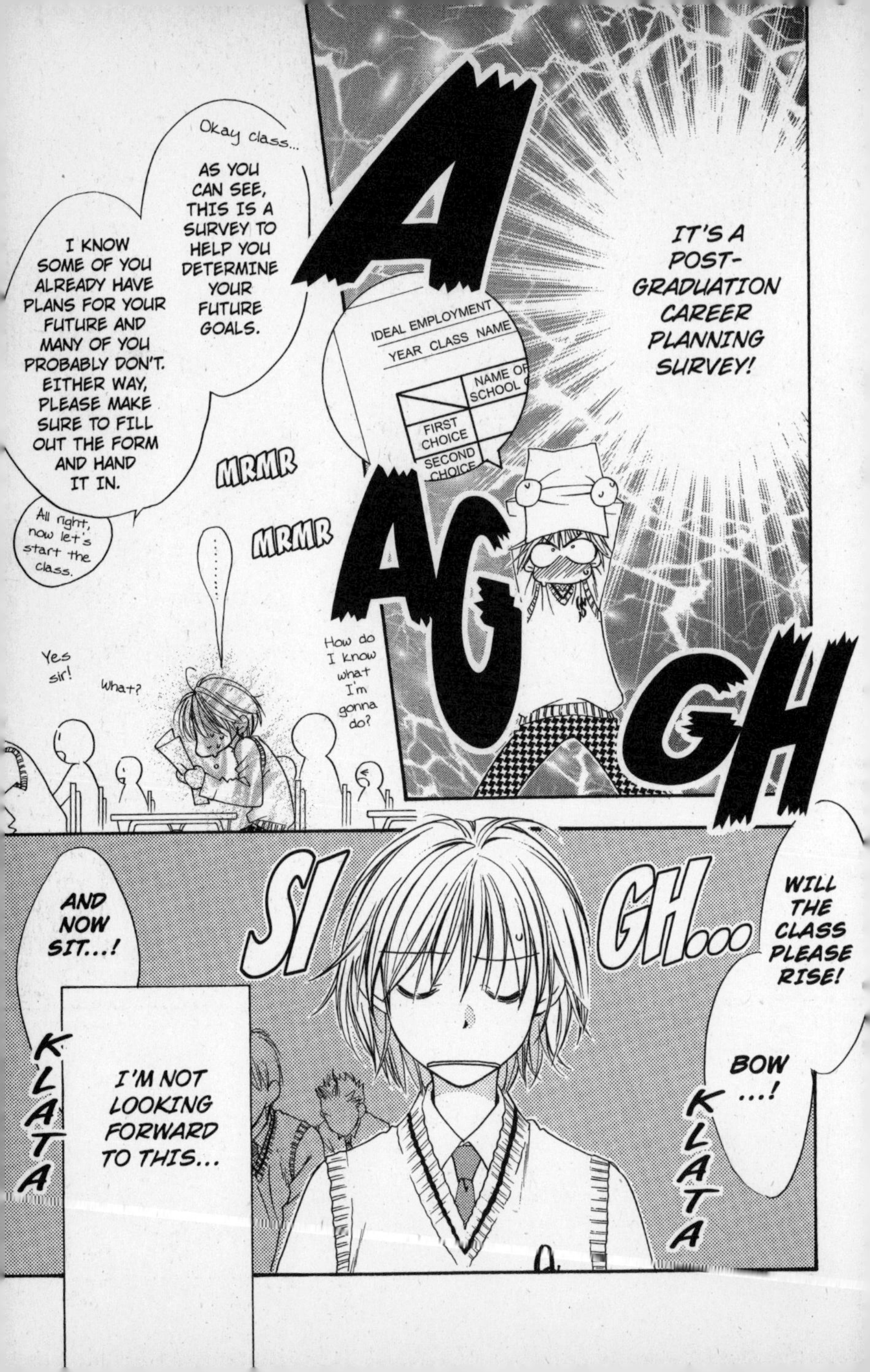
IT'S A POST-GRADUATION CAREER PLANNING SURVEY!
AAGH
IDEAL EMPLOYMENT
YEAR CLASS NAME
NAME OF SCHOOL
FIRST CHOICE
SECOND CHOICE
Okay class...
AS YOU CAN SEE, THIS IS A SURVEY TO HELP YOU DETERMINE YOUR FUTURE GOALS.
I KNOW SOME OF YOU ALREADY HAVE PLANS FOR YOUR FUTURE AND MANY OF YOU PROBABLY DON'T. EITHER WAY, PLEASE MAKE SURE TO FILL OUT THE FORM AND HAND IT IN.
All right, now let's start the class.
MRMR
MRMR
......
How do I know what I'm gonna do?
What?
Yes sir!
WILL THE CLASS PLEASE RISE!
BOW ...!
KLATA
SIGH...
AND NOW SIT...!
KLATA
I'M NOT LOOKING FORWARD TO THIS...

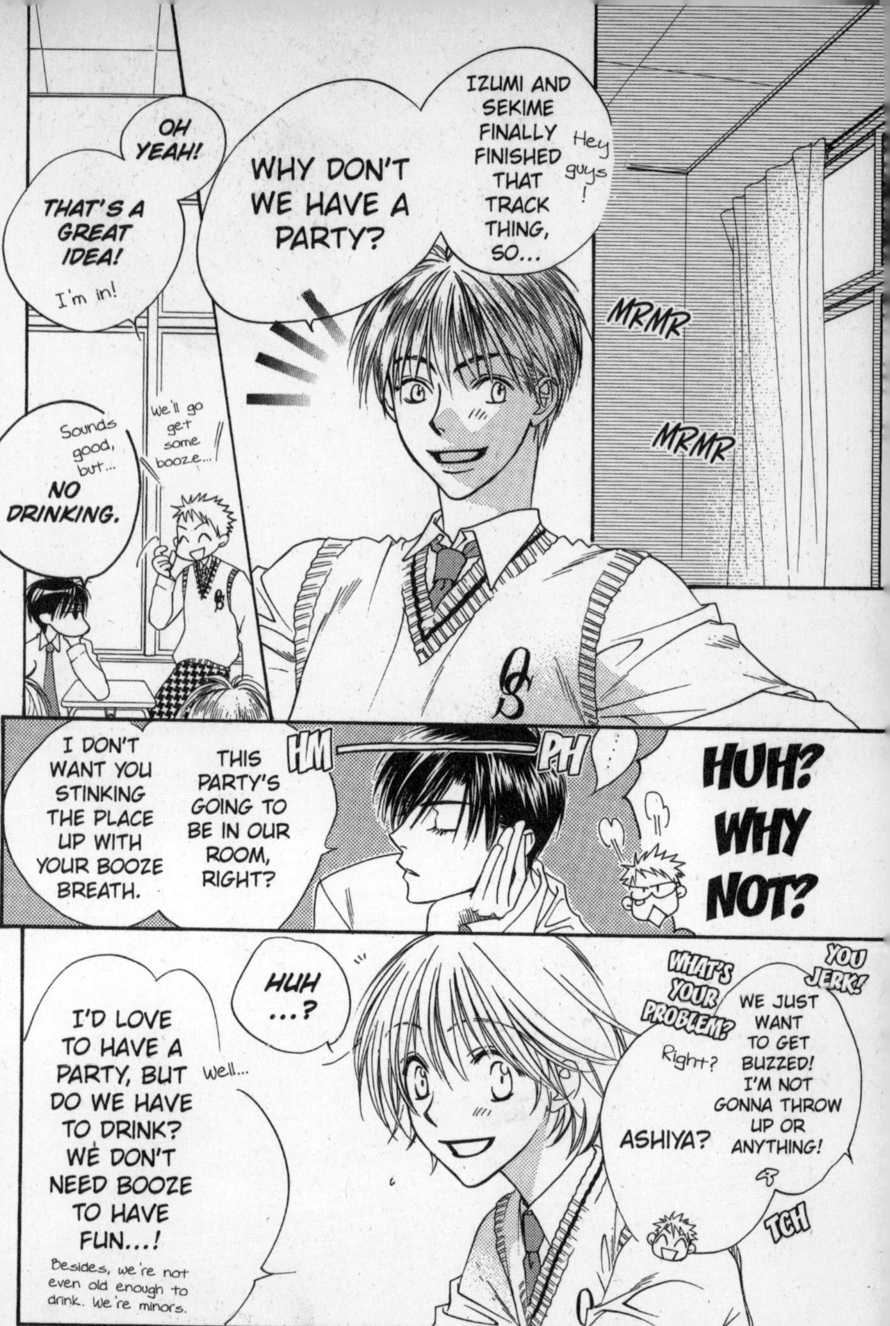
Hey guys!
IZUMI AND SEKIME FINALLY FINISHED THAT TRACK THING, SO...
WHY DON'T WE HAVE A PARTY?
MRMR
MRMR
OH YEAH! THAT'S A GREAT IDEA!
I'm in!
We'll go get some booze...
Sounds good, but... NO DRINKING.
HUH? WHY NOT?
HMPH
THIS PARTY'S GOING TO BE IN OUR ROOM, RIGHT?
I DON'T WANT YOU STINKING THE PLACE UP WITH YOUR BOOZE BREATH.
YOU JERK!
WHAT'S YOUR PROBLEM?
WE JUST WANT TO GET BUZZED! I'M NOT GONNA THROW UP OR ANYTHING!
Right?
TCH
ASHIYA?
HUH...?
Well...
I'D LOVE TO HAVE A PARTY, BUT DO WE HAVE TO DRINK? WE DON'T NEED BOOZE TO HAVE FUN...!
Besides, we're not even old enough to drink. We're minors.

SCHOOL

There are things about my high school that seem to be different from other schools... For example, we used to spend an entire month rehearsing for our graduation ceremony. The way our campus was laid out was kind of unique too. I tried to explain the layout to my assistants, but they didn't quite get it... Maybe the reason Osaka High is so unique is that it's based on my high school. Or maybe not! I'm glad that so many of you readers like the fact that Osaka High is a little different.

I heard that other schools don't rehearse that long.

...
Um...
SORRY, I CAN'T MAKE IT.
Gotta pass.
NOT OLD ENOUGH?!
WHY ARE YOU TRYING TO ACT ALL GOODY TWO-SHOES? YOU'RE NOT FOOLING ANYONE!
SHUT UP! I AM NOT A GOODY TWO-SHOES!
HUH?!
He got a haircut.
Huh? WHY CAN'T YOU COME, SEKIME?
HEY! WHAT'S WRONG? WHY CAN'T YOU HANG OUT?
HMPH
I need your support here!
Calm down, you guys.
I'VE GOT PLANS, THAT'S ALL.

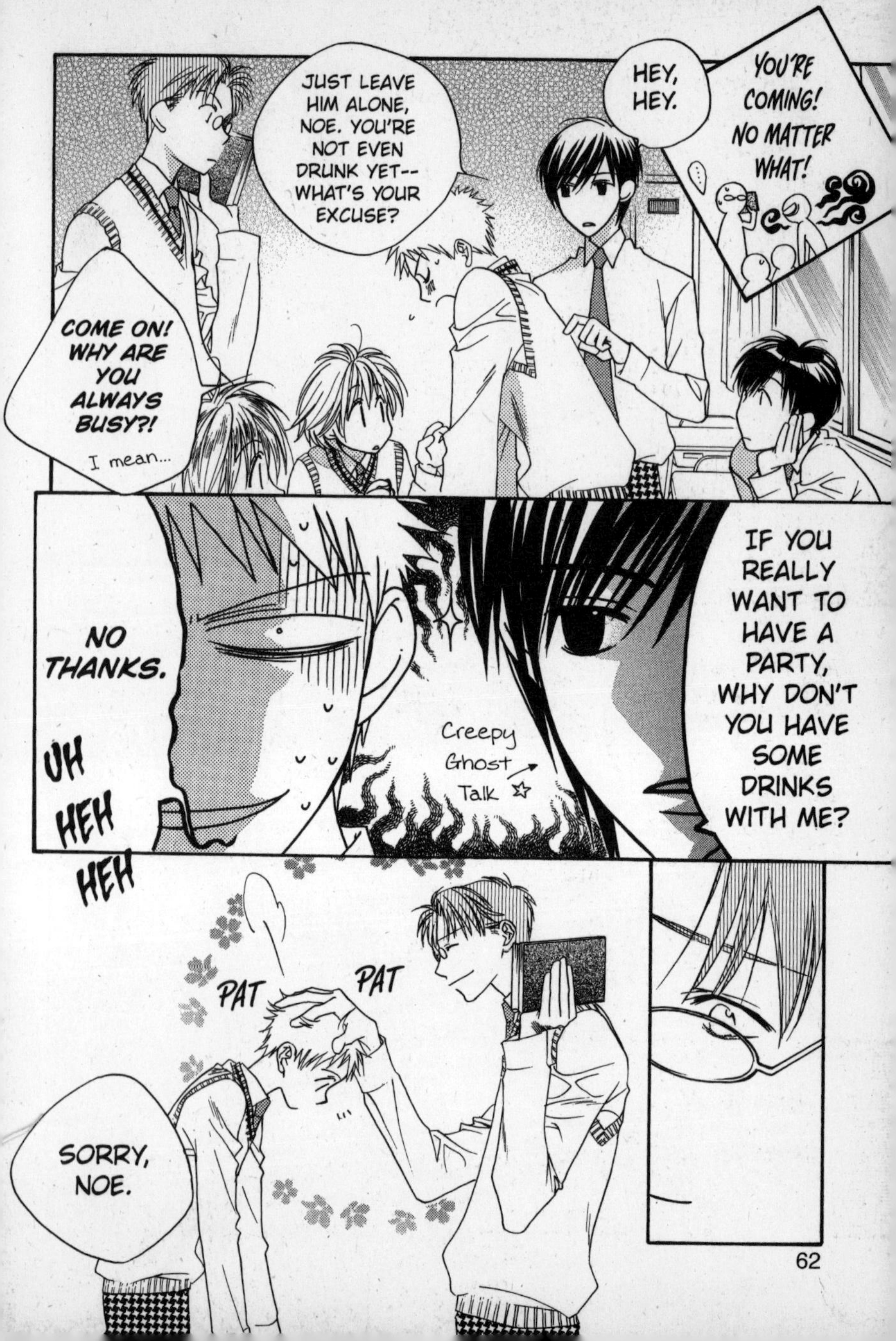
YOU'RE COMING! NO MATTER WHAT!
HEY, HEY.
JUST LEAVE HIM ALONE, NOE. YOU'RE NOT EVEN DRUNK YET--WHAT'S YOUR EXCUSE?
COME ON! WHY ARE YOU ALWAYS BUSY?!
I mean...
IF YOU REALLY WANT TO HAVE A PARTY, WHY DON'T YOU HAVE SOME DRINKS WITH ME?
Creepy Ghost Talk
NO THANKS.
UH HEH HEH
PAT PAT
SORRY, NOE.

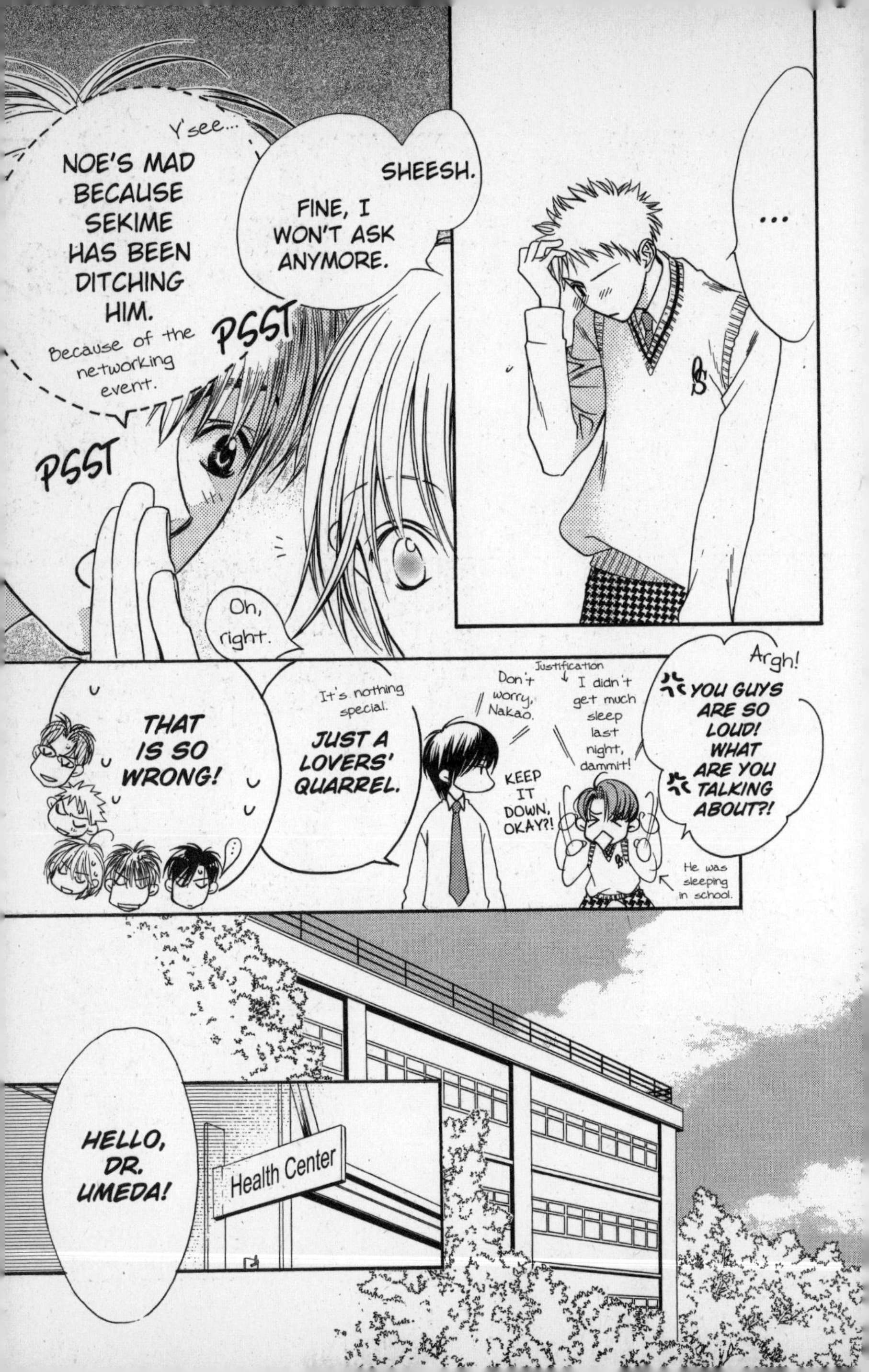
...
SHEESH.
FINE, I WON'T ASK ANYMORE.
Y'see...
NOE'S MAD BECAUSE SEKIME HAS BEEN DITCHING HIM.
Because of the networking event.
PSST
PSST
Oh, right.
Argh!
YOU GUYS ARE SO LOUD! WHAT ARE YOU TALKING ABOUT?!
He was sleeping in school.
Justification
I didn't get much sleep last night, dammit!
Don't worry, Nakao.
KEEP IT DOWN, OKAY?!
It's nothing special.
JUST A LOVERS' QUARREL.
THAT IS SO WRONG!
Health Center
HELLO, DR. UMEDA!

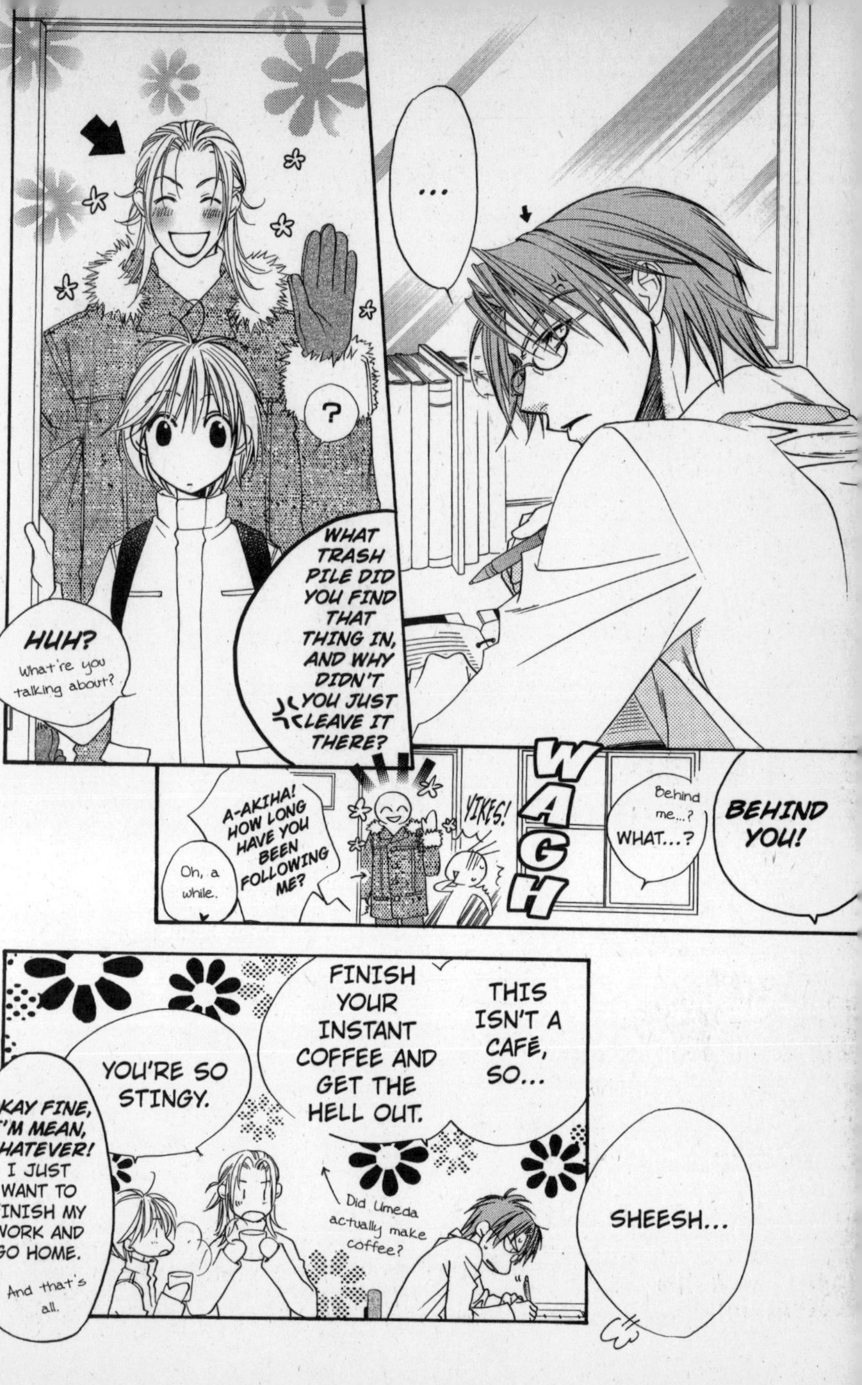
...
?
WHAT TRASH PILE DID YOU FIND THAT THING IN, AND WHY DIDN'T YOU JUST LEAVE IT THERE?
HUH? What're you talking about?
BEHIND YOU!
Behind me...? WHAT...?
WAGH
YIKES!
A-AKIHA! HOW LONG HAVE YOU BEEN FOLLOWING ME?
Oh, a while.
SHEESH...
THIS ISN'T A CAFÉ, SO...
FINISH YOUR INSTANT COFFEE AND GET THE HELL OUT.
Did Umeda actually make coffee?
YOU'RE SO STINGY.
OKAY FINE, I'M MEAN, WHATEVER! I JUST WANT TO FINISH MY WORK AND GO HOME.
And that's all.

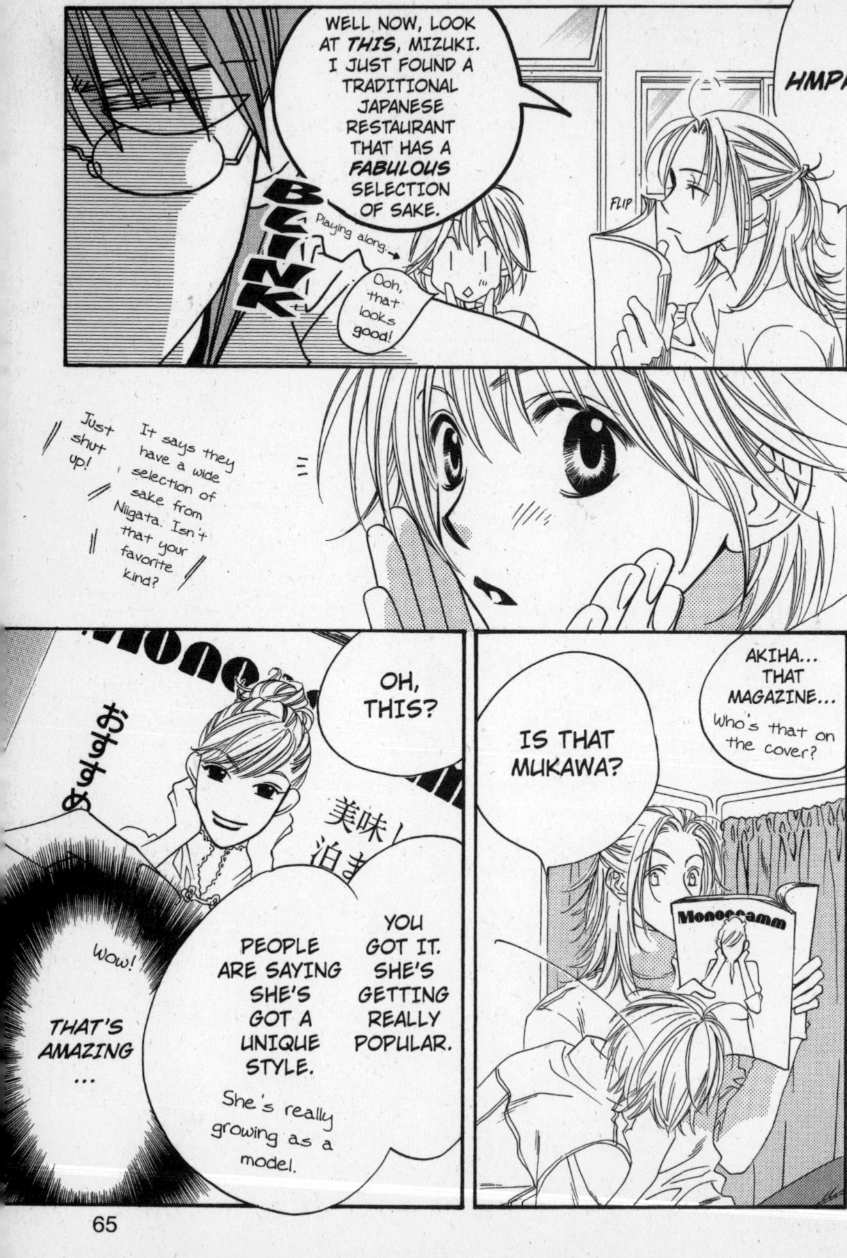
HMPH.
WELL NOW, LOOK AT THIS, MIZUKI. I JUST FOUND A TRADITIONAL JAPANESE RESTAURANT THAT HAS A FABULOUS SELECTION OF SAKE.
FLIP
BLINK
Playing along...
Ooh, that looks good!
It says they have a wide selection of sake from Niigata. Isn't that your favorite kind?
Just shut up!
AKIHA... THAT MAGAZINE...
Who's that on the cover?
IS THAT MUKAWA?
OH, THIS?
おすすめ
YOU GOT IT. SHE'S GETTING REALLY POPULAR.
PEOPLE ARE SAYING SHE'S GOT A UNIQUE STYLE.
She's really growing as a model.
Wow!
THAT'S AMAZING...

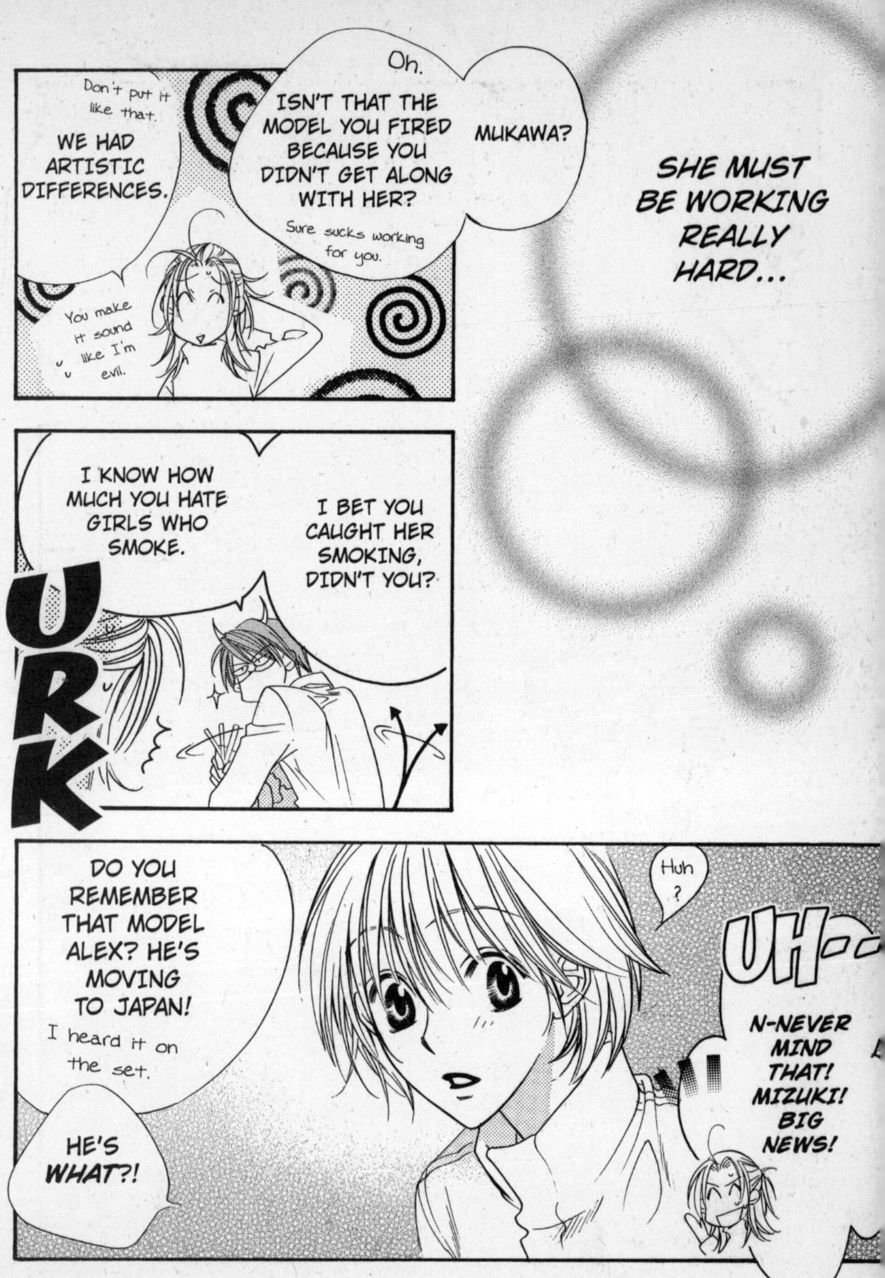
SHE MUST BE WORKING REALLY HARD...
Oh.
MUKAWA?
ISN'T THAT THE MODEL YOU FIRED BECAUSE YOU DIDN'T GET ALONG WITH HER?
Sure sucks working for you.
Don't put it like that.
WE HAD ARTISTIC DIFFERENCES.
You make it sound like I'm evil.
I BET YOU CAUGHT HER SMOKING, DIDN'T YOU?
I KNOW HOW MUCH YOU HATE GIRLS WHO SMOKE.
URK
Huh?
UH--
N-NEVER MIND THAT! MIZUKI! BIG NEWS!
DO YOU REMEMBER THAT MODEL ALEX? HE'S MOVING TO JAPAN!
I heard it on the set.
HE'S WHAT?!

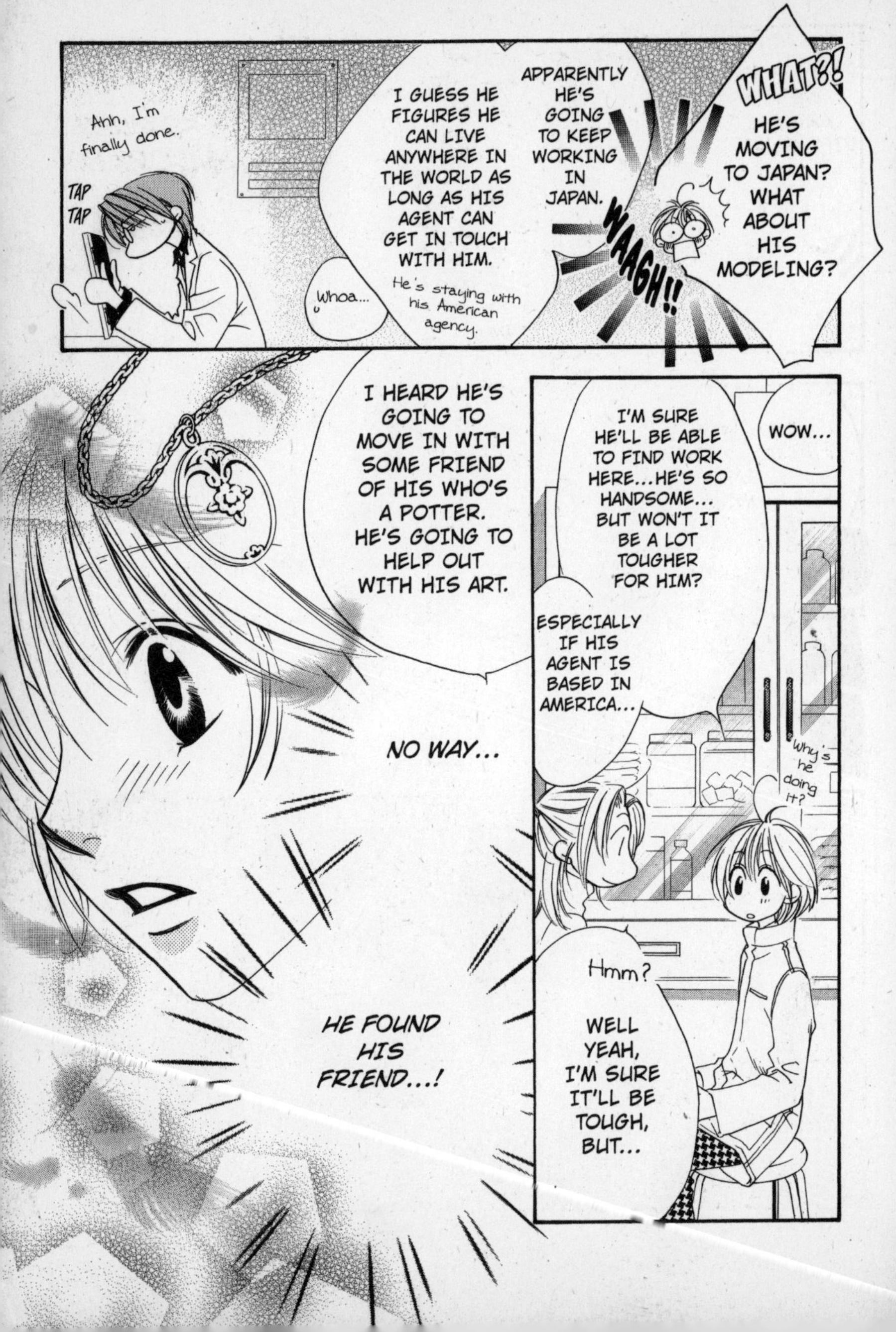
WHAT?!
HE'S MOVING TO JAPAN? WHAT ABOUT HIS MODELING?
WAAGH!!
APPARENTLY HE'S GOING TO KEEP WORKING IN JAPAN.
I GUESS HE FIGURES HE CAN LIVE ANYWHERE IN THE WORLD AS LONG AS HIS AGENT CAN GET IN TOUCH WITH HIM.
He's staying with his American agency.
Whoa...
Ahh, I'm finally done.
TAP TAP
WOW...
I'M SURE HE'LL BE ABLE TO FIND WORK HERE...HE'S SO HANDSOME... BUT WON'T IT BE A LOT TOUGHER FOR HIM?
ESPECIALLY IF HIS AGENT IS BASED IN AMERICA...
Why's he doing it?
Hmm?
WELL YEAH, I'M SURE IT'LL BE TOUGH, BUT...
I HEARD HE'S GOING TO MOVE IN WITH SOME FRIEND OF HIS WHO'S A POTTER. HE'S GOING TO HELP OUT WITH HIS ART.
NO WAY...
HE FOUND HIS FRIEND...!

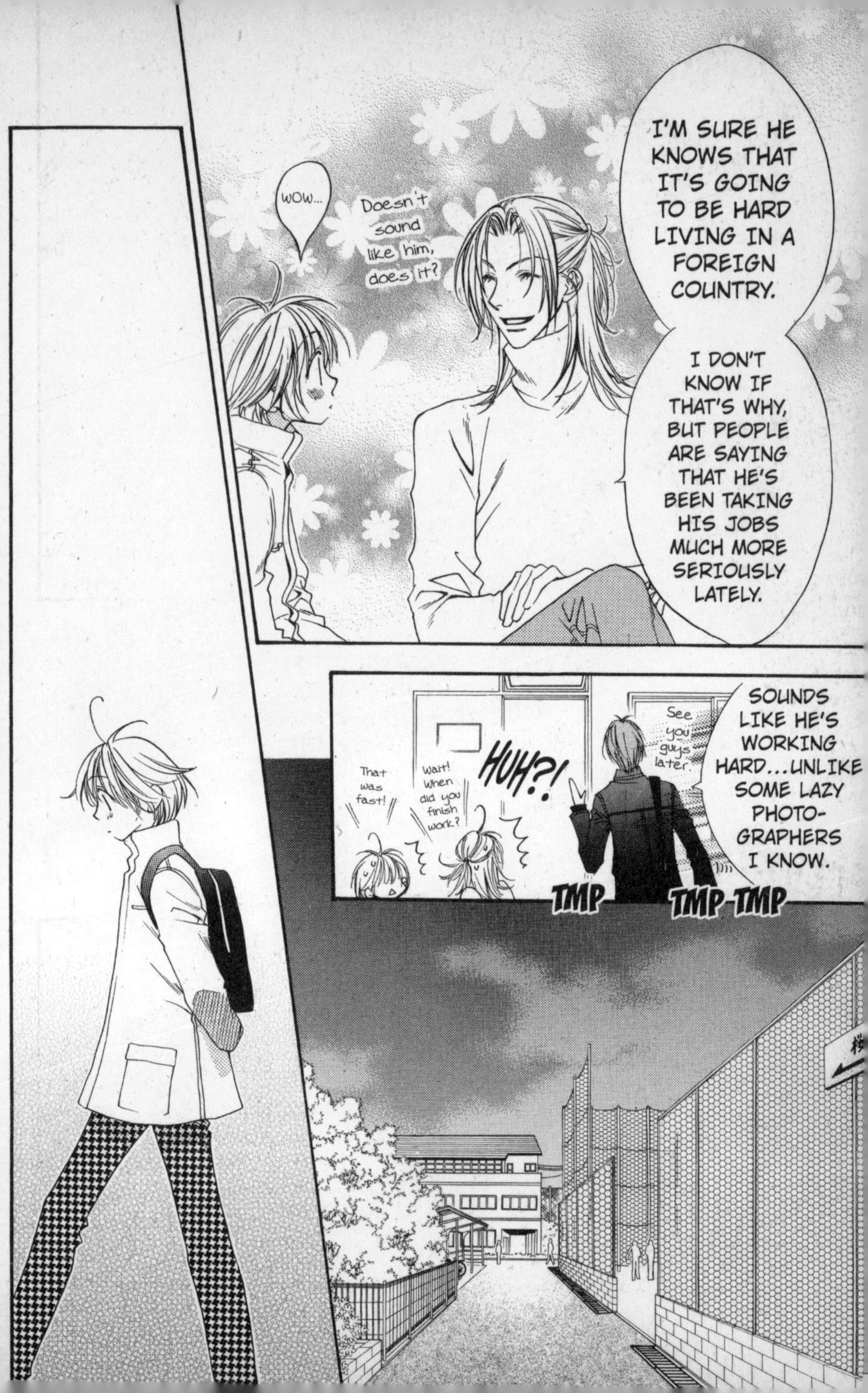
I'M SURE HE KNOWS THAT IT'S GOING TO BE HARD LIVING IN A FOREIGN COUNTRY.
I DON'T KNOW IF THAT'S WHY, BUT PEOPLE ARE SAYING THAT HE'S BEEN TAKING HIS JOBS MUCH MORE SERIOUSLY LATELY.
Doesn't sound like him, does it?
WOW...
SOUNDS LIKE HE'S WORKING HARD...UNLIKE SOME LAZY PHOTO-GRAPHERS I KNOW.
See you guys later.
HUH?!
Wait! When did you finish work?
That was fast!
TMP TMP
TMP

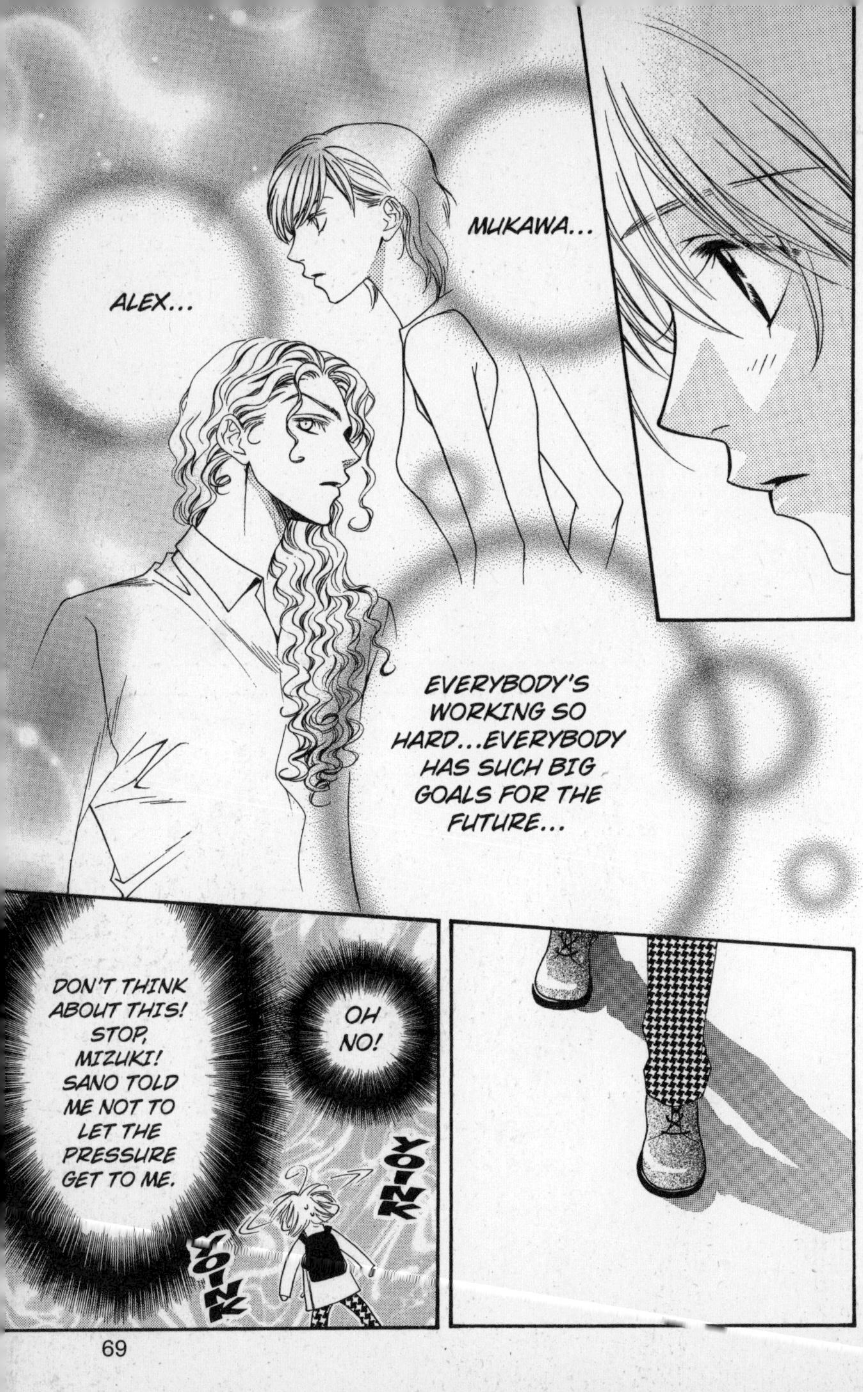
MUKAWA...
ALEX...
EVERYBODY'S WORKING SO HARD...EVERYBODY HAS SUCH BIG GOALS FOR THE FUTURE...
OH NO!
DON'T THINK ABOUT THIS! STOP, MIZUKI! SANO TOLD ME NOT TO LET THE PRESSURE GET TO ME.
YOINK
YOINK

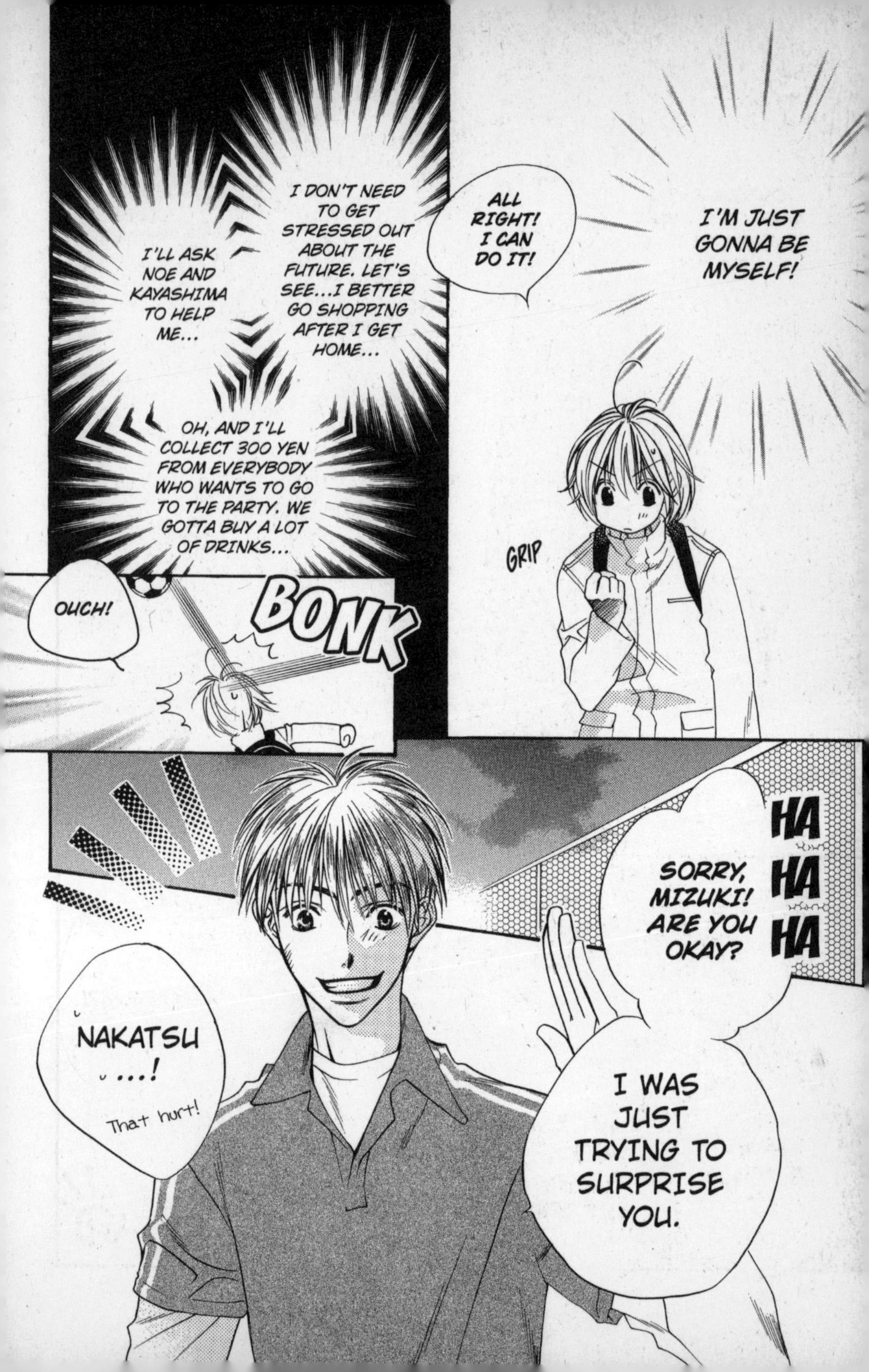
I'M JUST GONNA BE MYSELF!
ALL RIGHT! I CAN DO IT!
GRIP
I DON'T NEED TO GET STRESSED OUT ABOUT THE FUTURE. LET'S SEE...I BETTER GO SHOPPING AFTER I GET HOME...
I'LL ASK NOE AND KAYASHIMA TO HELP ME...
OH, AND I'LL COLLECT 300 YEN FROM EVERYBODY WHO WANTS TO GO TO THE PARTY. WE GOTTA BUY A LOT OF DRINKS...
BONK
OUCH!
HA HA HA
SORRY, MIZUKI! ARE YOU OKAY?
I WAS JUST TRYING TO SURPRISE YOU.
NAKATSU ...!
That hurt!

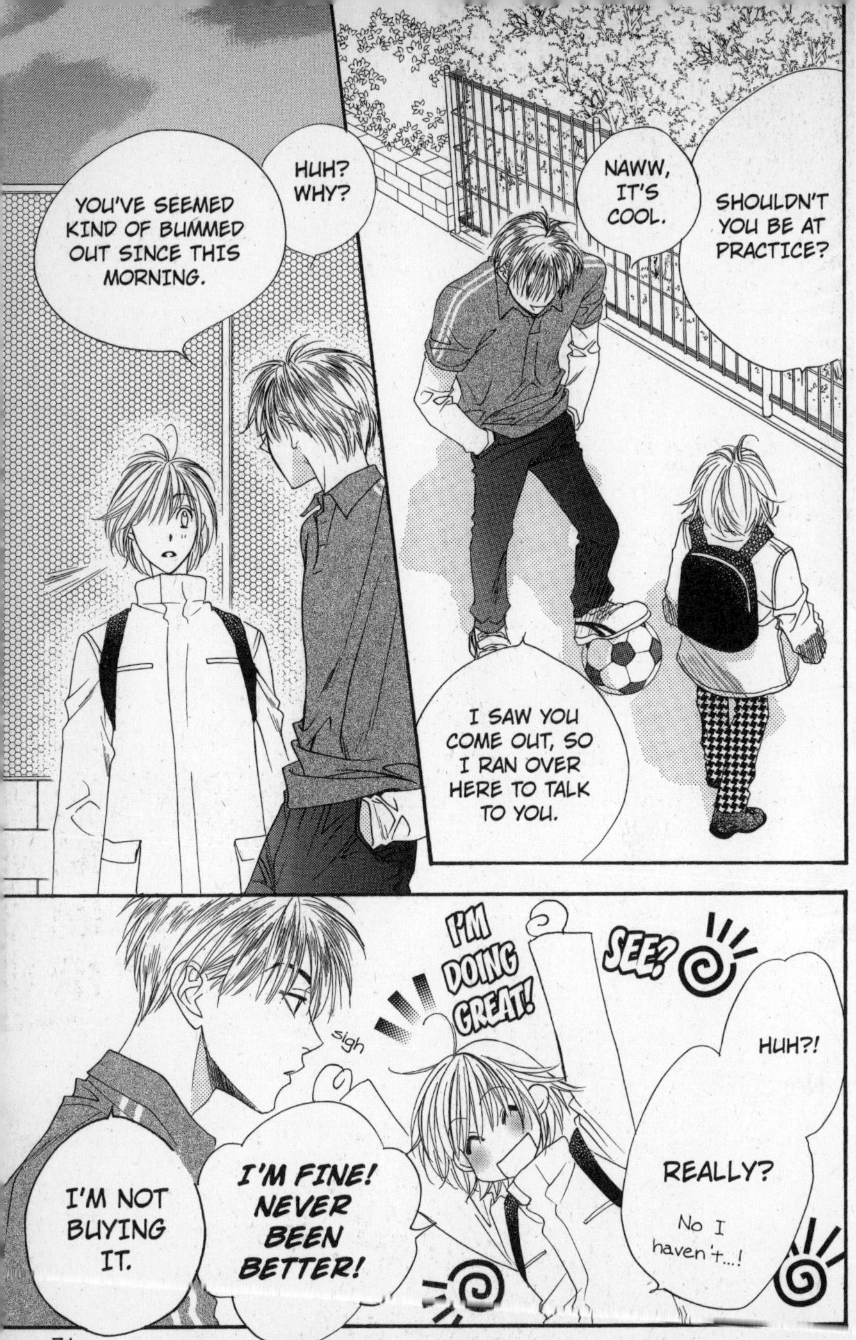

SHOULDN'T YOU BE AT PRACTICE?
NAWW, IT'S COOL.
I SAW YOU COME OUT, SO I RAN OVER HERE TO TALK TO YOU.
HUH? WHY?
YOU'VE SEEMED KIND OF BUMMED OUT SINCE THIS MORNING.
HUH?!
REALLY?
No I haven't...!
SEE?
I'M DOING GREAT!
I'M FINE! NEVER BEEN BETTER!
sigh
I'M NOT BUYING IT.

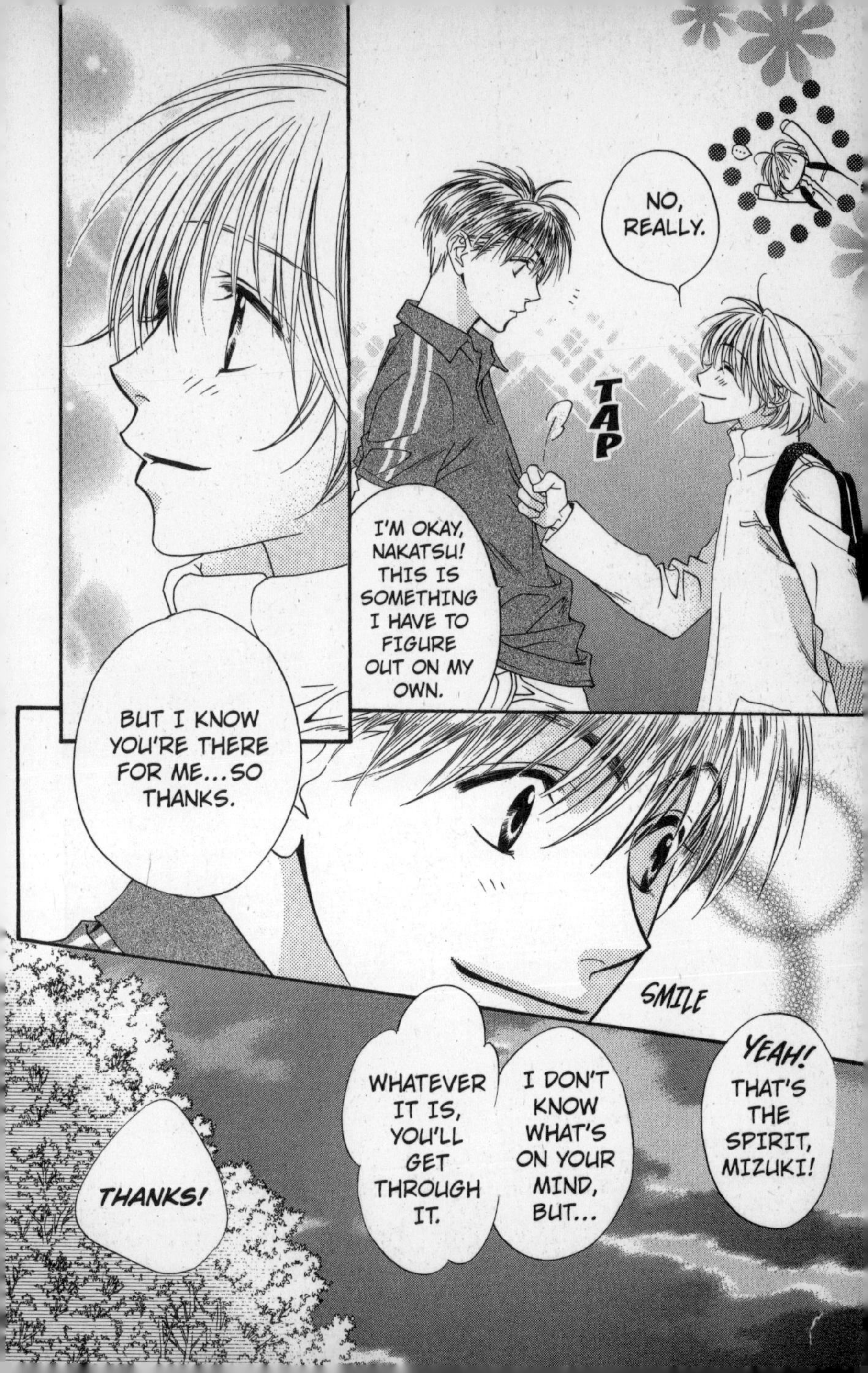
NO, REALLY.
TAP
I'M OKAY, NAKATSU! THIS IS SOMETHING I HAVE TO FIGURE OUT ON MY OWN.
BUT I KNOW YOU'RE THERE FOR ME...SO THANKS.
SMILE
YEAH! THAT'S THE SPIRIT, MIZUKI!
I DON'T KNOW WHAT'S ON YOUR MIND, BUT...
WHATEVER IT IS, YOU'LL GET THROUGH IT.
THANKS!

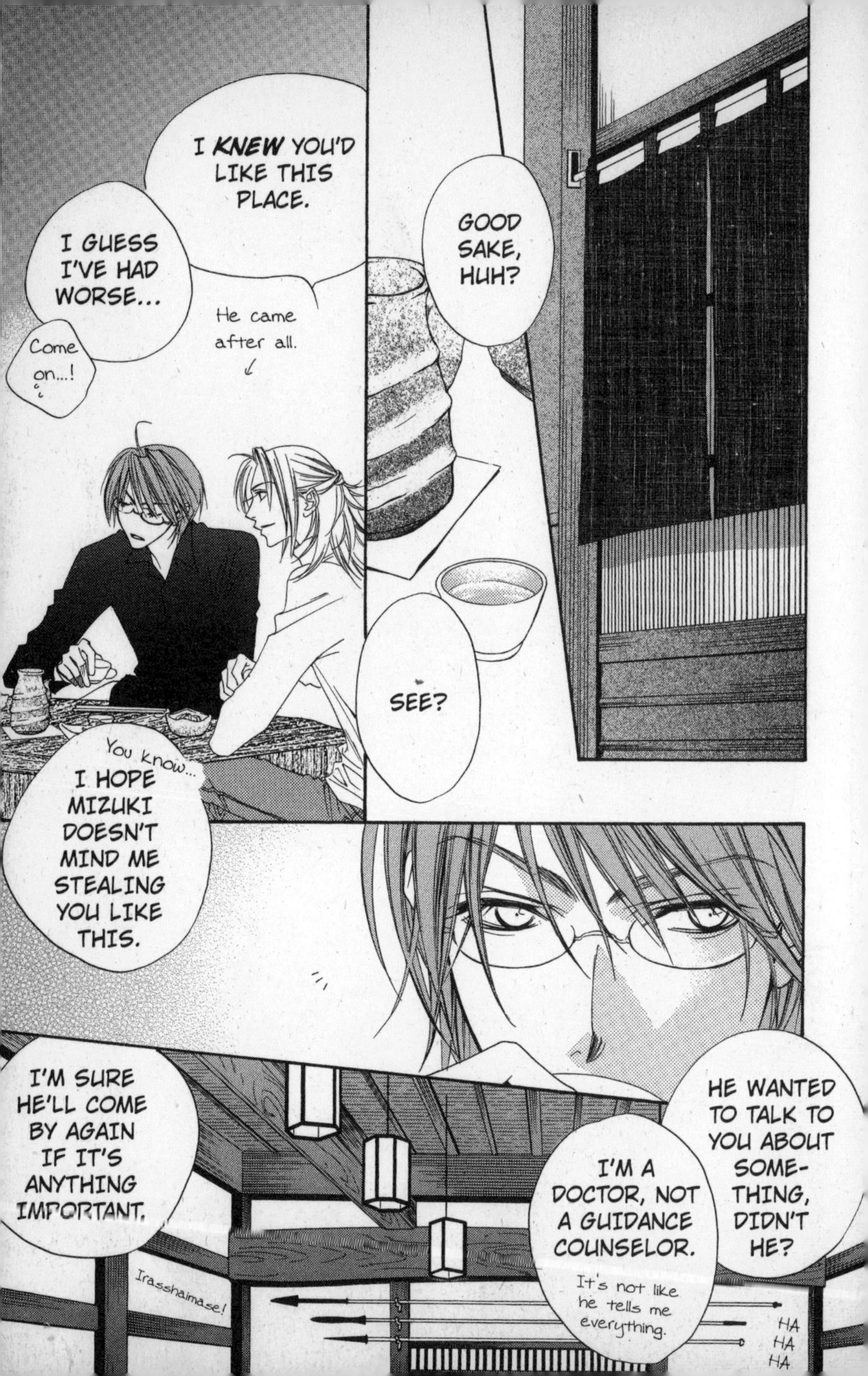
GOOD SAKE, HUH?
SEE?
I KNEW YOU'D LIKE THIS PLACE.
I GUESS I'VE HAD WORSE...
He came after all.
Come on...!
You know...
I HOPE MIZUKI DOESN'T MIND ME STEALING YOU LIKE THIS.
HE WANTED TO TALK TO YOU ABOUT SOME-THING, DIDN'T HE?
I'M A DOCTOR, NOT A GUIDANCE COUNSELOR.
It's not like he tells me everything.
HA HA HA
I'M SURE HE'LL COME BY AGAIN IF IT'S ANYTHING IMPORTANT.
Irasshaimase!

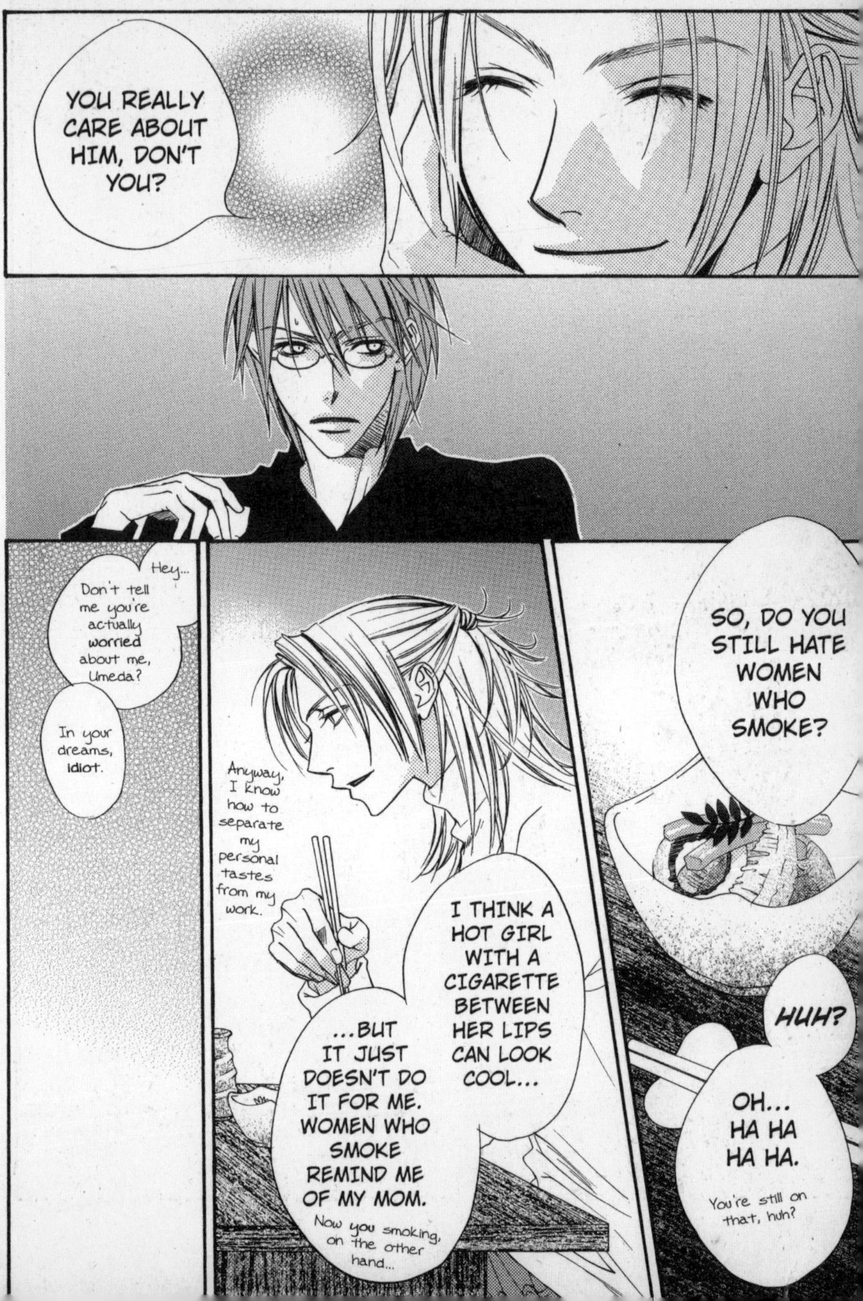
YOU REALLY CARE ABOUT HIM, DON'T YOU?
SO, DO YOU STILL HATE WOMEN WHO SMOKE?
HUH?
OH... HA HA HA HA.
You're still on that, huh?
I THINK A HOT GIRL WITH A CIGARETTE BETWEEN HER LIPS CAN LOOK COOL...
...BUT IT JUST DOESN'T DO IT FOR ME. WOMEN WHO SMOKE REMIND ME OF MY MOM.
Now you smoking, on the other hand...
Anyway, I know how to separate my personal tastes from my work.
Hey... Don't tell me you're actually worried about me, Umeda?
In your dreams, idiot.

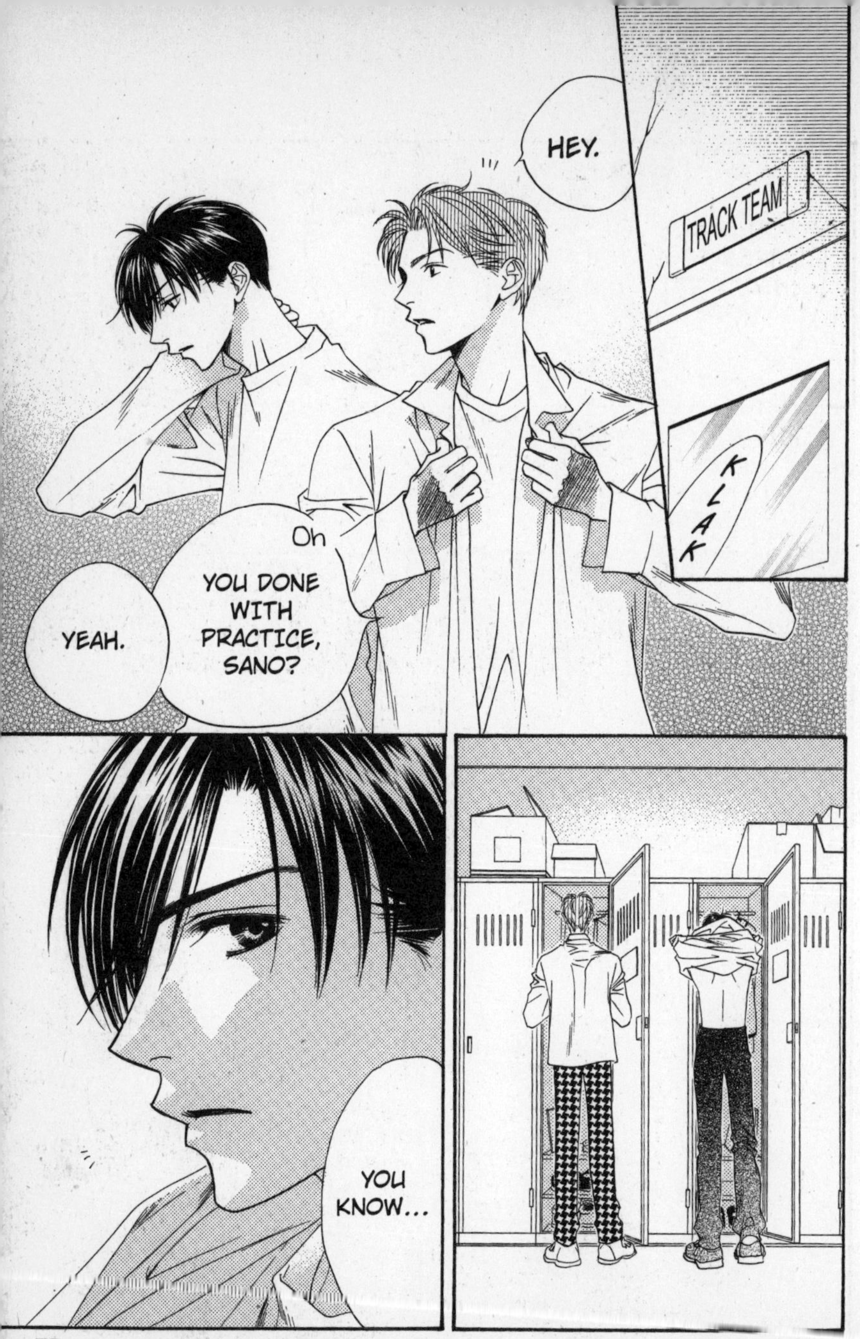
TRACK TEAM
KLAK
HEY.
Oh
YOU DONE WITH PRACTICE, SANO?
YEAH.
YOU KNOW...

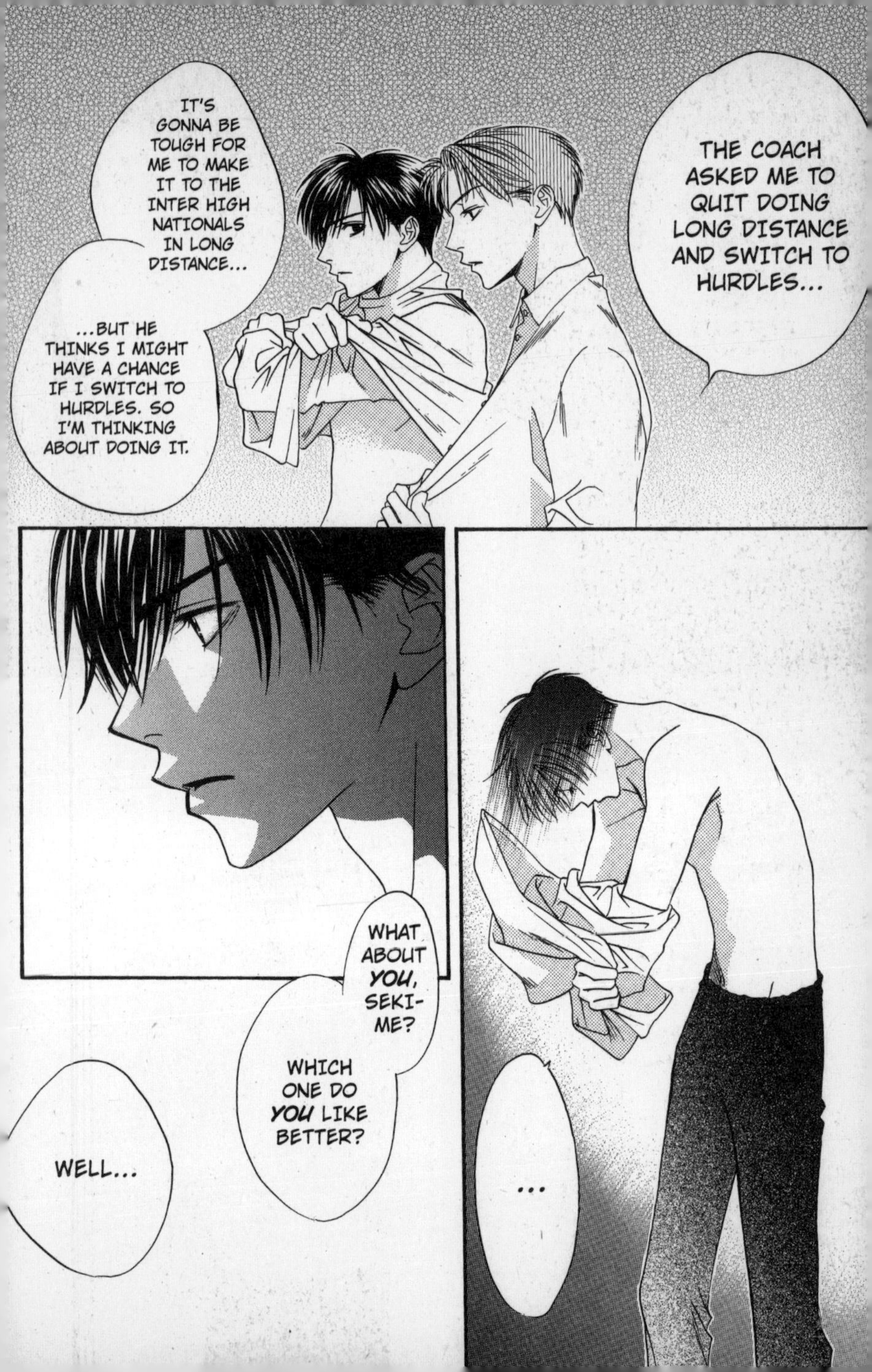
THE COACH ASKED ME TO QUIT DOING LONG DISTANCE AND SWITCH TO HURDLES...
IT'S GONNA BE TOUGH FOR ME TO MAKE IT TO THE INTER HIGH NATIONALS IN LONG DISTANCE...
...BUT HE THINKS I MIGHT HAVE A CHANCE IF I SWITCH TO HURDLES. SO I'M THINKING ABOUT DOING IT.
WHAT ABOUT *YOU*, SEKI-ME?
WHICH ONE DO *YOU* LIKE BETTER?
...
WELL...

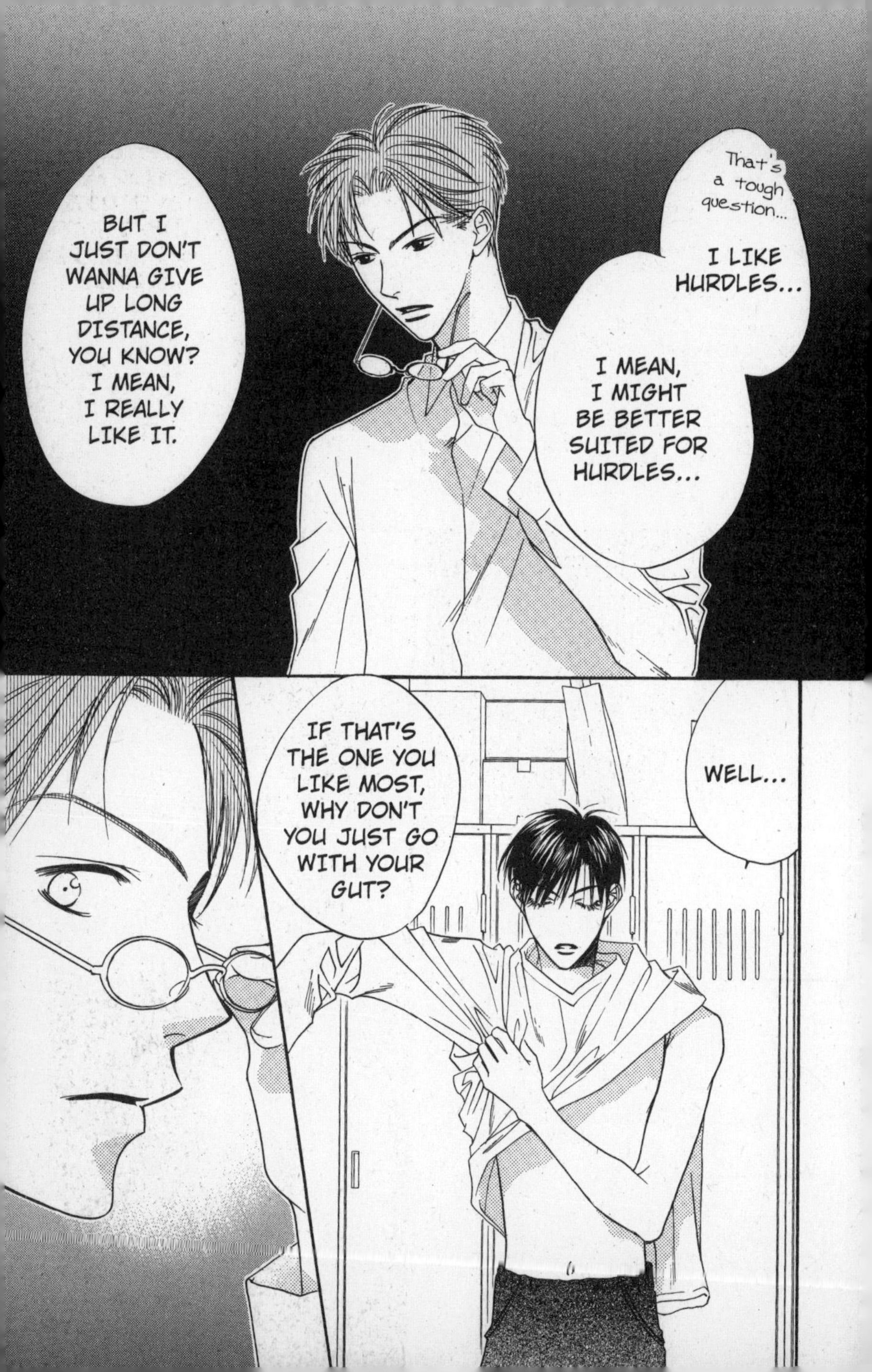
That's a tough question...
I LIKE HURDLES...
I MEAN, I MIGHT BE BETTER SUITED FOR HURDLES...
BUT I JUST DON'T WANNA GIVE UP LONG DISTANCE, YOU KNOW? I MEAN, I REALLY LIKE IT.
WELL...
IF THAT'S THE ONE YOU LIKE MOST, WHY DON'T YOU JUST GO WITH YOUR GUT?

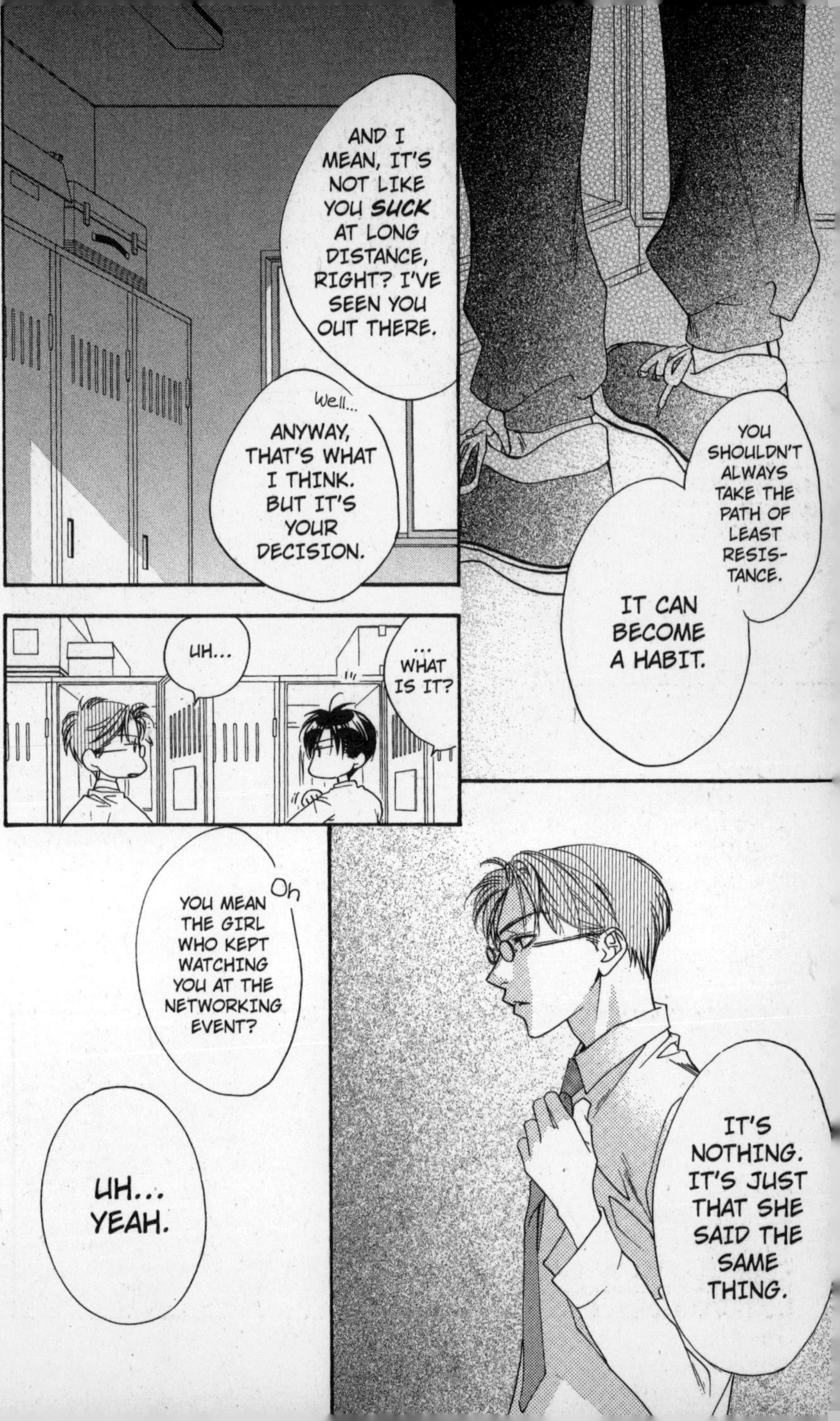
YOU SHOULDN'T ALWAYS TAKE THE PATH OF LEAST RESIS-TANCE.
IT CAN BECOME A HABIT.
AND I MEAN, IT'S NOT LIKE YOU SUCK AT LONG DISTANCE, RIGHT? I'VE SEEN YOU OUT THERE.
Well...
ANYWAY, THAT'S WHAT I THINK. BUT IT'S YOUR DECISION.
... WHAT IS IT?
UH...
IT'S NOTHING. IT'S JUST THAT SHE SAID THE SAME THING.
Oh
YOU MEAN THE GIRL WHO KEPT WATCHING YOU AT THE NETWORKING EVENT?
UH... YEAH.

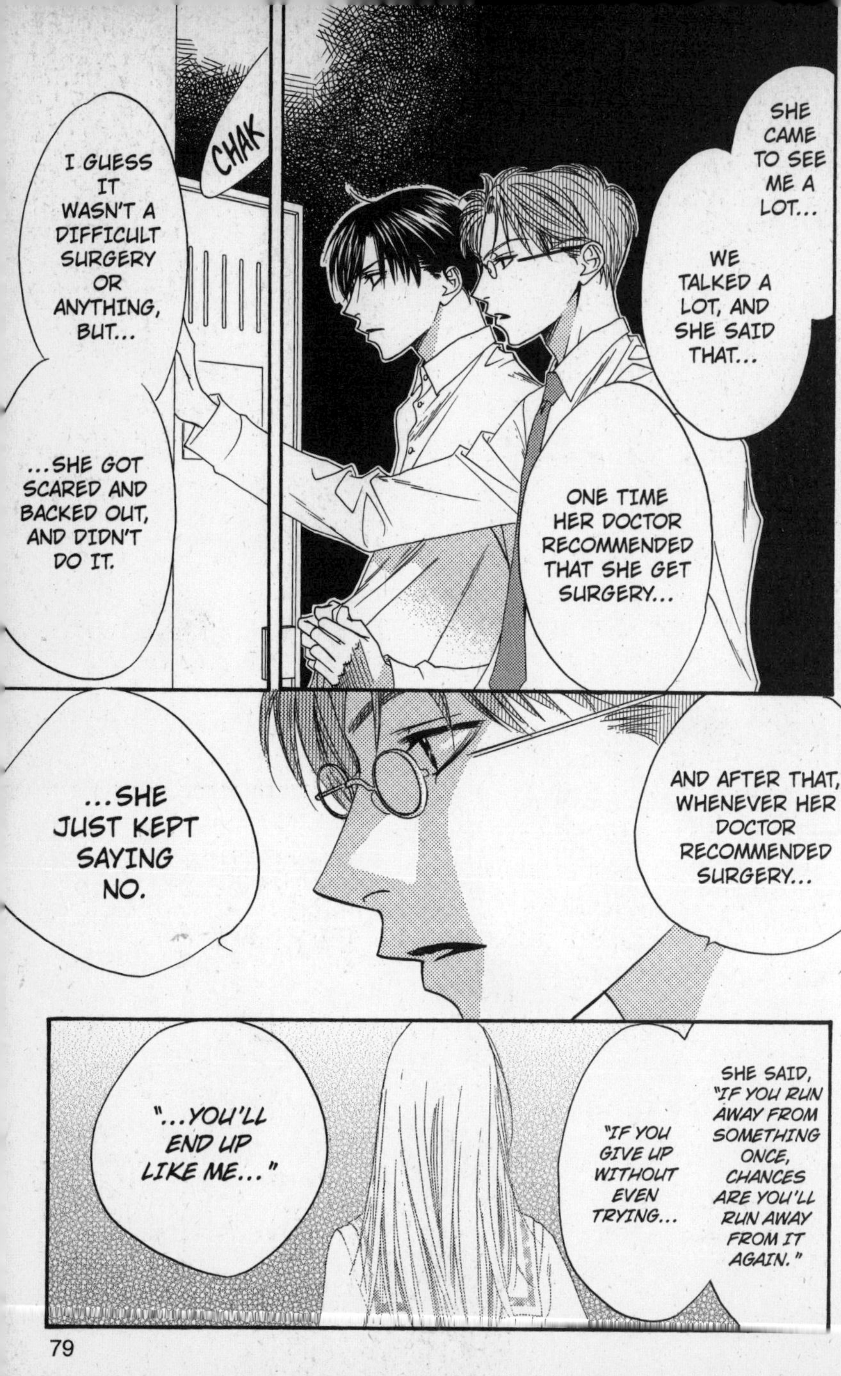
SHE CAME TO SEE ME A LOT...
WE TALKED A LOT, AND SHE SAID THAT...
ONE TIME HER DOCTOR RECOMMENDED THAT SHE GET SURGERY...
CHAK
I GUESS IT WASN'T A DIFFICULT SURGERY OR ANYTHING, BUT...
...SHE GOT SCARED AND BACKED OUT, AND DIDN'T DO IT.
AND AFTER THAT, WHENEVER HER DOCTOR RECOMMENDED SURGERY...
...SHE JUST KEPT SAYING NO.
SHE SAID, "IF YOU RUN AWAY FROM SOMETHING ONCE, CHANCES ARE YOU'LL RUN AWAY FROM IT AGAIN."
"IF YOU GIVE UP WITHOUT EVEN TRYING...
...YOU'LL END UP LIKE ME..."

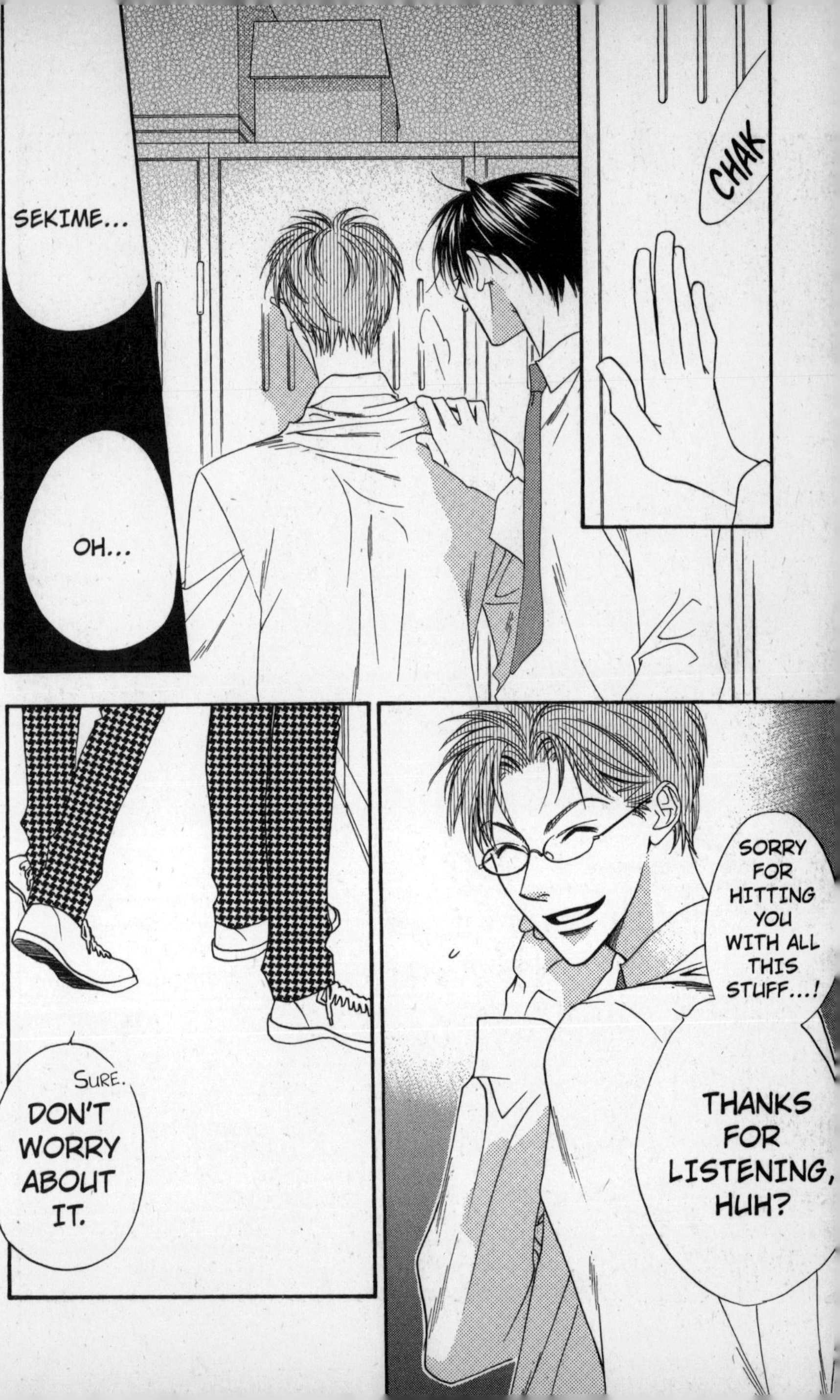
CHAK
SEKIME...
OH...
SORRY FOR HITTING YOU WITH ALL THIS STUFF...!
THANKS FOR LISTENING, HUH?
SURE.
DON'T WORRY ABOUT IT.

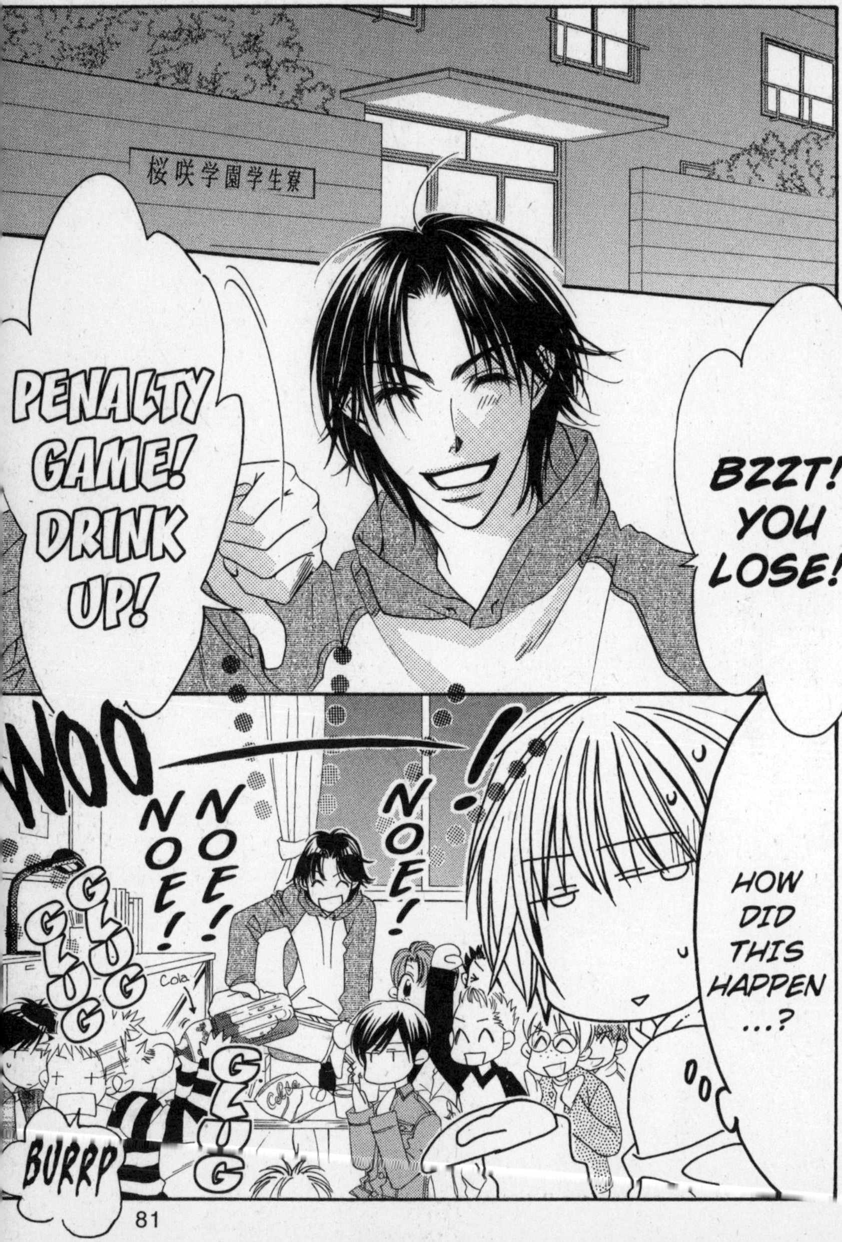
桜咲学園学生寮
BZZT! YOU LOSE!
PENALTY GAME! DRINK UP!
HOW DID THIS HAPPEN ...?
NOE!
NOE!
NOE!
WOO
GLUG GLUG
Cola
GLUG GLUG
BURRP

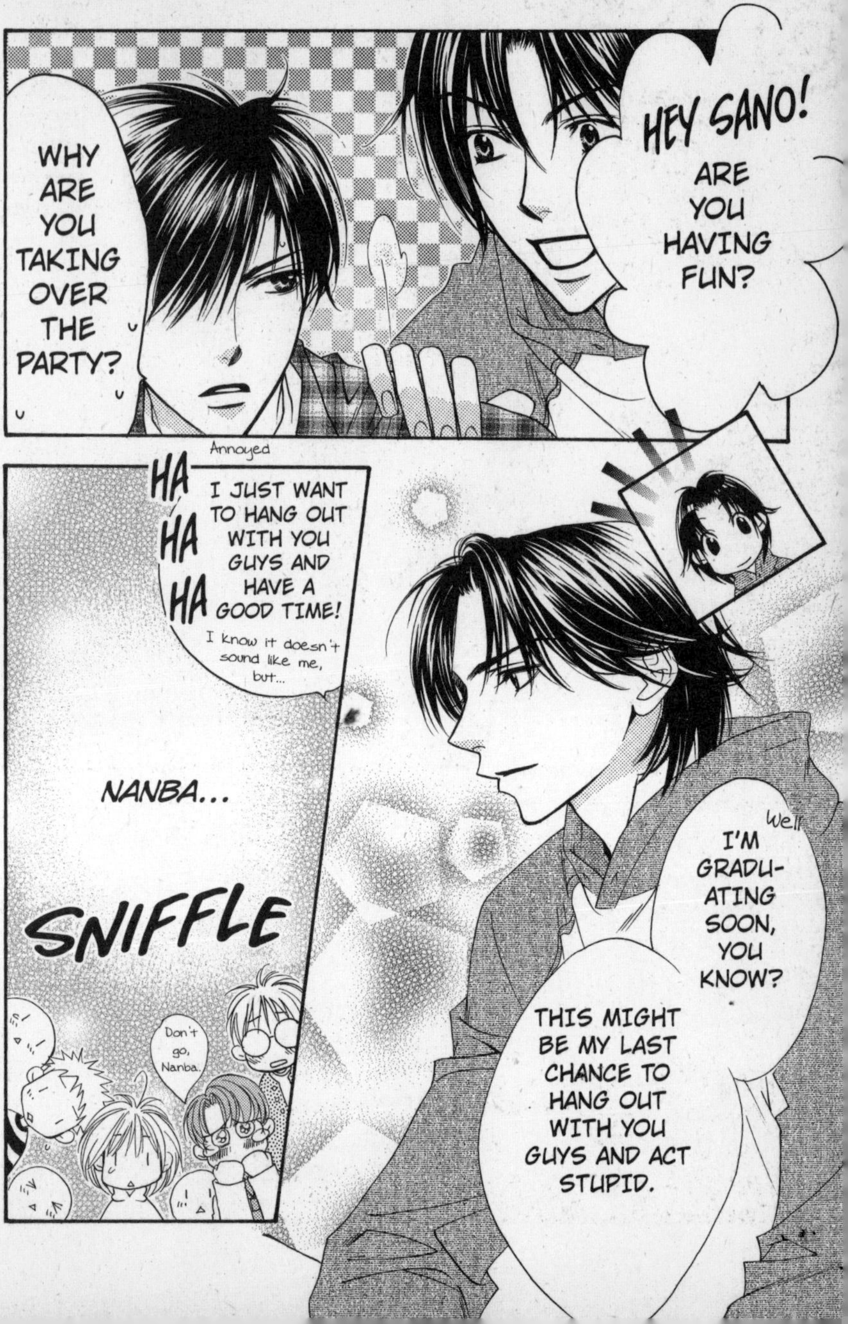
HEY SANO!
ARE YOU HAVING FUN?
WHY ARE YOU TAKING OVER THE PARTY?
Annoyed
HA HA HA
I JUST WANT TO HANG OUT WITH YOU GUYS AND HAVE A GOOD TIME!
I know it doesn't sound like me, but...
Well
I'M GRADUATING SOON, YOU KNOW?
THIS MIGHT BE MY LAST CHANCE TO HANG OUT WITH YOU GUYS AND ACT STUPID.
NANBA...
SNIFFLE
Don't go, Nanba.

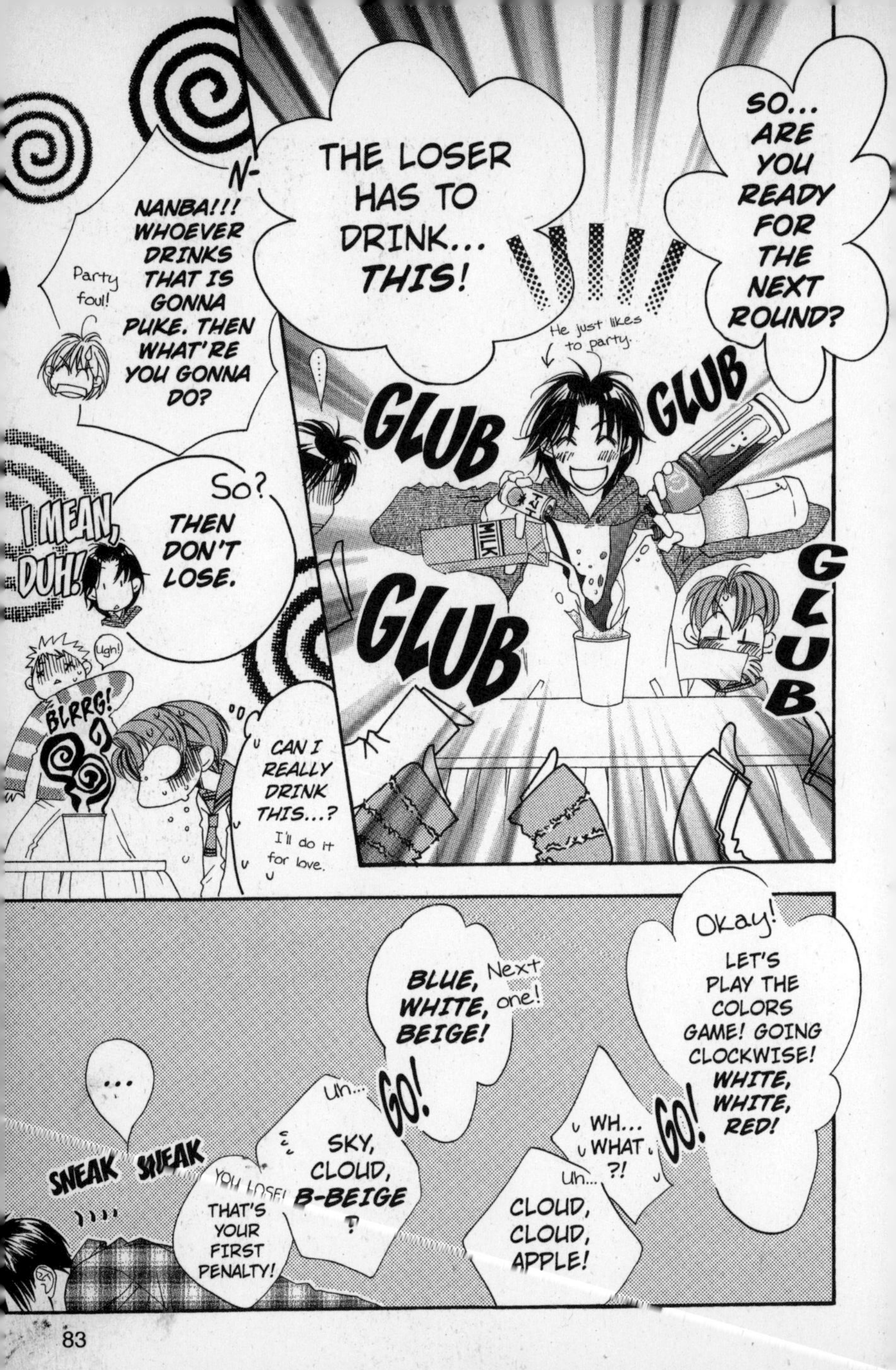
SO... ARE YOU READY FOR THE NEXT ROUND?
THE LOSER HAS TO DRINK... THIS!
He just likes to party.
GLUB
GLUB
GLUB
GLUB
N-NANBA!!! WHOEVER DRINKS THAT IS GONNA PUKE. THEN WHAT'RE YOU GONNA DO?
Party foul!
So? THEN DON'T LOSE.
I MEAN, DUH!
Ugh!
BLRRG!
CAN I REALLY DRINK THIS...?
I'll do it for love.
Okay! LET'S PLAY THE COLORS GAME! GOING CLOCKWISE! WHITE, WHITE, RED!
GO!
WH... WHAT?!
Uh... CLOUD, CLOUD, APPLE!
BLUE, WHITE, BEIGE!
Next one!
GO!
Uh... SKY, CLOUD, B-BEIGE?
YOU LOSE! THAT'S YOUR FIRST PENALTY!
...
SNEAK SNEAK

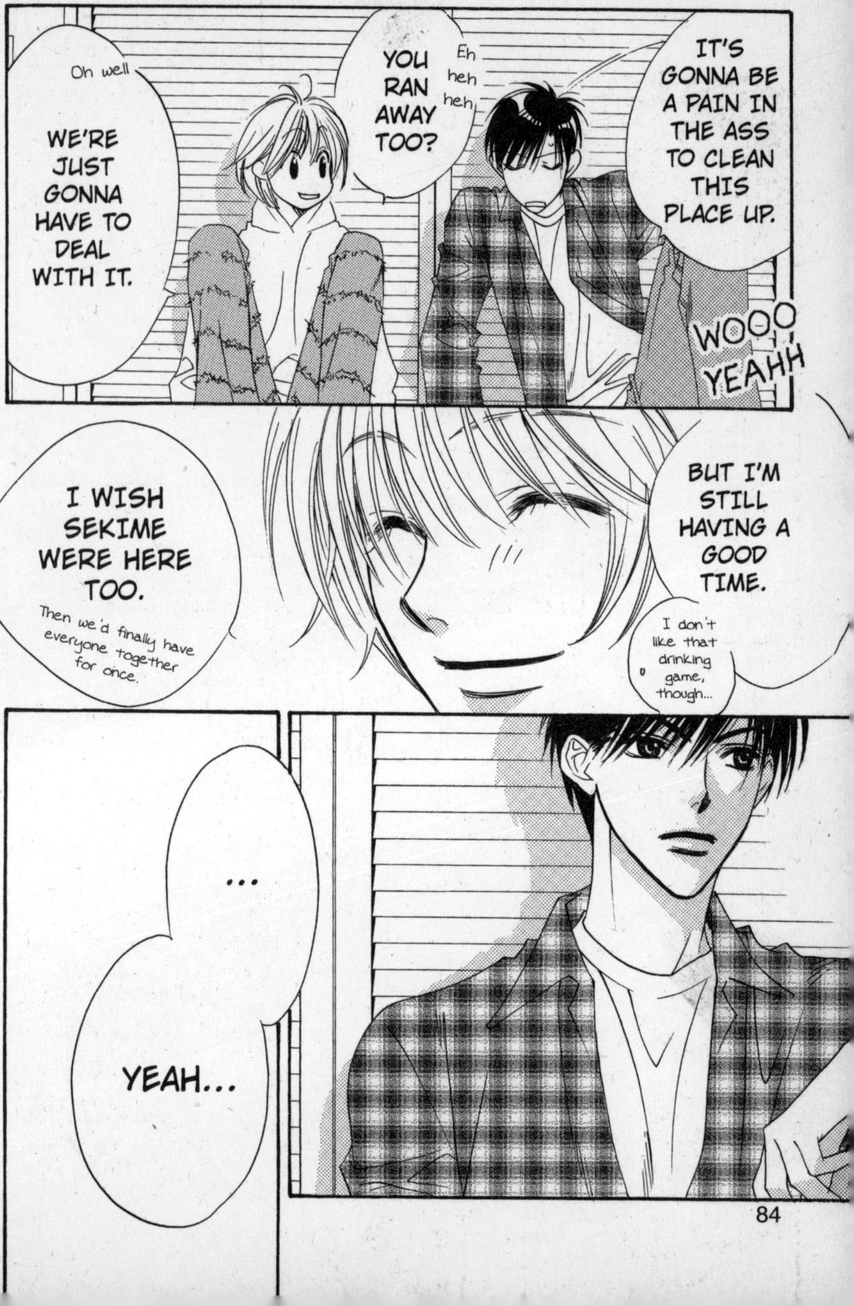
IT'S GONNA BE A PAIN IN THE ASS TO CLEAN THIS PLACE UP.
WOOO YEAHH
Eh heh heh
YOU RAN AWAY TOO?
Oh well
WE'RE JUST GONNA HAVE TO DEAL WITH IT.
BUT I'M STILL HAVING A GOOD TIME.
I don't like that drinking game, though...
I WISH SEKIME WERE HERE TOO.
Then we'd finally have everyone together for once.
...
YEAH...

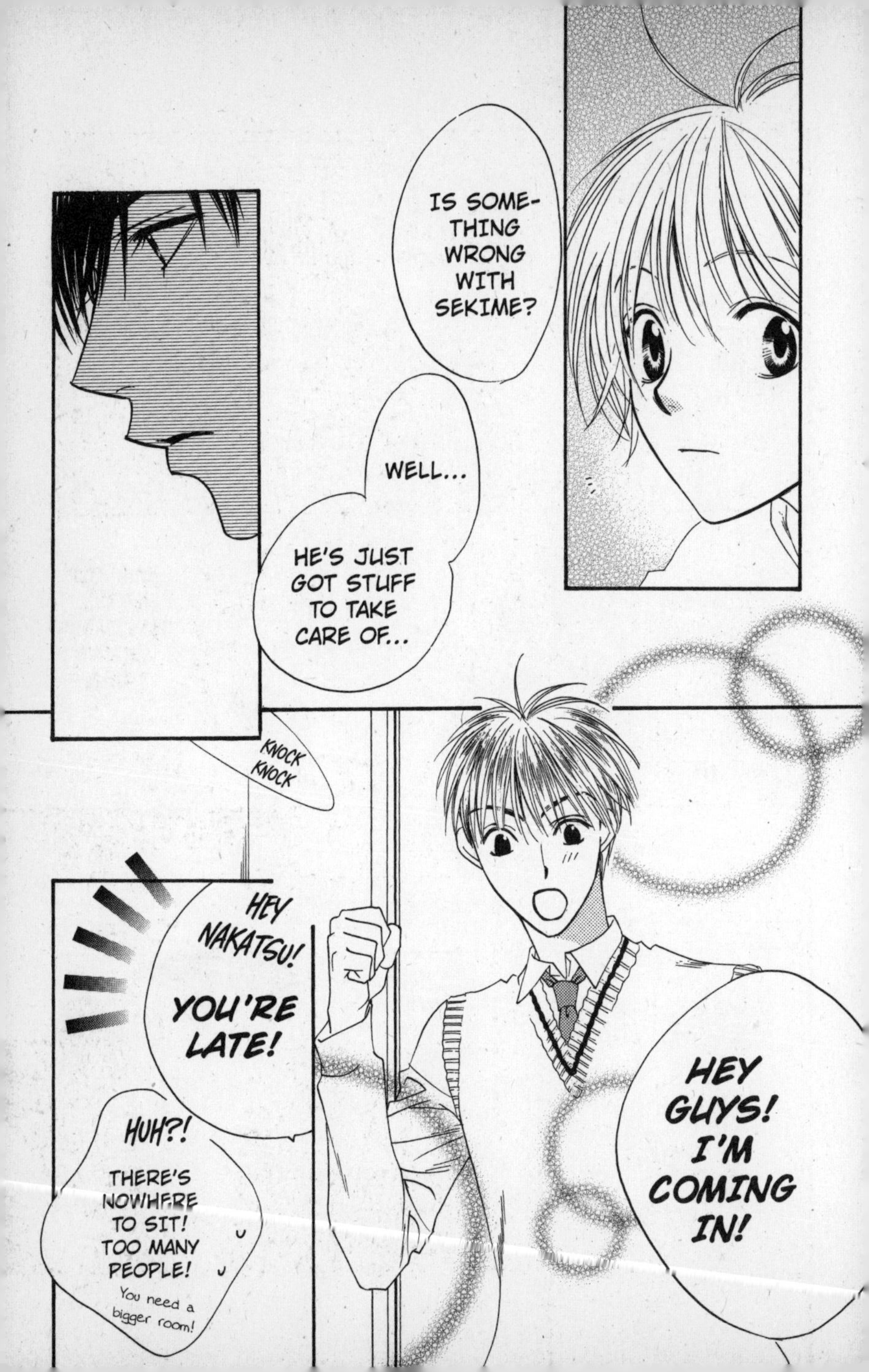
IS SOME-THING WRONG WITH SEKIME?
WELL...
HE'S JUST GOT STUFF TO TAKE CARE OF...
KNOCK KNOCK
HEY GUYS! I'M COMING IN!
HEY NAKATSU!
YOU'RE LATE!
HUH?!
THERE'S NOWHERE TO SIT! TOO MANY PEOPLE!
You need a bigger room!

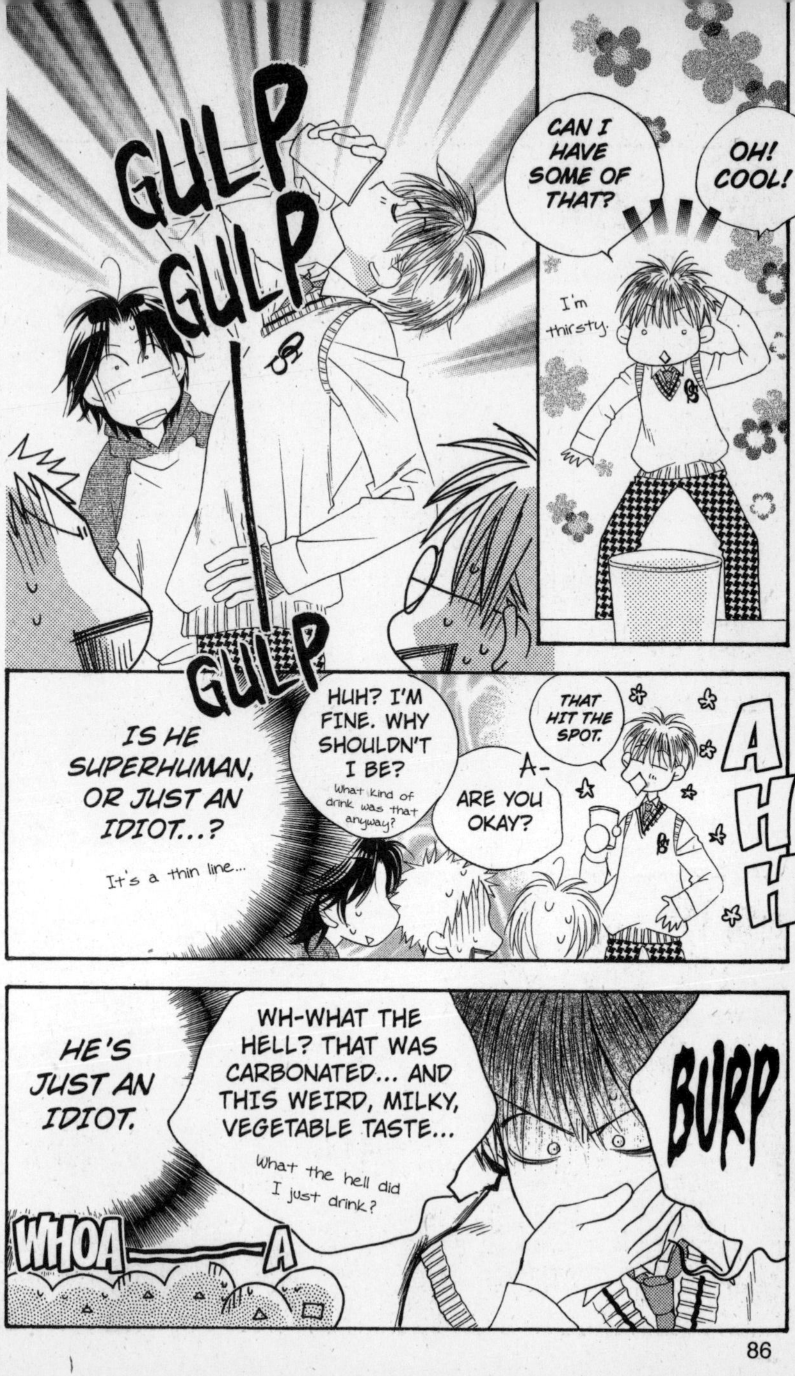
OH! COOL!
CAN I HAVE SOME OF THAT?
I'm thirsty.
GULP
GULP
GULP
AHHH
THAT HIT THE SPOT.
A-
ARE YOU OKAY?
HUH? I'M FINE. WHY SHOULDN'T I BE?
What kind of drink was that anyway?
IS HE SUPERHUMAN, OR JUST AN IDIOT...?
It's a thin line...
BURP
WH-WHAT THE HELL? THAT WAS CARBONATED... AND THIS WEIRD, MILKY, VEGETABLE TASTE...
What the hell did I just drink?
HE'S JUST AN IDIOT.
WHOA——A

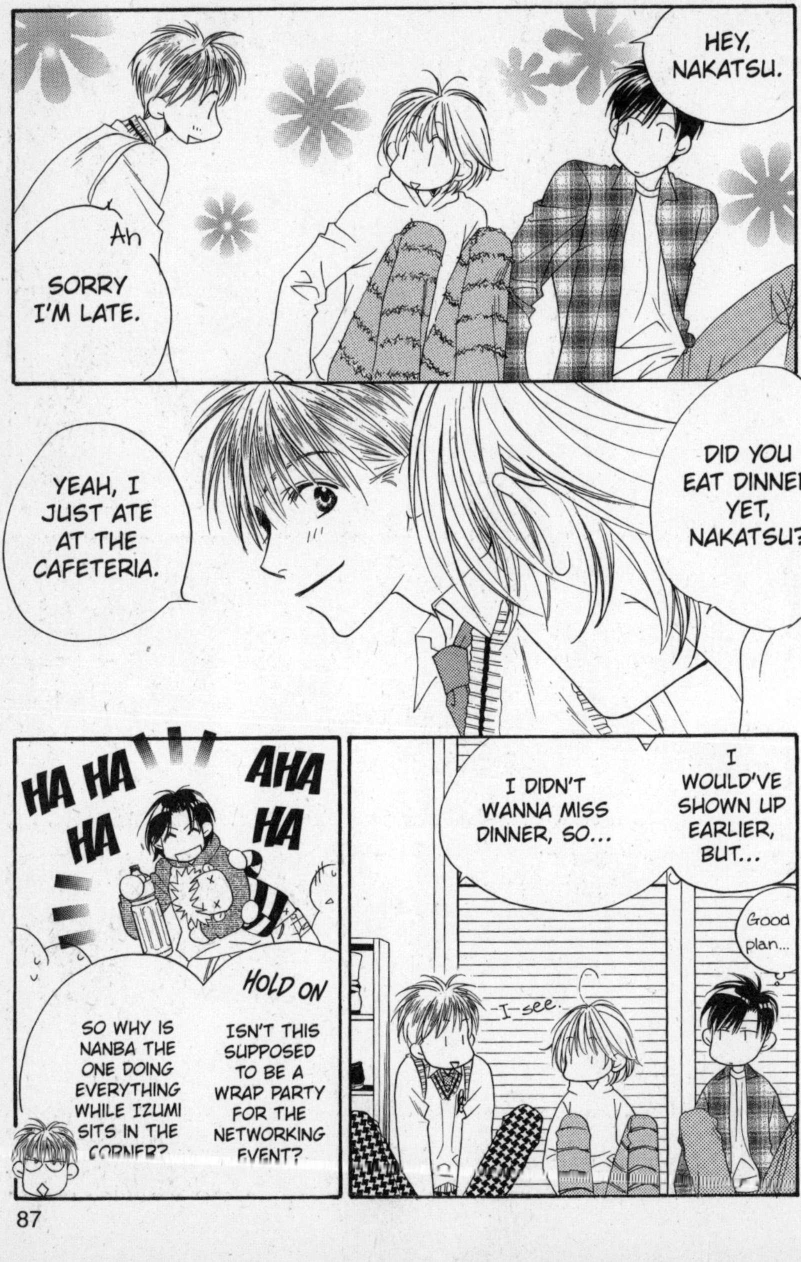
HEY, NAKATSU.
Ah
SORRY I'M LATE.
DID YOU EAT DINNER YET, NAKATSU?
YEAH, I JUST ATE AT THE CAFETERIA.
I WOULD'VE SHOWN UP EARLIER, BUT...
I DIDN'T WANNA MISS DINNER, SO...
Good plan...
I see.
AHA HA
HA HA HA
HOLD ON
ISN'T THIS SUPPOSED TO BE A WRAP PARTY FOR THE NETWORKING EVENT?
SO WHY IS NANBA THE ONE DOING EVERYTHING WHILE IZUMI SITS IN THE CORNER?

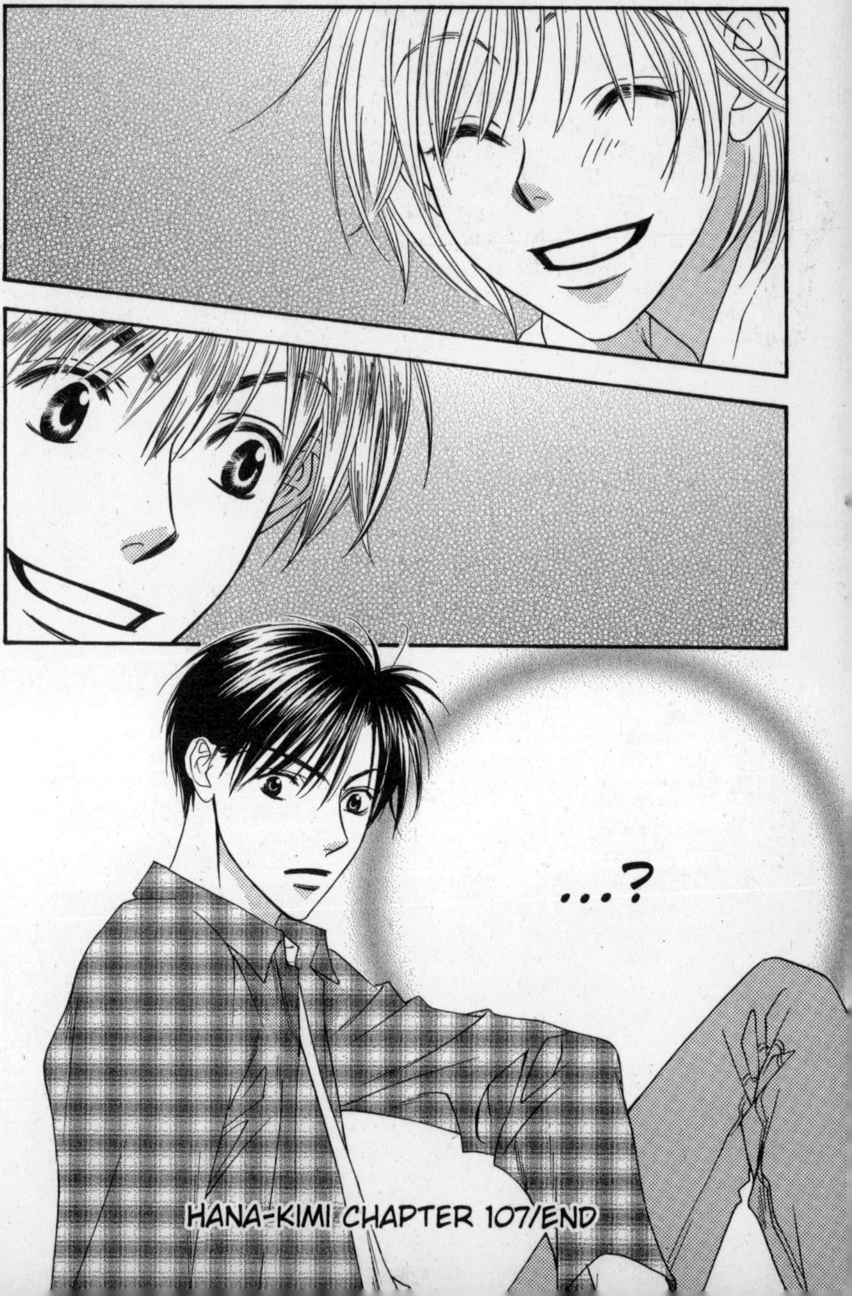
...?
HANA-KIMI CHAPTER 107/END

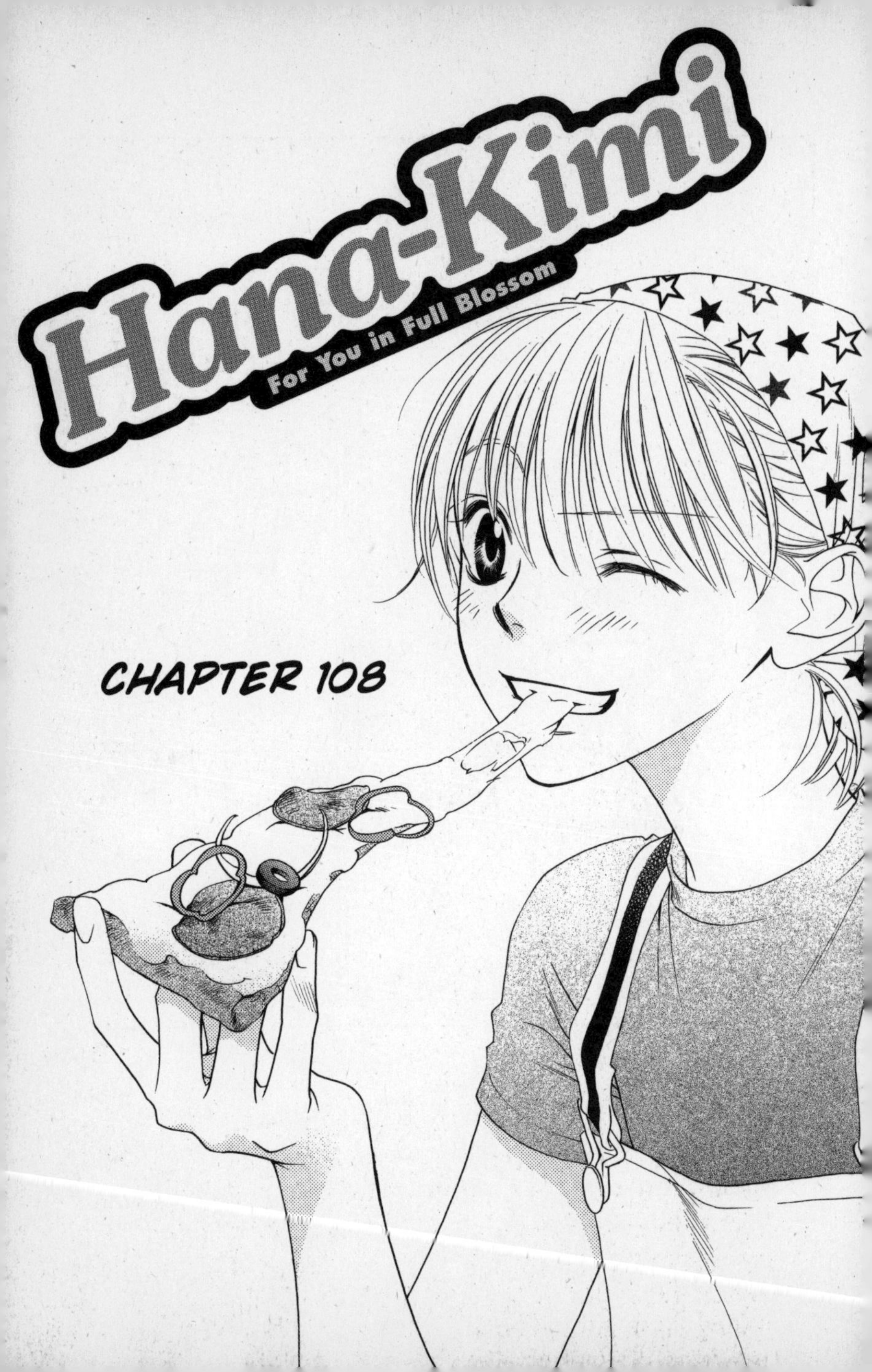
Hana-Kimi
For You in Full Blossom
CHAPTER 108

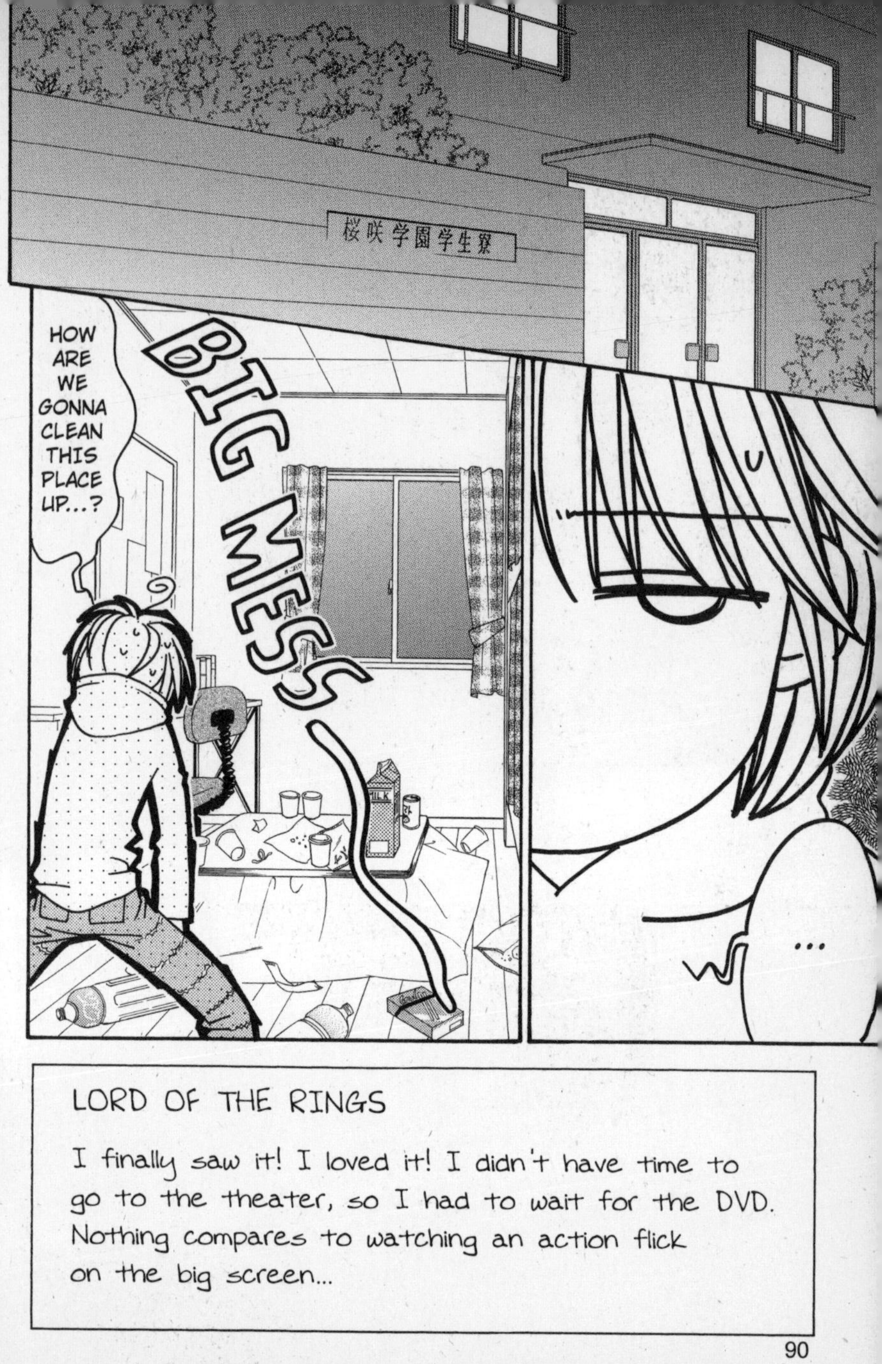
桜咲学園学生寮
...
HOW ARE WE GONNA CLEAN THIS PLACE UP...?
BIG MESS

LORD OF THE RINGS

I finally saw it! I loved it! I didn't have time to go to the theater, so I had to wait for the DVD. Nothing compares to watching an action flick on the big screen...

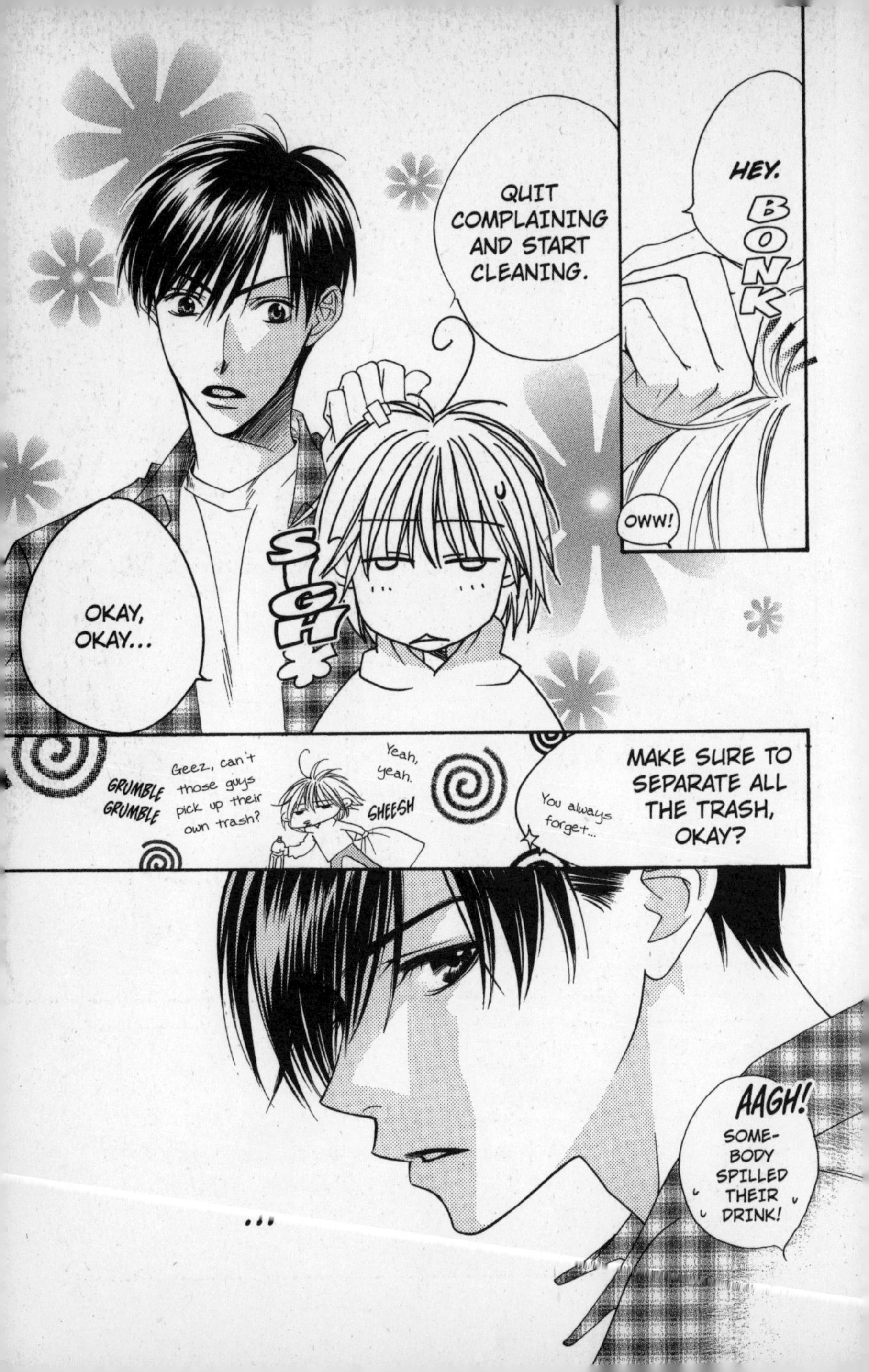
HEY.
BONK
OWW!
QUIT COMPLAINING AND START CLEANING.
SIGH
OKAY, OKAY...
MAKE SURE TO SEPARATE ALL THE TRASH, OKAY?
You always forget...
Yeah, yeah.
SHEESH
Geez, can't those guys pick up their own trash?
GRUMBLE GRUMBLE
AAGH! SOME-BODY SPILLED THEIR DRINK!
...

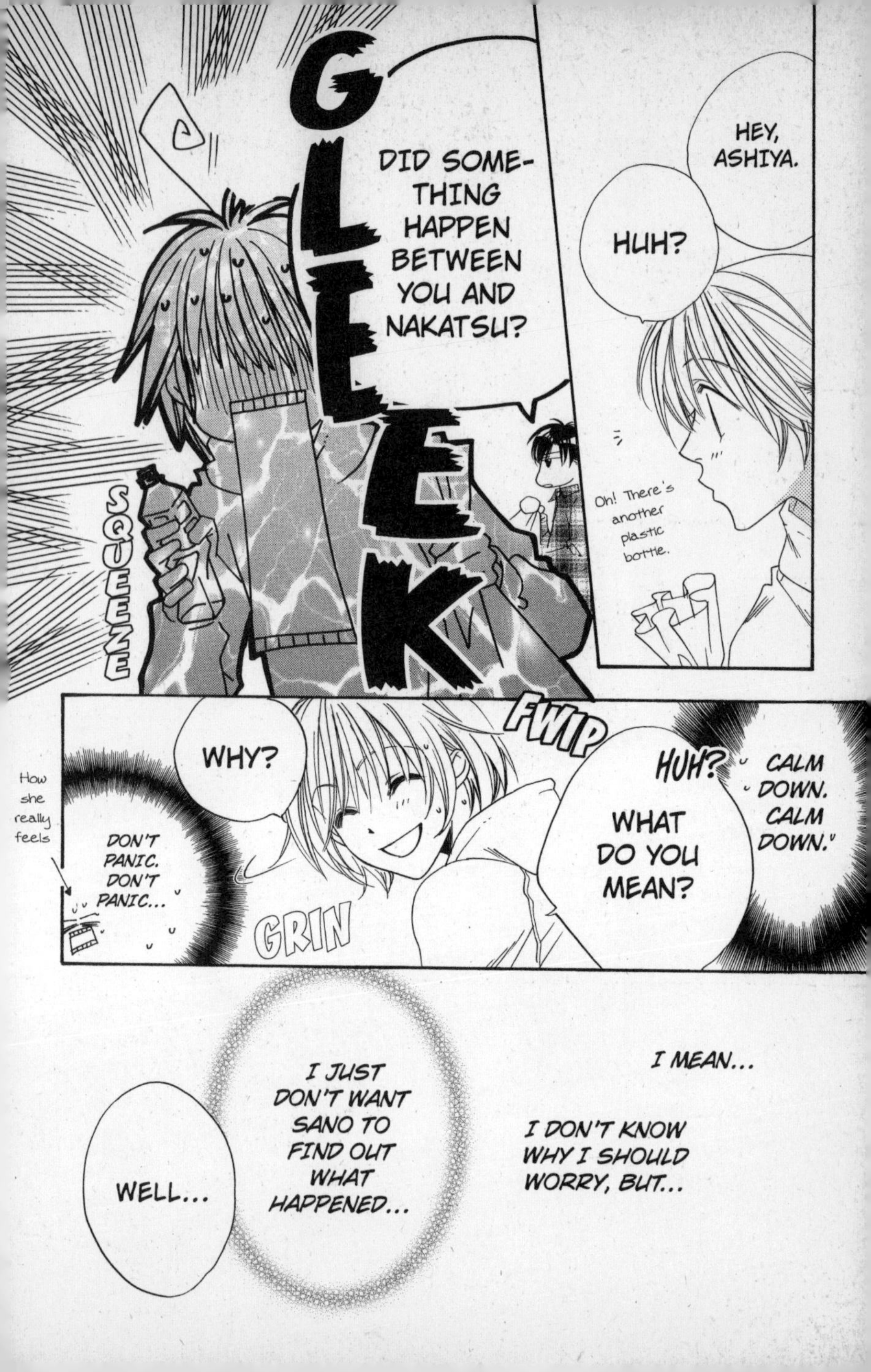
HEY, ASHIYA.
HUH?
Oh! There's another plastic bottle.
GLEEK
DID SOME-THING HAPPEN BETWEEN YOU AND NAKATSU?
SQUEEZE
FWIP
CALM DOWN. CALM DOWN.
HUH?
WHAT DO YOU MEAN?
WHY?
GRIN
DON'T PANIC. DON'T PANIC...
How she really feels
I MEAN...
I DON'T KNOW WHY I SHOULD WORRY, BUT...
I JUST DON'T WANT SANO TO FIND OUT WHAT HAPPENED...
WELL...

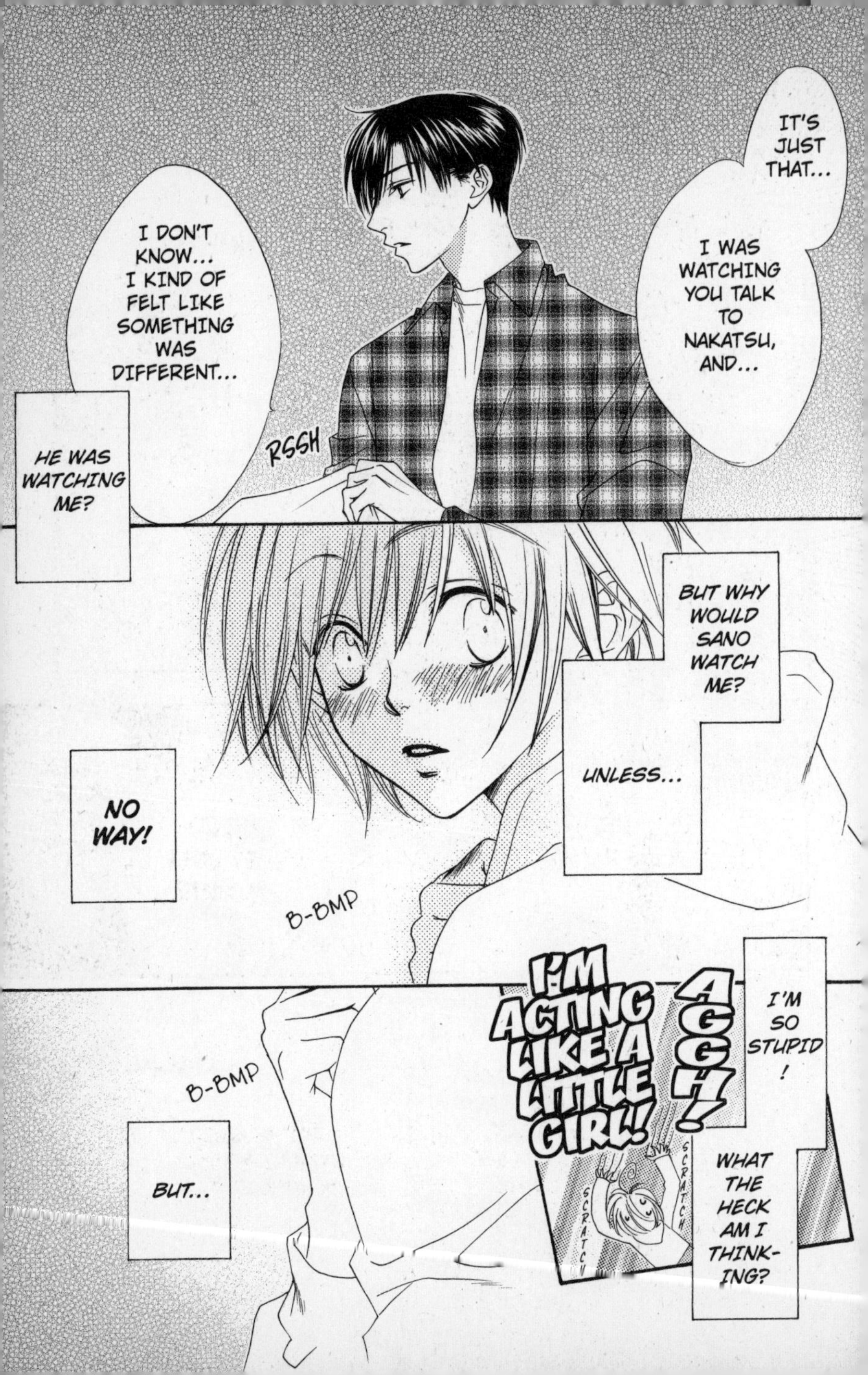
IT'S JUST THAT...
I WAS WATCHING YOU TALK TO NAKATSU, AND...
I DON'T KNOW... I KIND OF FELT LIKE SOMETHING WAS DIFFERENT...
RSSH
HE WAS WATCHING ME?
BUT WHY WOULD SANO WATCH ME?
UNLESS...
NO WAY!
B-BMP
I'M SO STUPID!
WHAT THE HECK AM I THINKING?
AGGH!
I'M ACTING LIKE A LITTLE GIRL!
SCRATCH
SCRATCH
B-BMP
BUT...

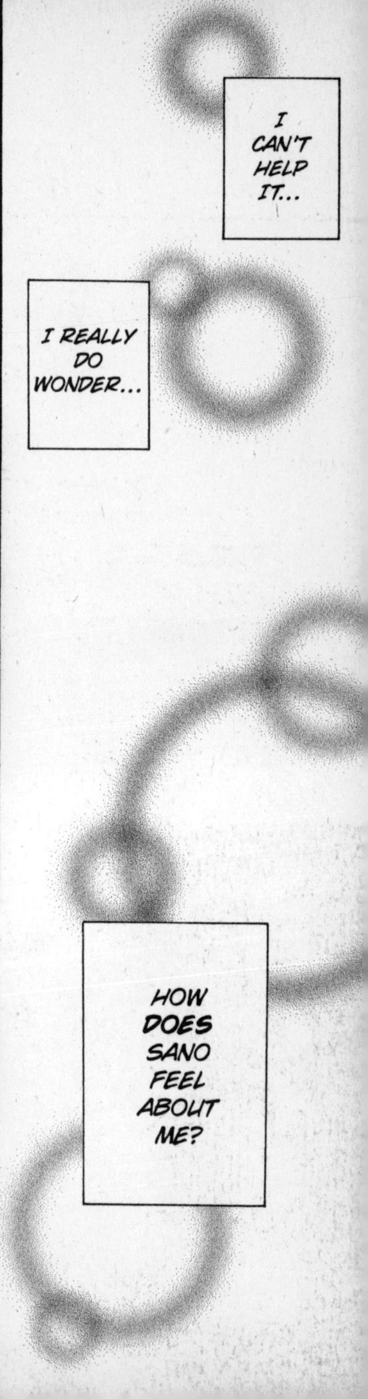
I CAN'T HELP IT...
I REALLY DO WONDER...
HOW DOES SANO FEEL ABOUT ME?

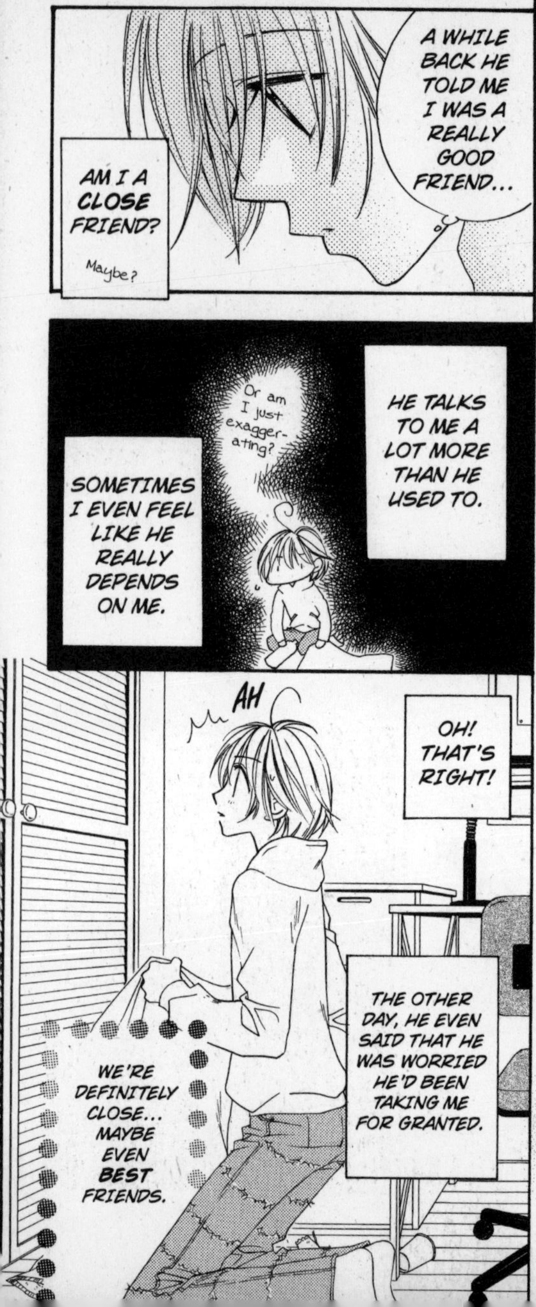
A WHILE BACK HE TOLD ME I WAS A REALLY GOOD FRIEND...
AM I A CLOSE FRIEND?
Maybe?
HE TALKS TO ME A LOT MORE THAN HE USED TO.
Or am I just exagger-ating?
SOMETIMES I EVEN FEEL LIKE HE REALLY DEPENDS ON ME.
OH! THAT'S RIGHT!
AH
THE OTHER DAY, HE EVEN SAID THAT HE WAS WORRIED HE'D BEEN TAKING ME FOR GRANTED.
WE'RE DEFINITELY CLOSE... MAYBE EVEN BEST FRIENDS.

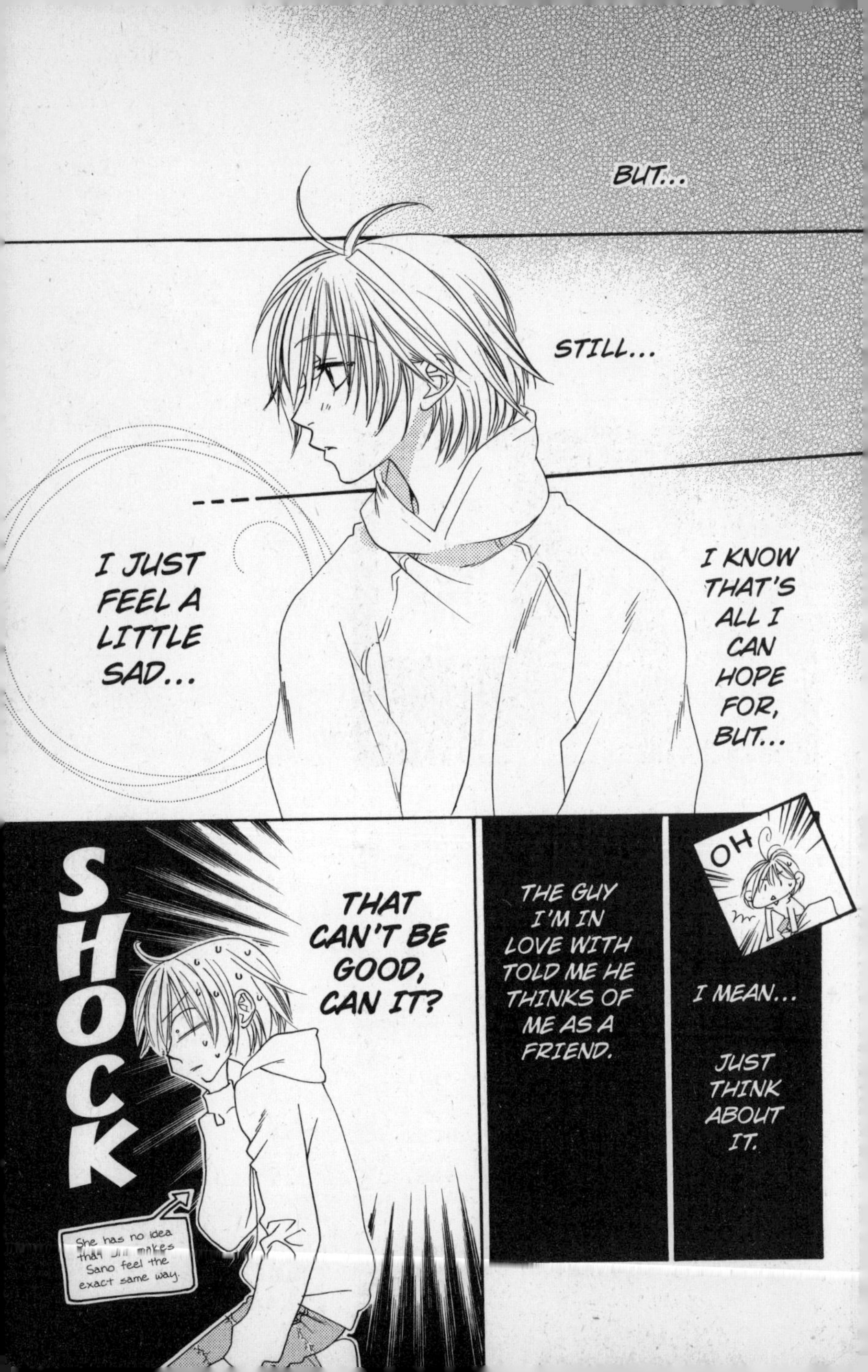
BUT...
STILL...

I KNOW THAT'S ALL I CAN HOPE FOR, BUT...
I JUST FEEL A LITTLE SAD...
OH
I MEAN...
JUST THINK ABOUT IT.
THE GUY I'M IN LOVE WITH TOLD ME HE THINKS OF ME AS A FRIEND.
SHOCK
THAT CAN'T BE GOOD, CAN IT?
She has no idea that [illegible] makes Sano feel the exact same way.

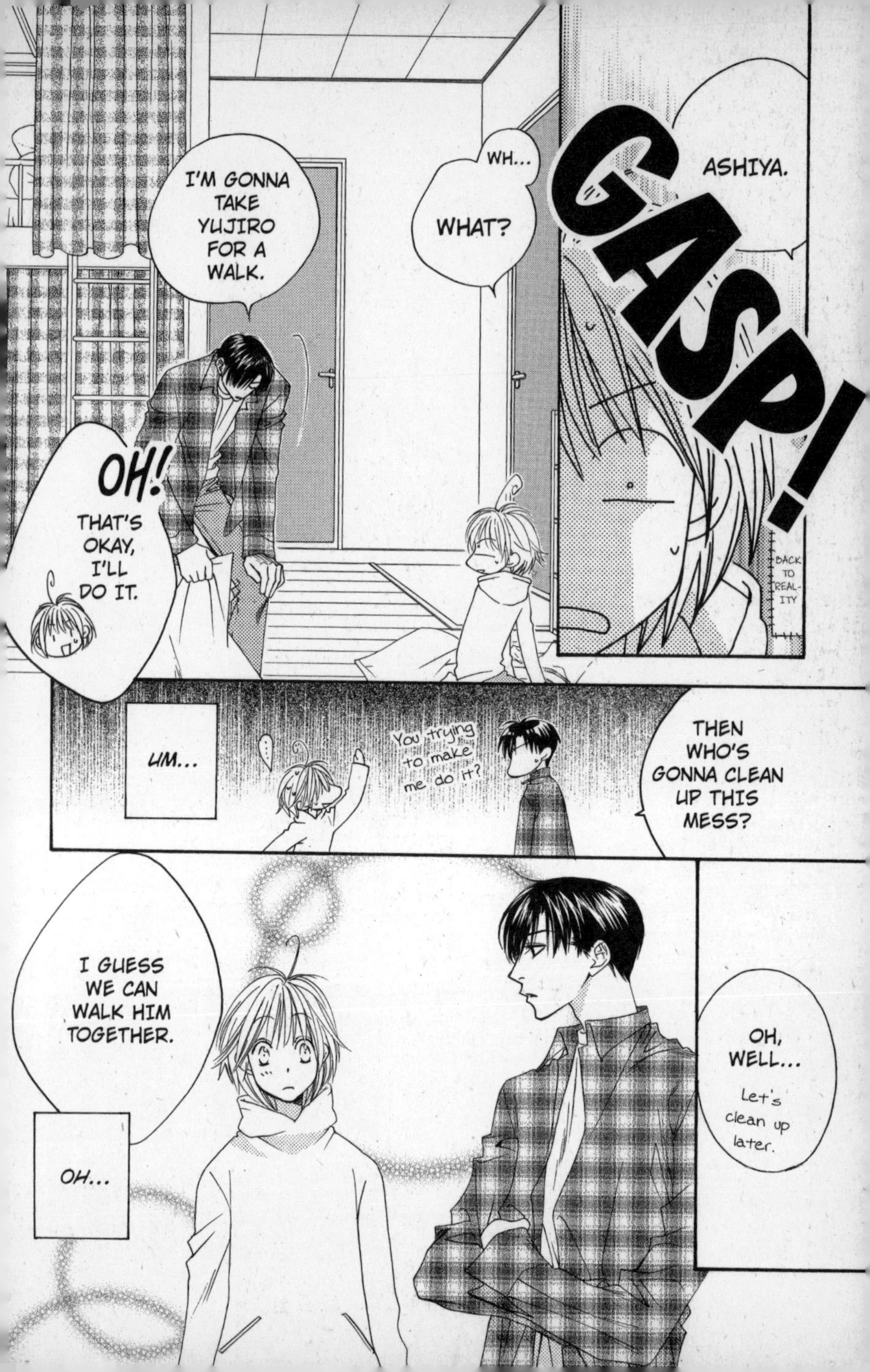
ASHIYA.
GASP!
BACK TO REAL-ITY
WH... WHAT?
I'M GONNA TAKE YUJIRO FOR A WALK.
OH! THAT'S OKAY, I'LL DO IT.
THEN WHO'S GONNA CLEAN UP THIS MESS?
You trying to make me do it?
UM...
OH, WELL...
Let's clean up later.
I GUESS WE CAN WALK HIM TOGETHER.
OH...

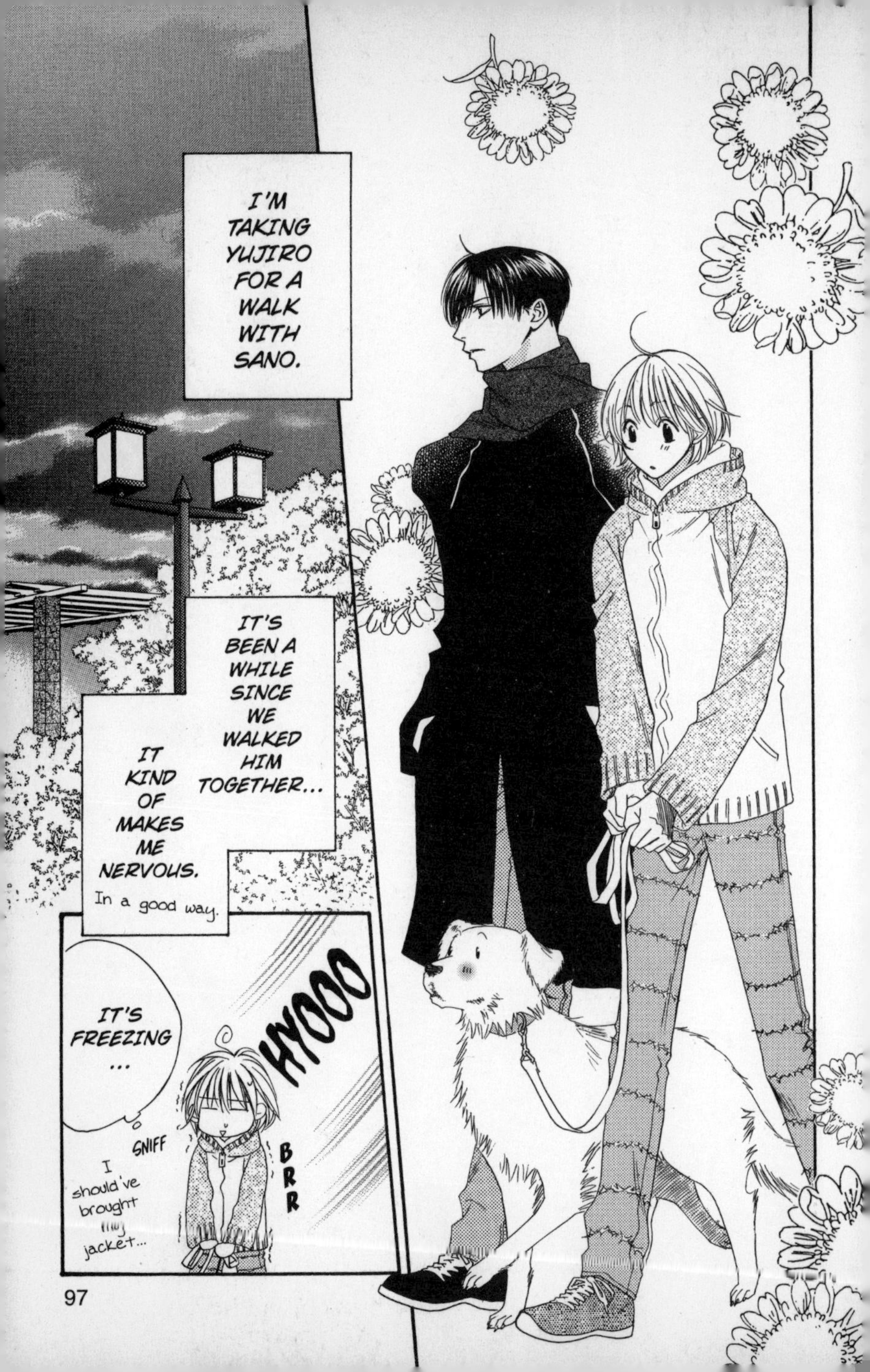
I'M TAKING YUJIRO FOR A WALK WITH SANO.
IT'S BEEN A WHILE SINCE WE WALKED HIM TOGETHER...
IT KIND OF MAKES ME NERVOUS.
In a good way.
HYOOO
IT'S FREEZING...
SNIFF
BRR
I should've brought my jacket...

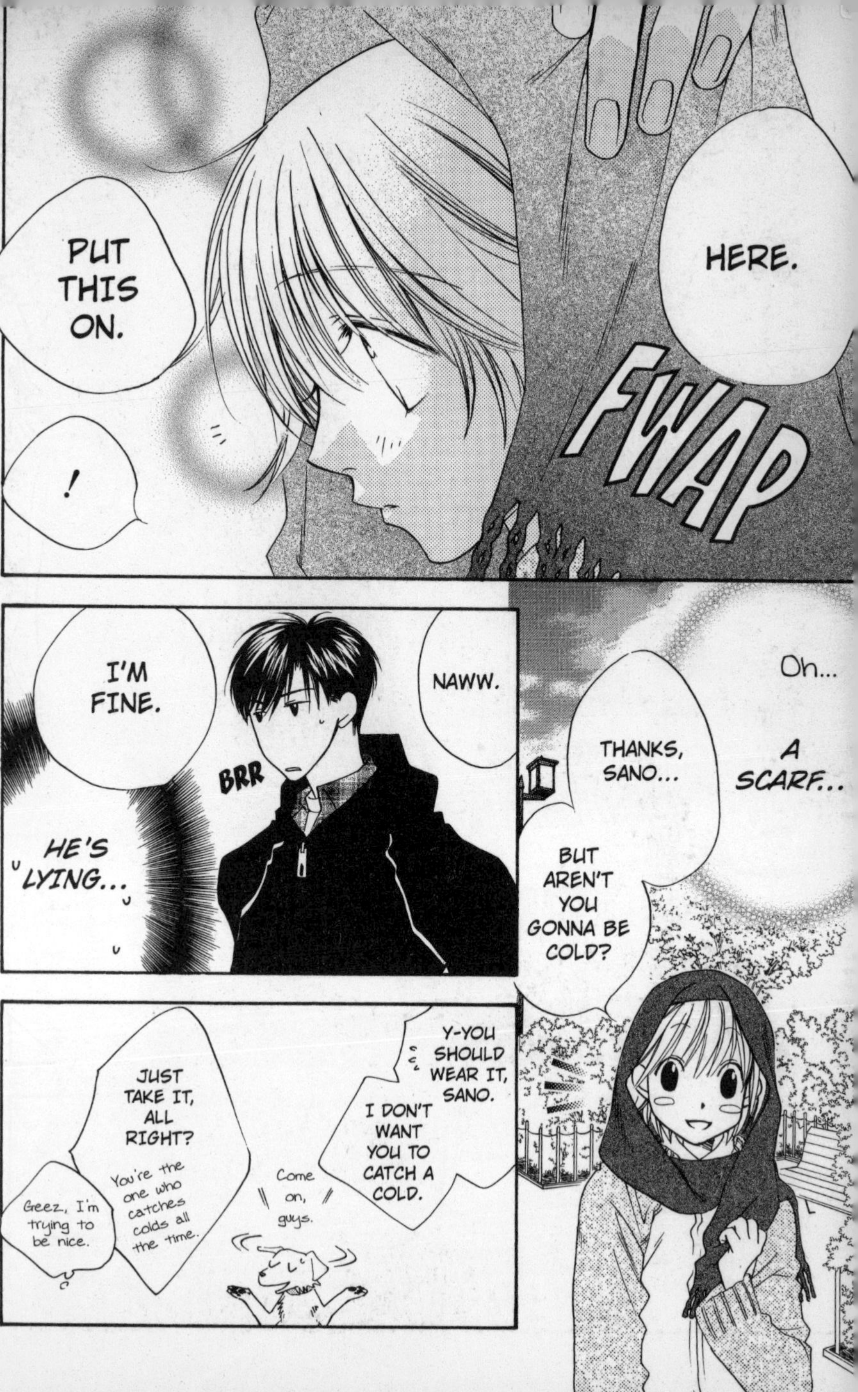
HERE.
FWAP
PUT THIS ON.
!
Oh...
A SCARF...
THANKS, SANO...
BUT AREN'T YOU GONNA BE COLD?
NAWW.
BRR
I'M FINE.
HE'S LYING...
Y-YOU SHOULD WEAR IT, SANO.
I DON'T WANT YOU TO CATCH A COLD.
JUST TAKE IT, ALL RIGHT?
You're the one who catches colds all the time.
Come on, guys.
Geez, I'm trying to be nice.

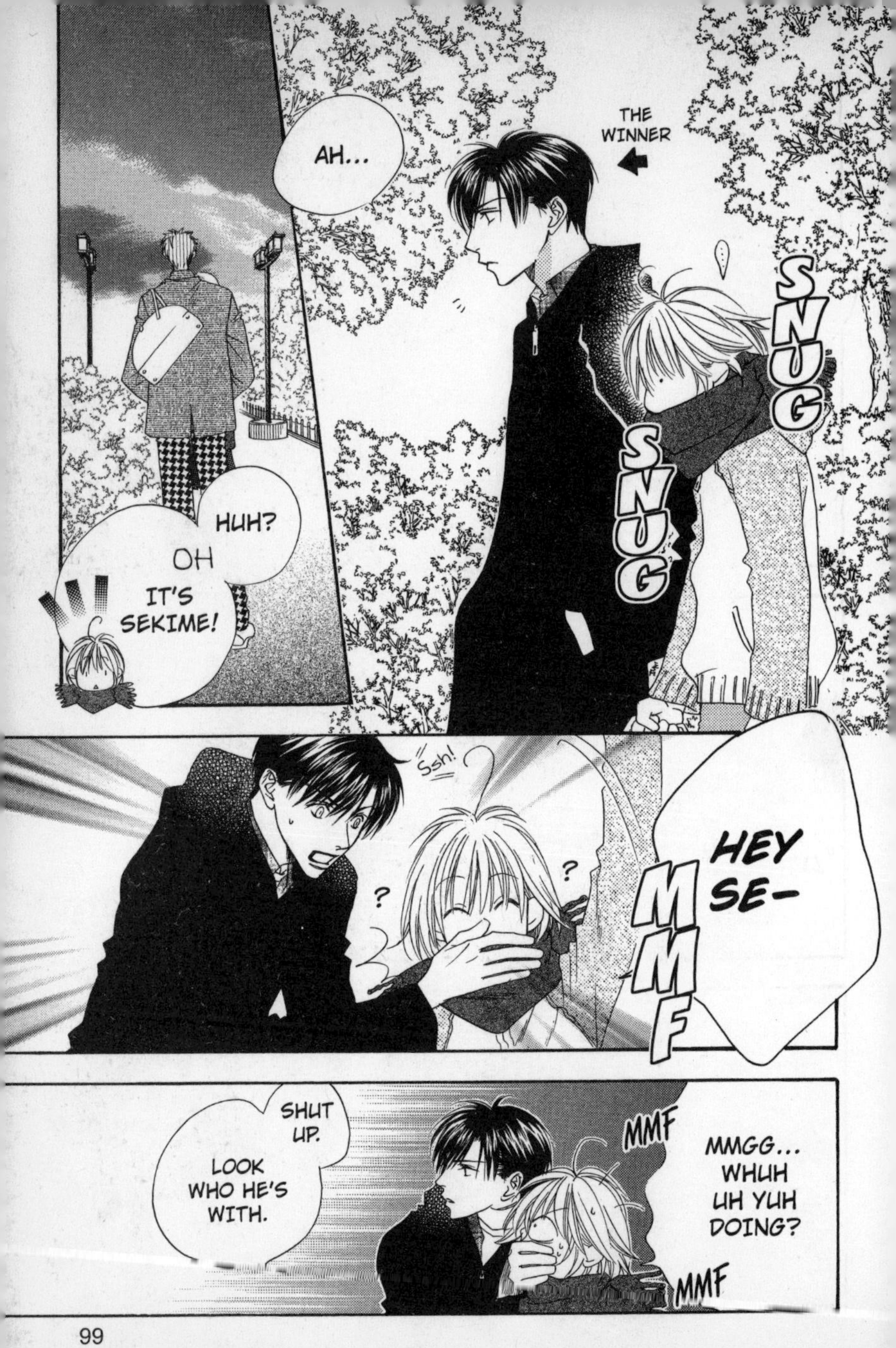

THE WINNER
AH...
SNUG
SNUG
HUH? OH IT'S SEKIME!
HEY SE—
MMMF
Ssh!
MMGG... WHUH UH YUH DOING?
MMF
MMF
SHUT UP.
LOOK WHO HE'S WITH.

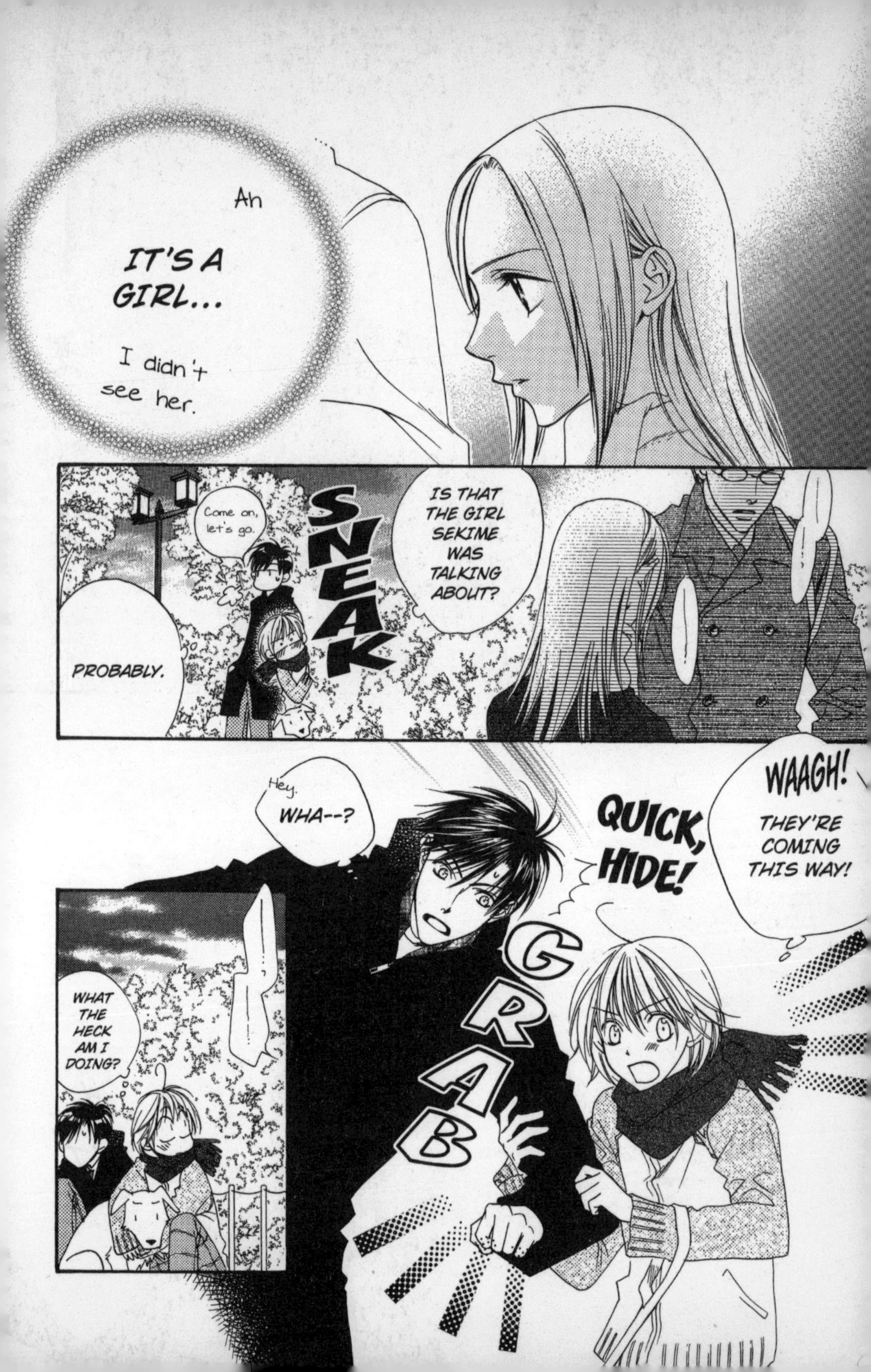
An
IT'S A GIRL...
I didn't see her.
IS THAT THE GIRL SEKIME WAS TALKING ABOUT?
SNEAK
PROBABLY.
Come on, let's go.
WAAGH!
THEY'RE COMING THIS WAY!
QUICK, HIDE!
GRAB
Hey.
WHA--?
WHAT THE HECK AM I DOING?

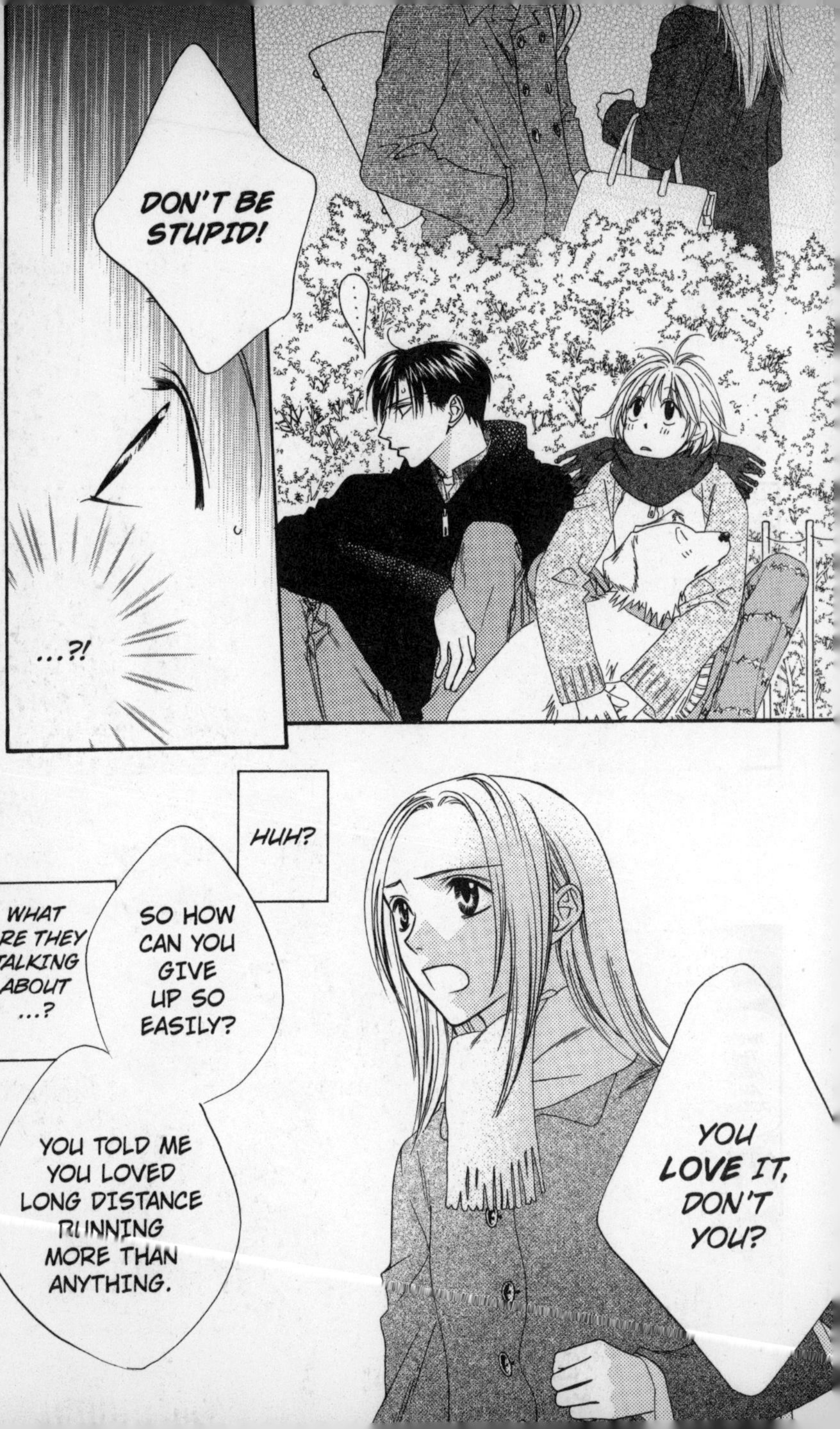
DON'T BE STUPID!
...?!
HUH?
SO HOW CAN YOU GIVE UP SO EASILY?
WHAT ARE THEY TALKING ABOUT ...?
YOU LOVE IT, DON'T YOU?
YOU TOLD ME YOU LOVED LONG DISTANCE RUNNING MORE THAN ANYTHING.

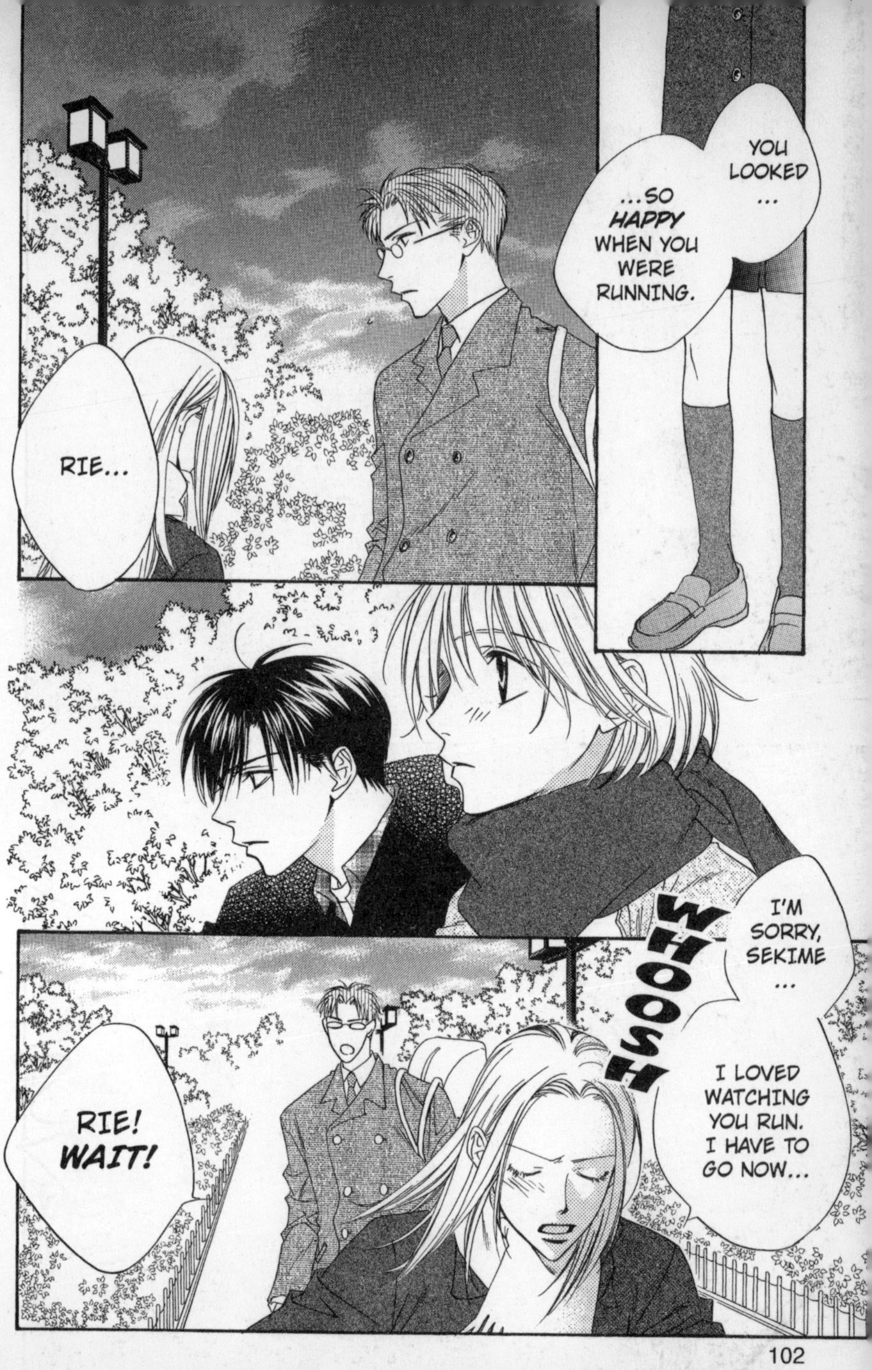
YOU LOOKED ... ...SO HAPPY WHEN YOU WERE RUNNING.
RIE...
WHOOSH
I'M SORRY, SEKIME ...
I LOVED WATCHING YOU RUN. I HAVE TO GO NOW...
RIE! WAIT!

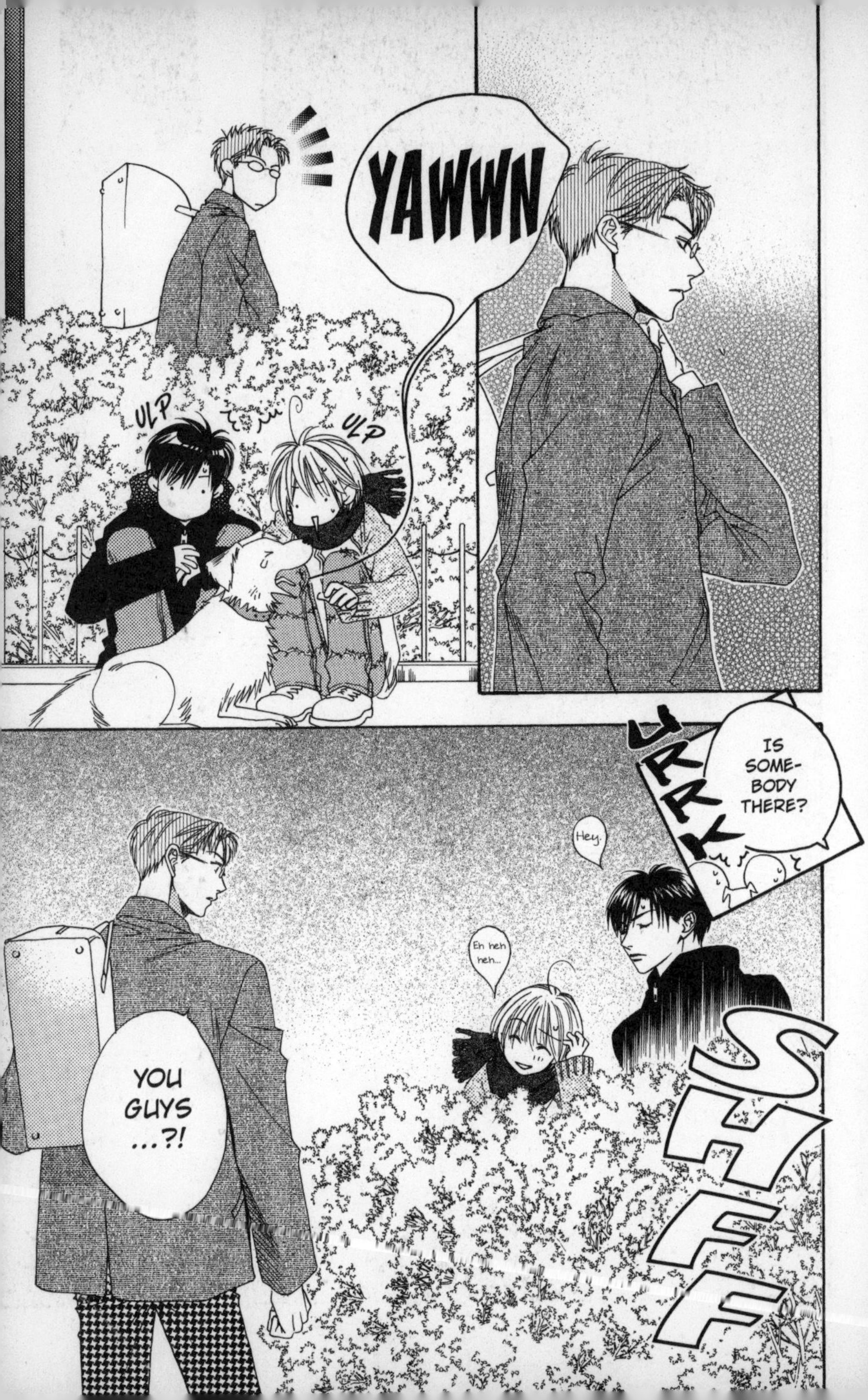
YAWWN
ULP
ULP
URRK
IS SOME-BODY THERE?
Hey.
SHFFF
Eh heh heh...
YOU GUYS ...?!

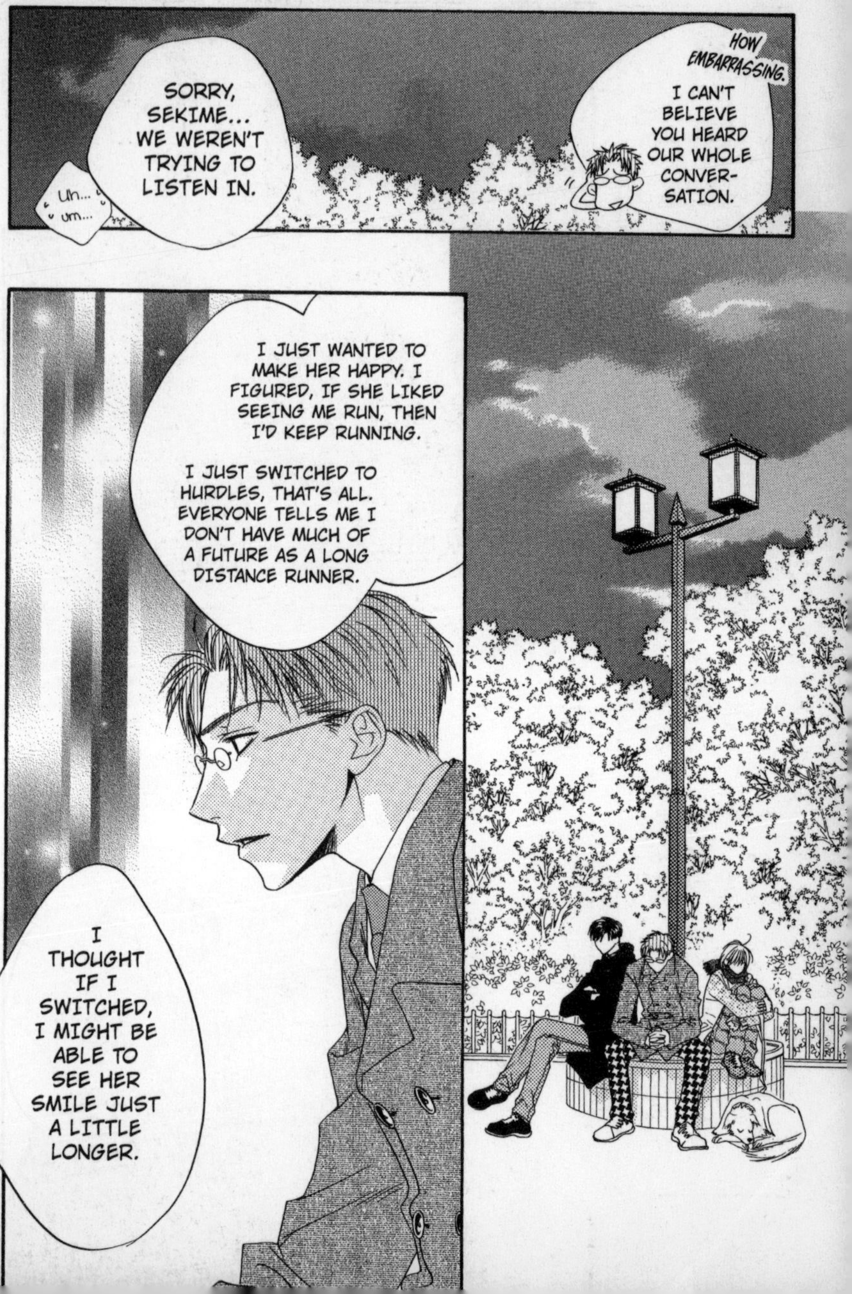
HOW EMBARRASSING.
I CAN'T BELIEVE YOU HEARD OUR WHOLE CONVER-SATION.
SORRY, SEKIME... WE WEREN'T TRYING TO LISTEN IN.
Uh... um...
I JUST WANTED TO MAKE HER HAPPY. I FIGURED, IF SHE LIKED SEEING ME RUN, THEN I'D KEEP RUNNING.
I JUST SWITCHED TO HURDLES, THAT'S ALL. EVERYONE TELLS ME I DON'T HAVE MUCH OF A FUTURE AS A LONG DISTANCE RUNNER.
I THOUGHT IF I SWITCHED, I MIGHT BE ABLE TO SEE HER SMILE JUST A LITTLE LONGER.

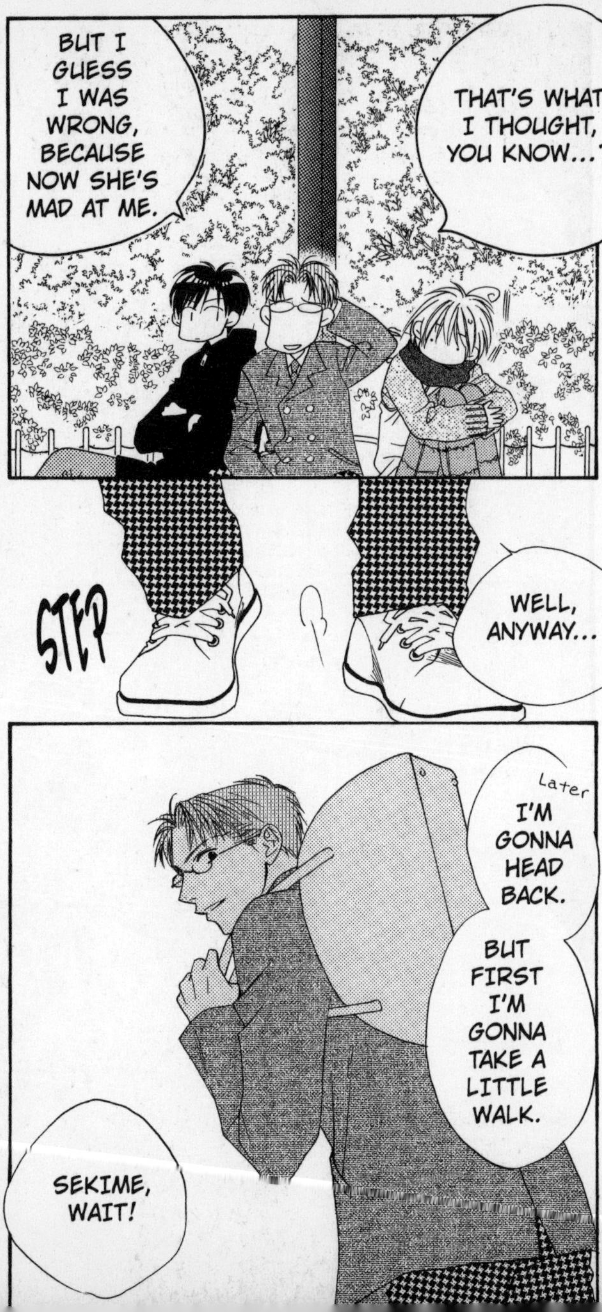
THAT'S WHAT I THOUGHT, YOU KNOW...?
BUT I GUESS I WAS WRONG, BECAUSE NOW SHE'S MAD AT ME.
WELL, ANYWAY...
STEP
Later
I'M GONNA HEAD BACK.
BUT FIRST I'M GONNA TAKE A LITTLE WALK.
SEKIME, WAIT!

♥

ALL ABOUT THE CHARACTERS

First up, Sekime! Did you notice that Sekime got a hair cut? He had long hair when I introduced him for the first time, but I always wanted to change it. I thought this story was the perfect chance, so I did it! Sekime got a makeover! Ever since his hairstyle changed, he's become much more popular.

Next up is Shin. He seemed so mysterious at the end of his last appearance, but in the end he was as popular as the main characters. Shin and I both thought long and hard about how we were gonna end that final scene. Ha ha! At one point, Shin was gonna tell Mizuki, "I don't know why I have these feelings for you!" But we decided against that.

Sorry I've been neglecting you, Sekime.

Thanks-S_kime

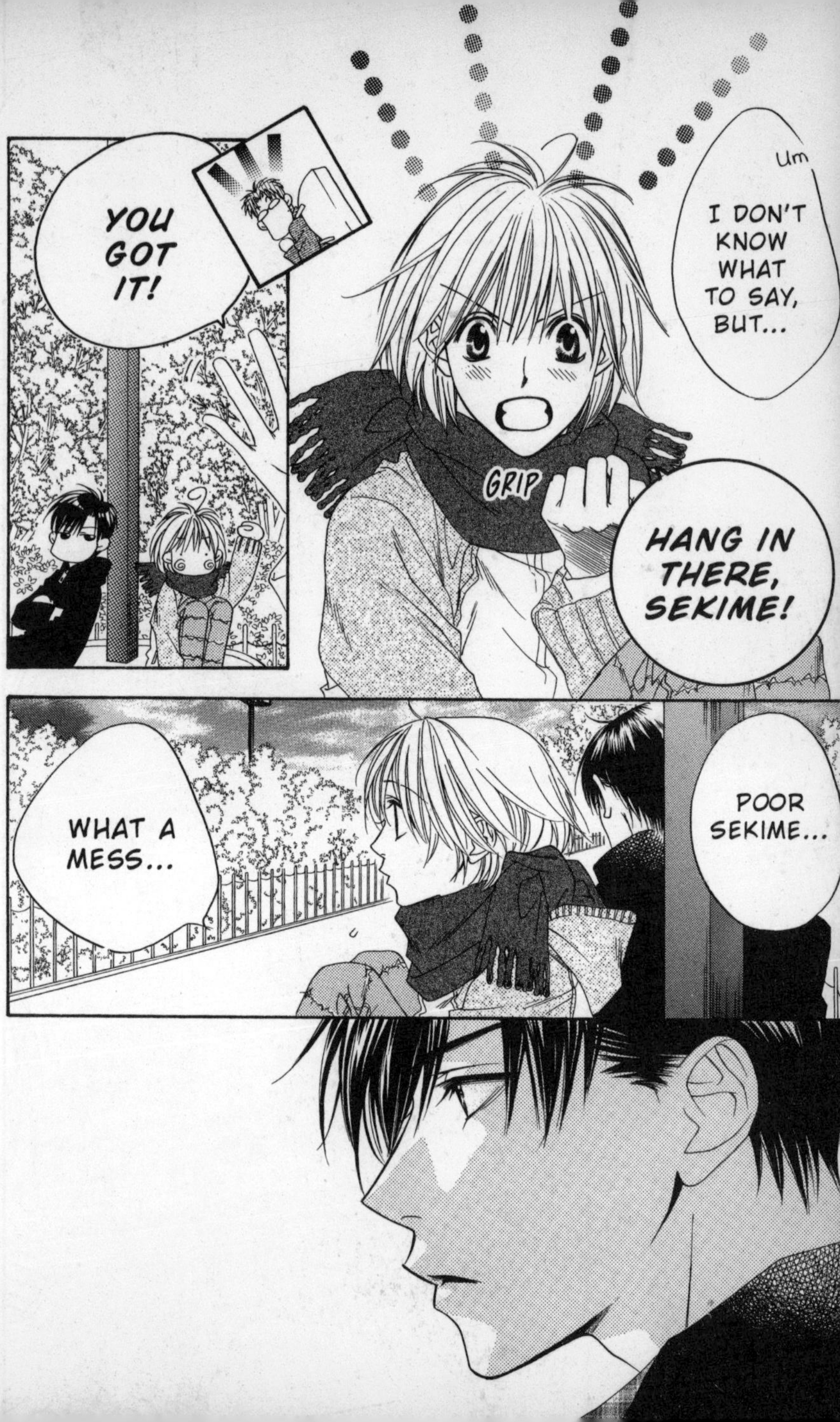
Um
I DON'T KNOW WHAT TO SAY, BUT...
GRIP
HANG IN THERE, SEKIME!
YOU GOT IT!
POOR SEKIME...
WHAT A MESS...

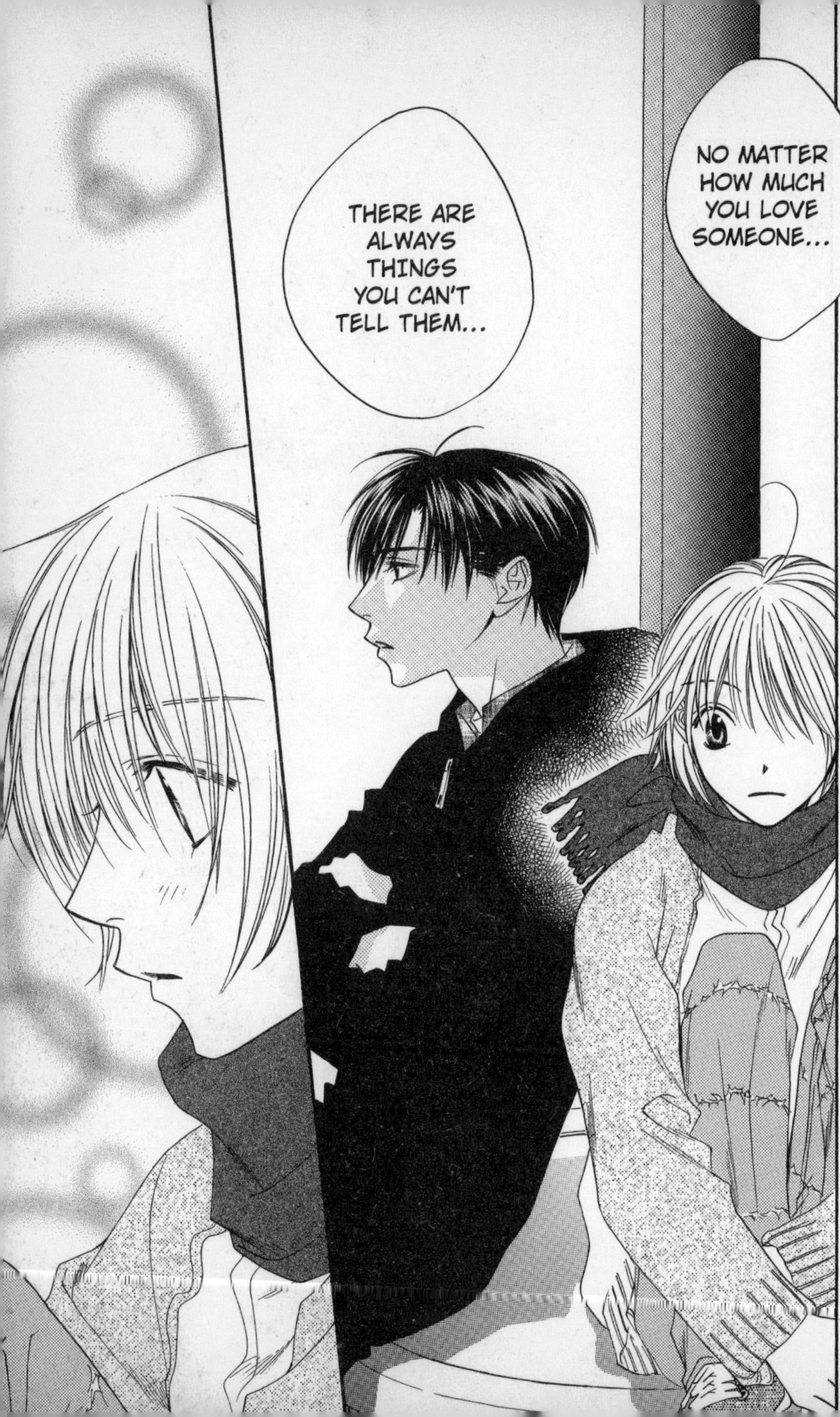
NO MATTER HOW MUCH YOU LOVE SOMEONE...
THERE ARE ALWAYS THINGS YOU CAN'T TELL THEM...

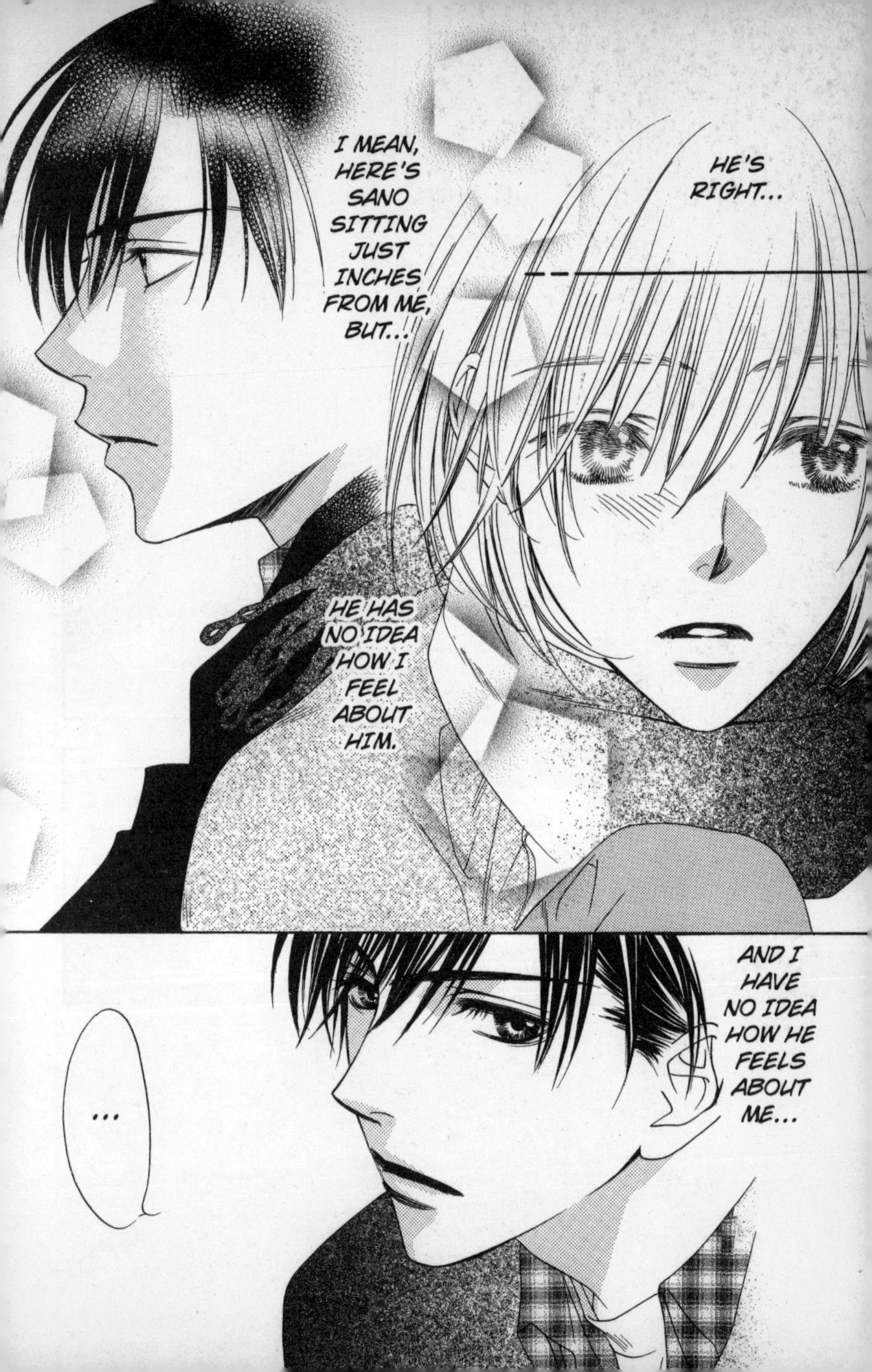
HE'S RIGHT...
I MEAN, HERE'S SANO SITTING JUST INCHES FROM ME, BUT...
HE HAS NO IDEA HOW I FEEL ABOUT HIM.
AND I HAVE NO IDEA HOW HE FEELS ABOUT ME...
...

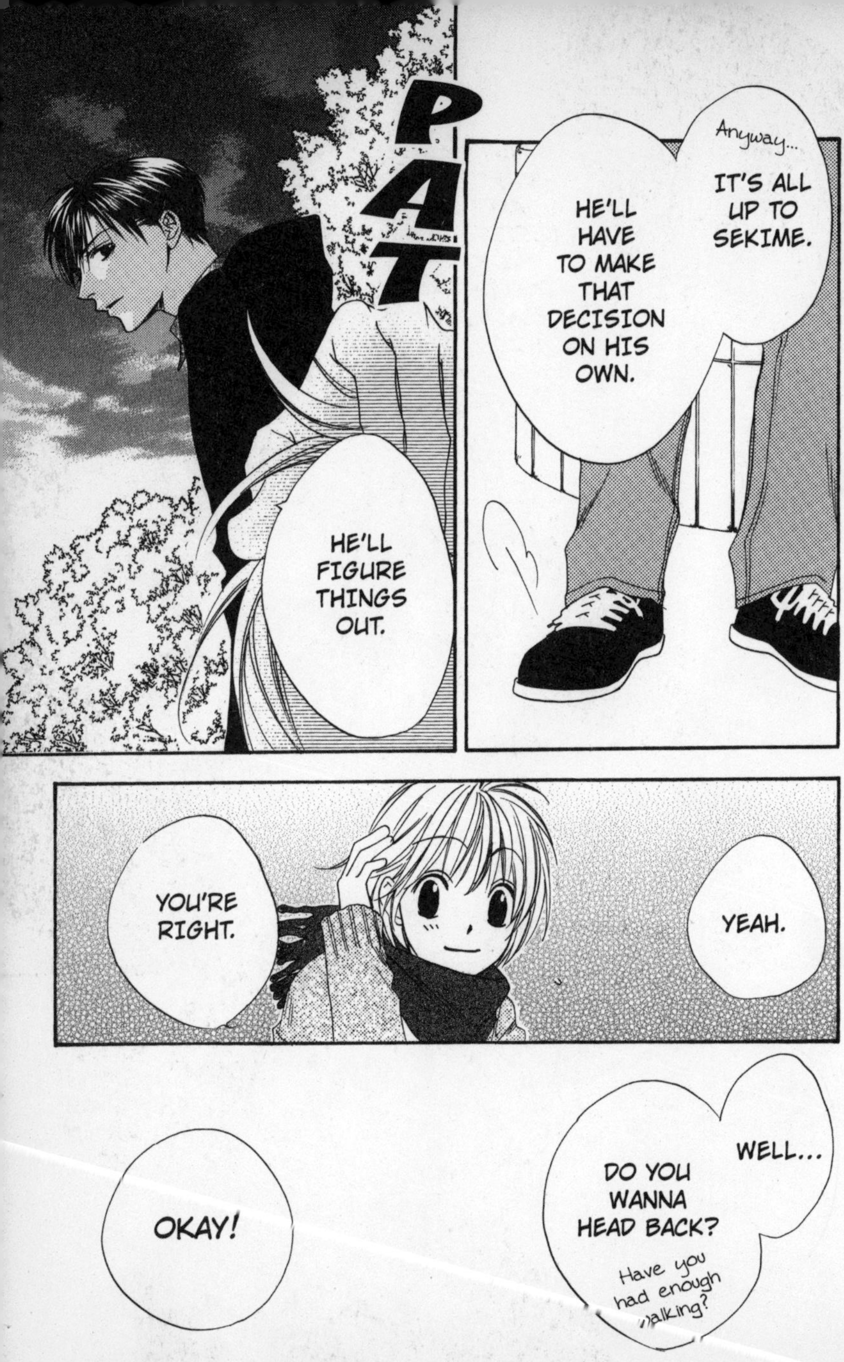
Anyway...
IT'S ALL UP TO SEKIME.
HE'LL HAVE TO MAKE THAT DECISION ON HIS OWN.
PAT
HE'LL FIGURE THINGS OUT.
YEAH.
YOU'RE RIGHT.
WELL... DO YOU WANNA HEAD BACK?
Have you had enough walking?
OKAY!

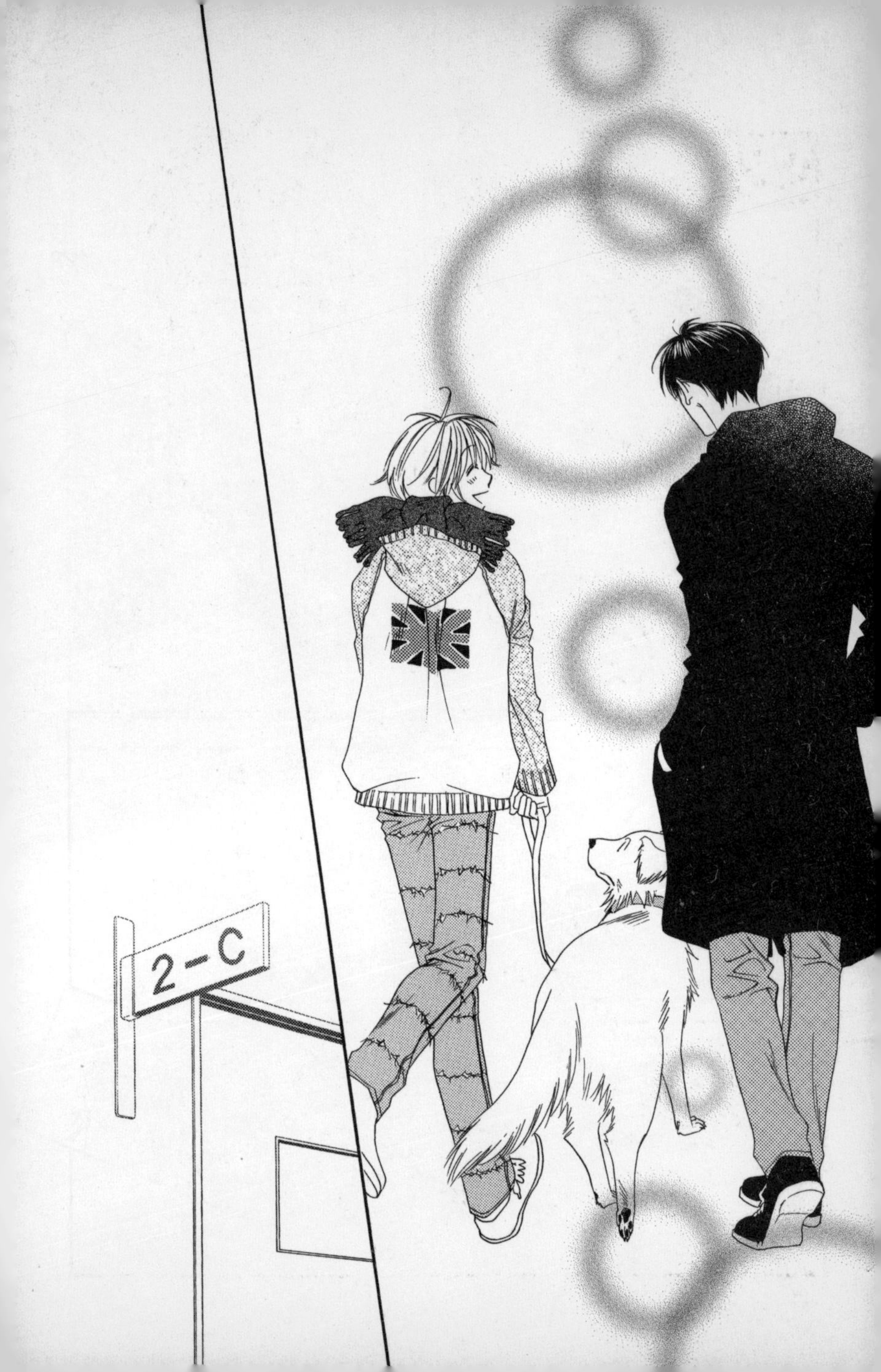
2-C

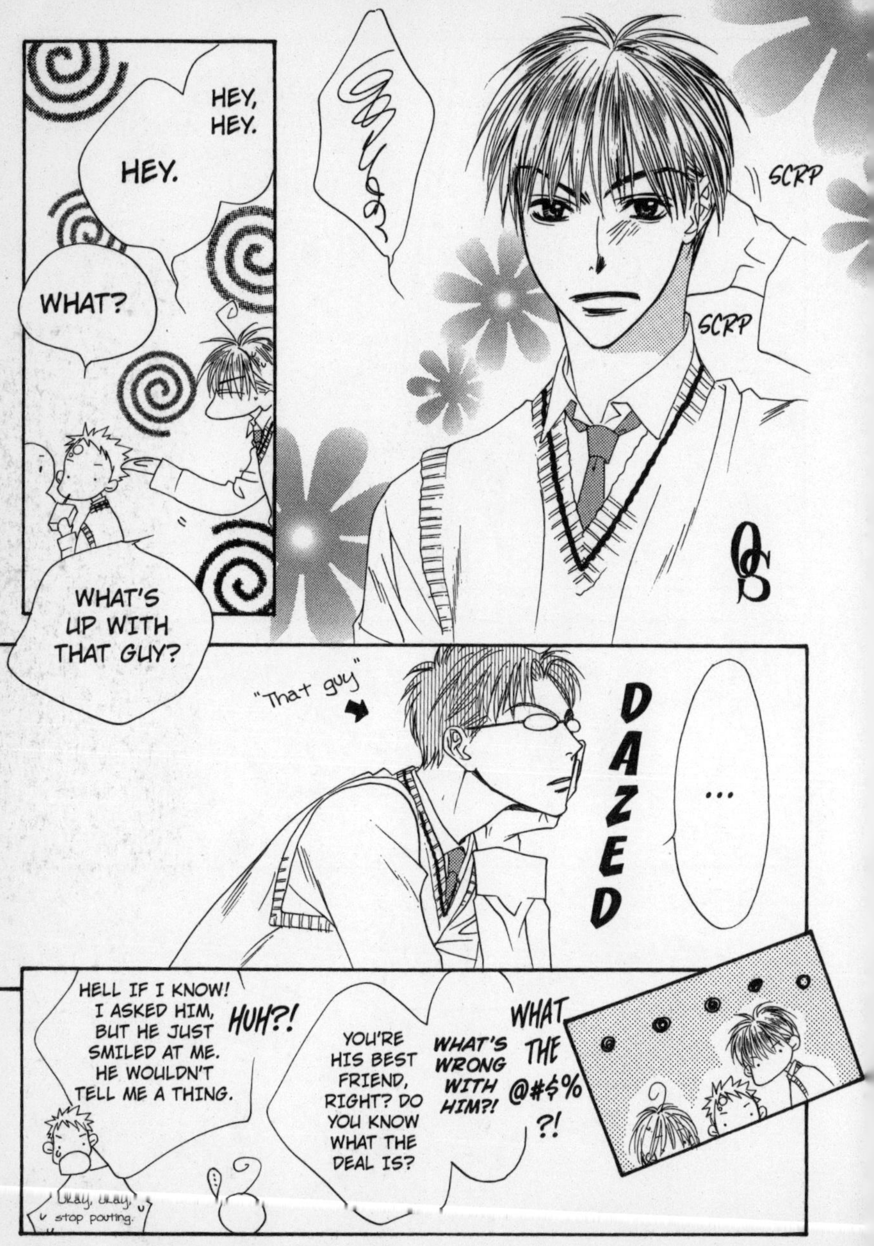
SCRP
SCRP
HEY, HEY.
HEY.
WHAT?
WHAT'S UP WITH THAT GUY?
"That guy"
DAZED
...
WHAT THE @#$% ?!
WHAT'S WRONG WITH HIM?!
YOU'RE HIS BEST FRIEND, RIGHT? DO YOU KNOW WHAT THE DEAL IS?
HUH?!
HELL IF I KNOW! I ASKED HIM, BUT HE JUST SMILED AT ME. HE WOULDN'T TELL ME A THING.
Okay, okay, stop pouting.

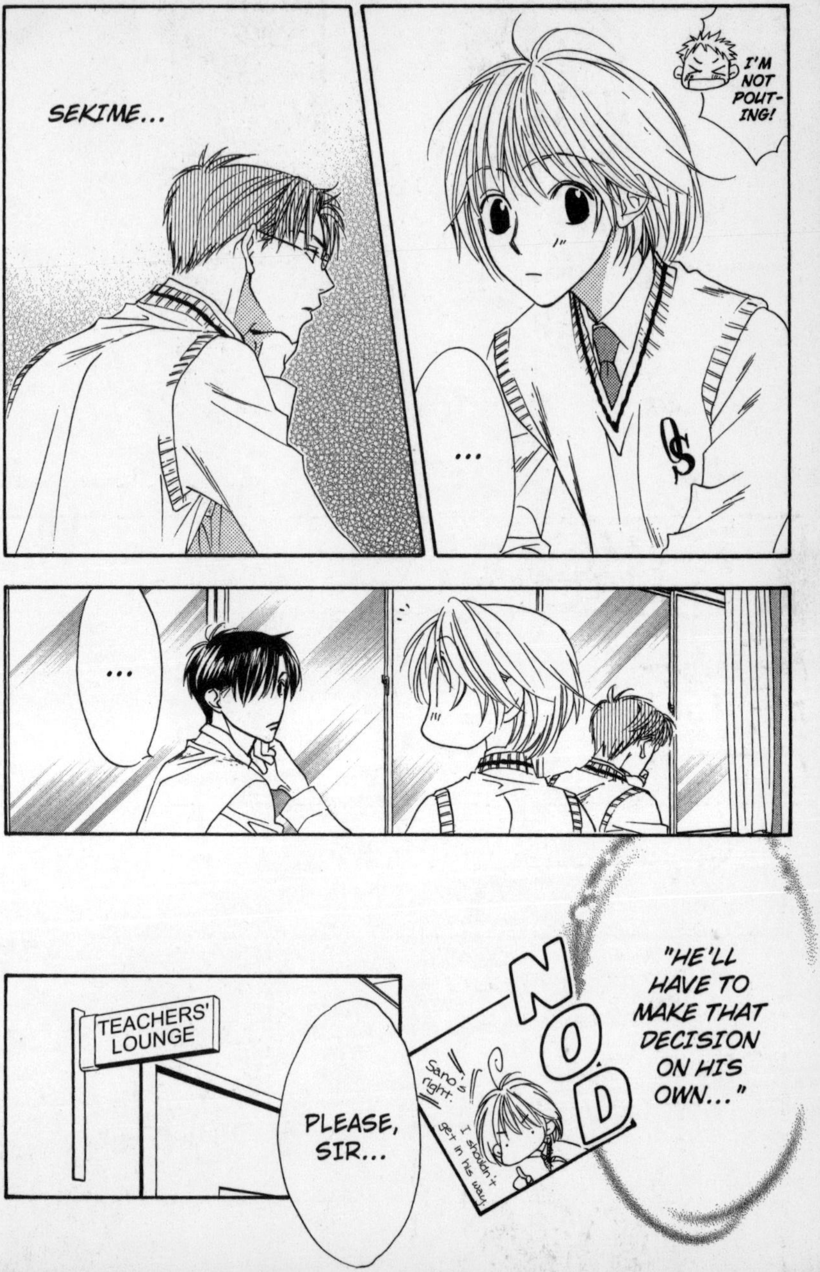
I'M NOT POUT-ING!
...
SEKIME...
...
"HE'LL HAVE TO MAKE THAT DECISION ON HIS OWN..."
NOD
Sano's right.
I shouldn't get in his way.
TEACHERS' LOUNGE
PLEASE, SIR...

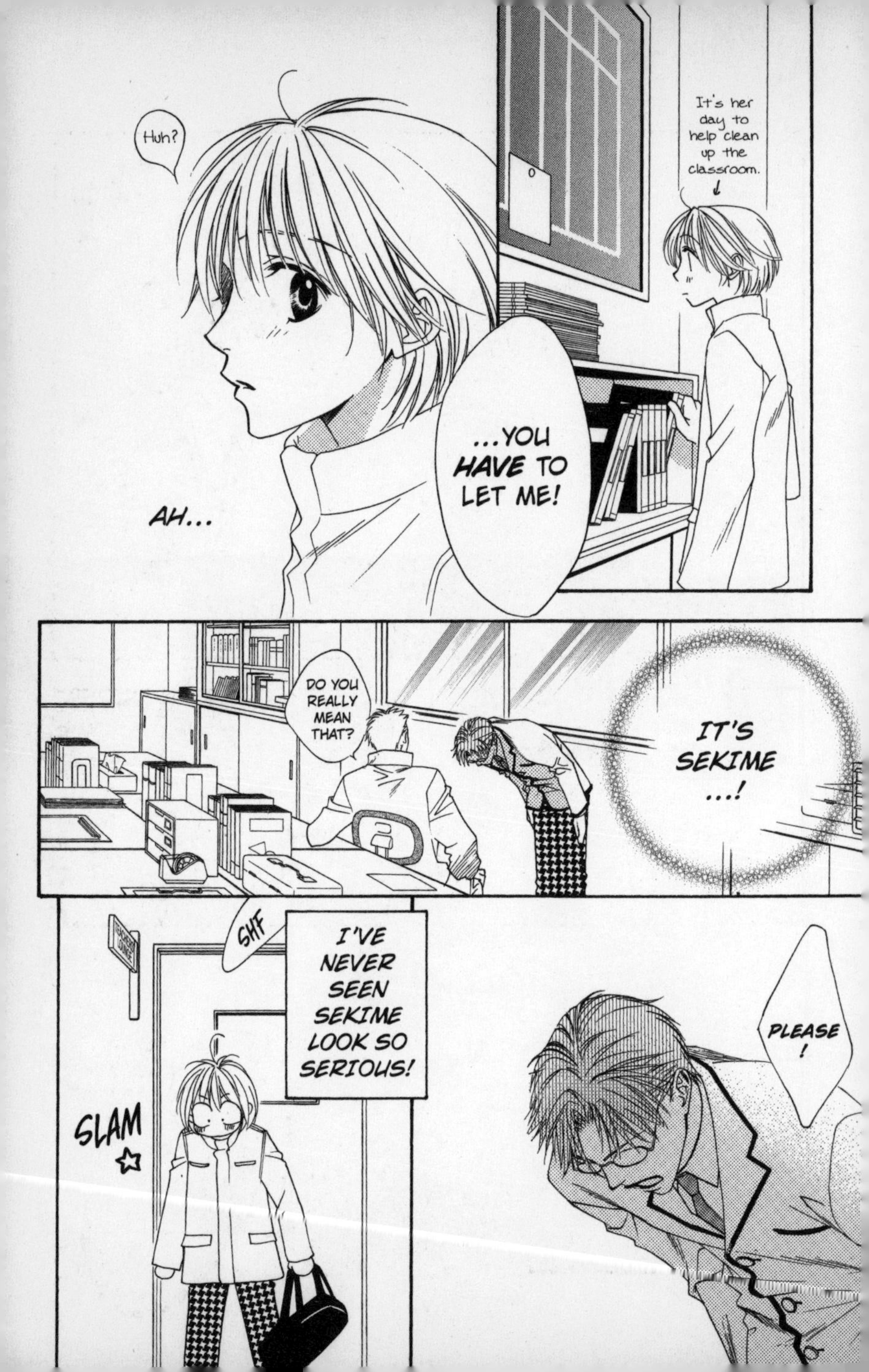
It's her day to help clean up the classroom.
...YOU HAVE TO LET ME!
Huh?
AH...
IT'S SEKIME ...!
DO YOU REALLY MEAN THAT?
PLEASE !
SHF
I'VE NEVER SEEN SEKIME LOOK SO SERIOUS!
SLAM

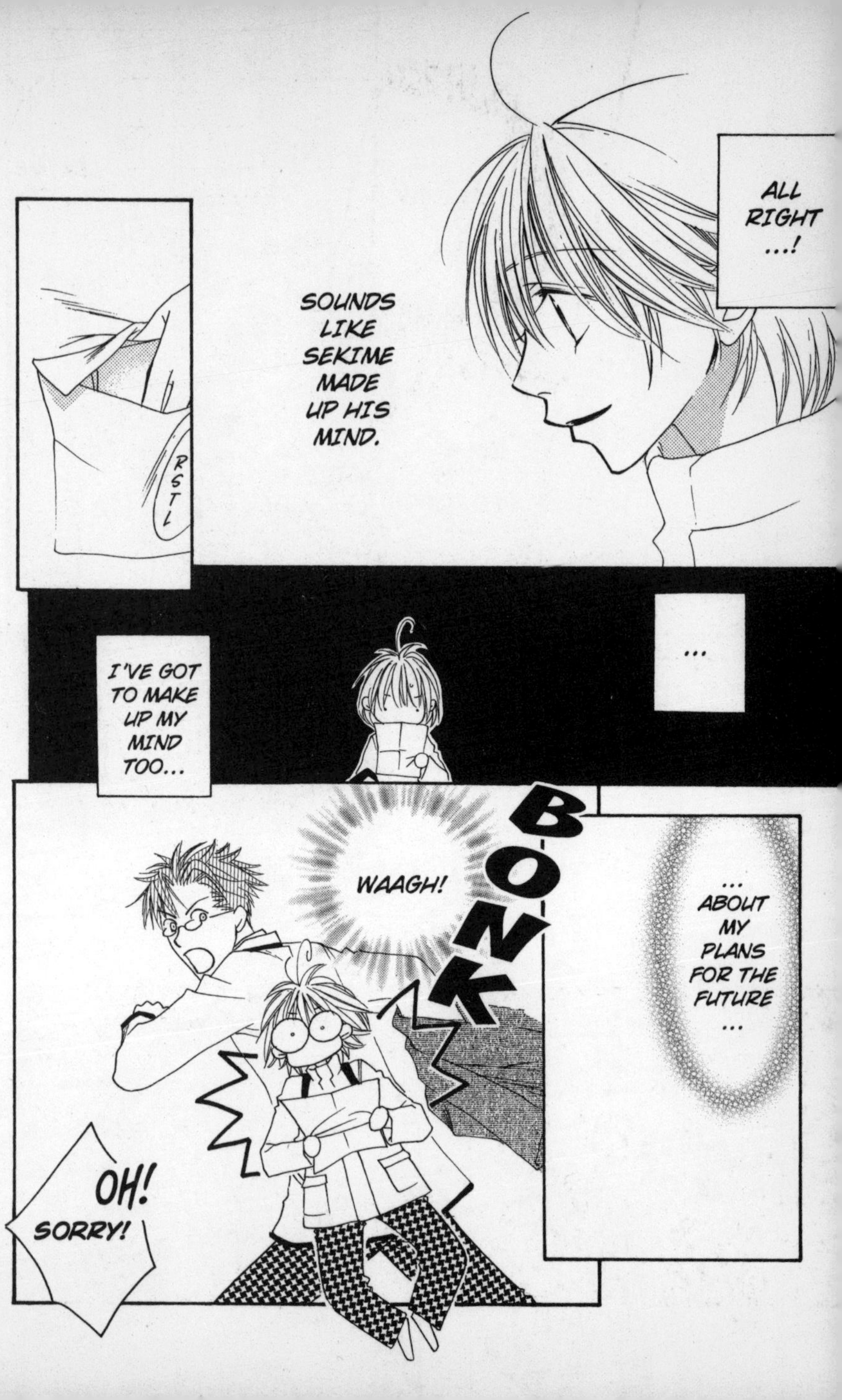
ALL RIGHT ...!
SOUNDS LIKE SEKIME MADE UP HIS MIND.
RSTL
...
I'VE GOT TO MAKE UP MY MIND TOO...
... ABOUT MY PLANS FOR THE FUTURE ...
BONK
WAAGH!
OH!
SORRY!

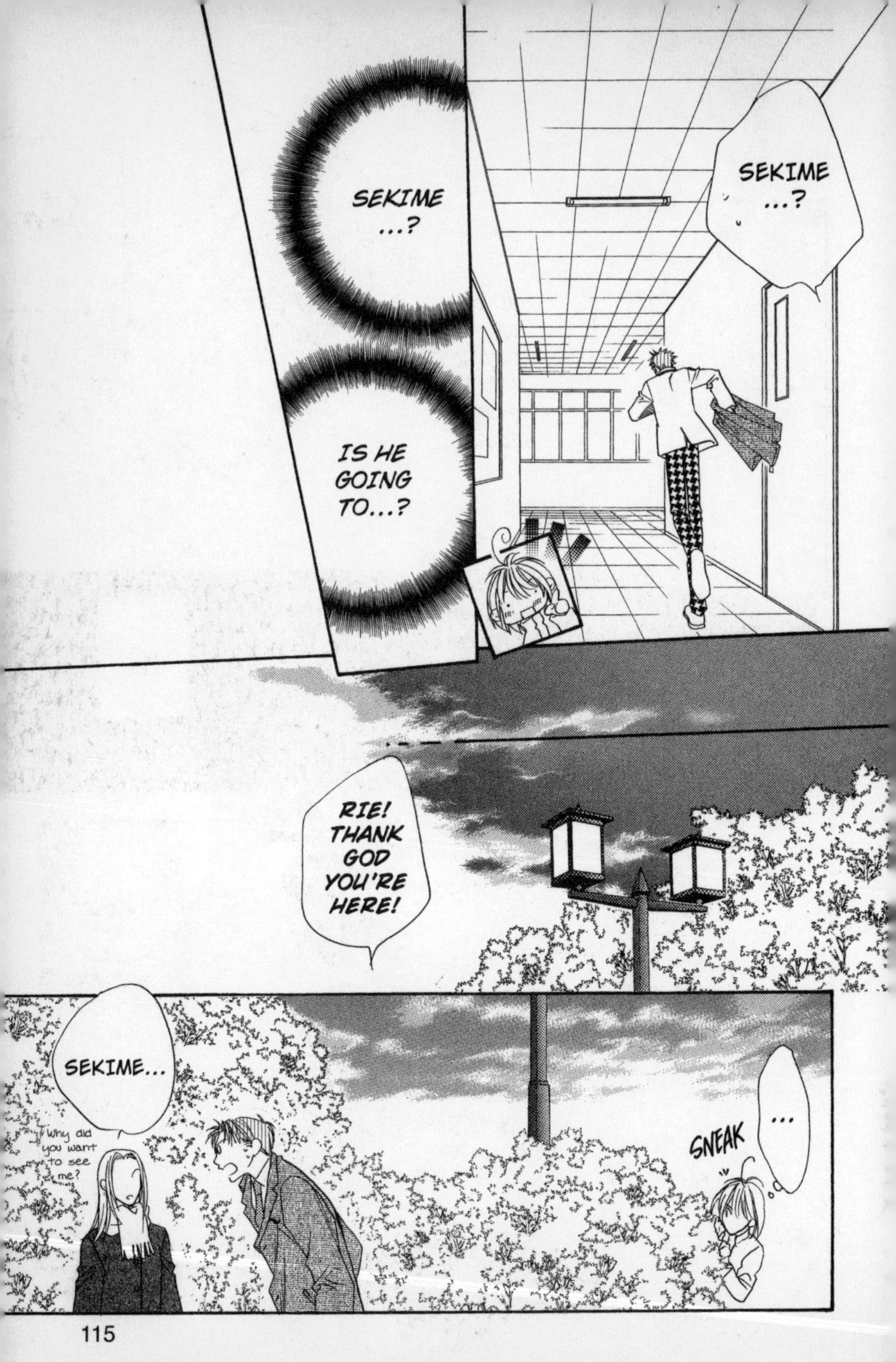
SEKIME ...?
SEKIME ...?
IS HE GOING TO...?
RIE! THANK GOD YOU'RE HERE!
...
SNEAK
SEKIME...
Why did you want to see me?

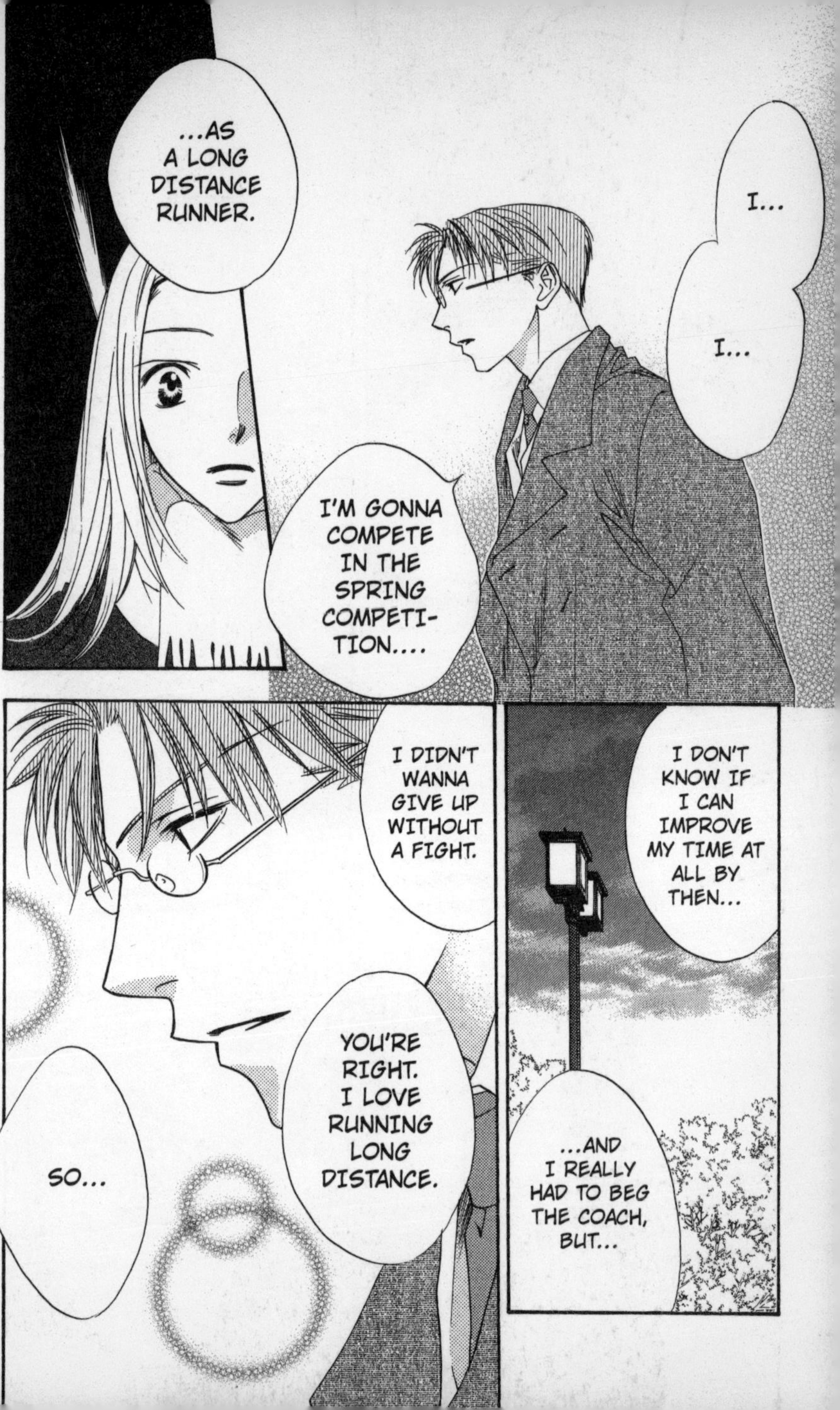
I...
I...
I'M GONNA COMPETE IN THE SPRING COMPETITION....
...AS A LONG DISTANCE RUNNER.
I DON'T KNOW IF I CAN IMPROVE MY TIME AT ALL BY THEN...
...AND I REALLY HAD TO BEG THE COACH, BUT...
I DIDN'T WANNA GIVE UP WITHOUT A FIGHT.
YOU'RE RIGHT. I LOVE RUNNING LONG DISTANCE.
SO...

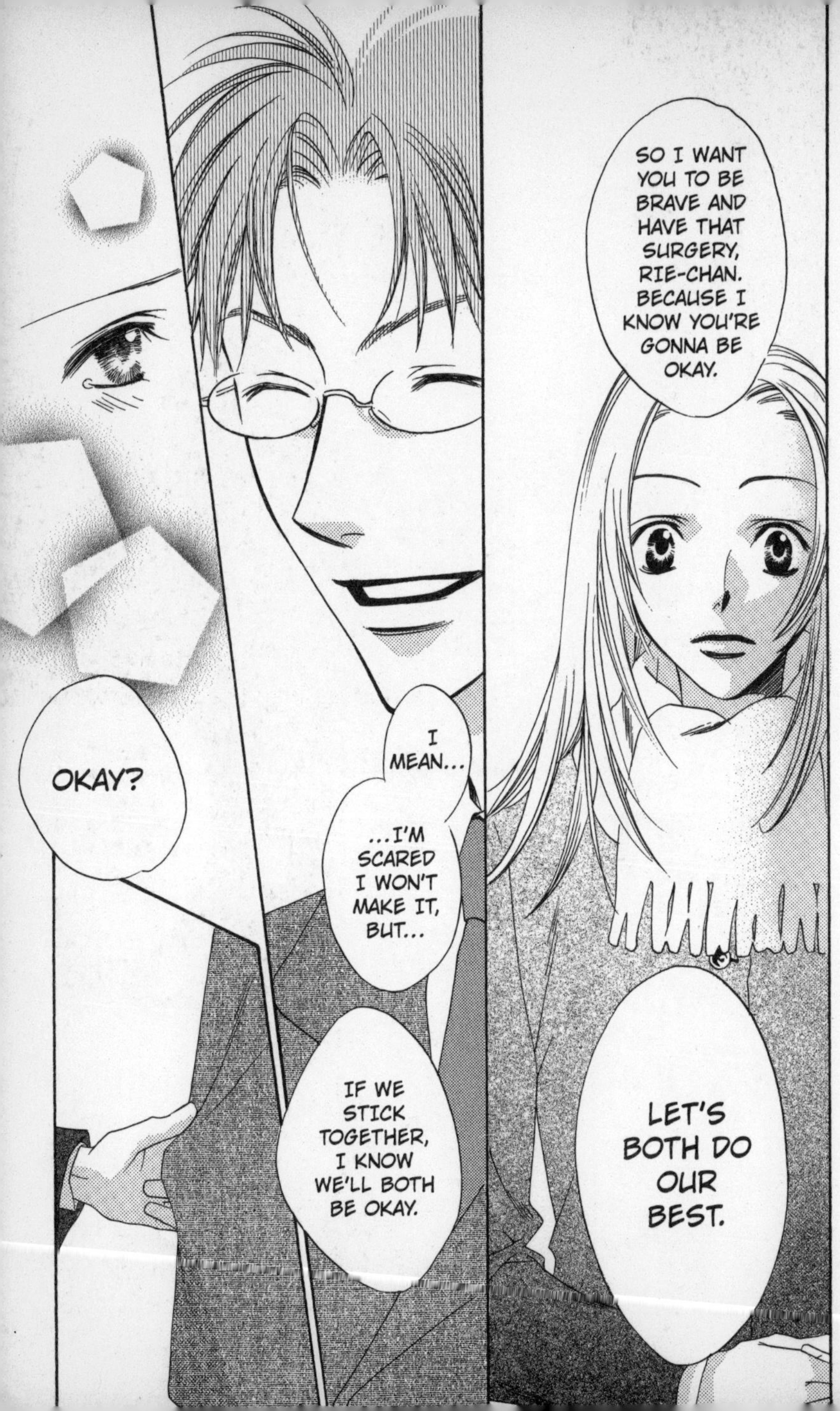
SO I WANT YOU TO BE BRAVE AND HAVE THAT SURGERY, RIE-CHAN. BECAUSE I KNOW YOU'RE GONNA BE OKAY.
LET'S BOTH DO OUR BEST.
I MEAN...
...I'M SCARED I WON'T MAKE IT, BUT...
IF WE STICK TOGETHER, I KNOW WE'LL BOTH BE OKAY.
OKAY?

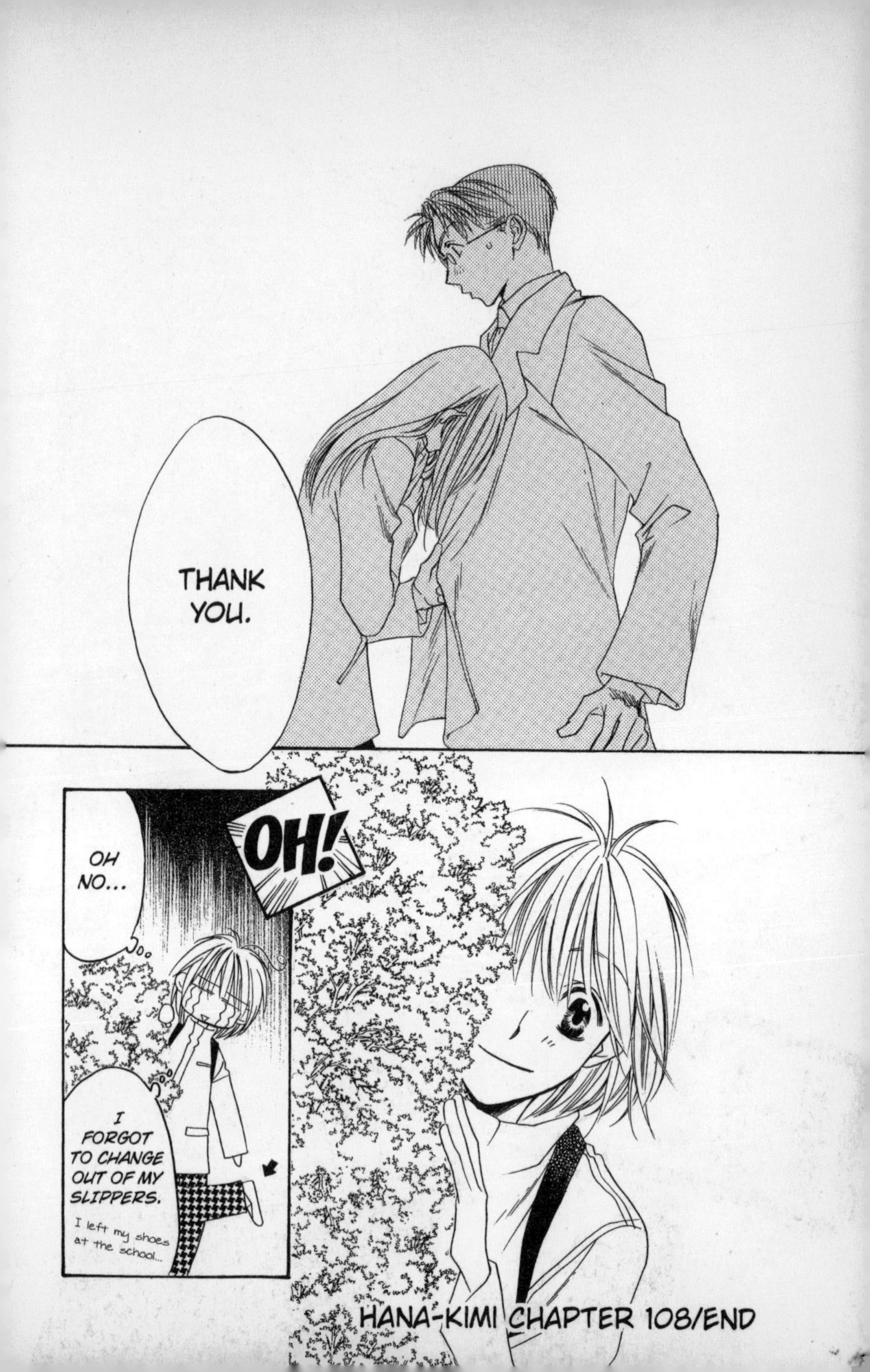
THANK YOU.
OH!
OH NO...
I FORGOT TO CHANGE OUT OF MY SLIPPERS.
I left my shoes at the school...
HANA-KIMI CHAPTER 108/END

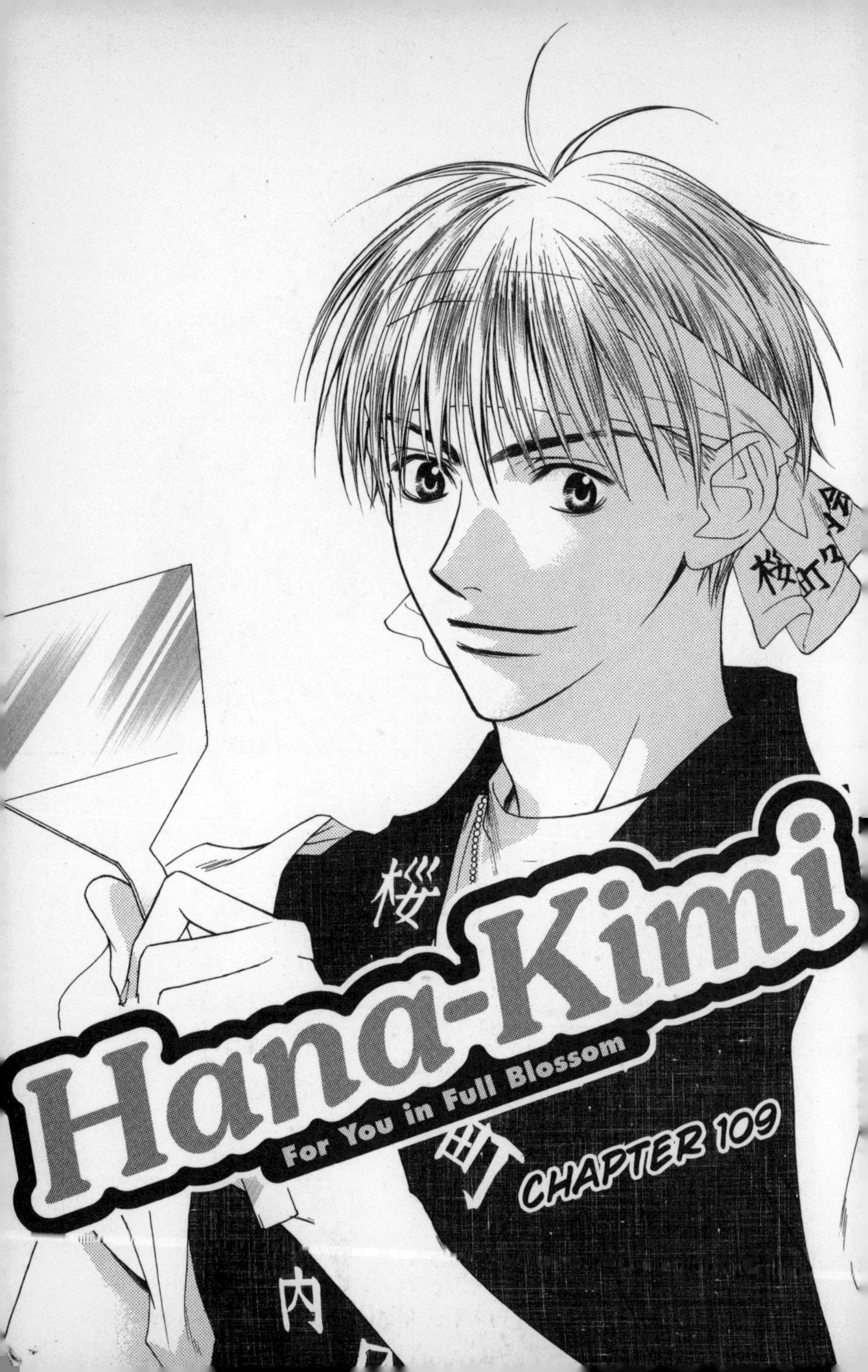
Hana-Kimi
For You in Full Blossom
CHAPTER 109

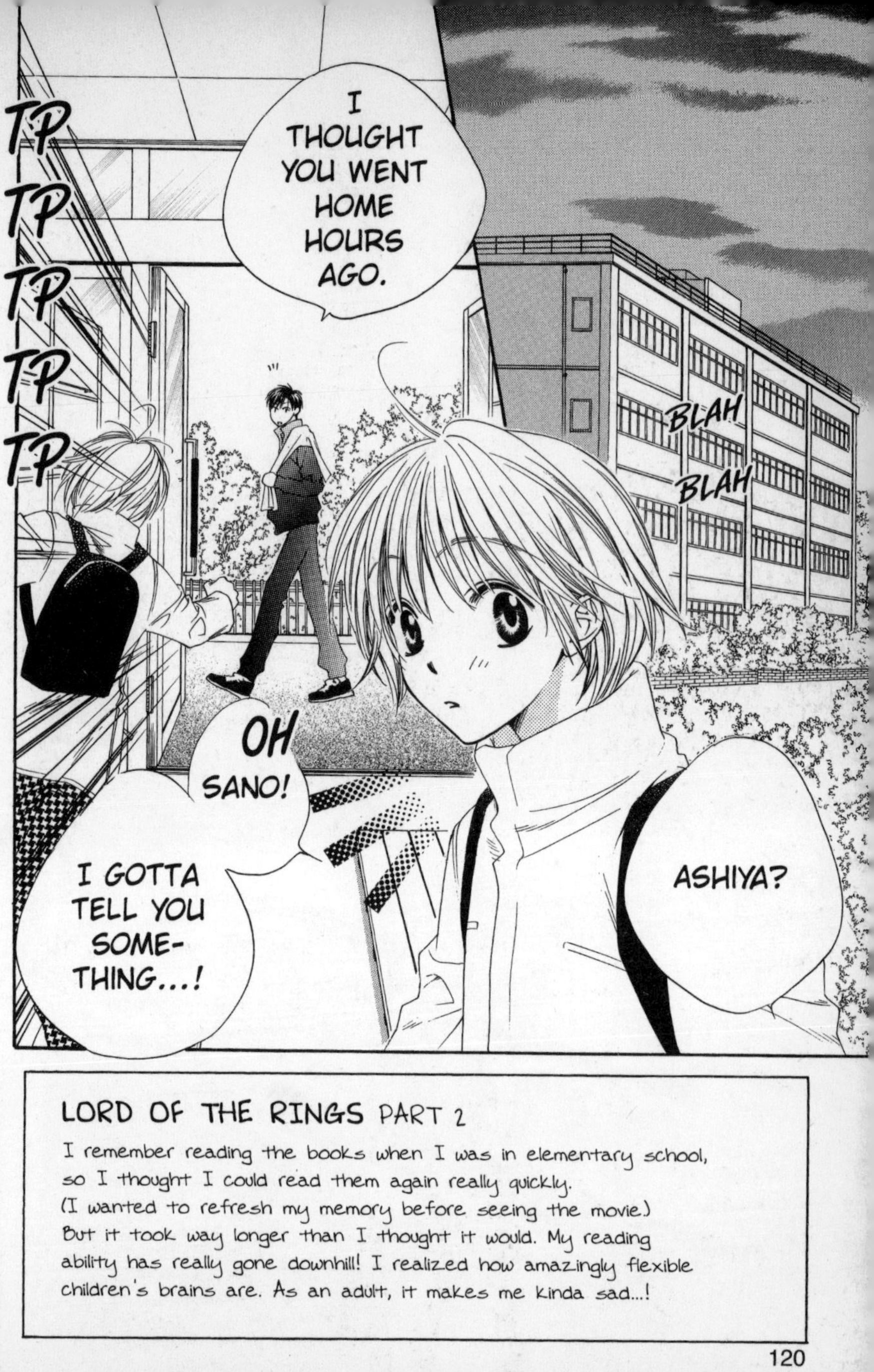
I THOUGHT YOU WENT HOME HOURS AGO.
BLAH BLAH
TP TP TP TP TP
ASHIYA?
OH SANO!
I GOTTA TELL YOU SOME-THING...!

LORD OF THE RINGS PART 2

I remember reading the books when I was in elementary school, so I thought I could read them again really quickly. (I wanted to refresh my memory before seeing the movie.) But it took way longer than I thought it would. My reading ability has really gone downhill! I realized how amazingly flexible children's brains are. As an adult, it makes me kinda sad...!

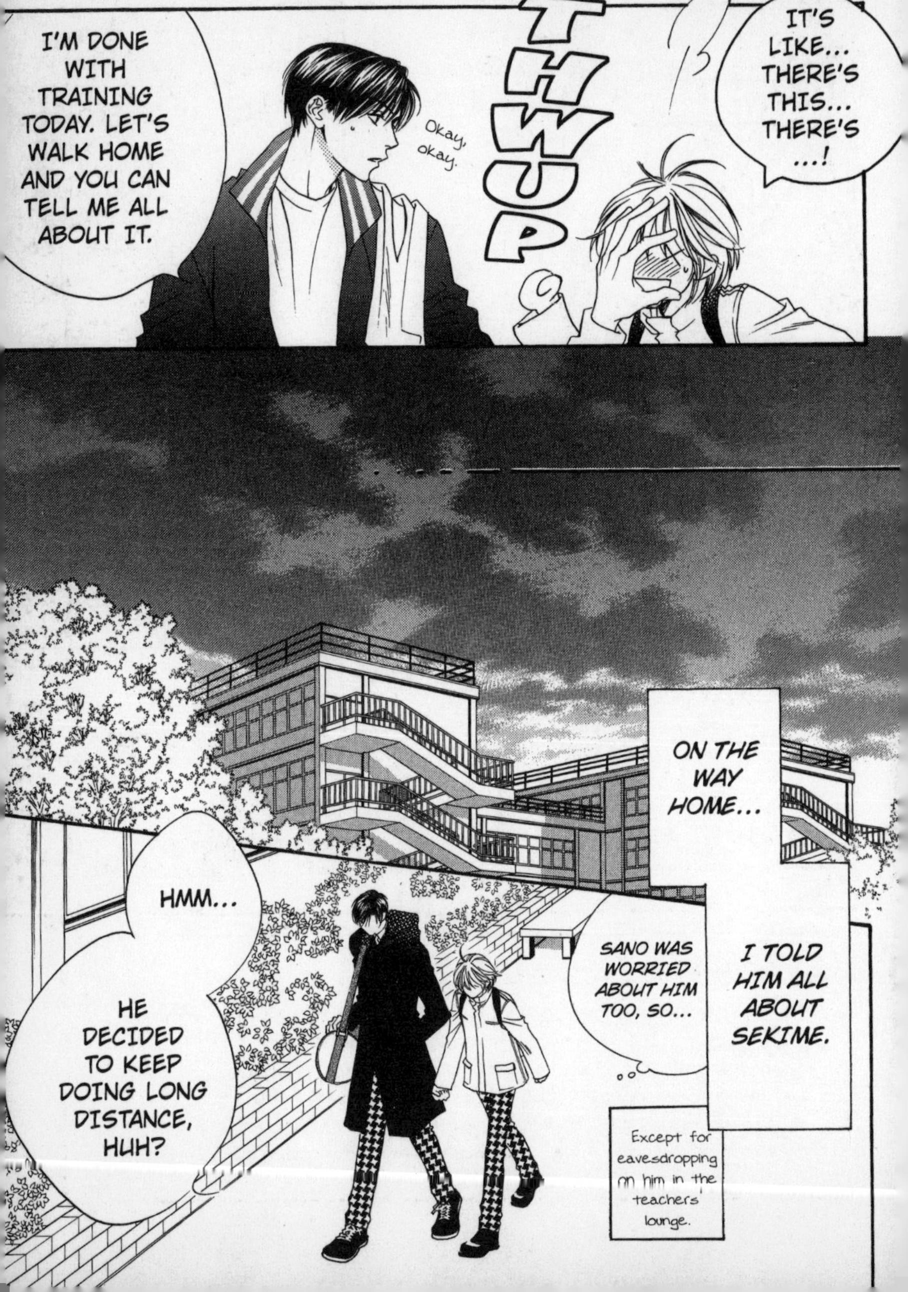
IT'S LIKE... THERE'S THIS... THERE'S ...!
THWUP
Okay, okay.
I'M DONE WITH TRAINING TODAY. LET'S WALK HOME AND YOU CAN TELL ME ALL ABOUT IT.
ON THE WAY HOME...
I TOLD HIM ALL ABOUT SEKIME.
SANO WAS WORRIED ABOUT HIM TOO, SO...
Except for eavesdropping on him in the teachers' lounge.
HMM...
HE DECIDED TO KEEP DOING LONG DISTANCE, HUH?

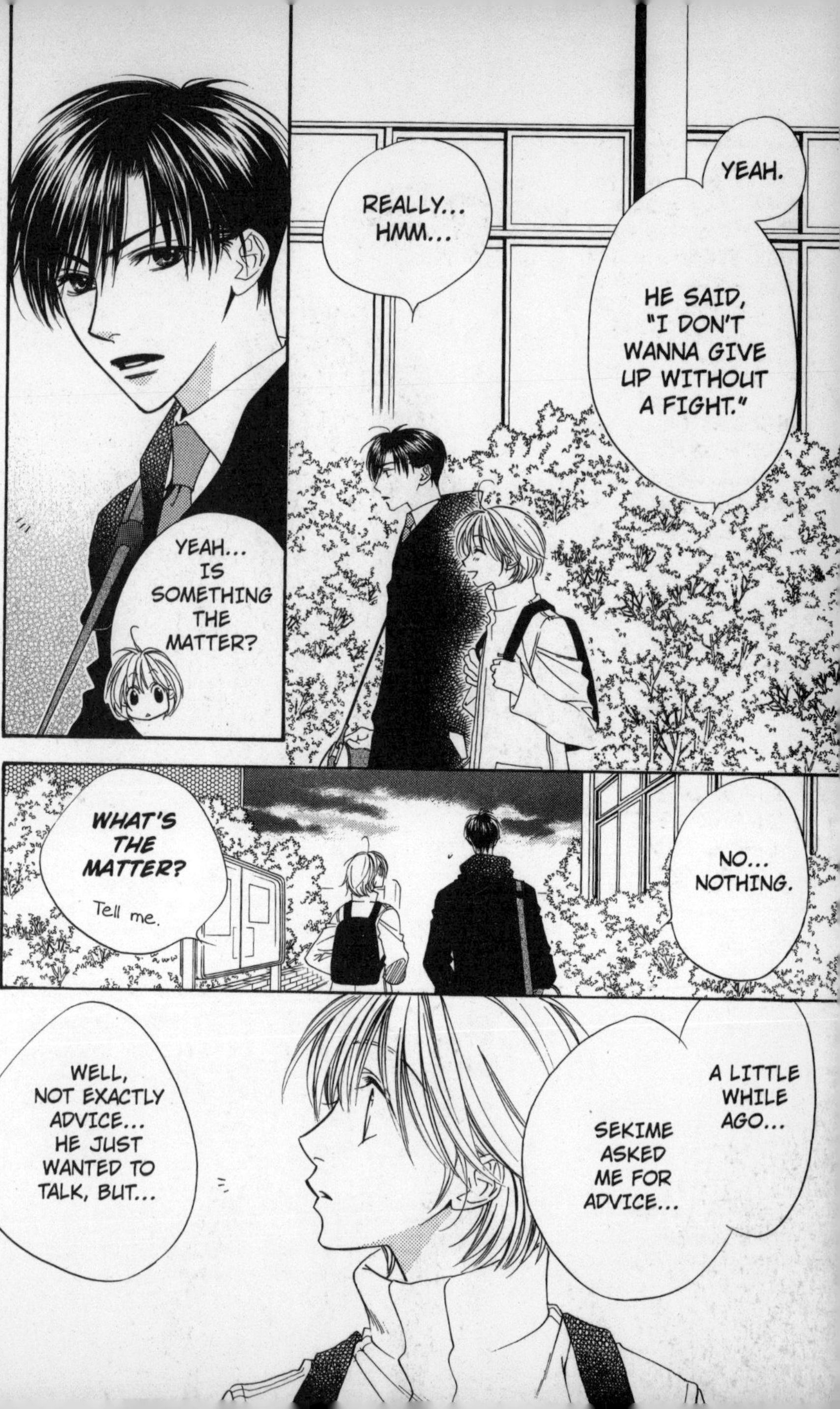
YEAH.
HE SAID, "I DON'T WANNA GIVE UP WITHOUT A FIGHT."
REALLY... HMM...
YEAH... IS SOMETHING THE MATTER?
NO... NOTHING.
WHAT'S THE MATTER?
Tell me.
A LITTLE WHILE AGO...
SEKIME ASKED ME FOR ADVICE...
WELL, NOT EXACTLY ADVICE... HE JUST WANTED TO TALK, BUT...

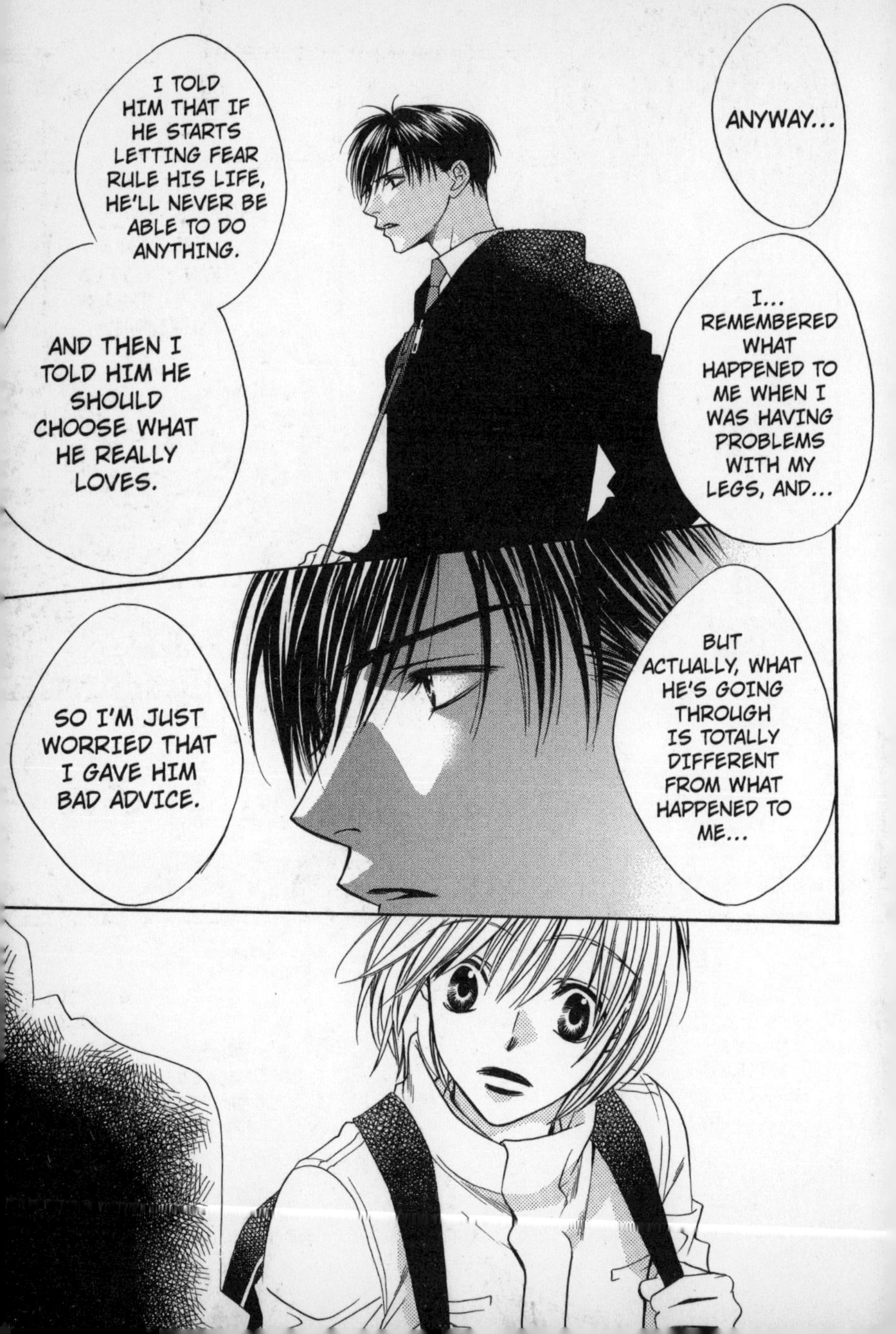
ANYWAY...
I... REMEMBERED WHAT HAPPENED TO ME WHEN I WAS HAVING PROBLEMS WITH MY LEGS, AND...
I TOLD HIM THAT IF HE STARTS LETTING FEAR RULE HIS LIFE, HE'LL NEVER BE ABLE TO DO ANYTHING.
AND THEN I TOLD HIM HE SHOULD CHOOSE WHAT HE REALLY LOVES.
BUT ACTUALLY, WHAT HE'S GOING THROUGH IS TOTALLY DIFFERENT FROM WHAT HAPPENED TO ME...
SO I'M JUST WORRIED THAT I GAVE HIM BAD ADVICE.

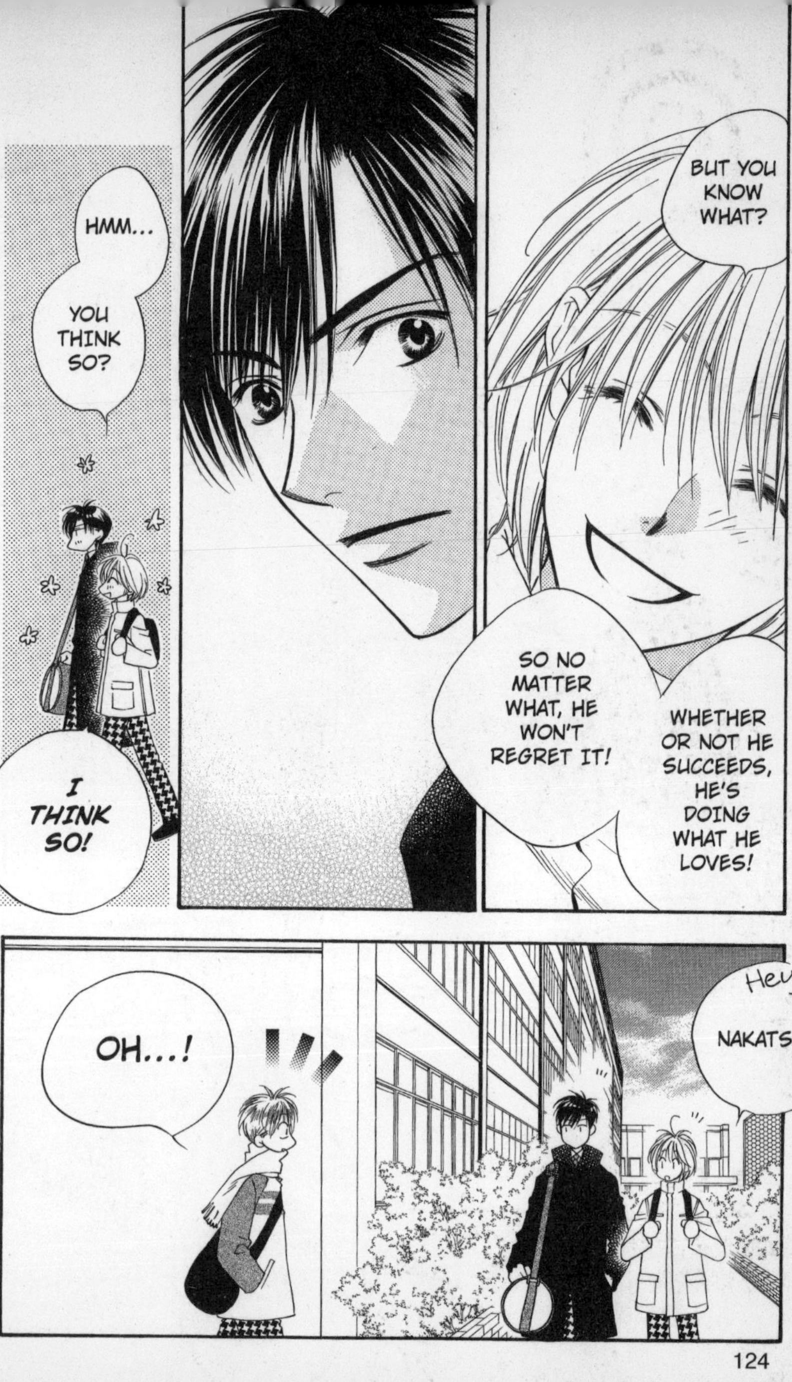
BUT YOU KNOW WHAT?
WHETHER OR NOT HE SUCCEEDS, HE'S DOING WHAT HE LOVES!
SO NO MATTER WHAT, HE WON'T REGRET IT!
HMM...
YOU THINK SO?
I THINK SO!
Hey
NAKATSU.
OH...!

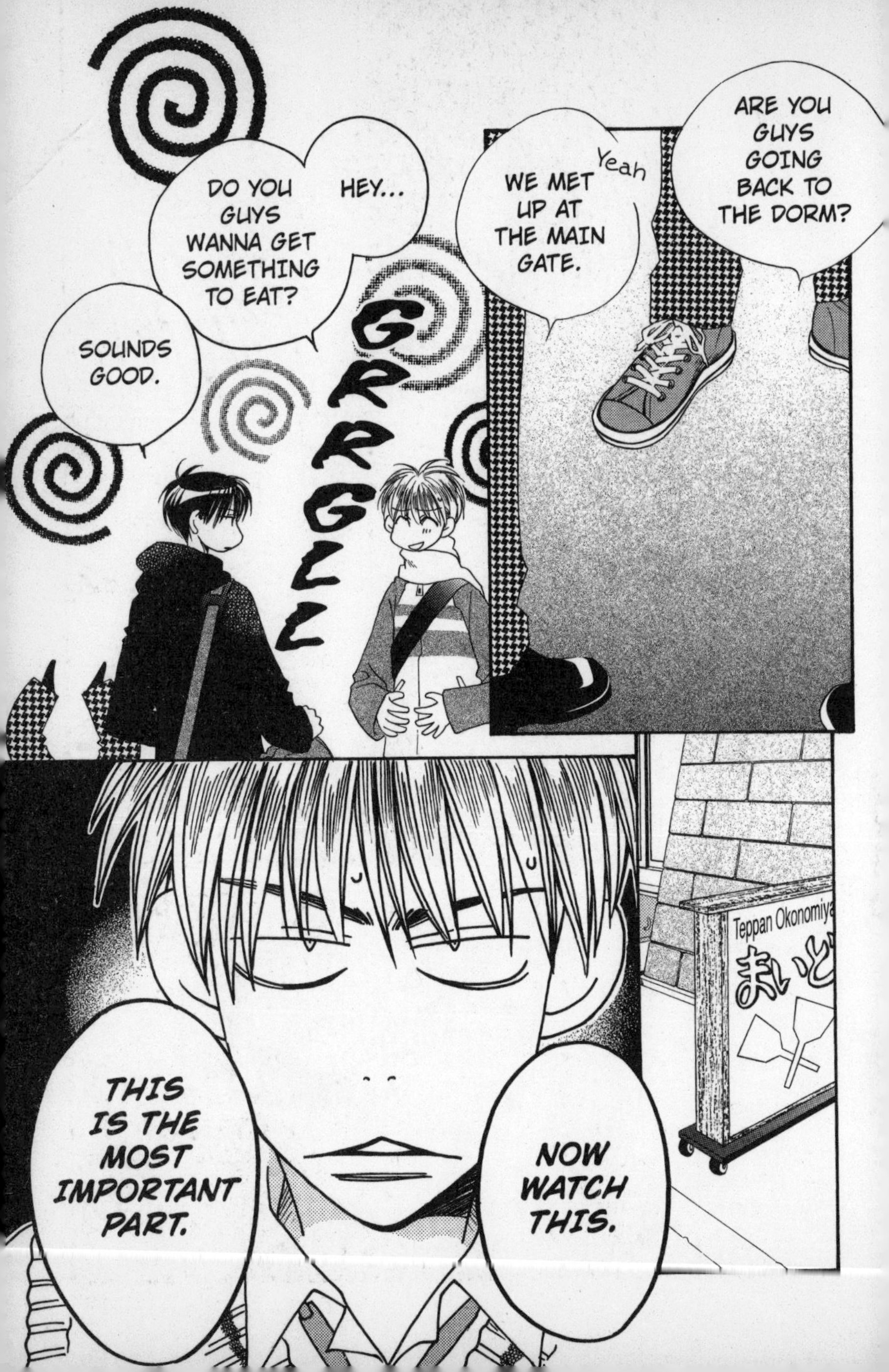
ARE YOU GUYS GOING BACK TO THE DORM?
Yeah
WE MET UP AT THE MAIN GATE.
HEY...
DO YOU GUYS WANNA GET SOMETHING TO EAT?
SOUNDS GOOD.
GRRGLL
Teppan Okonomiya
まいど
NOW WATCH THIS.
THIS IS THE MOST IMPORTANT PART.

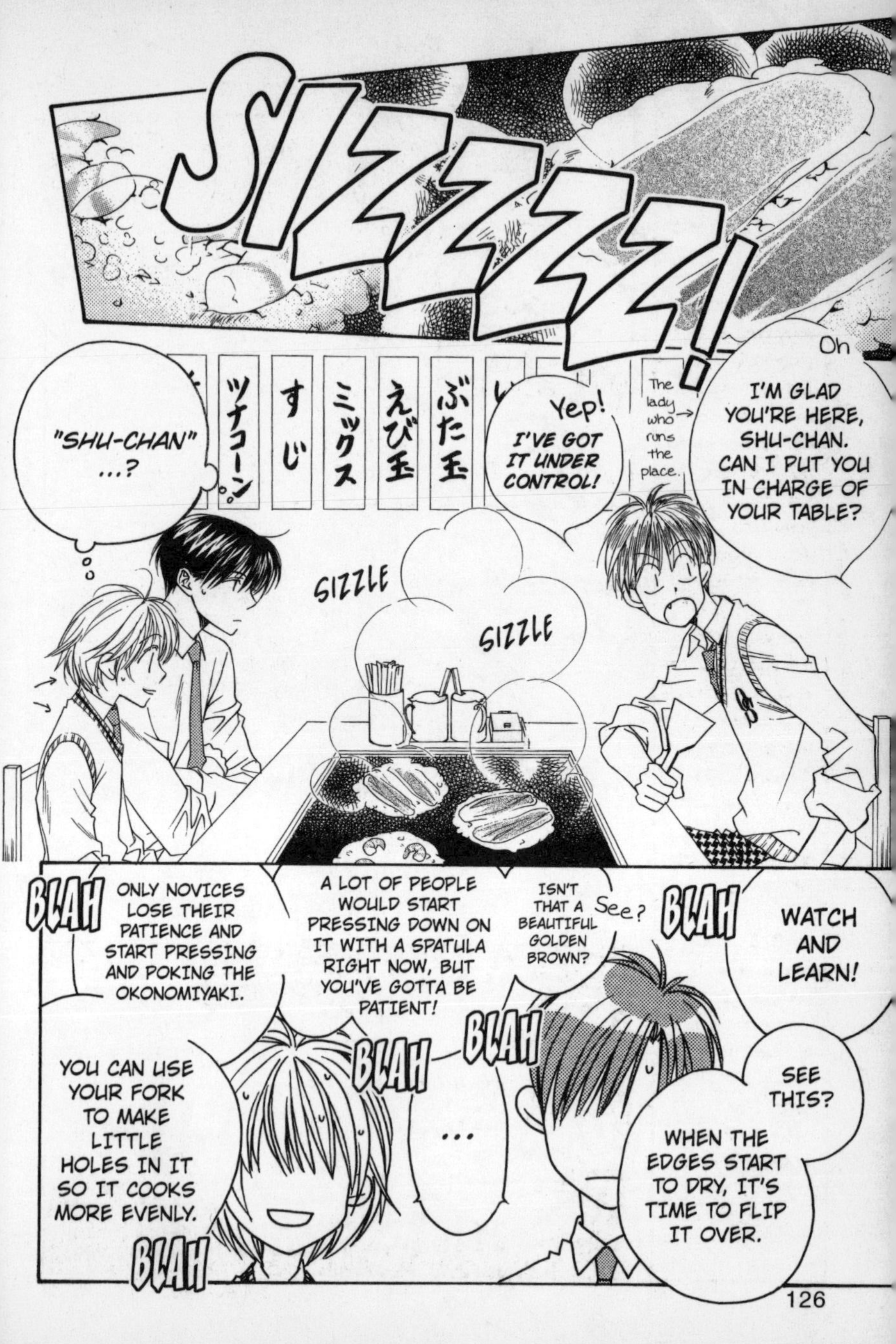
SIZZZZZ!
Oh
I'M GLAD YOU'RE HERE, SHU-CHAN. CAN I PUT YOU IN CHARGE OF YOUR TABLE?
The lady who runs the place.
Yep!
I'VE GOT IT UNDER CONTROL!
ぶた玉
えび玉
ミックス
すじ
ツナコーン
SIZZLE
SIZZLE
"SHU-CHAN"...?
WATCH AND LEARN!
BLAH
See?
ISN'T THAT A BEAUTIFUL GOLDEN BROWN?
A LOT OF PEOPLE WOULD START PRESSING DOWN ON IT WITH A SPATULA RIGHT NOW, BUT YOU'VE GOTTA BE PATIENT!
ONLY NOVICES LOSE THEIR PATIENCE AND START PRESSING AND POKING THE OKONOMIYAKI.
BLAH
SEE THIS?
WHEN THE EDGES START TO DRY, IT'S TIME TO FLIP IT OVER.
BLAH
BLAH
...
YOU CAN USE YOUR FORK TO MAKE LITTLE HOLES IN IT SO IT COOKS MORE EVENLY.
BLAH

「 vs 」

Um...I really don't know anything about baseball, but I'd love to go see a Hanshin vs. Kyojin game just to see the team mascots, Tracky and Giabbit, fight! When I was channel surfing, I happened to see the show "Craziest Moments in Baseball," and I got hooked. The team mascots were so hilarious! I laughed so hard I cried. My stomach hurt so bad. ✿ I don't have a favorite team, but I love Tracky. He's got such a bad temper.

"Sorry, I know that's a stupid reason..."

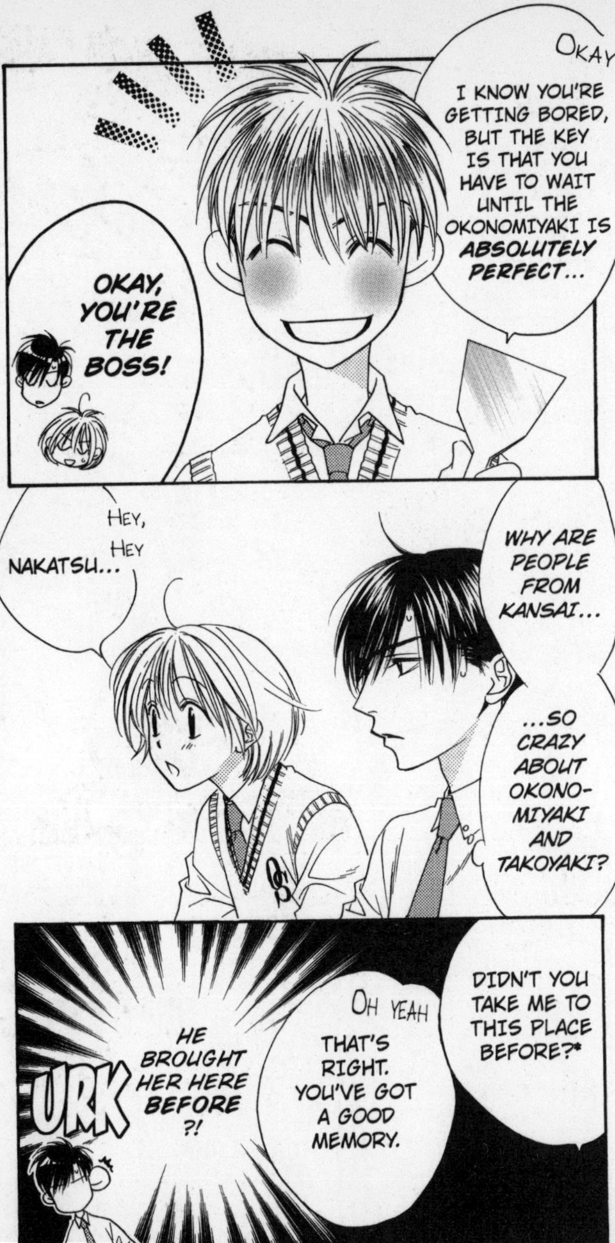

OKAY
I KNOW YOU'RE GETTING BORED, BUT THE KEY IS THAT YOU HAVE TO WAIT UNTIL THE OKONOMIYAKI IS ABSOLUTELY PERFECT...
OKAY, YOU'RE THE BOSS!
WHY ARE PEOPLE FROM KANSAI...
...SO CRAZY ABOUT OKONOMIYAKI AND TAKOYAKI?
HEY, HEY
NAKATSU...
DIDN'T YOU TAKE ME TO THIS PLACE BEFORE?*
OH YEAH
THAT'S RIGHT. YOU'VE GOT A GOOD MEMORY.
HE BROUGHT HER HERE BEFORE?!
URK

*SEE *HANA-KIMI* VOLUME 2!

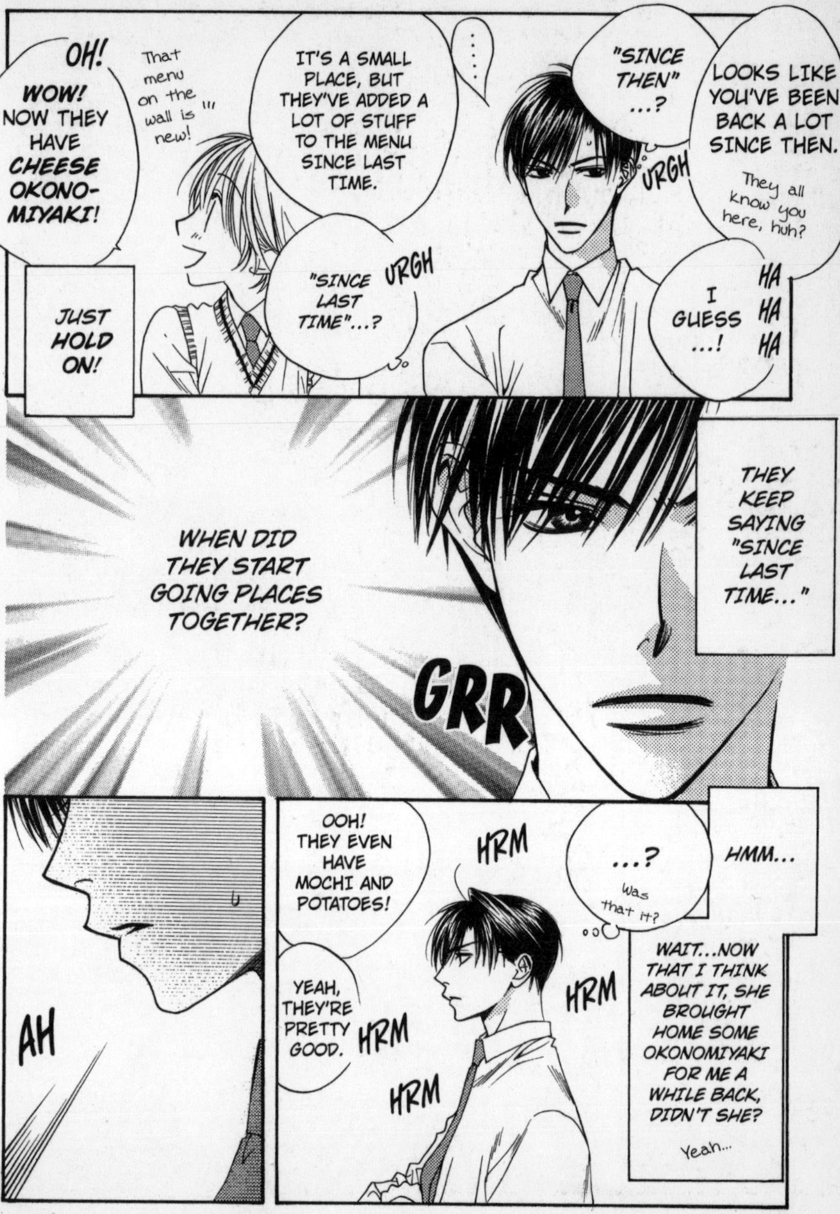
LOOKS LIKE YOU'VE BEEN BACK A LOT SINCE THEN.
They all know you here, huh?
HA HA HA
I GUESS ...!
"SINCE THEN" ...?
URGH
......
IT'S A SMALL PLACE, BUT THEY'VE ADDED A LOT OF STUFF TO THE MENU SINCE LAST TIME.
"SINCE LAST TIME"...?
URGH
That menu on the wall is new!
OH!
WOW! NOW THEY HAVE CHEESE OKONOMIYAKI!
JUST HOLD ON!
THEY KEEP SAYING "SINCE LAST TIME..."
GRR
WHEN DID THEY START GOING PLACES TOGETHER?
HMM...
...? Was that it?
HRM
OOH! THEY EVEN HAVE MOCHI AND POTATOES!
WAIT...NOW THAT I THINK ABOUT IT, SHE BROUGHT HOME SOME OKONOMIYAKI FOR ME A WHILE BACK, DIDN'T SHE?
Yeah...
HRM
YEAH, THEY'RE PRETTY GOOD.
HRM
HRM
AH

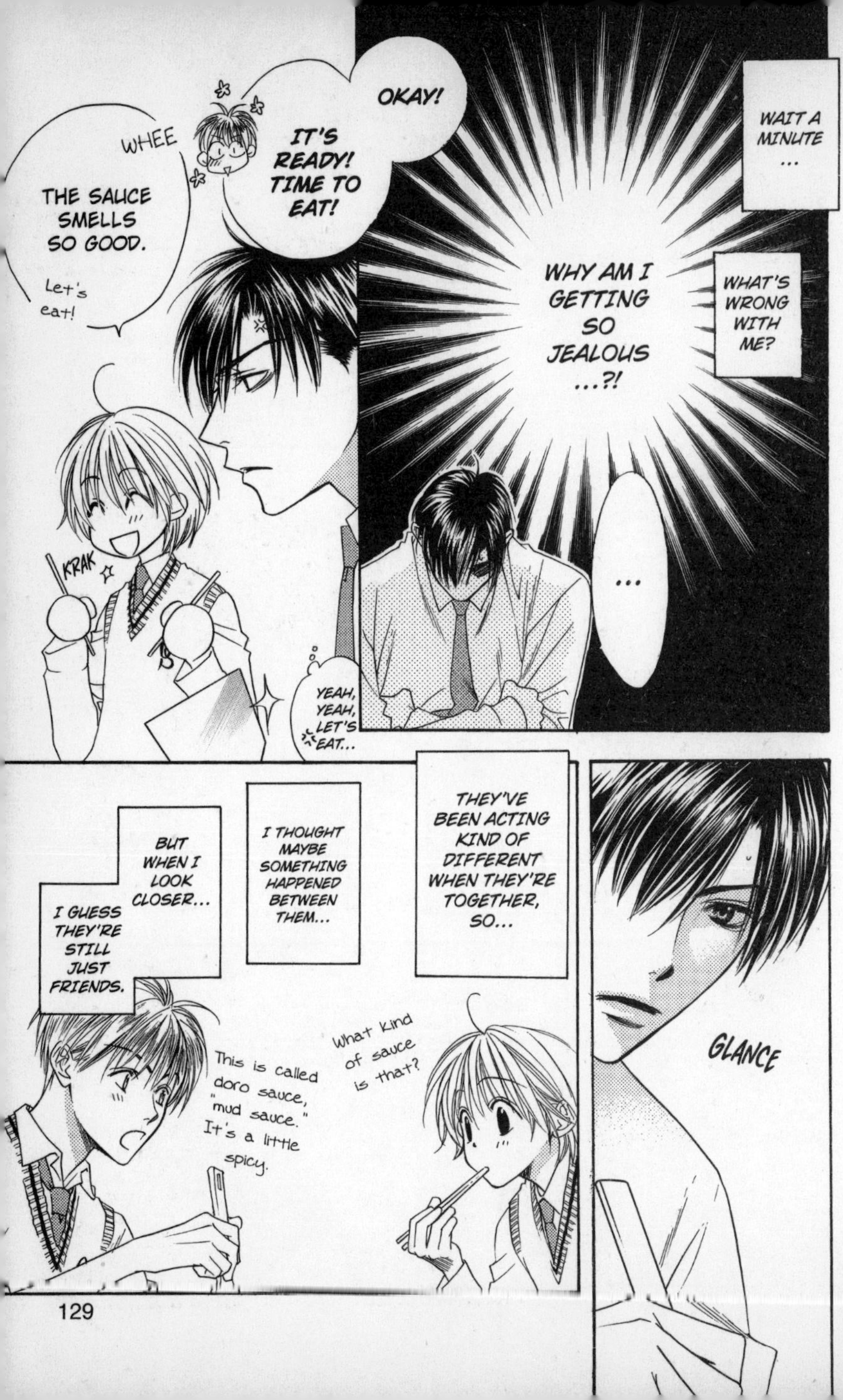
WAIT A MINUTE ...
WHAT'S WRONG WITH ME?
WHY AM I GETTING SO JEALOUS ...?!
...
OKAY!
IT'S READY! TIME TO EAT!
WHEE
THE SAUCE SMELLS SO GOOD.
Let's eat!
KRAK
YEAH, YEAH, LET'S EAT...
GLANCE
THEY'VE BEEN ACTING KIND OF DIFFERENT WHEN THEY'RE TOGETHER, SO...
I THOUGHT MAYBE SOMETHING HAPPENED BETWEEN THEM...
BUT WHEN I LOOK CLOSER...
I GUESS THEY'RE STILL JUST FRIENDS.
What kind of sauce is that?
This is called doro sauce, "mud sauce." It's a little spicy.

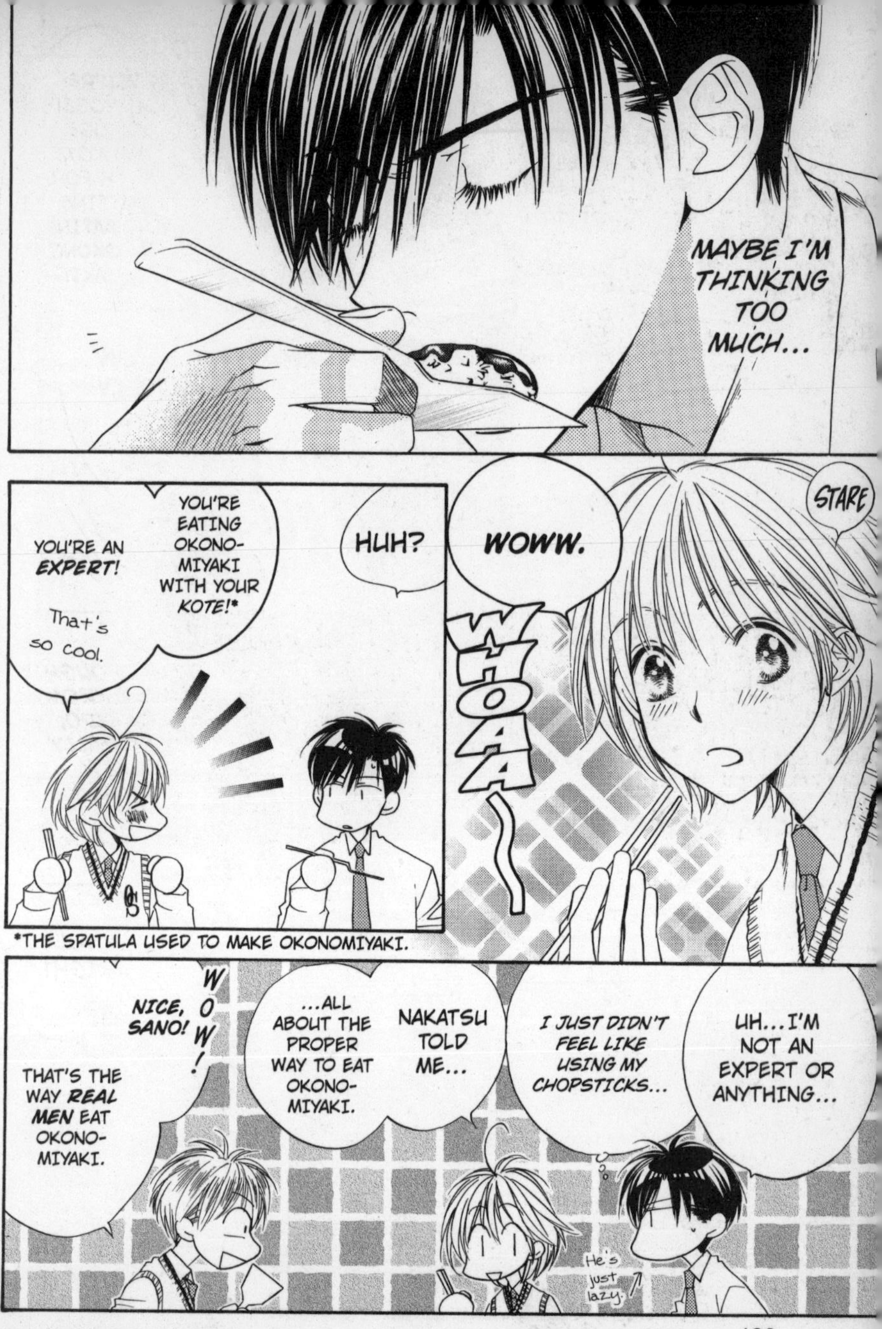
MAYBE I'M THINKING TOO MUCH...
STARE
WOWW.
WHOAA~
HUH?
YOU'RE EATING OKONOMIYAKI WITH YOUR KOTE!*
YOU'RE AN EXPERT!
That's so cool.
*THE SPATULA USED TO MAKE OKONOMIYAKI.
UH...I'M NOT AN EXPERT OR ANYTHING...
I JUST DIDN'T FEEL LIKE USING MY CHOPSTICKS...
NAKATSU TOLD ME...
...ALL ABOUT THE PROPER WAY TO EAT OKONOMIYAKI.
He's just lazy.
WOW!
NICE, SANO!
THAT'S THE WAY REAL MEN EAT OKONOMIYAKI.

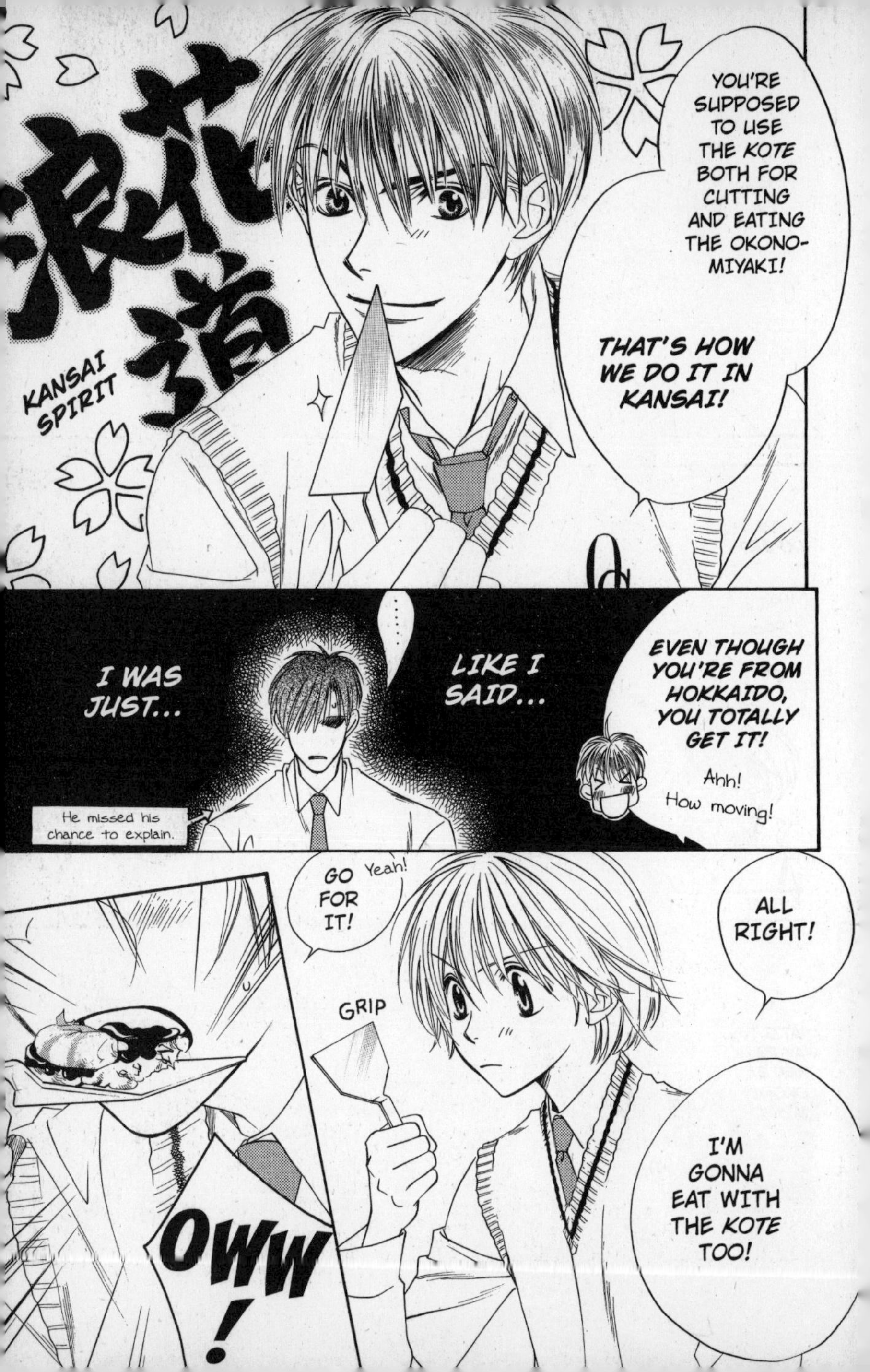
YOU'RE SUPPOSED TO USE THE KOTE BOTH FOR CUTTING AND EATING THE OKONO-MIYAKI!
THAT'S HOW WE DO IT IN KANSAI!
KANSAI SPIRIT
EVEN THOUGH YOU'RE FROM HOKKAIDO, YOU TOTALLY GET IT!
Ahh! How moving!
LIKE I SAID...
......
I WAS JUST...
He missed his chance to explain.
ALL RIGHT!
I'M GONNA EAT WITH THE KOTE TOO!
GO FOR IT!
Yeah!
GRIP
OWW!

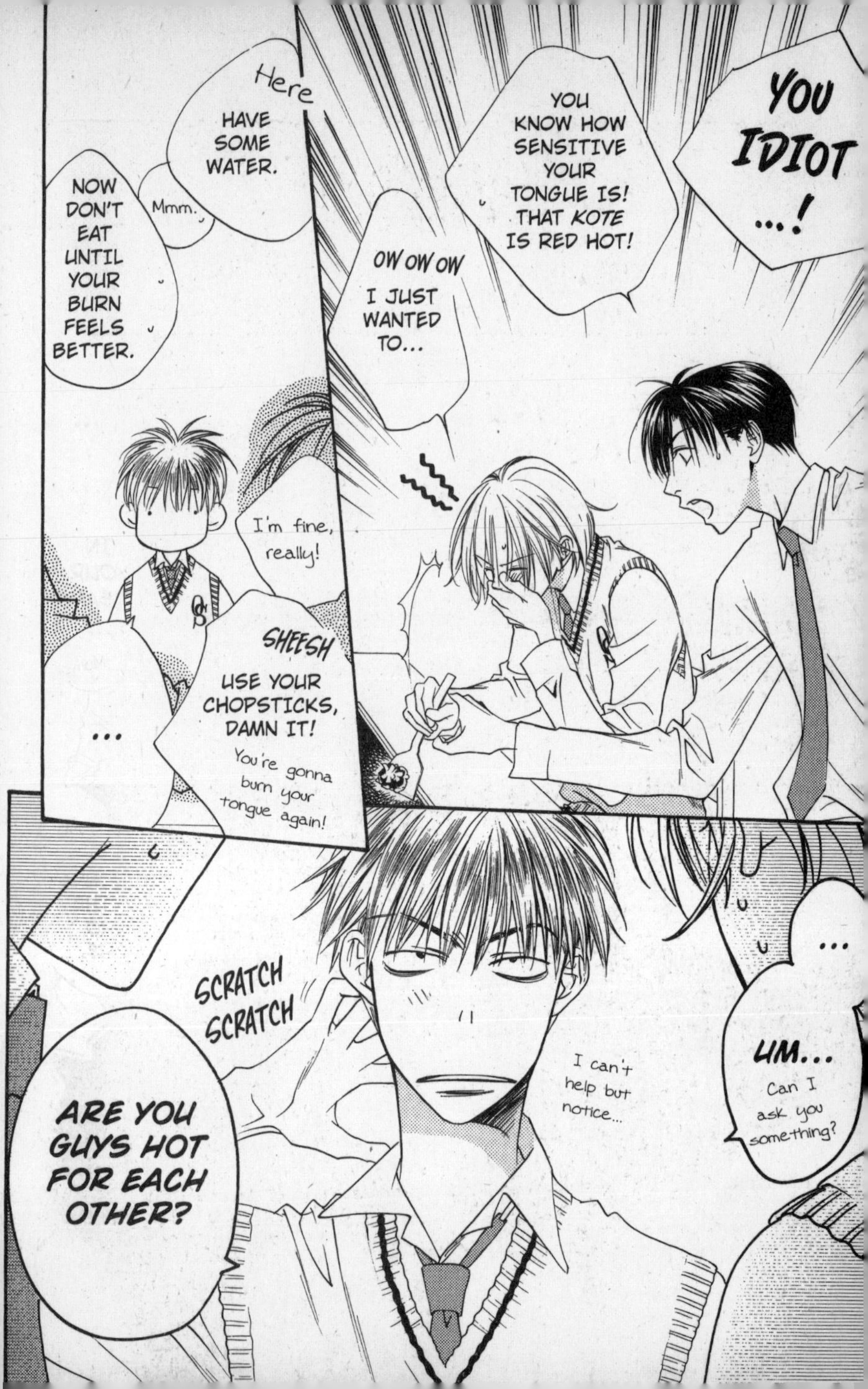
YOU IDIOT ...!
YOU KNOW HOW SENSITIVE YOUR TONGUE IS! THAT KOTE IS RED HOT!
OW OW OW
I JUST WANTED TO...
Here
HAVE SOME WATER.
Mmm.
NOW DON'T EAT UNTIL YOUR BURN FEELS BETTER.
I'm fine, really!
SHEESH
USE YOUR CHOPSTICKS, DAMN IT!
You're gonna burn your tongue again!
...
...
UM...
Can I ask you something?
I can't help but notice...
SCRATCH SCRATCH
ARE YOU GUYS HOT FOR EACH OTHER?

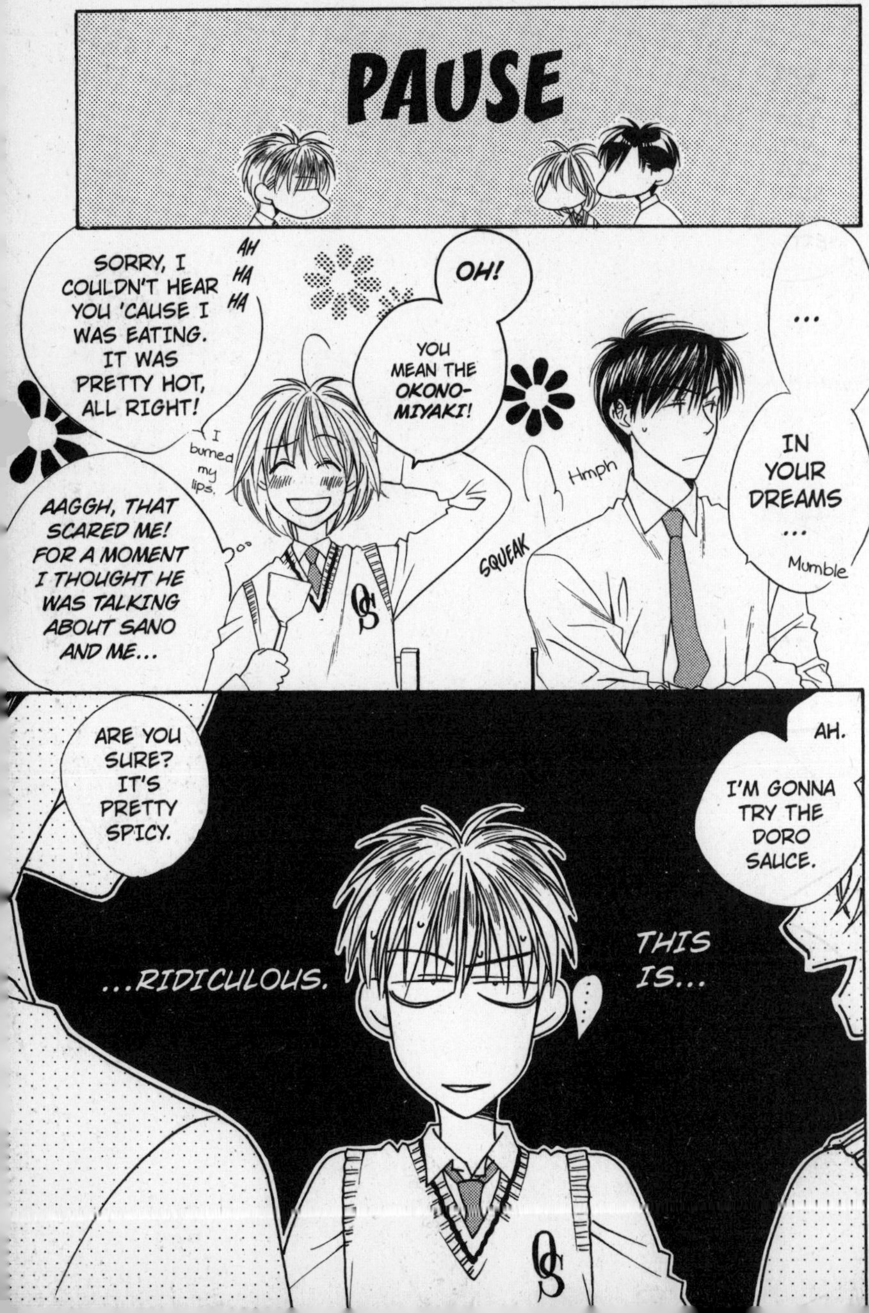
PAUSE
...
IN YOUR DREAMS...
Mumble
Hmph
SQUEAK
OH!
YOU MEAN THE OKONO-MIYAKI!
AH HA HA
SORRY, I COULDN'T HEAR YOU 'CAUSE I WAS EATING. IT WAS PRETTY HOT, ALL RIGHT!
I burned my lips.
AAGGH, THAT SCARED ME! FOR A MOMENT I THOUGHT HE WAS TALKING ABOUT SANO AND ME...
AH.
I'M GONNA TRY THE DORO SAUCE.
ARE YOU SURE? IT'S PRETTY SPICY.
THIS IS...
...RIDICULOUS.

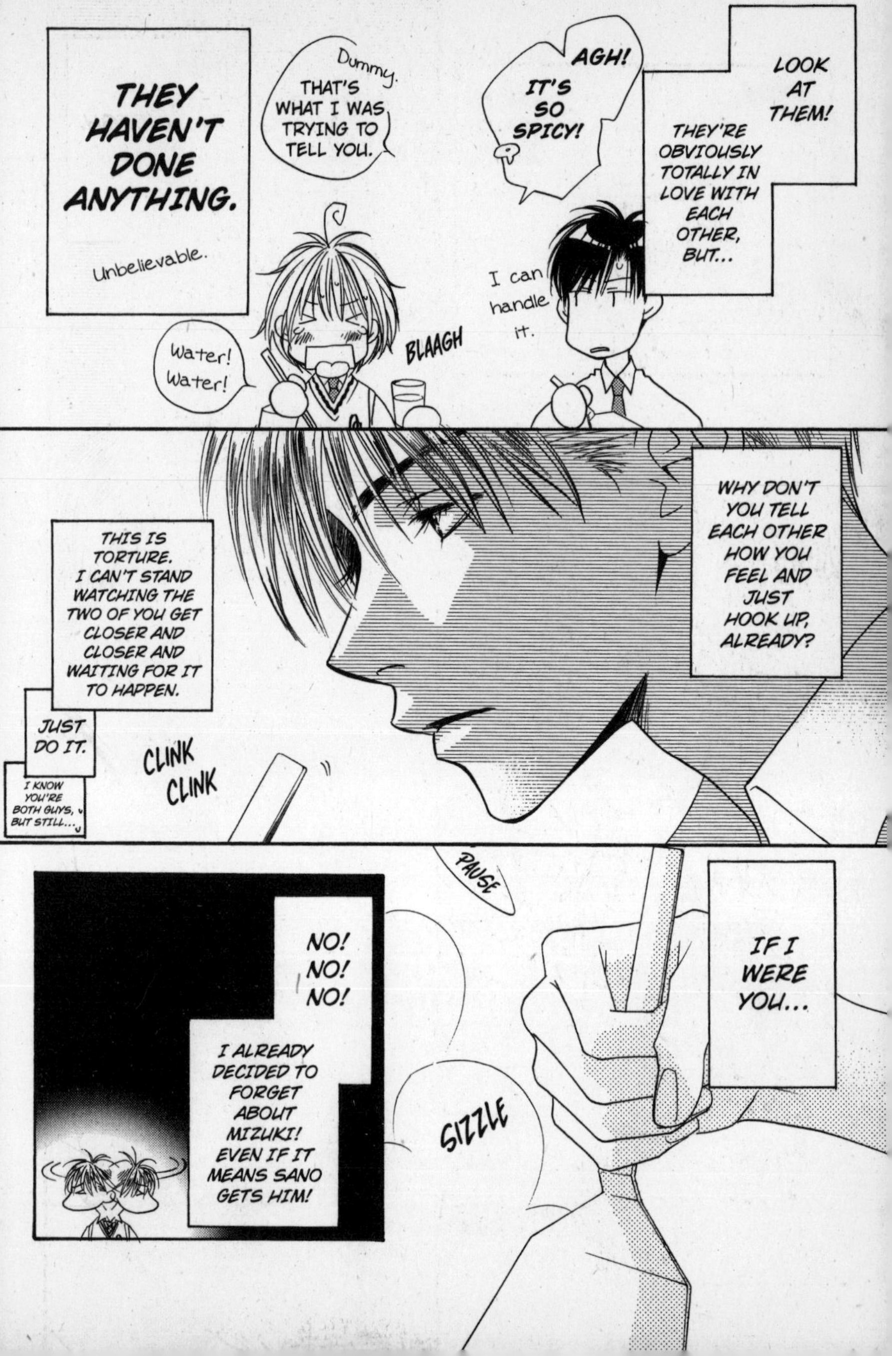
LOOK AT THEM!
THEY'RE OBVIOUSLY TOTALLY IN LOVE WITH EACH OTHER, BUT...
AGH! IT'S SO SPICY!
I can handle it.
Dummy.
THAT'S WHAT I WAS TRYING TO TELL YOU.
BLAAGH
Water! Water!
THEY HAVEN'T DONE ANYTHING.
Unbelievable.
WHY DON'T YOU TELL EACH OTHER HOW YOU FEEL AND JUST HOOK UP, ALREADY?
THIS IS TORTURE. I CAN'T STAND WATCHING THE TWO OF YOU GET CLOSER AND CLOSER AND WAITING FOR IT TO HAPPEN.
CLINK CLINK
JUST DO IT.
I KNOW YOU'RE BOTH GUYS, BUT STILL...
PAUSE
IF I WERE YOU...
SIZZLE
NO! NO! NO!
I ALREADY DECIDED TO FORGET ABOUT MIZUKI! EVEN IF IT MEANS SANO GETS HIM!

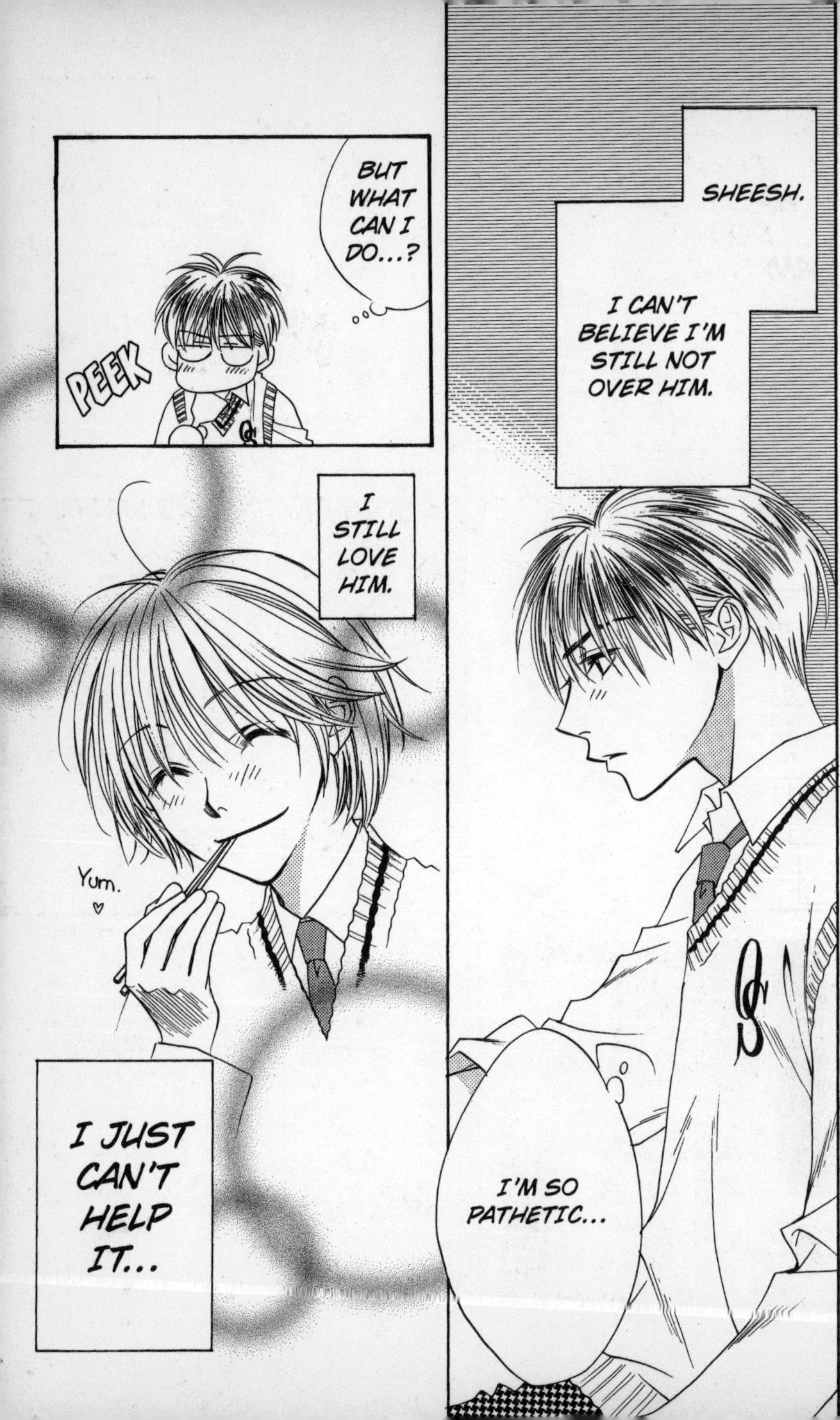
SHEESH.
I CAN'T BELIEVE I'M STILL NOT OVER HIM.
I'M SO PATHETIC...
BUT WHAT CAN I DO...?
PEEK
I STILL LOVE HIM.
Yum.
I JUST CAN'T HELP IT...

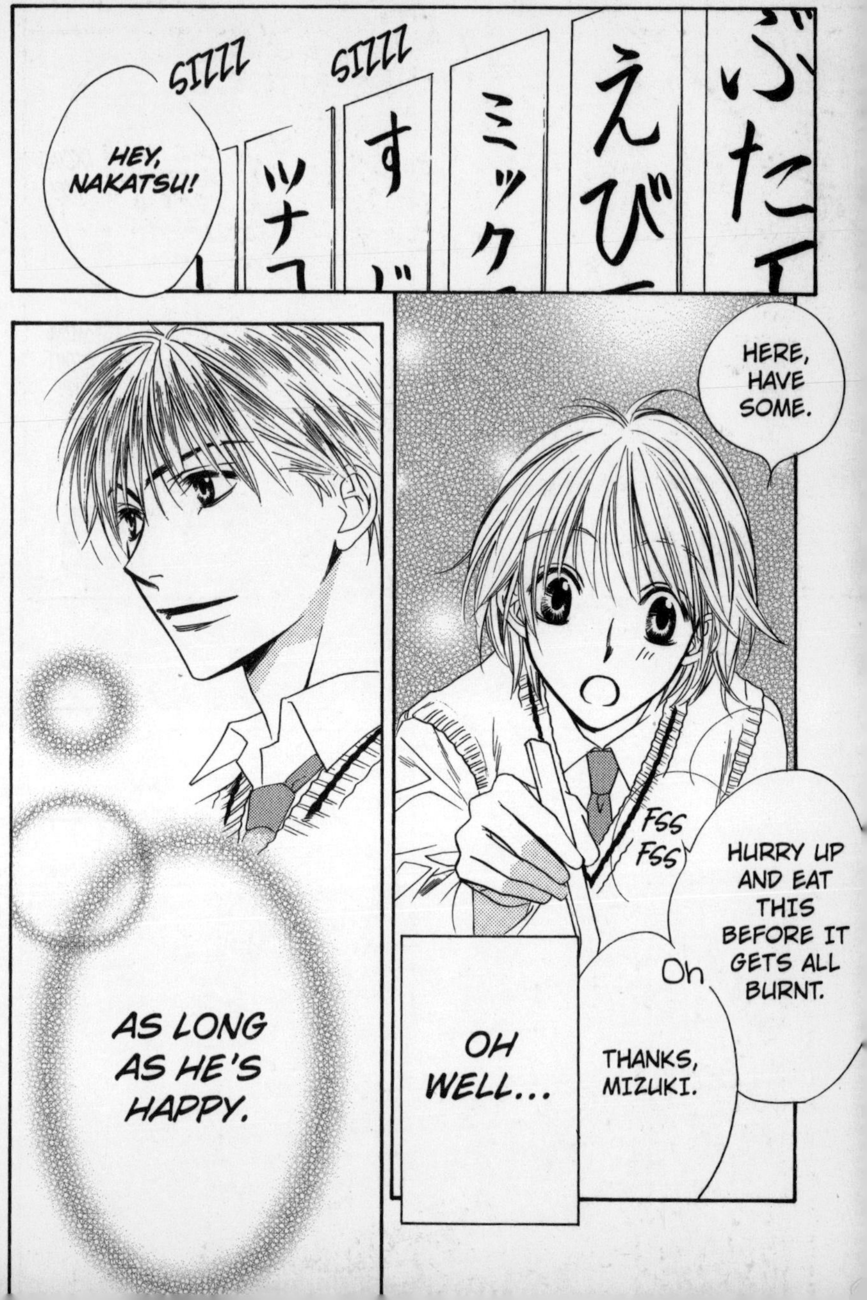
ぶた
えび
ミック
す
ツナ
SIZZZ
SIZZZ
HEY, NAKATSU!
HERE, HAVE SOME.
FSS FSS
HURRY UP AND EAT THIS BEFORE IT GETS ALL BURNT.
Oh
THANKS, MIZUKI.
OH WELL...
AS LONG AS HE'S HAPPY.

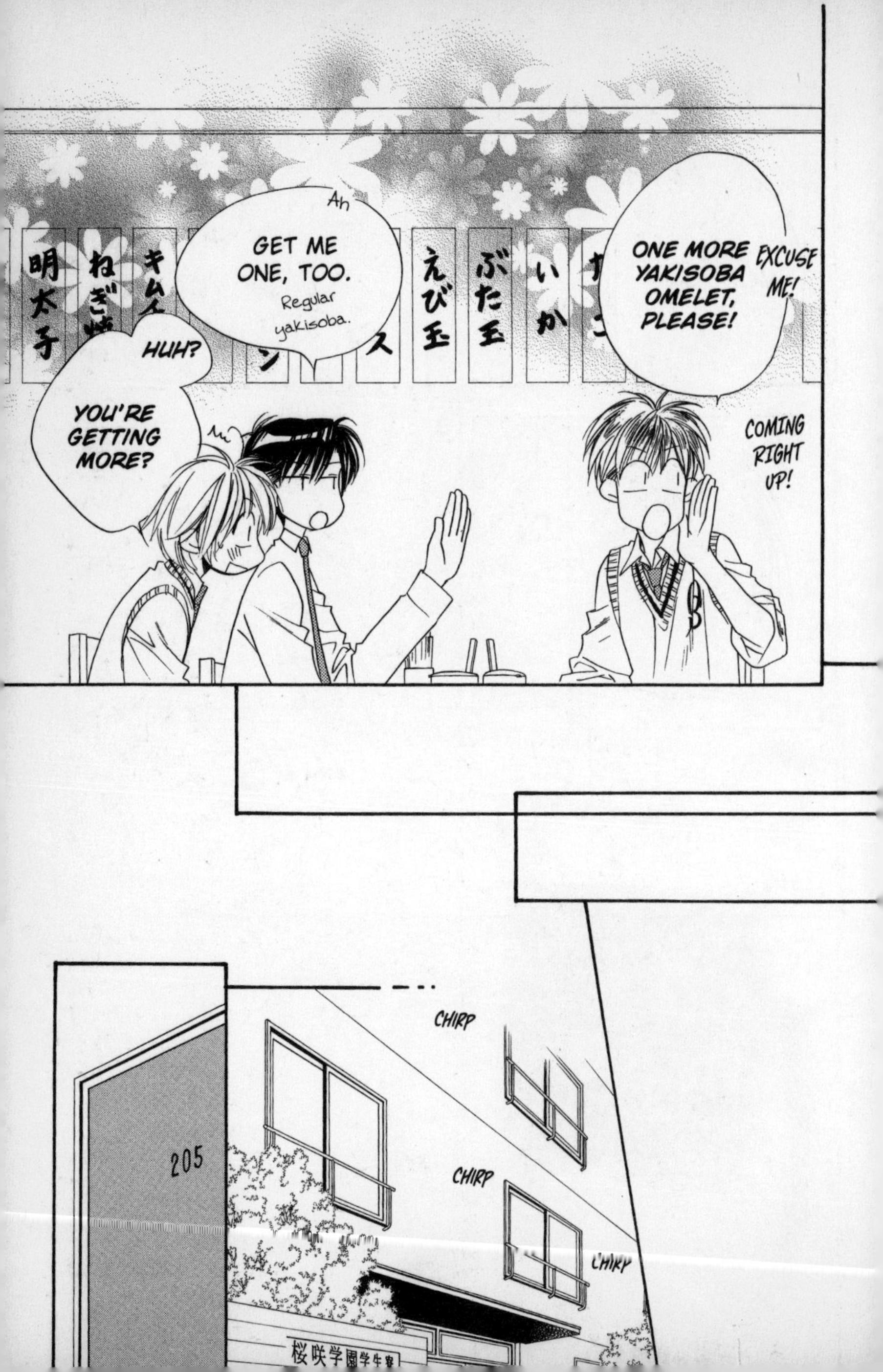
EXCUSE ME!
ONE MORE YAKISOBA OMELET, PLEASE!
COMING RIGHT UP!
いか
ぶた玉
えび玉
Ah
GET ME ONE, TOO.
Regular yakisoba.
明太子
HUH?
YOU'RE GETTING MORE?
CHIRP
CHIRP
CHIRP
205
桜咲学園学生寮

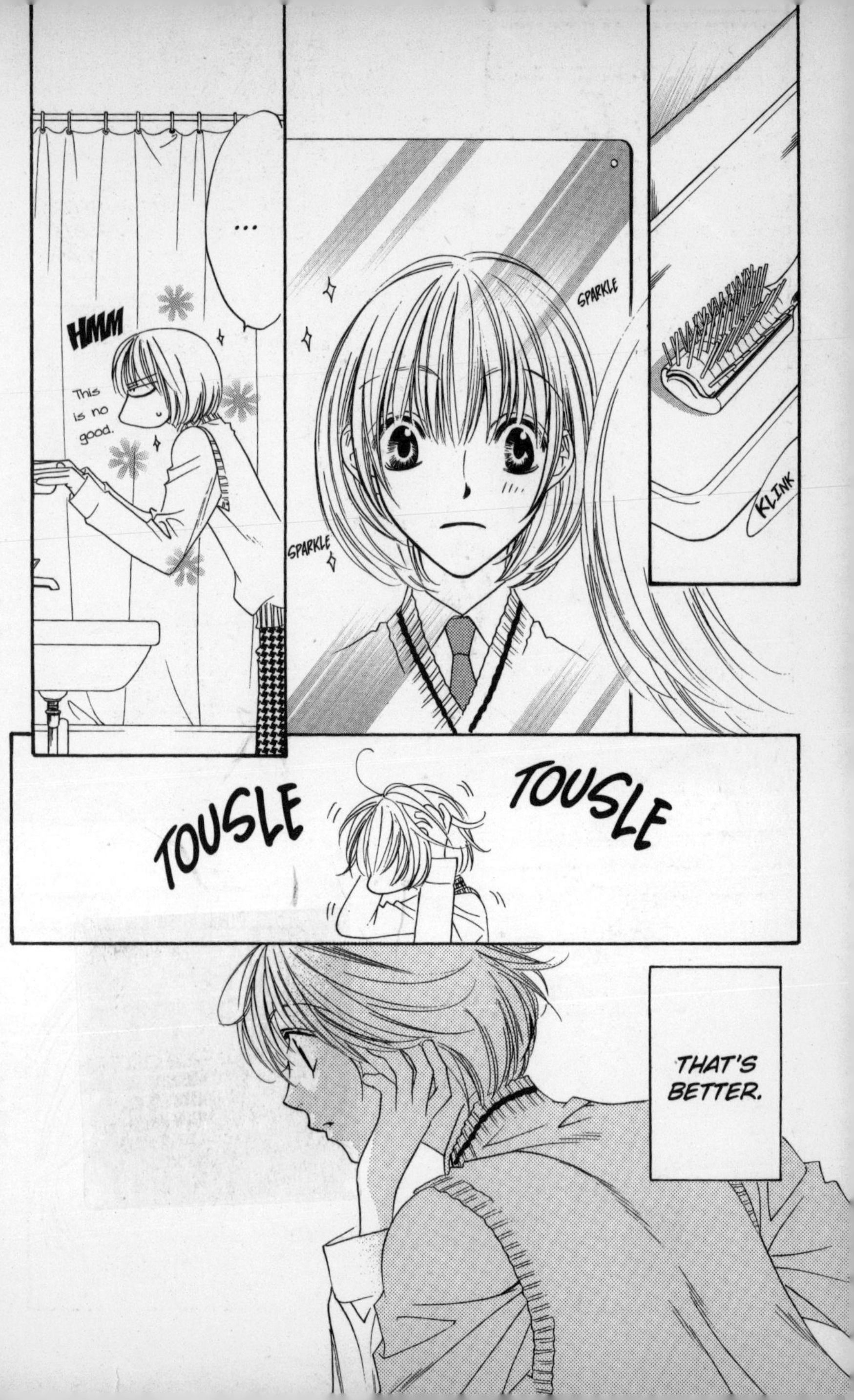
KLINK
SPARKLE
SPARKLE
...
HMMM
This is no good.
TOUSLE
TOUSLE
THAT'S BETTER.

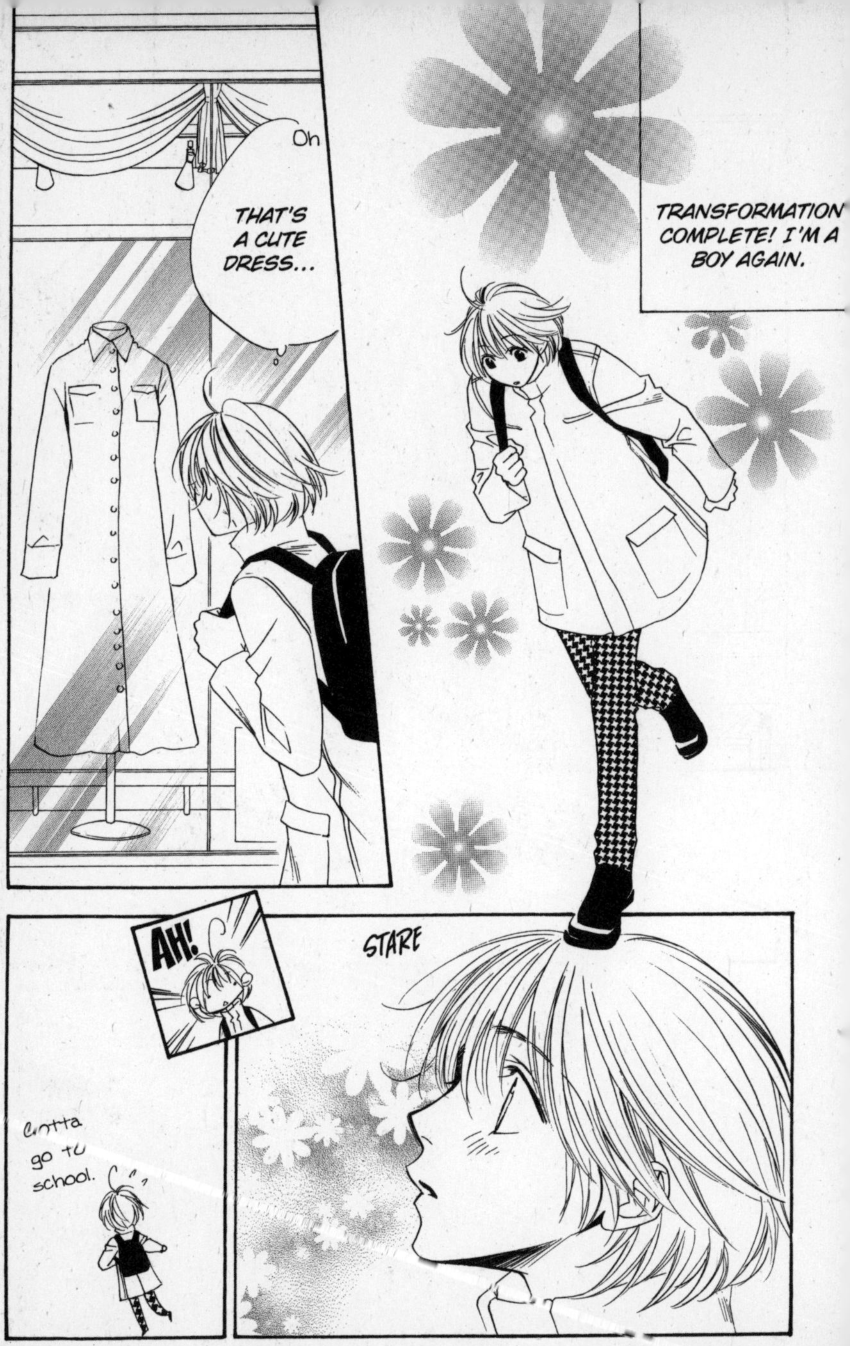
TRANSFORMATION COMPLETE! I'M A BOY AGAIN.
Oh
THAT'S A CUTE DRESS...
STARE
AH!
Gotta go to school.

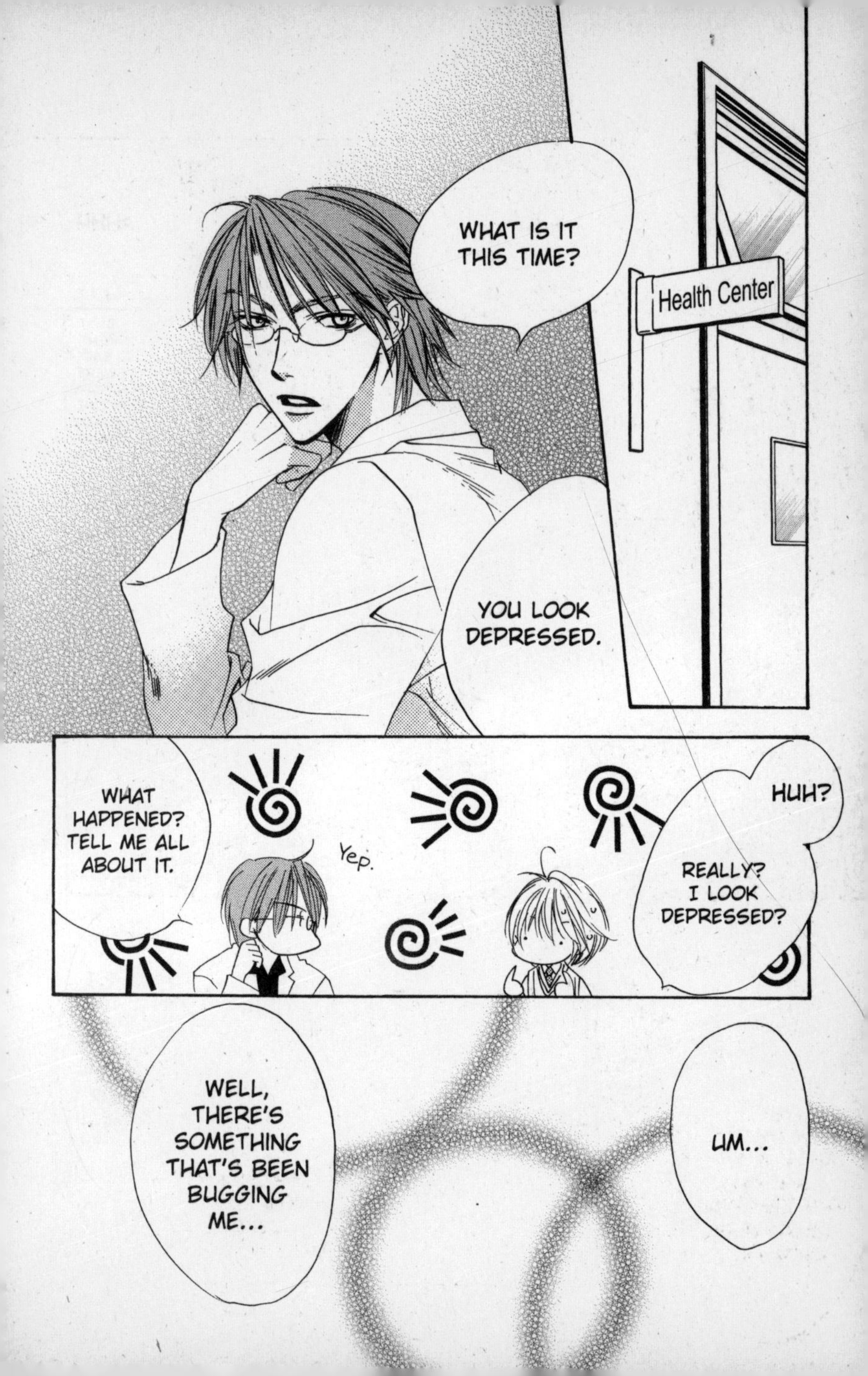
Health Center
WHAT IS IT THIS TIME?
YOU LOOK DEPRESSED.
HUH?
REALLY? I LOOK DEPRESSED?
Yep.
WHAT HAPPENED? TELL ME ALL ABOUT IT.
UM...
WELL, THERE'S SOMETHING THAT'S BEEN BUGGING ME...

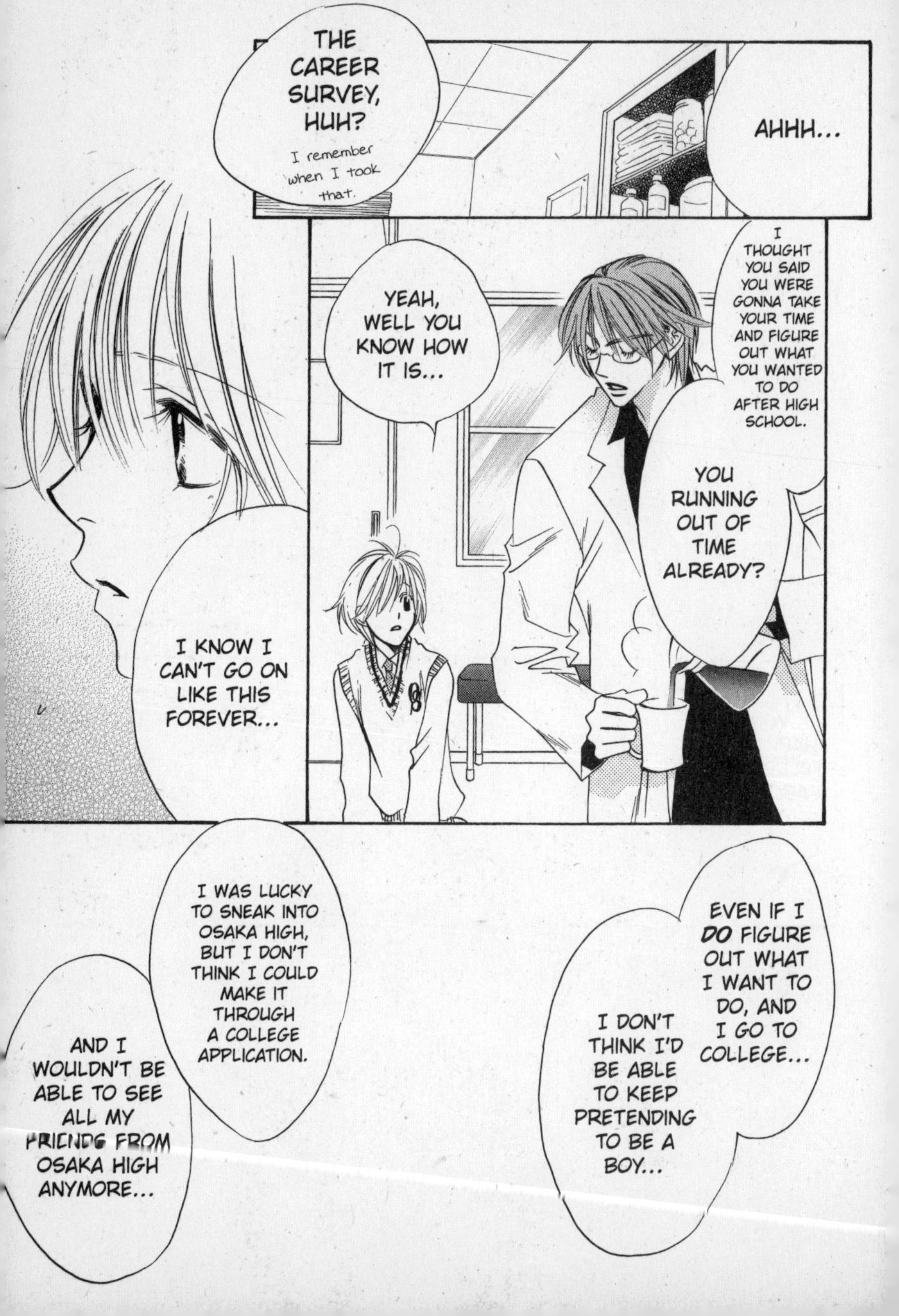
AHHH...
THE CAREER SURVEY, HUH?
I remember when I took that.
I THOUGHT YOU SAID YOU WERE GONNA TAKE YOUR TIME AND FIGURE OUT WHAT YOU WANTED TO DO AFTER HIGH SCHOOL.
YOU RUNNING OUT OF TIME ALREADY?
YEAH, WELL YOU KNOW HOW IT IS...
I KNOW I CAN'T GO ON LIKE THIS FOREVER...
EVEN IF I *DO* FIGURE OUT WHAT I WANT TO DO, AND I GO TO COLLEGE...
I DON'T THINK I'D BE ABLE TO KEEP PRETENDING TO BE A BOY...
I WAS LUCKY TO SNEAK INTO OSAKA HIGH, BUT I DON'T THINK I COULD MAKE IT THROUGH A COLLEGE APPLICATION.
AND I WOULDN'T BE ABLE TO SEE ALL MY FRIENDS FROM OSAKA HIGH ANYMORE...

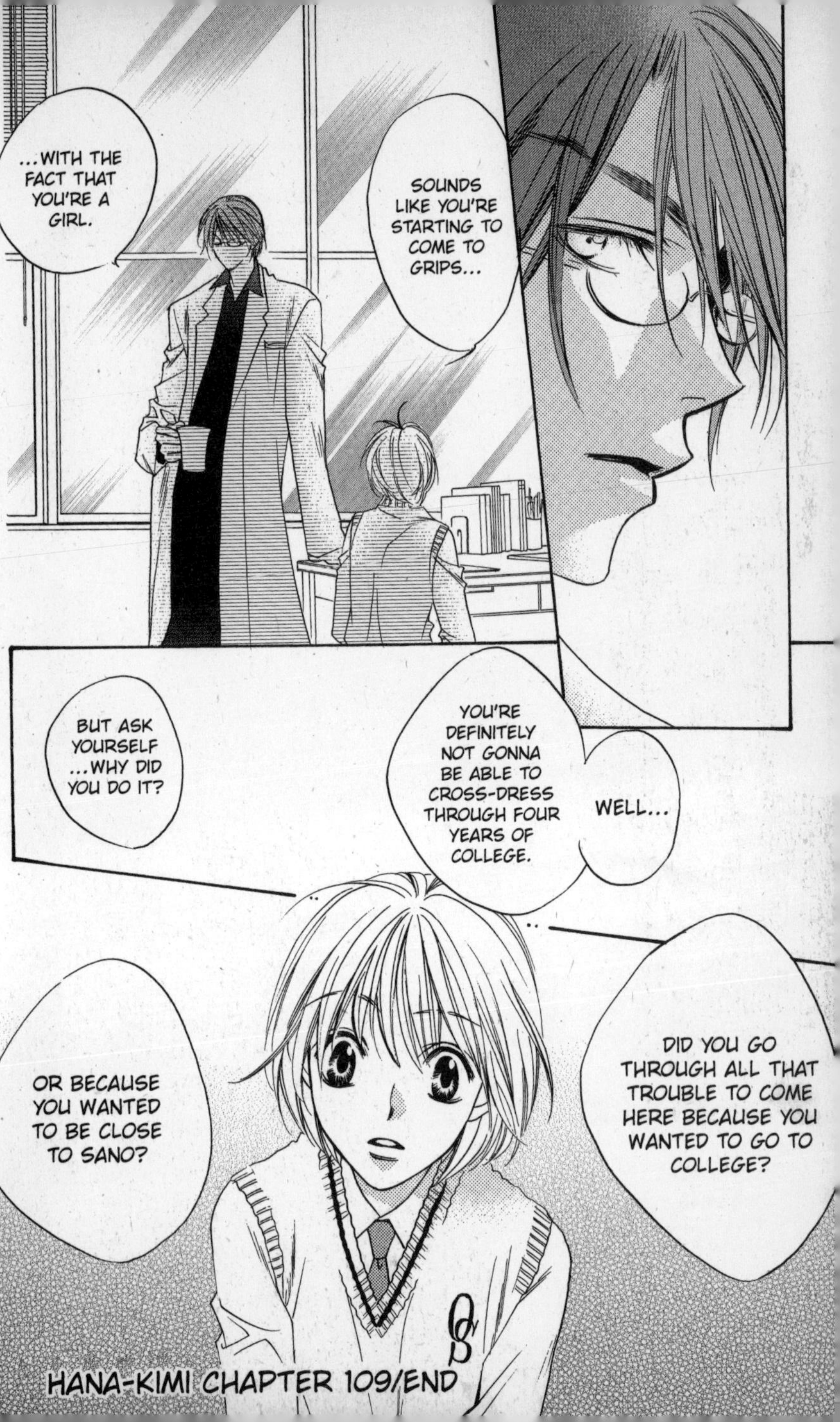
SOUNDS LIKE YOU'RE STARTING TO COME TO GRIPS...
...WITH THE FACT THAT YOU'RE A GIRL.
WELL...
YOU'RE DEFINITELY NOT GONNA BE ABLE TO CROSS-DRESS THROUGH FOUR YEARS OF COLLEGE.
BUT ASK YOURSELF ...WHY DID YOU DO IT?
DID YOU GO THROUGH ALL THAT TROUBLE TO COME HERE BECAUSE YOU WANTED TO GO TO COLLEGE?
OR BECAUSE YOU WANTED TO BE CLOSE TO SANO?
HANA-KIMI CHAPTER 109/END

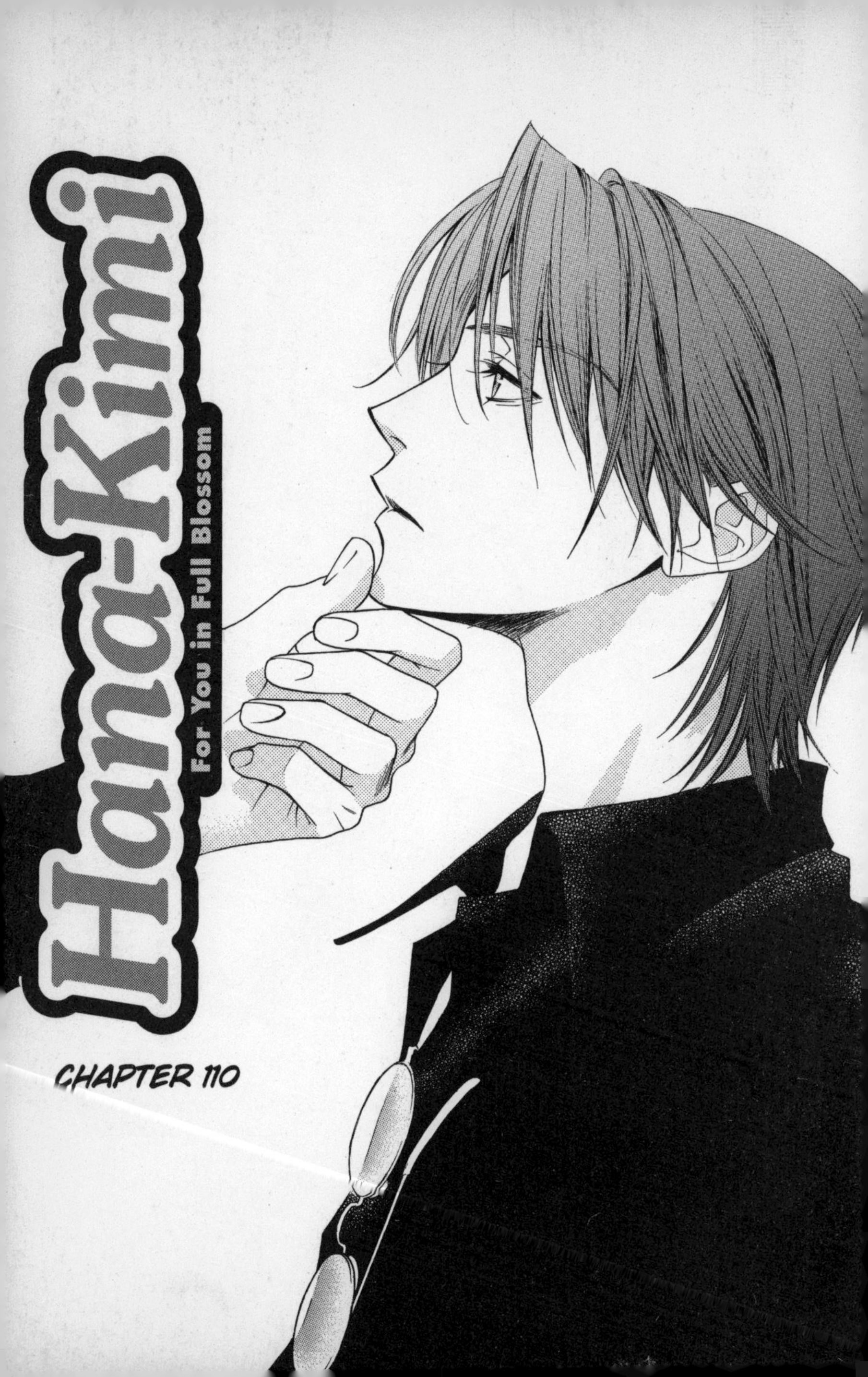
Hana-Kimi
For You in Full Blossom
CHAPTER 110

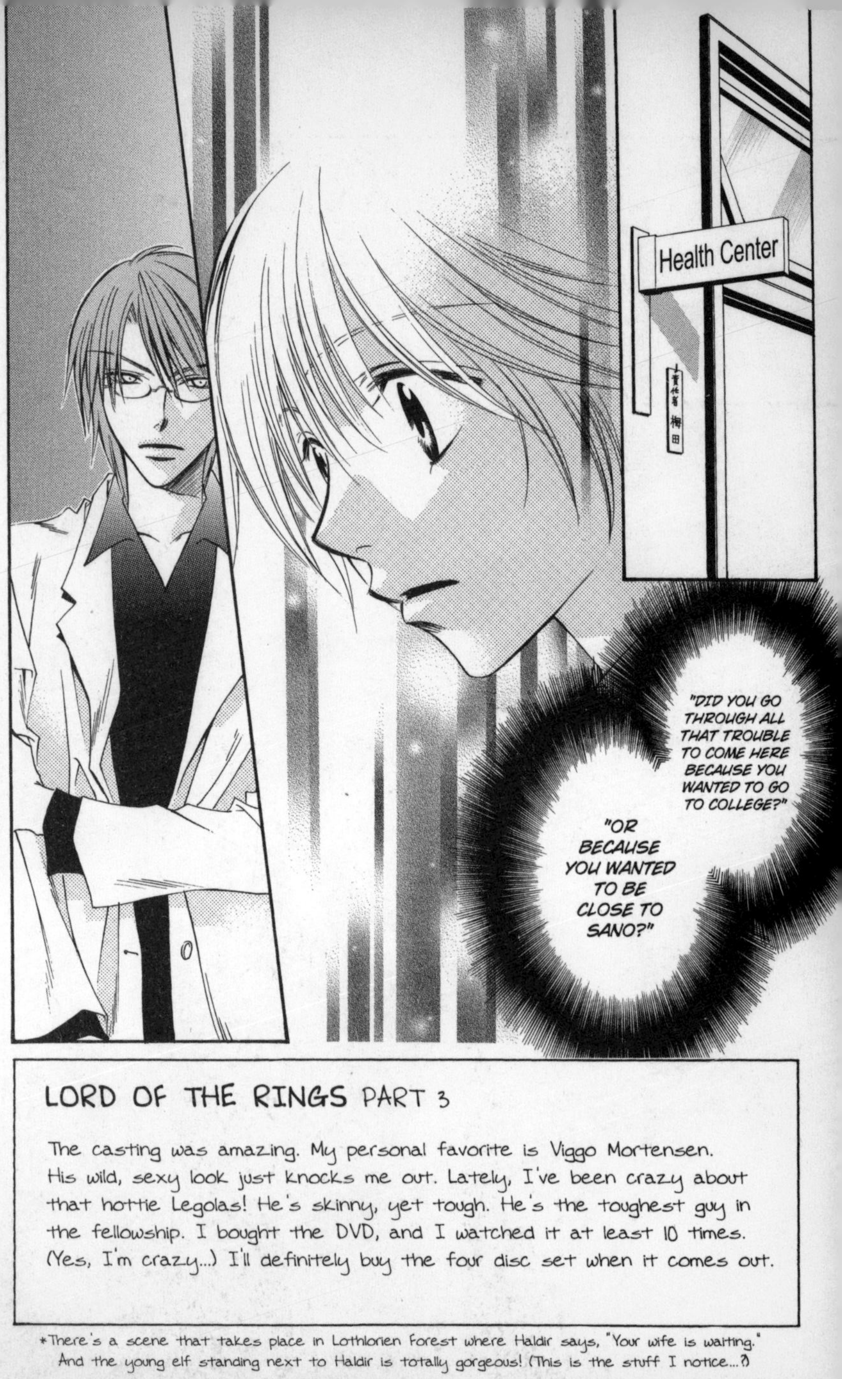
Health Center
責任者 梅田
"DID YOU GO THROUGH ALL THAT TROUBLE TO COME HERE BECAUSE YOU WANTED TO GO TO COLLEGE?"
"OR BECAUSE YOU WANTED TO BE CLOSE TO SANO?"

LORD OF THE RINGS PART 3

The casting was amazing. My personal favorite is Viggo Mortensen. His wild, sexy look just knocks me out. Lately, I've been crazy about that hottie Legolas! He's skinny, yet tough. He's the toughest guy in the fellowship. I bought the DVD, and I watched it at least 10 times. (Yes, I'm crazy...) I'll definitely buy the four disc set when it comes out.

*There's a scene that takes place in Lothlorien Forest where Haldir says, "Your wife is waiting." And the young elf standing next to Haldir is totally gorgeous! (This is the stuff I notice...?)

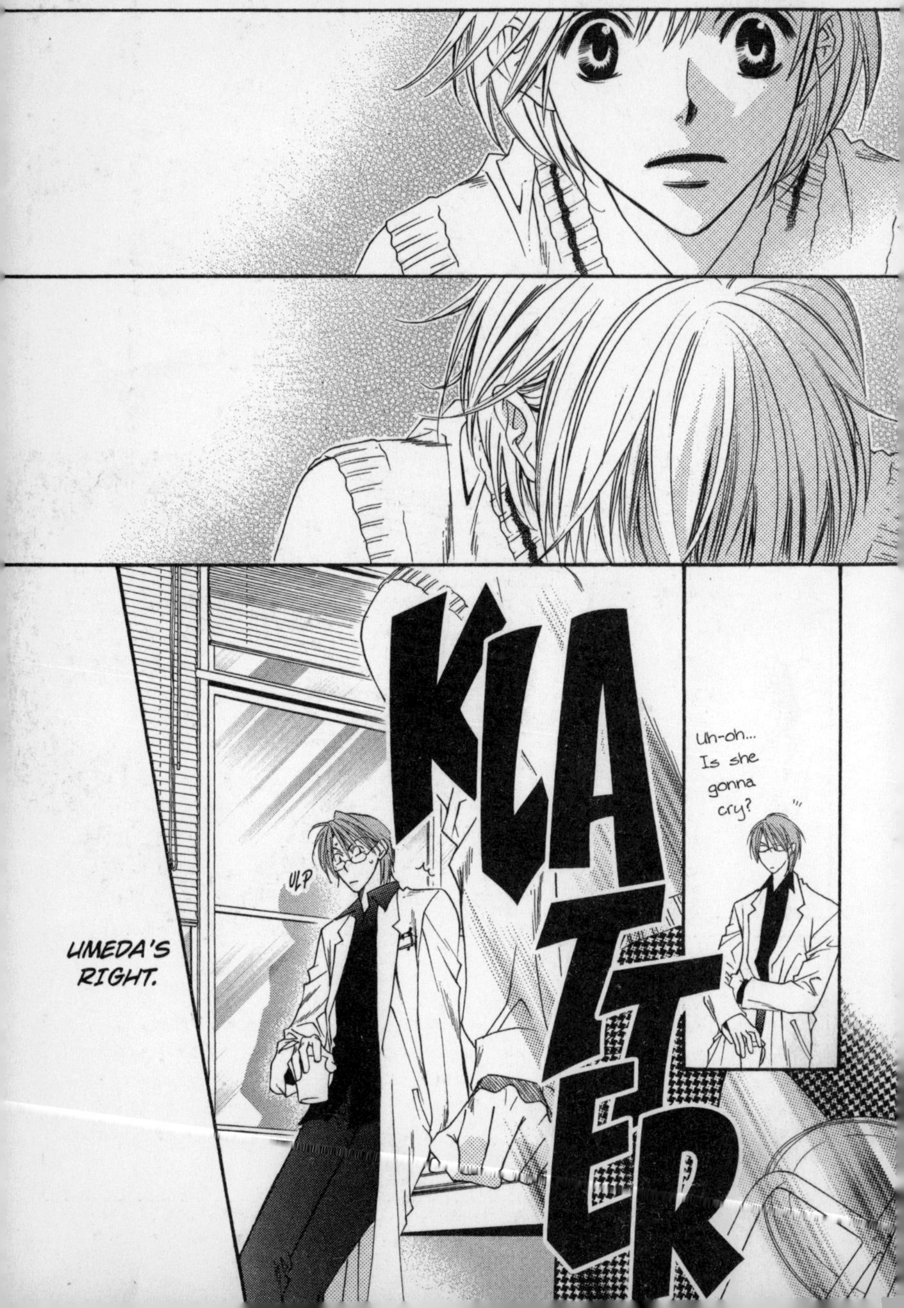
Uh-oh... Is she gonna cry?
KLATTER
ULP
UMEDA'S RIGHT.

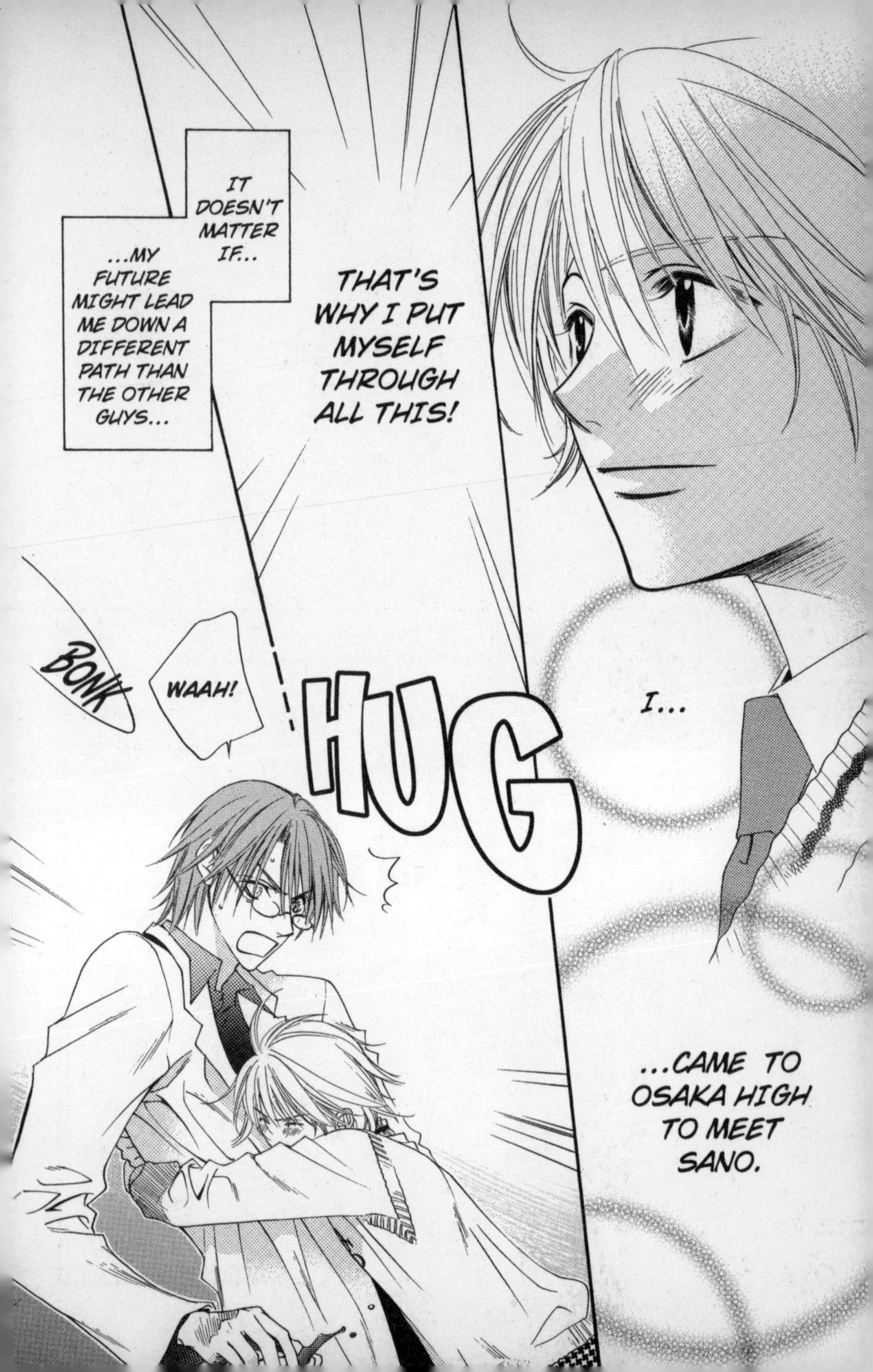
I...
...CAME TO OSAKA HIGH TO MEET SANO.
THAT'S WHY I PUT MYSELF THROUGH ALL THIS!
IT DOESN'T MATTER IF...
...MY FUTURE MIGHT LEAD ME DOWN A DIFFERENT PATH THAN THE OTHER GUYS...
HUG
WAAH!
BONK

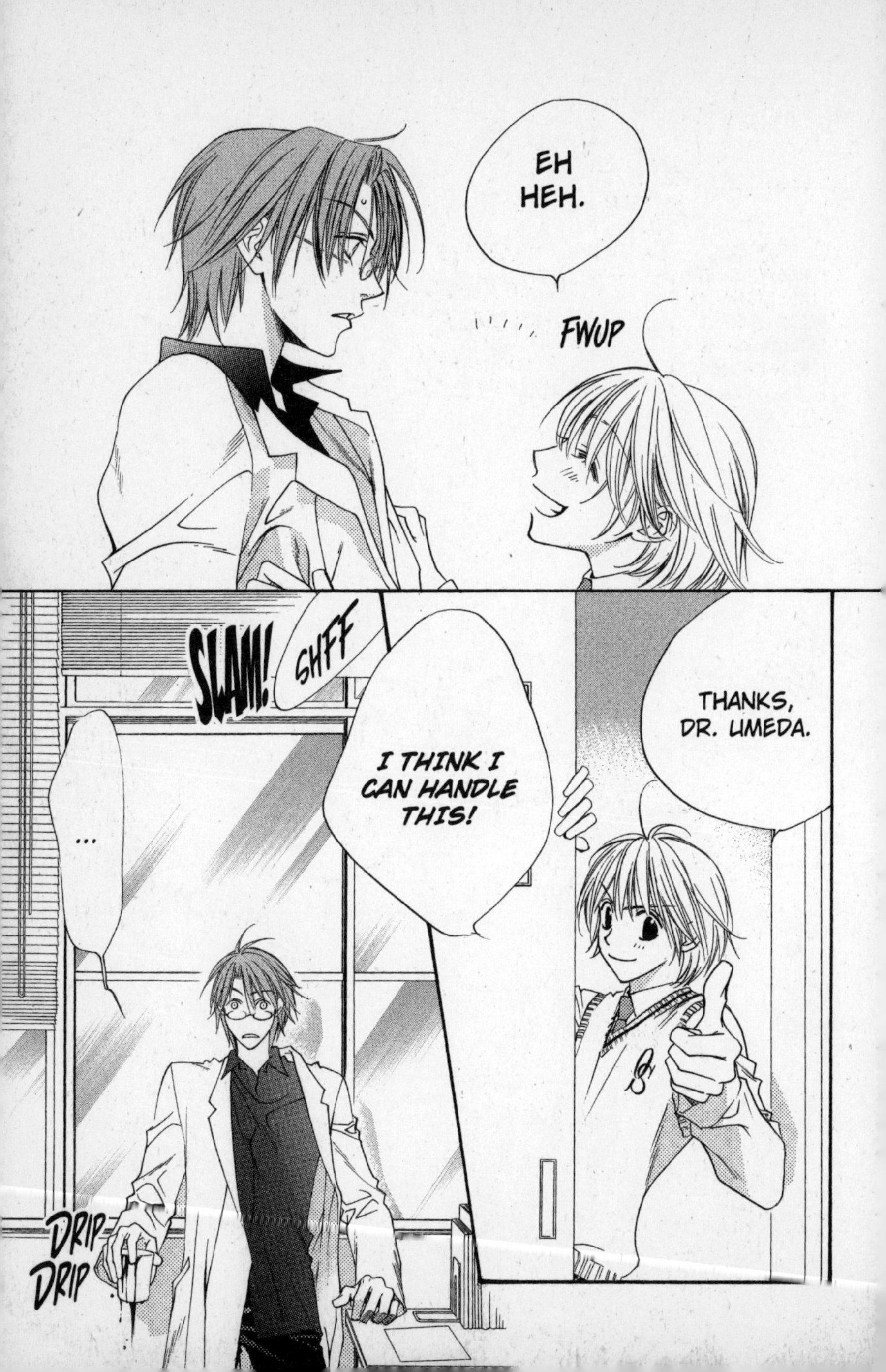
EH HEH.
FWUP
THANKS, DR. UMEDA.
I THINK I CAN HANDLE THIS!
SHFF
SLAM!
...
DRIP DRIP

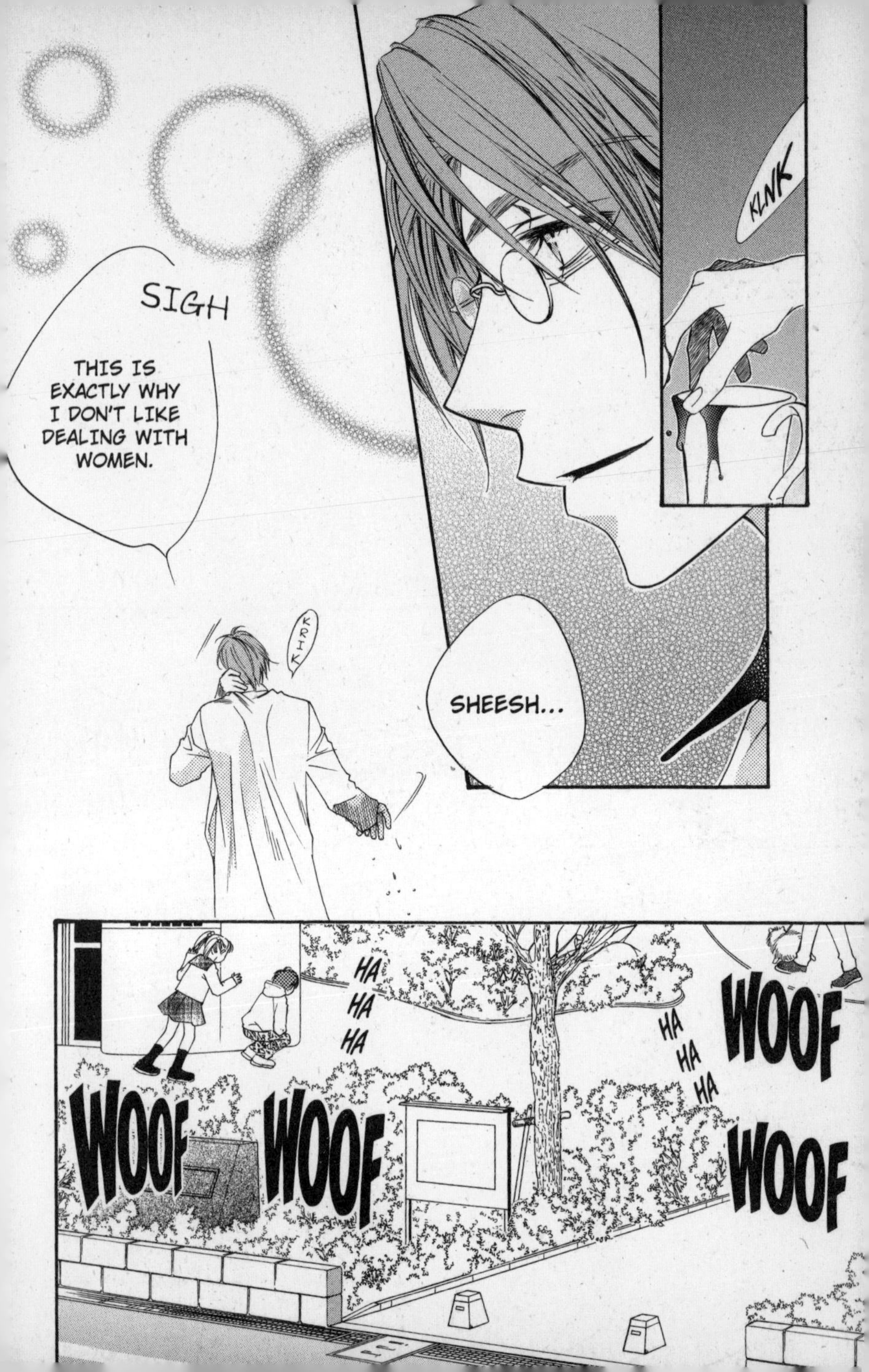
KLNK
SHEESH...
SIGH
THIS IS EXACTLY WHY I DON'T LIKE DEALING WITH WOMEN.
KRIK
WOOF
HA HA HA
WOOF
HA HA HA
WOOF
WOOF

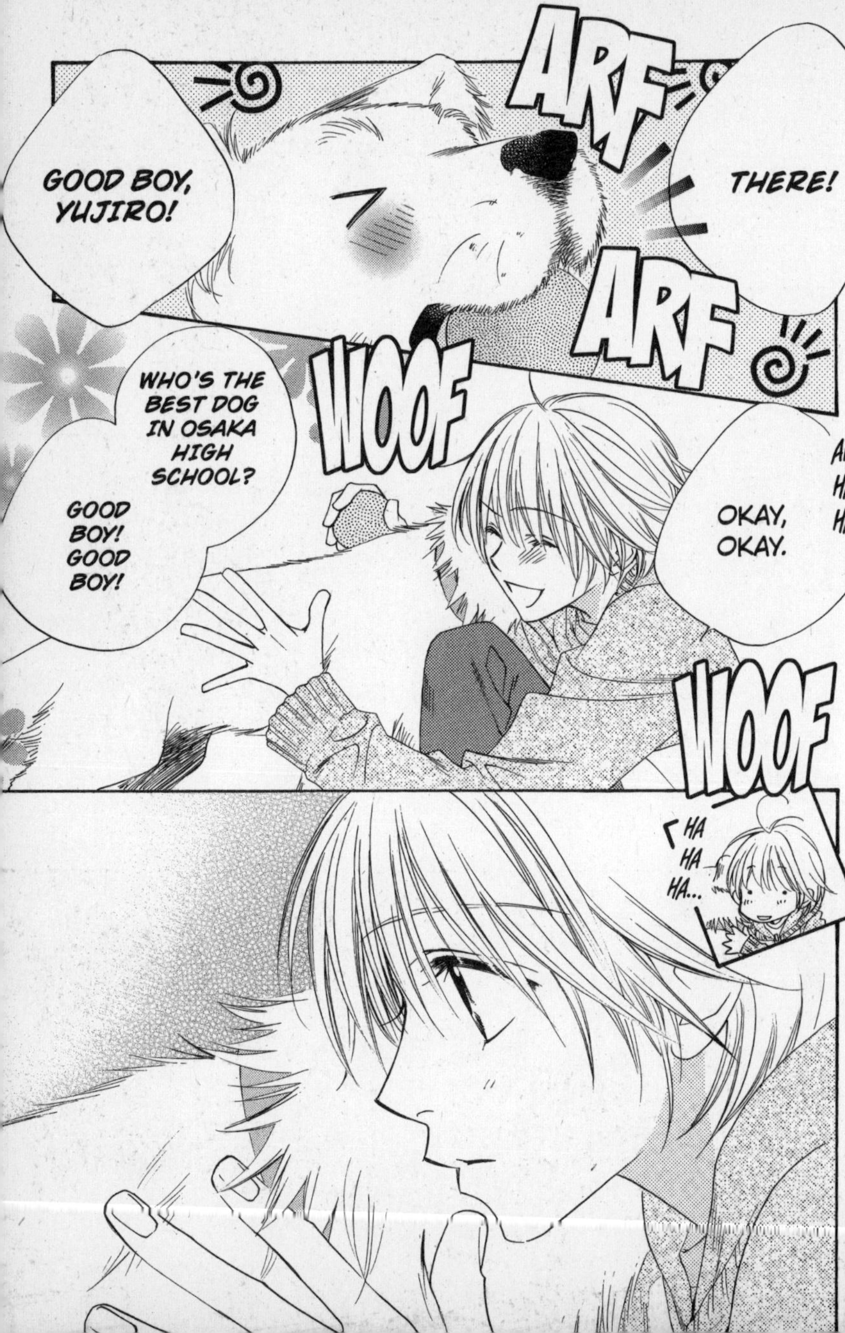
ARF
ARF
THERE!
GOOD BOY, YUJIRO!
AH HA HA
OKAY, OKAY.
WOOF
WHO'S THE BEST DOG IN OSAKA HIGH SCHOOL?
GOOD BOY! GOOD BOY!
WOOF
HA HA HA...

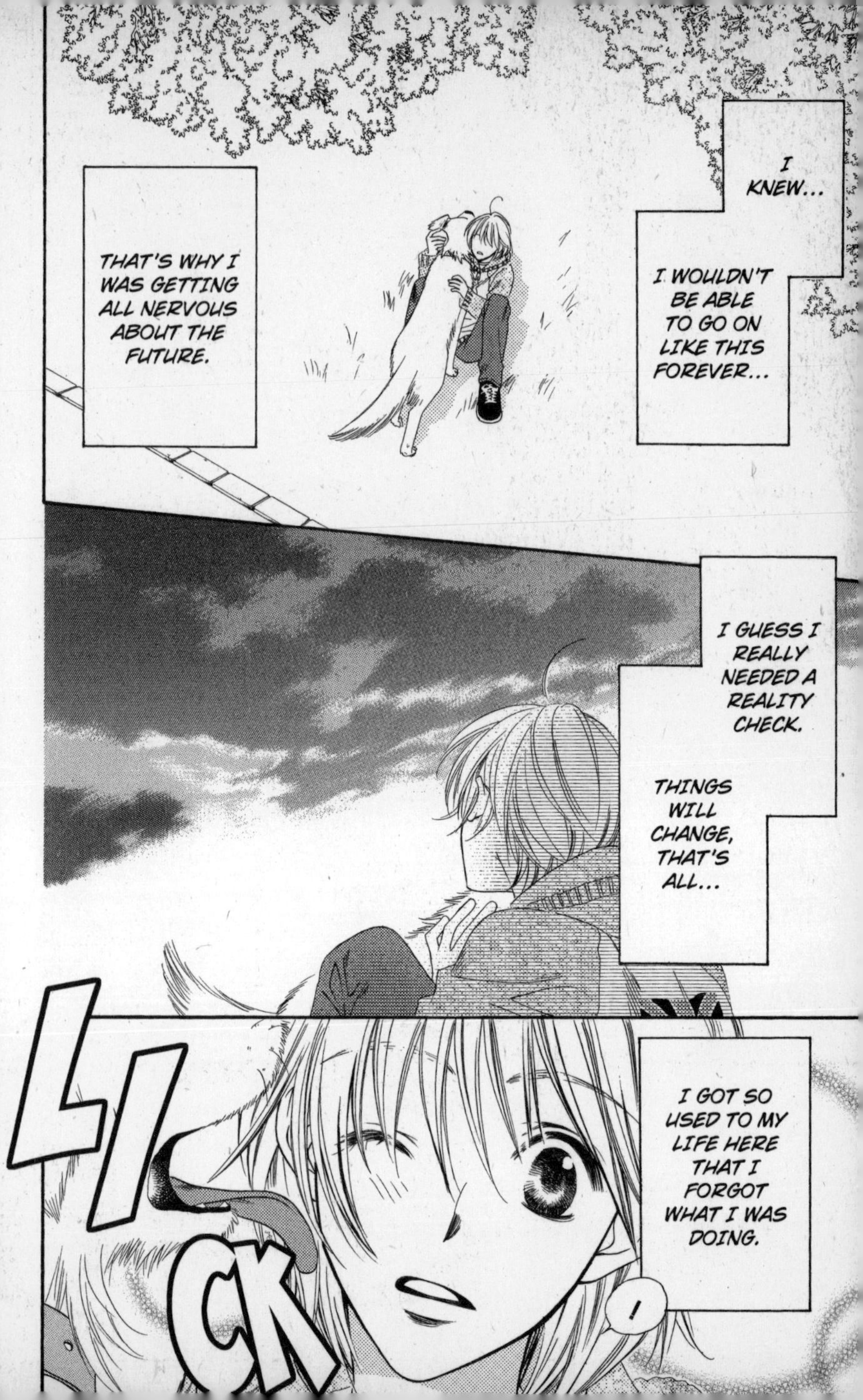
I KNEW...
I WOULDN'T BE ABLE TO GO ON LIKE THIS FOREVER...
THAT'S WHY I WAS GETTING ALL NERVOUS ABOUT THE FUTURE.
I GUESS I REALLY NEEDED A REALITY CHECK.
THINGS WILL CHANGE, THAT'S ALL...
I GOT SO USED TO MY LIFE HERE THAT I FORGOT WHAT I WAS DOING.
!
LICK

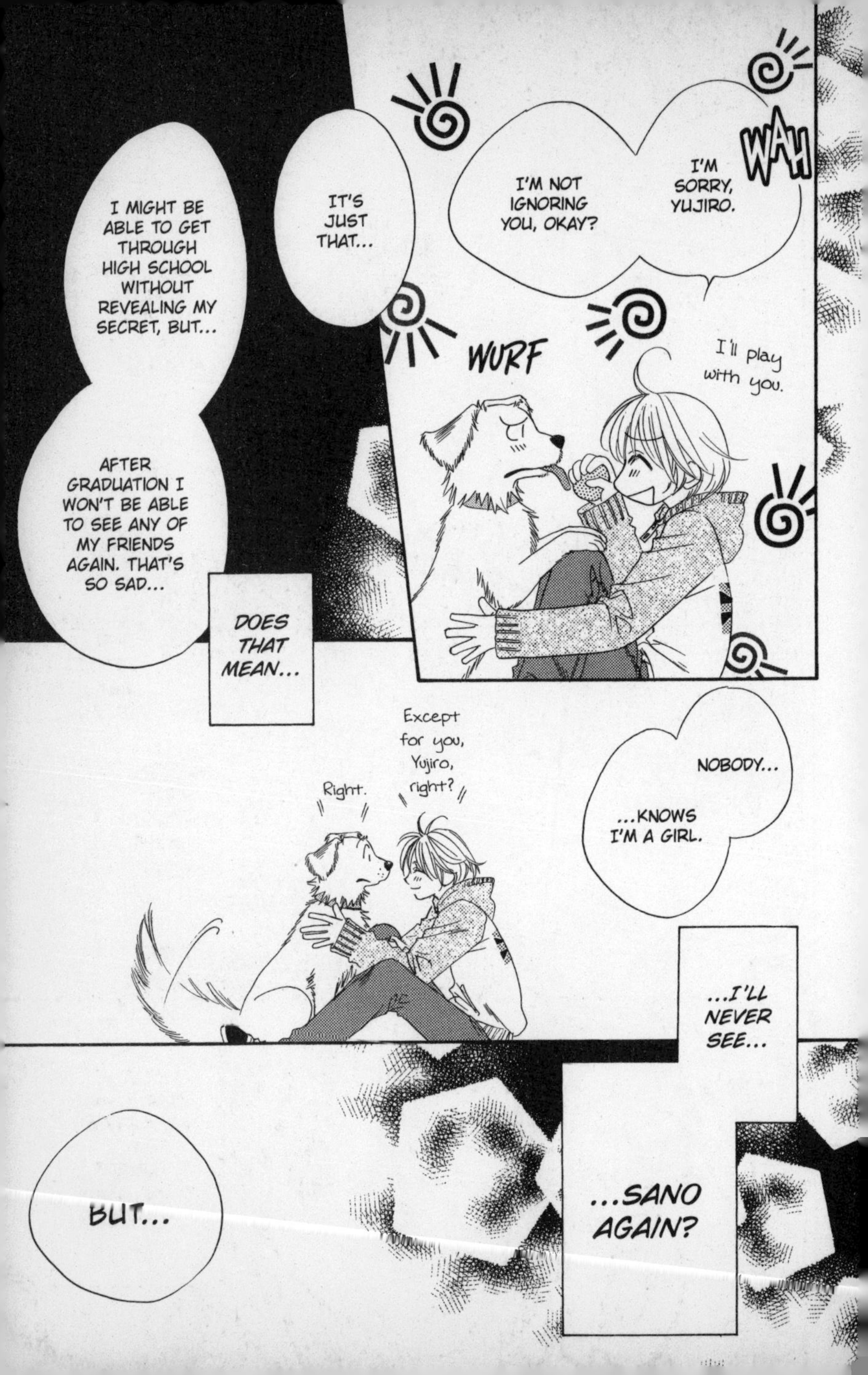
WAH
I'M SORRY, YUJIRO.
I'M NOT IGNORING YOU, OKAY?
IT'S JUST THAT...
WURF
I'll play with you.
I MIGHT BE ABLE TO GET THROUGH HIGH SCHOOL WITHOUT REVEALING MY SECRET, BUT...
AFTER GRADUATION I WON'T BE ABLE TO SEE ANY OF MY FRIENDS AGAIN. THAT'S SO SAD...
DOES THAT MEAN...
NOBODY...
...KNOWS I'M A GIRL.
Except for you, Yujiro, right?
Right.
...I'LL NEVER SEE...
...SANO AGAIN?
BUT...

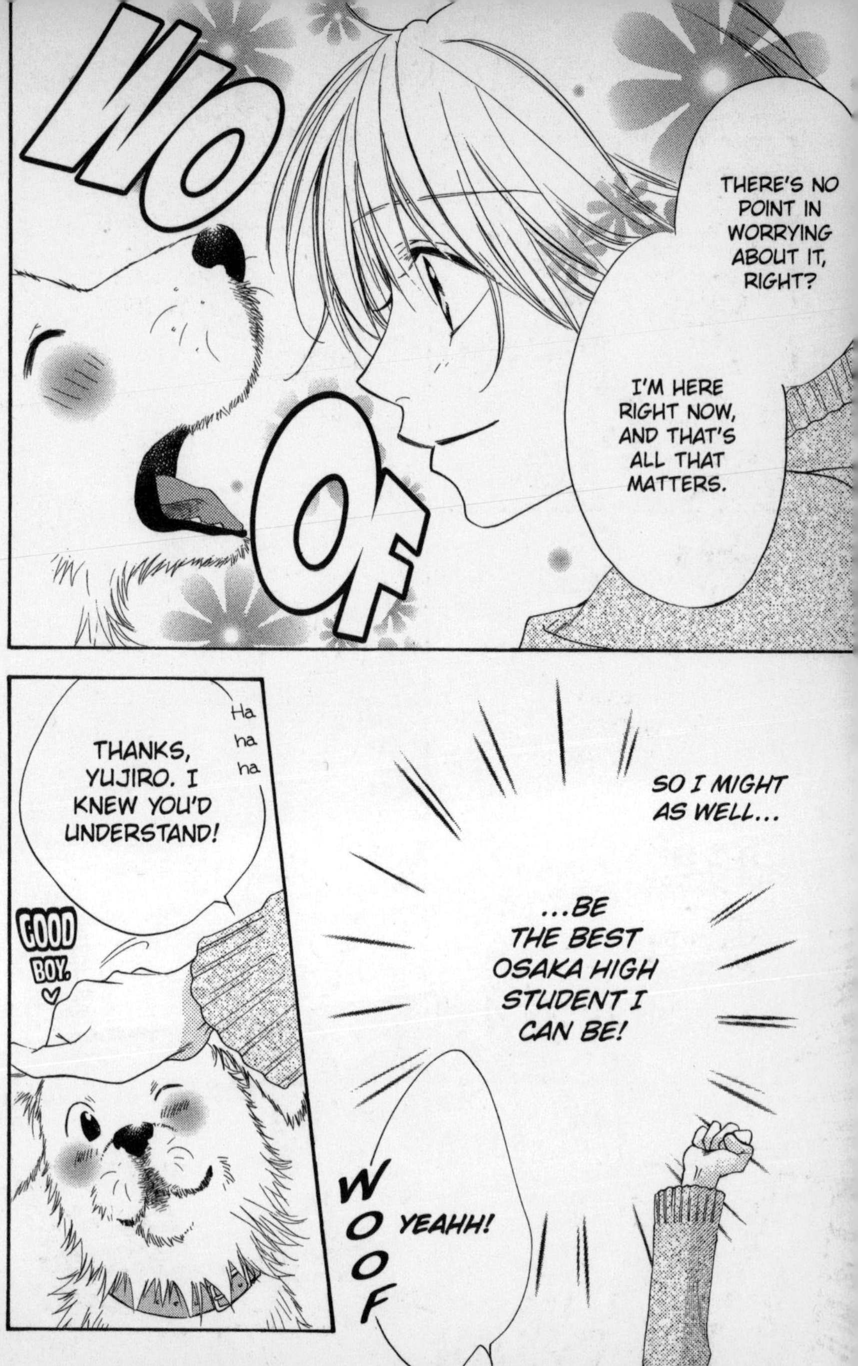
THERE'S NO POINT IN WORRYING ABOUT IT, RIGHT?
I'M HERE RIGHT NOW, AND THAT'S ALL THAT MATTERS.
WOOF
SO I MIGHT AS WELL...
...BE THE BEST OSAKA HIGH STUDENT I CAN BE!
YEAHH!
WOOF
Ha ha ha
THANKS, YUJIRO. I KNEW YOU'D UNDERSTAND!
GOOD BOY. ♥

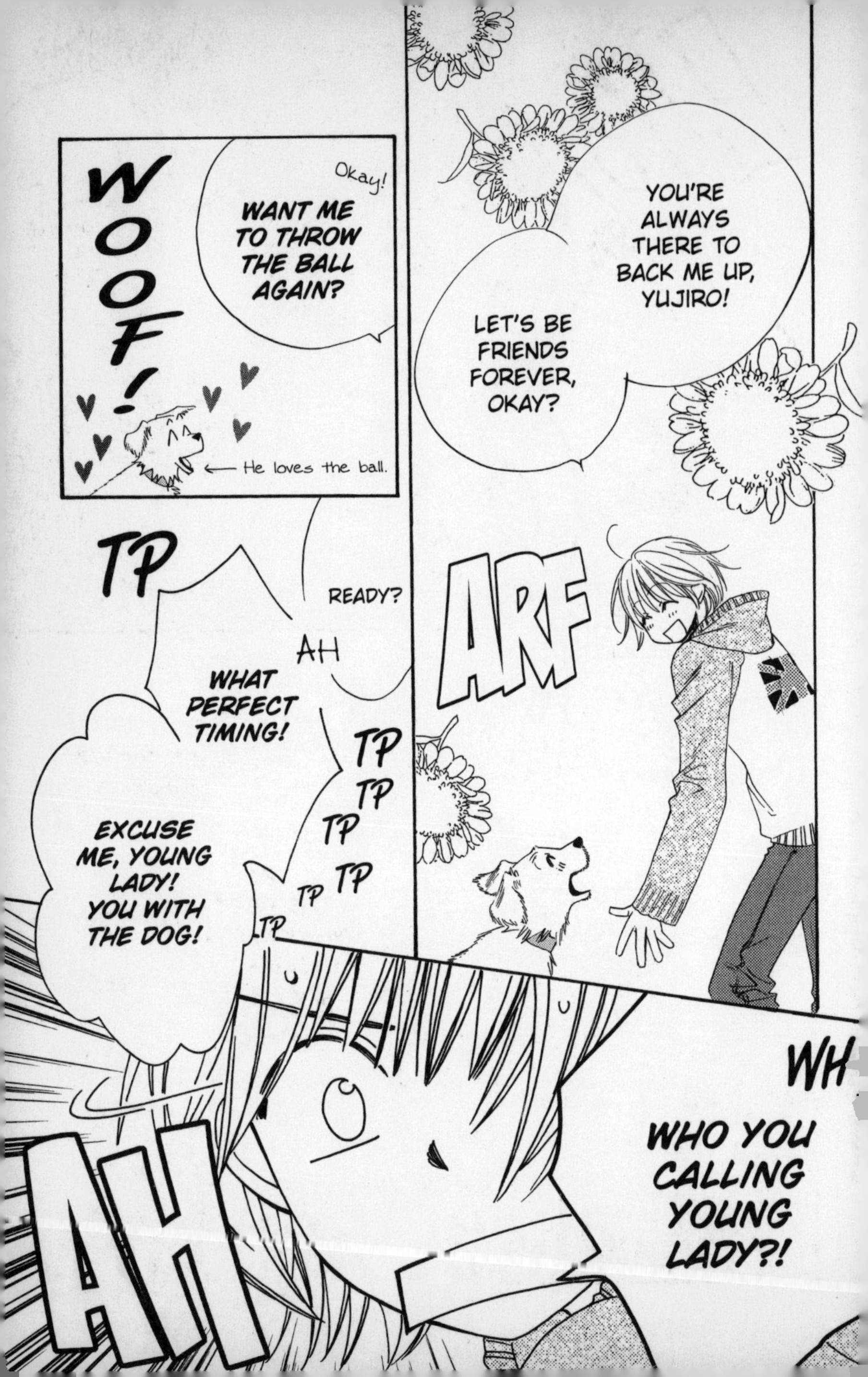

YOU'RE ALWAYS THERE TO BACK ME UP, YUJIRO!
LET'S BE FRIENDS FOREVER, OKAY?
ARF
Okay!
WANT ME TO THROW THE BALL AGAIN?
WOOF!
He loves the ball.
READY?
TP
AH
WHAT PERFECT TIMING!
TP TP TP TP TP TP
EXCUSE ME, YOUNG LADY! YOU WITH THE DOG!
WH
WHO YOU CALLING YOUNG LADY?!
AH

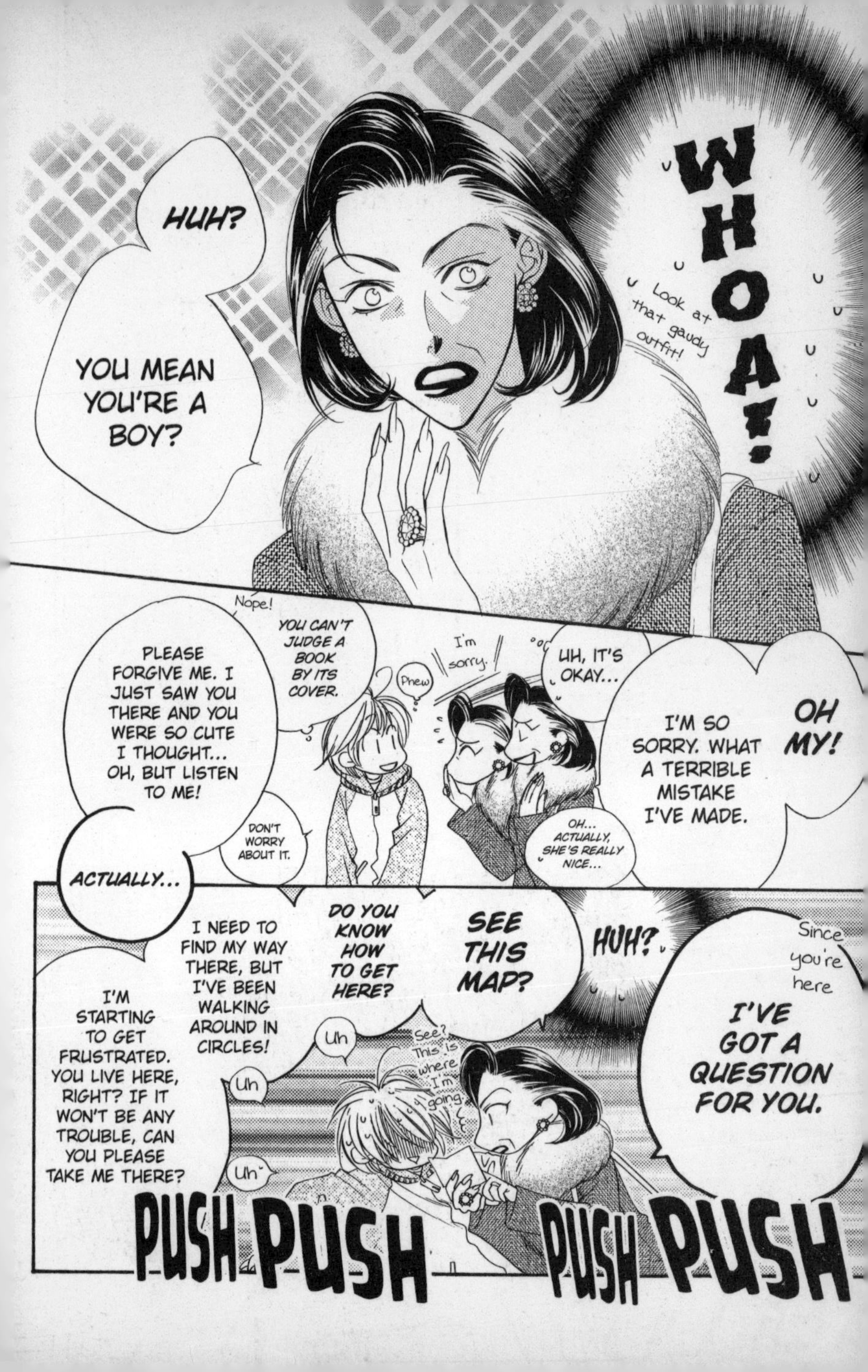
WHOA!
Look at that gaudy outfit!
HUH?
YOU MEAN YOU'RE A BOY?
OH MY!
I'M SO SORRY. WHAT A TERRIBLE MISTAKE I'VE MADE.
UH, IT'S OKAY...
I'm sorry.
OH... ACTUALLY, SHE'S REALLY NICE...
Phew
YOU CAN'T JUDGE A BOOK BY ITS COVER.
Nope!
PLEASE FORGIVE ME. I JUST SAW YOU THERE AND YOU WERE SO CUTE I THOUGHT... OH, BUT LISTEN TO ME!
DON'T WORRY ABOUT IT.
ACTUALLY...
Since you're here
I'VE GOT A QUESTION FOR YOU.
HUH?
SEE THIS MAP?
DO YOU KNOW HOW TO GET HERE?
I NEED TO FIND MY WAY THERE, BUT I'VE BEEN WALKING AROUND IN CIRCLES!
I'M STARTING TO GET FRUSTRATED. YOU LIVE HERE, RIGHT? IF IT WON'T BE ANY TROUBLE, CAN YOU PLEASE TAKE ME THERE?
See? This is where I'm going.
Uh
Uh
Uh
PUSH PUSH
PUSH PUSH

MEET THE PARENTS

Here we go! Here comes Nakatsu's mom! She's the stereotypical Osaka woman. I was worried the readers wouldn't accept her, but she's actually been pretty popular. Thanks, everybody. When I first thought about Nakatsu's mom, I imagined a gorgeous lady, like Shima Iwashita in a kimono, but considering Nakatsu's personality, I thought that wouldn't be quite right. So that's how I came up with Nakatsu's mom. (I didn't decide on her look until the last minute.) I added a little Kansai flavor.

Nakatsu trapped inside Shima Iwashita's body.

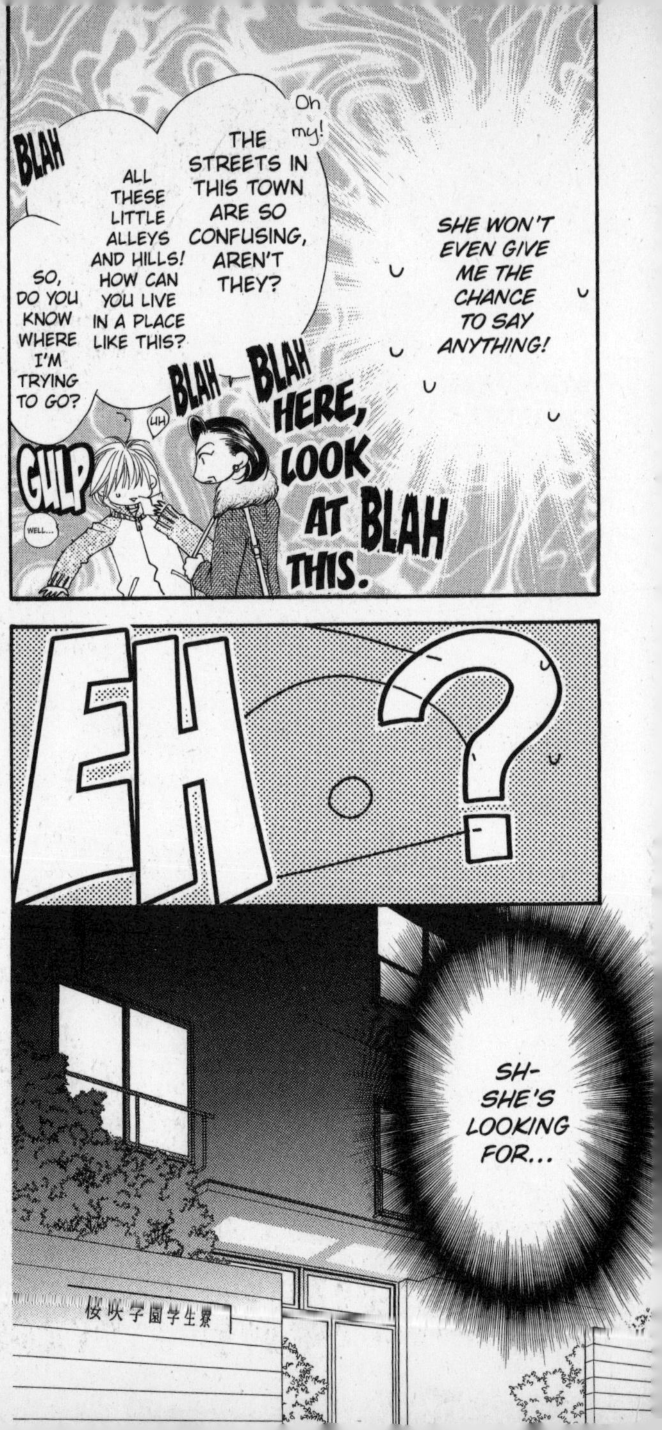
SHE WON'T EVEN GIVE ME THE CHANCE TO SAY ANYTHING!
Oh my!
THE STREETS IN THIS TOWN ARE SO CONFUSING, AREN'T THEY?
ALL THESE LITTLE ALLEYS AND HILLS! HOW CAN YOU LIVE IN A PLACE LIKE THIS?
BLAH
SO, DO YOU KNOW WHERE I'M TRYING TO GO?
BLAH
BLAH
HERE, LOOK AT THIS.
BLAH
UH
GULP
WELL...
EH?
SH- SHE'S LOOKING FOR...
桜咲学園学生寮

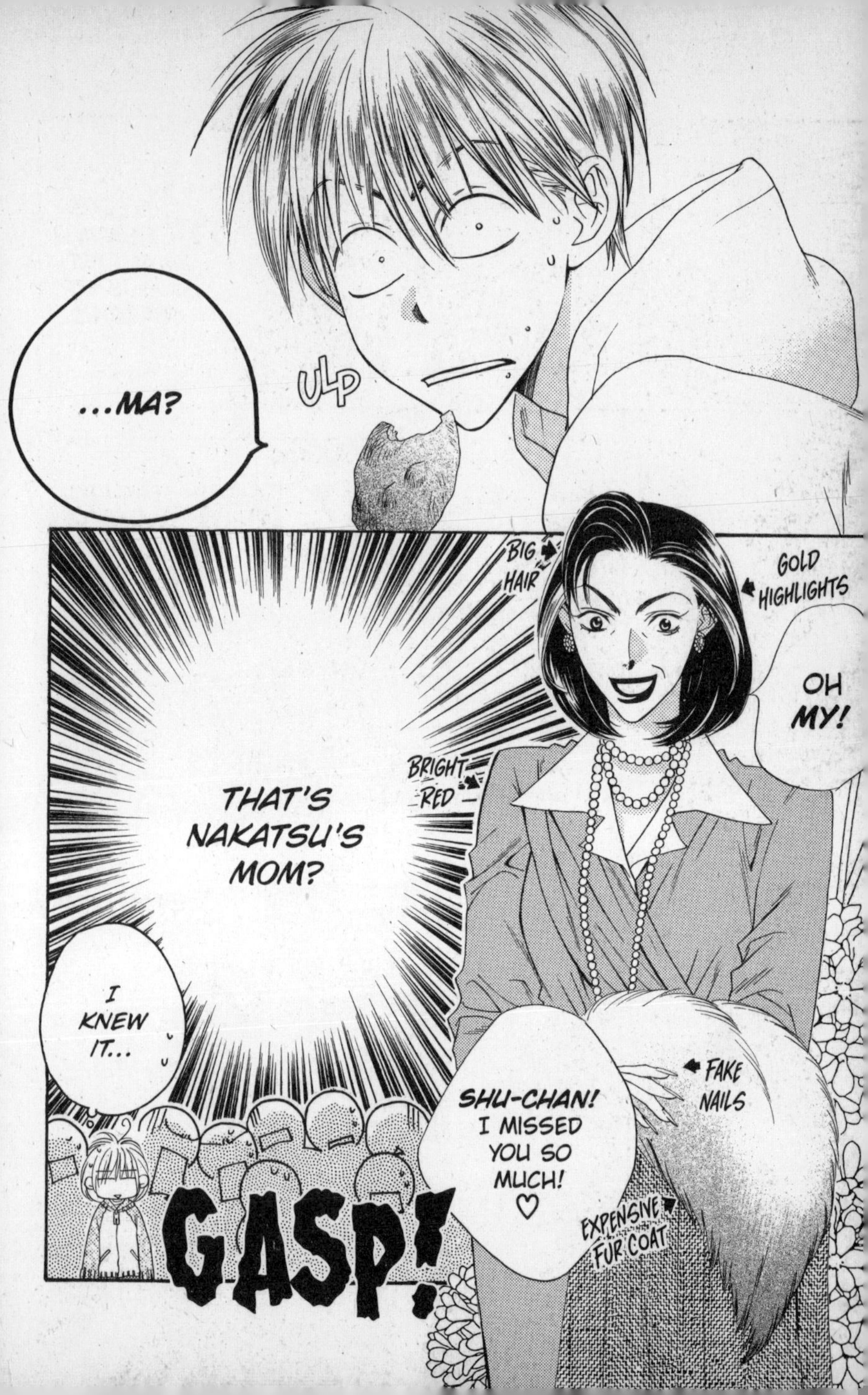
ULP
...MA?
GOLD HIGHLIGHTS
OH MY!
BIG HAIR
BRIGHT RED
THAT'S NAKATSU'S MOM?
FAKE NAILS
SHU-CHAN! I MISSED YOU SO MUCH! ♡
EXPENSIVE FUR COAT
I KNEW IT...
GASP!

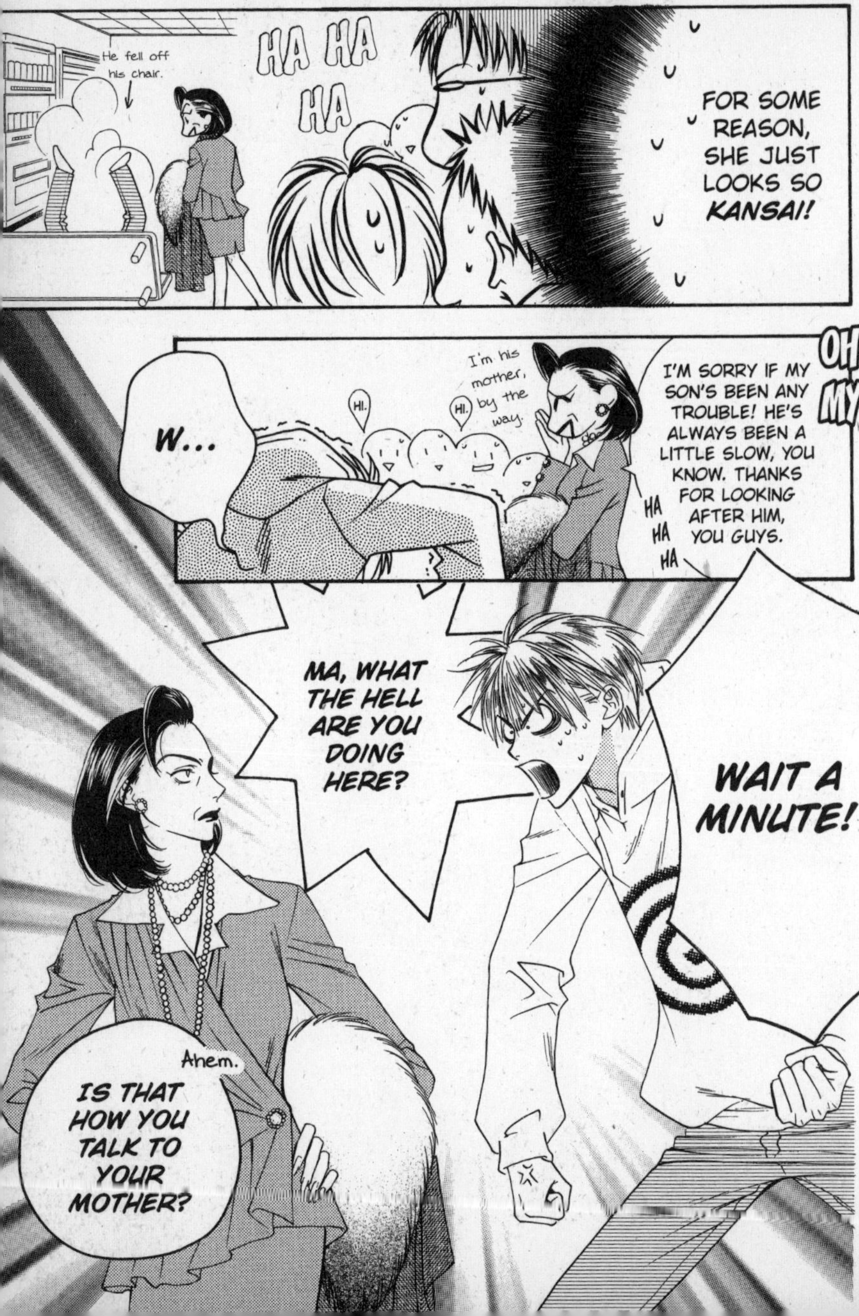
FOR SOME REASON, SHE JUST LOOKS SO *KANSAI!*
HA HA HA
He fell off his chair.
OH MY
I'M SORRY IF MY SON'S BEEN ANY TROUBLE! HE'S ALWAYS BEEN A LITTLE SLOW, YOU KNOW. THANKS FOR LOOKING AFTER HIM, YOU GUYS.
HA HA HA
I'm his mother, by the way.
HI.
HI.
W...
WAIT A MINUTE!
MA, WHAT THE HELL ARE YOU DOING HERE?
Ahem.
IS THAT HOW YOU TALK TO YOUR MOTHER?

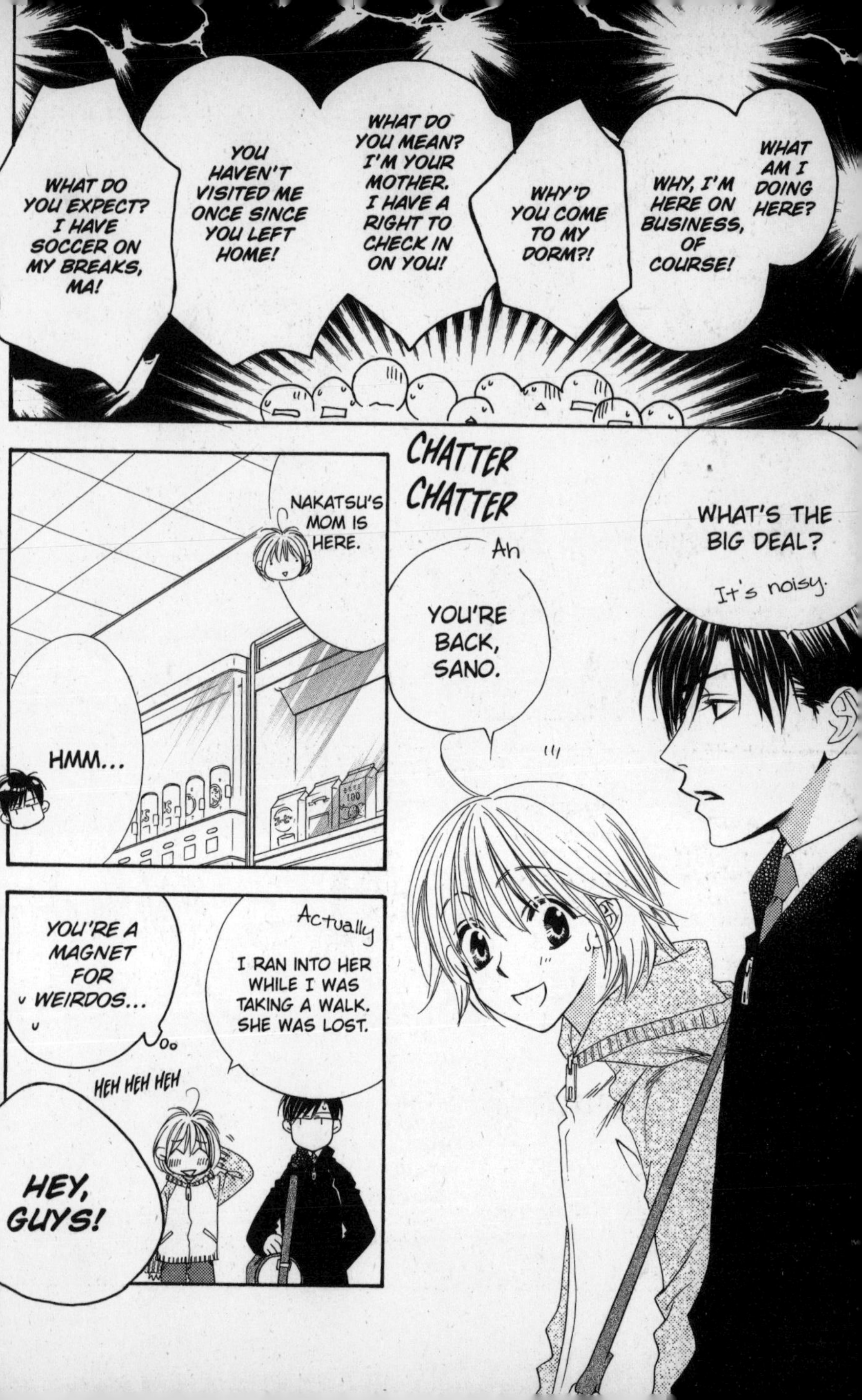
WHAT AM I DOING HERE?
WHY, I'M HERE ON BUSINESS, OF COURSE!
WHY'D YOU COME TO MY DORM?!
WHAT DO YOU MEAN? I'M YOUR MOTHER. I HAVE A RIGHT TO CHECK IN ON YOU!
YOU HAVEN'T VISITED ME ONCE SINCE YOU LEFT HOME!
WHAT DO YOU EXPECT? I HAVE SOCCER ON MY BREAKS, MA!
WHAT'S THE BIG DEAL?
It's noisy.
CHATTER CHATTER
Ah
YOU'RE BACK, SANO.
NAKATSU'S MOM IS HERE.
HMM...
Actually
I RAN INTO HER WHILE I WAS TAKING A WALK. SHE WAS LOST.
YOU'RE A MAGNET FOR WEIRDOS...
HEH HEH HEH
HEY, GUYS!

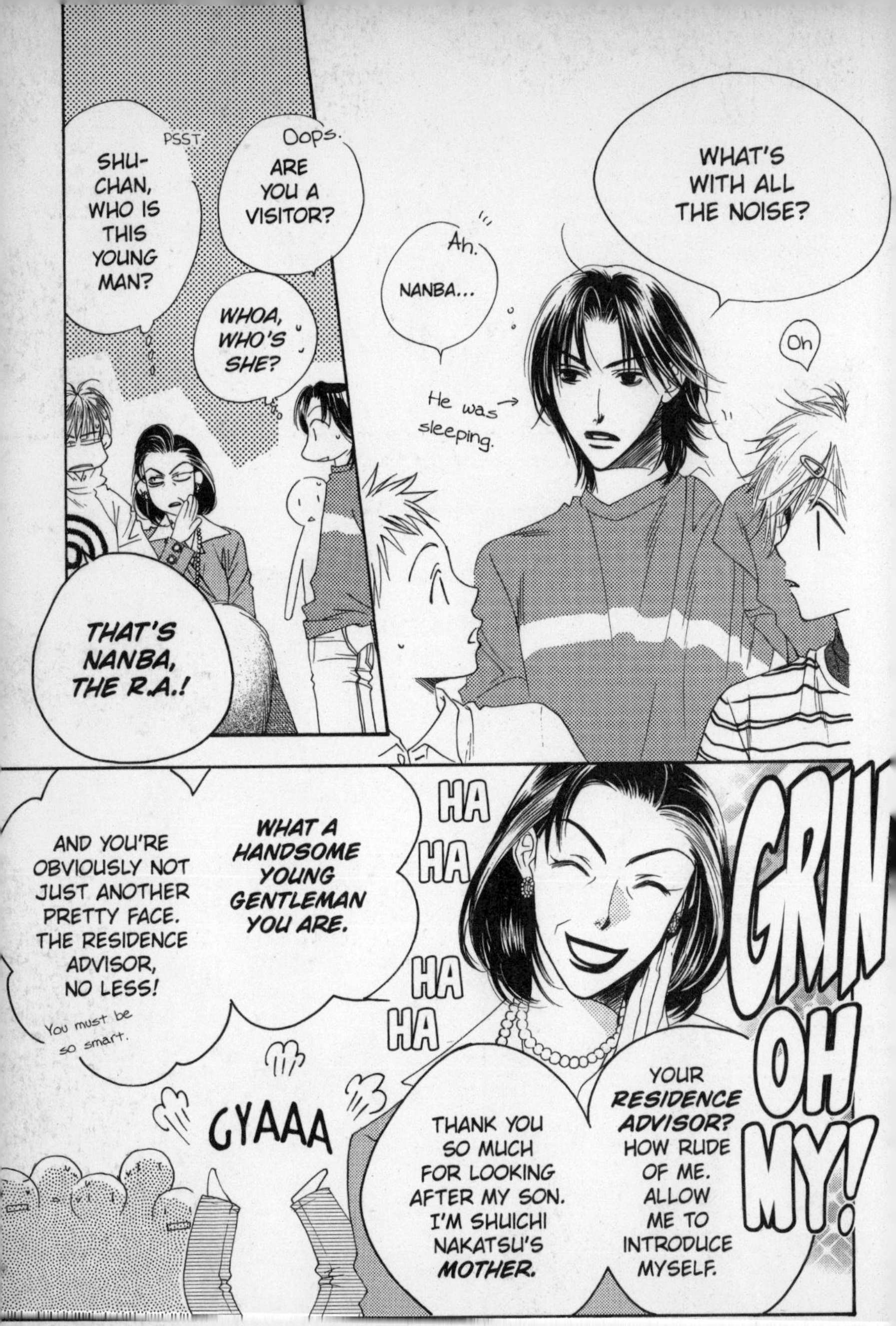
WHAT'S WITH ALL THE NOISE?
Oh
Ah.
NANBA...
He was sleeping.
Oops.
ARE YOU A VISITOR?
PSST.
SHU-CHAN, WHO IS THIS YOUNG MAN?
WHOA, WHO'S SHE?
THAT'S NANBA, THE R.A.!
GRIN
HA HA
WHAT A HANDSOME YOUNG GENTLEMAN YOU ARE.
HA HA
AND YOU'RE OBVIOUSLY NOT JUST ANOTHER PRETTY FACE. THE RESIDENCE ADVISOR, NO LESS!
You must be so smart.
OH MY!
YOUR RESIDENCE ADVISOR? HOW RUDE OF ME. ALLOW ME TO INTRODUCE MYSELF.
THANK YOU SO MUCH FOR LOOKING AFTER MY SON. I'M SHUICHI NAKATSU'S MOTHER.
GYAAA

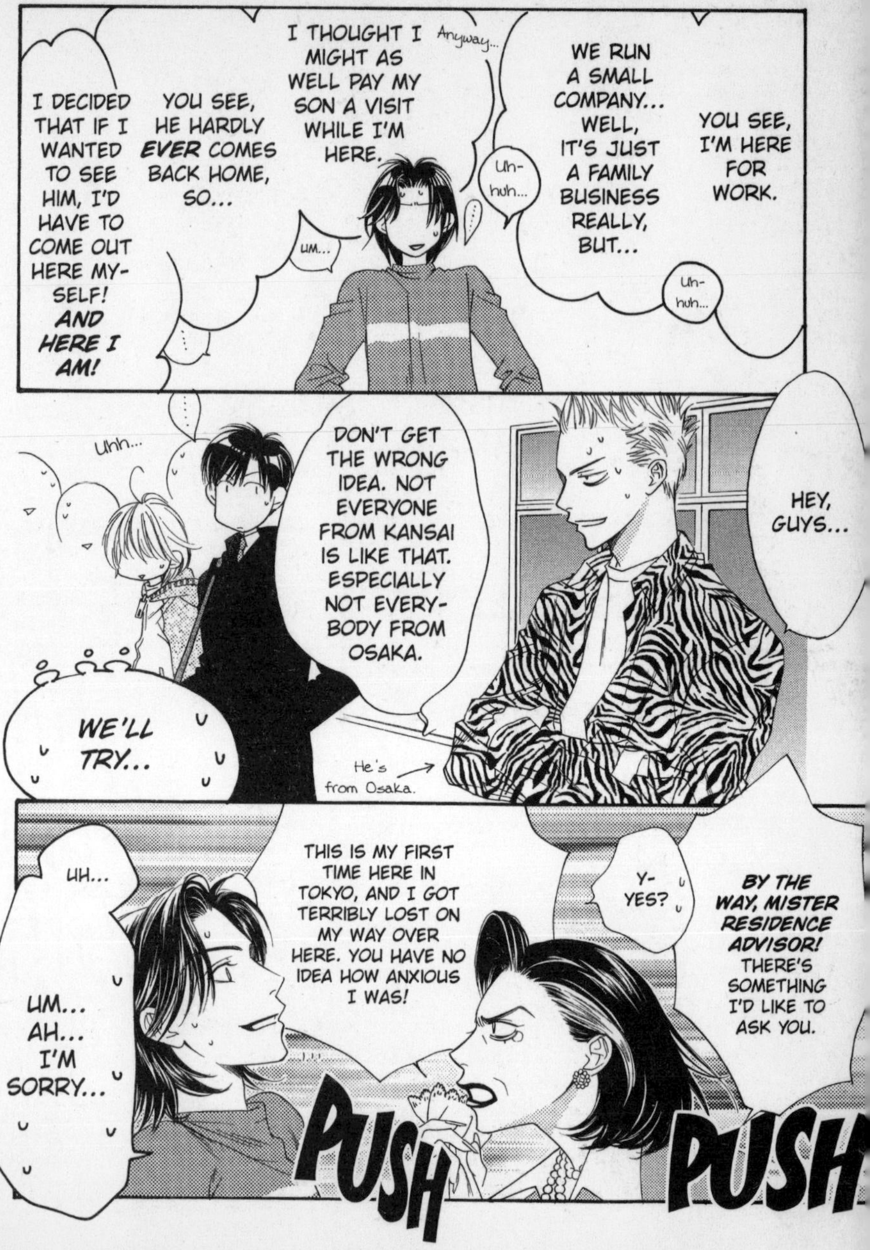
YOU SEE, I'M HERE FOR WORK.
Uh-huh...
WE RUN A SMALL COMPANY... WELL, IT'S JUST A FAMILY BUSINESS REALLY, BUT...
Uh-huh...
Anyway...
I THOUGHT I MIGHT AS WELL PAY MY SON A VISIT WHILE I'M HERE.
YOU SEE, HE HARDLY EVER COMES BACK HOME, SO...
UM...
I DECIDED THAT IF I WANTED TO SEE HIM, I'D HAVE TO COME OUT HERE MYSELF! AND HERE I AM!
HEY, GUYS...
DON'T GET THE WRONG IDEA. NOT EVERYONE FROM KANSAI IS LIKE THAT. ESPECIALLY NOT EVERYBODY FROM OSAKA.
He's from Osaka.
Uhh...
WE'LL TRY...
BY THE WAY, MISTER RESIDENCE ADVISOR! THERE'S SOMETHING I'D LIKE TO ASK YOU.
PUSH
Y-YES?
THIS IS MY FIRST TIME HERE IN TOKYO, AND I GOT TERRIBLY LOST ON MY WAY OVER HERE. YOU HAVE NO IDEA HOW ANXIOUS I WAS!
UH...
UM... AH... I'M SORRY...
PUSH

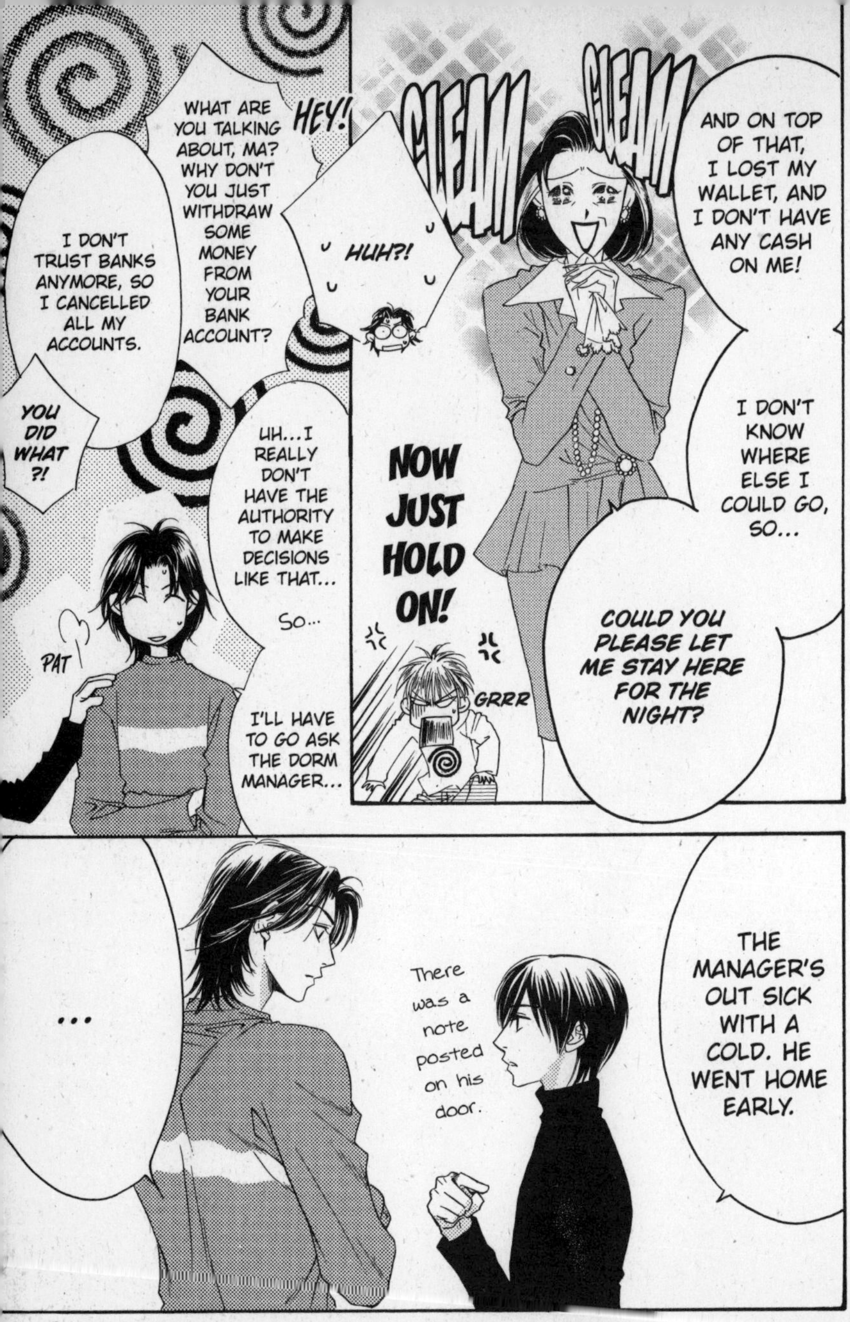
GLEAM GLEAM
AND ON TOP OF THAT, I LOST MY WALLET, AND I DON'T HAVE ANY CASH ON ME!
I DON'T KNOW WHERE ELSE I COULD GO, SO...
COULD YOU PLEASE LET ME STAY HERE FOR THE NIGHT?
NOW JUST HOLD ON!
GRRR
HEY!
HUH?!
WHAT ARE YOU TALKING ABOUT, MA? WHY DON'T YOU JUST WITHDRAW SOME MONEY FROM YOUR BANK ACCOUNT?
I DON'T TRUST BANKS ANYMORE, SO I CANCELLED ALL MY ACCOUNTS.
YOU DID WHAT?!
UH...I REALLY DON'T HAVE THE AUTHORITY TO MAKE DECISIONS LIKE THAT...
So...
I'LL HAVE TO GO ASK THE DORM MANAGER...
PAT
THE MANAGER'S OUT SICK WITH A COLD. HE WENT HOME EARLY.
There was a note posted on his door.
...

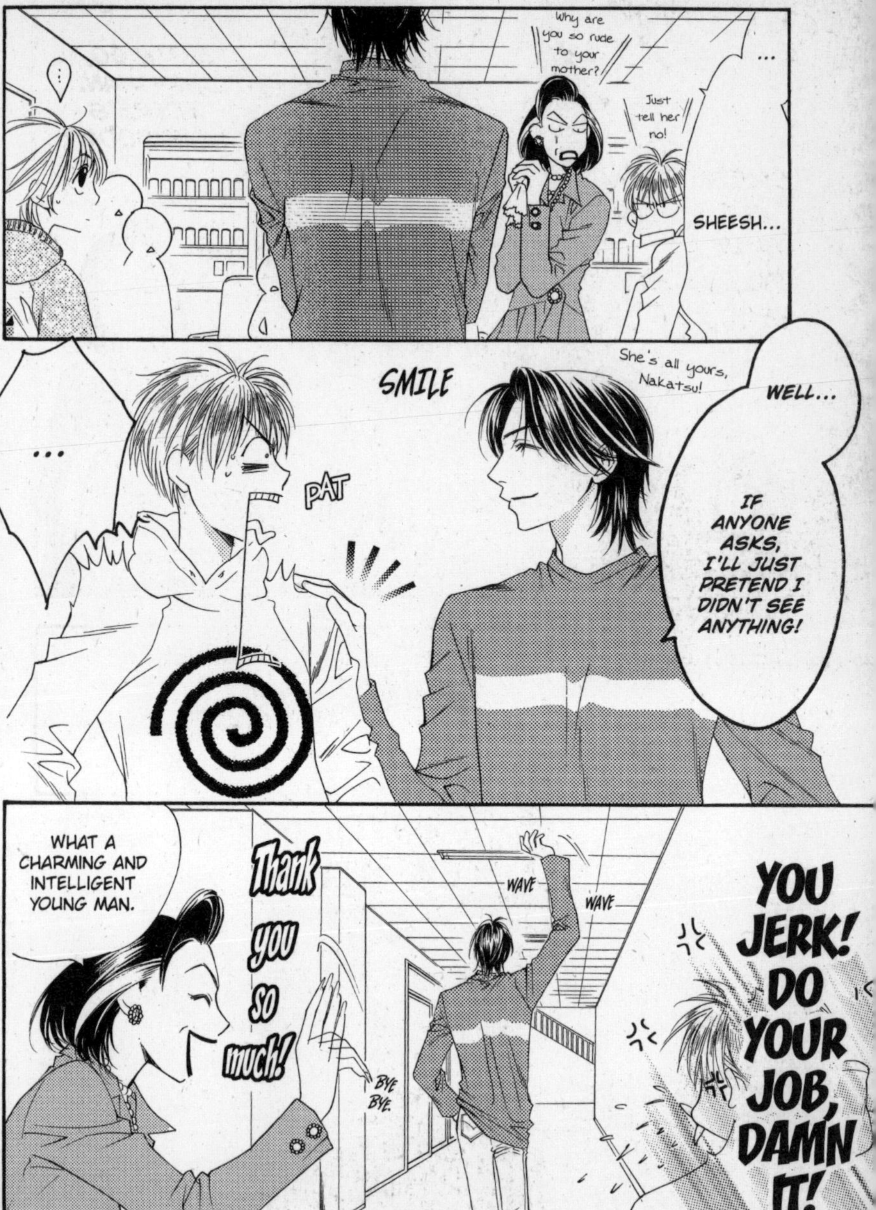
...
Why are you so rude to your mother?
Just tell her no!
SHEESH...
WELL...
IF ANYONE ASKS, I'LL JUST PRETEND I DIDN'T SEE ANYTHING!
She's all yours, Nakatsu!
SMILE
PAT
...
YOU JERK! DO YOUR JOB, DAMN IT!
WAVE
WAVE
BYE BYE.
Thank you so much!
WHAT A CHARMING AND INTELLIGENT YOUNG MAN.

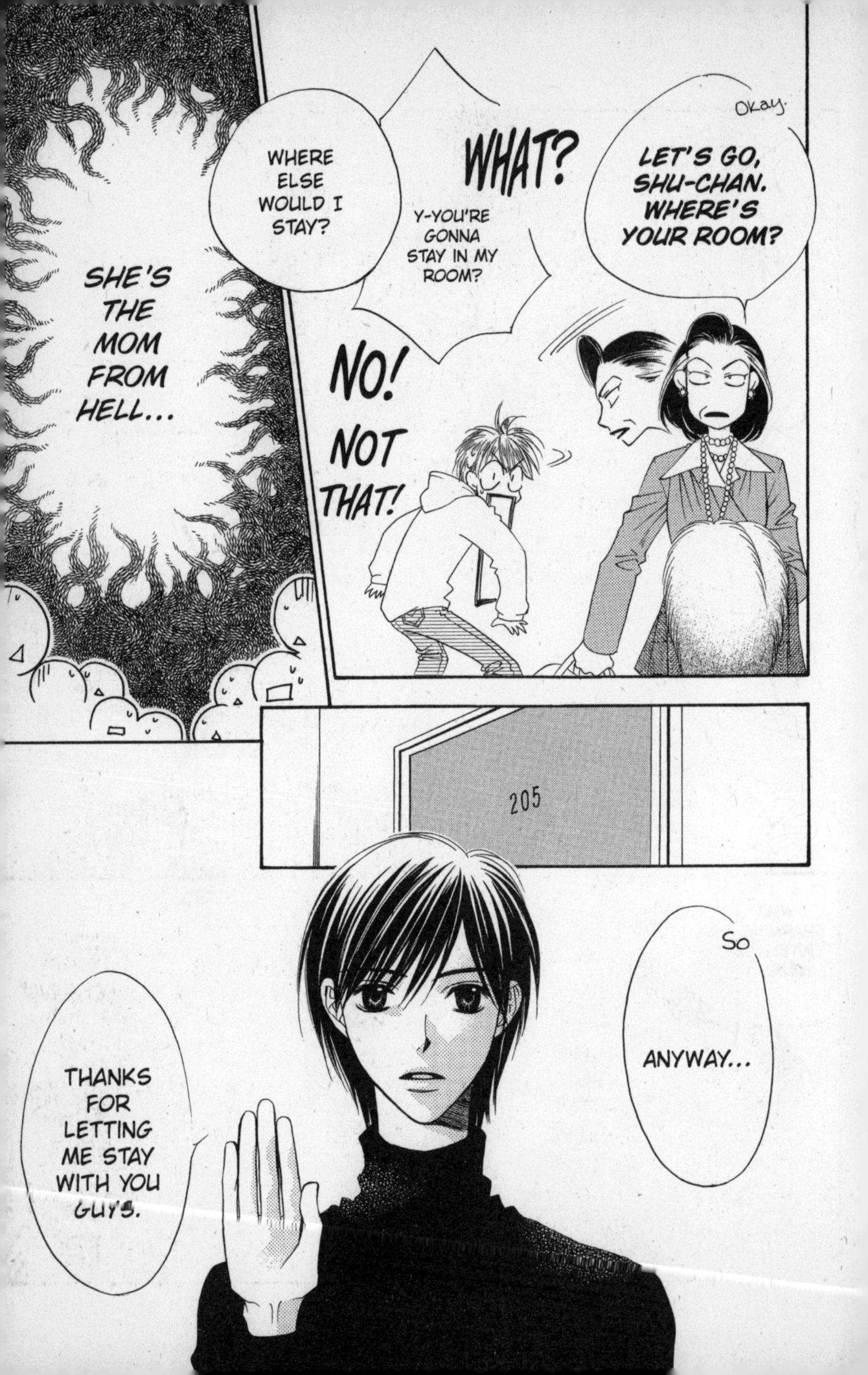

Okay.
LET'S GO, SHU-CHAN. WHERE'S YOUR ROOM?
WHAT?
Y-YOU'RE GONNA STAY IN MY ROOM?
WHERE ELSE WOULD I STAY?
NO! NOT THAT!
SHE'S THE MOM FROM HELL...
205
So
ANYWAY...
THANKS FOR LETTING ME STAY WITH YOU GUYS.

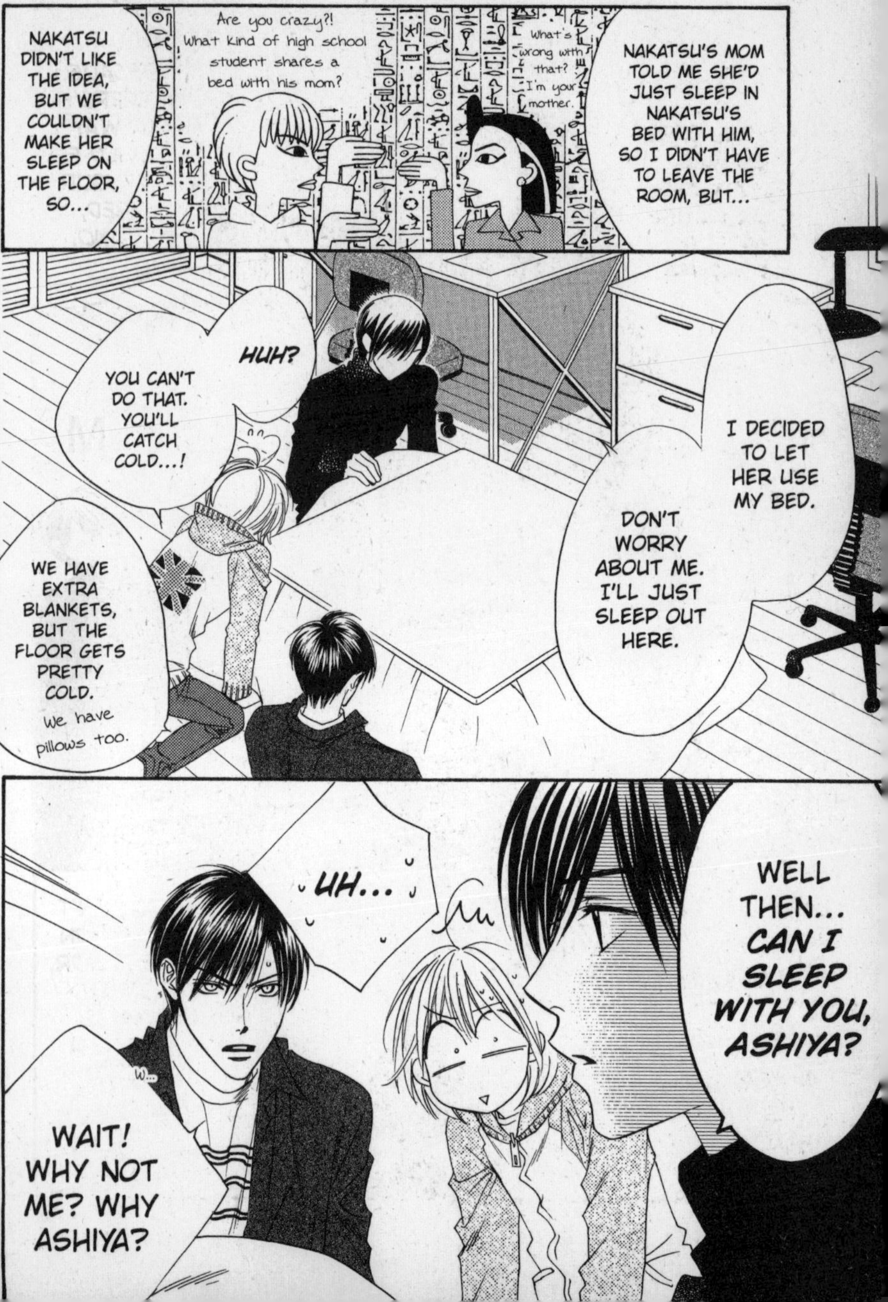

NAKATSU'S MOM TOLD ME SHE'D JUST SLEEP IN NAKATSU'S BED WITH HIM, SO I DIDN'T HAVE TO LEAVE THE ROOM, BUT...
Are you crazy?! What kind of high school student shares a bed with his mom?
What's wrong with that? I'm your mother.
NAKATSU DIDN'T LIKE THE IDEA, BUT WE COULDN'T MAKE HER SLEEP ON THE FLOOR, SO...
I DECIDED TO LET HER USE MY BED.
DON'T WORRY ABOUT ME. I'LL JUST SLEEP OUT HERE.
HUH?
YOU CAN'T DO THAT. YOU'LL CATCH COLD...!
WE HAVE EXTRA BLANKETS, BUT THE FLOOR GETS PRETTY COLD.
We have pillows too.
WELL THEN... CAN I SLEEP WITH YOU, ASHIYA?
UH...
W...
WAIT! WHY NOT ME? WHY ASHIYA?

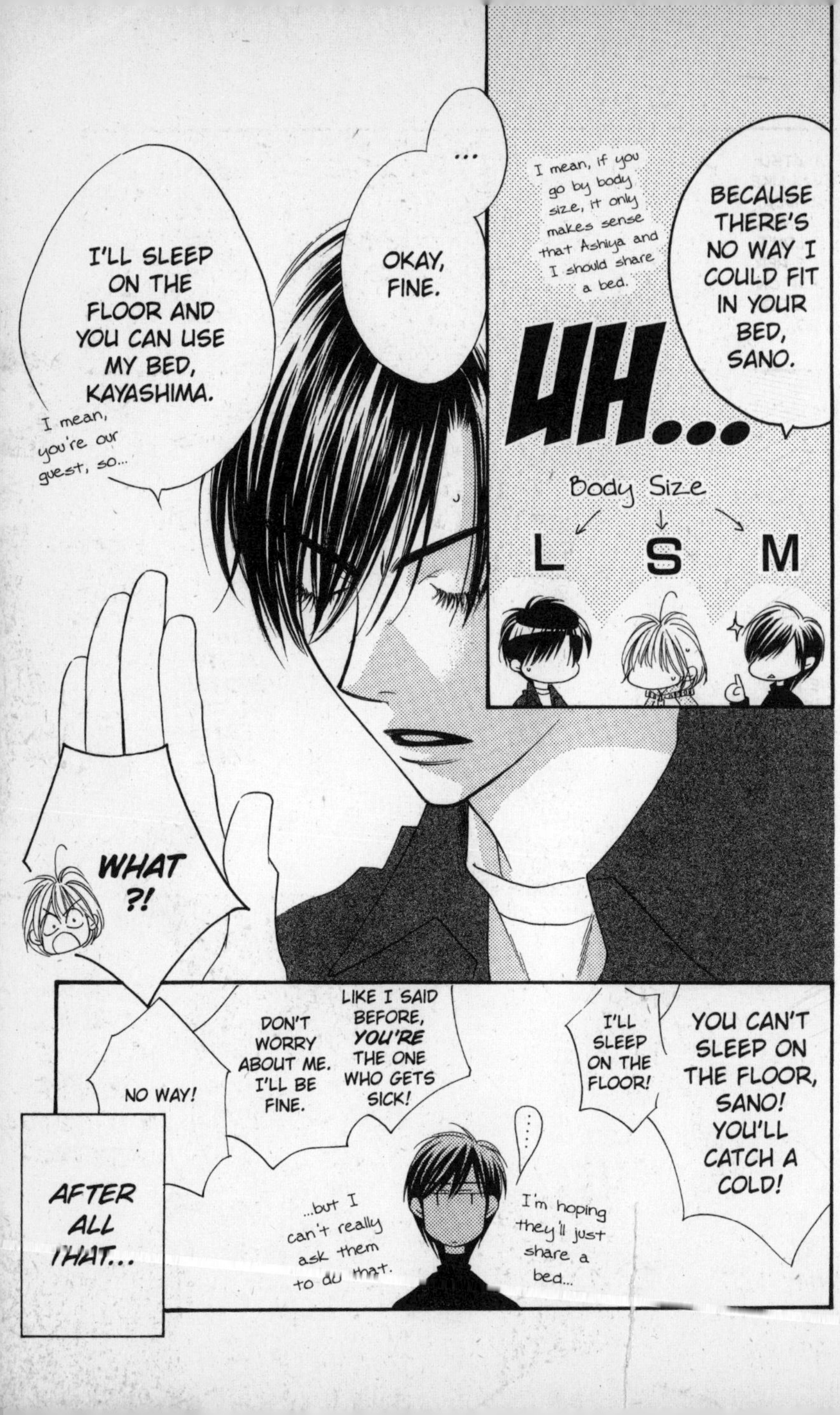
BECAUSE THERE'S NO WAY I COULD FIT IN YOUR BED, SANO.
UH...
I mean, if you go by body size, it only makes sense that Ashiya and I should share a bed.
Body Size
L
S
M
...
OKAY, FINE.
I'LL SLEEP ON THE FLOOR AND YOU CAN USE MY BED, KAYASHIMA.
I mean, you're our guest, so...
WHAT ?!
YOU CAN'T SLEEP ON THE FLOOR, SANO! YOU'LL CATCH A COLD!
I'LL SLEEP ON THE FLOOR!
...
I'm hoping they'll just share a bed...
LIKE I SAID BEFORE, *YOU'RE* THE ONE WHO GETS SICK!
DON'T WORRY ABOUT ME. I'LL BE FINE.
...but I can't really ask them to do that.
NO WAY!
AFTER ALL THAT...

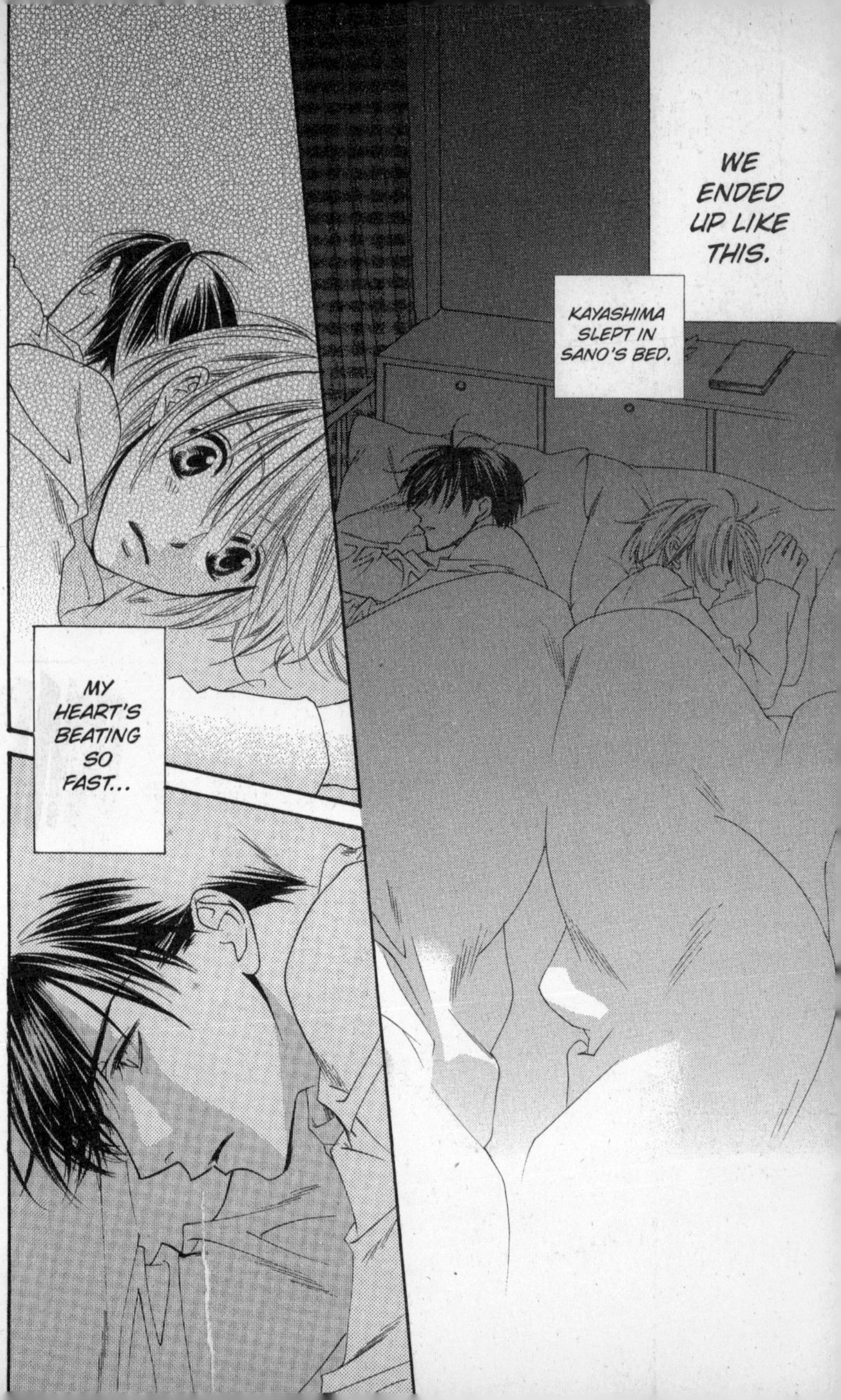
WE ENDED UP LIKE THIS.
KAYASHIMA SLEPT IN SANO'S BED.
MY HEART'S BEATING SO FAST...

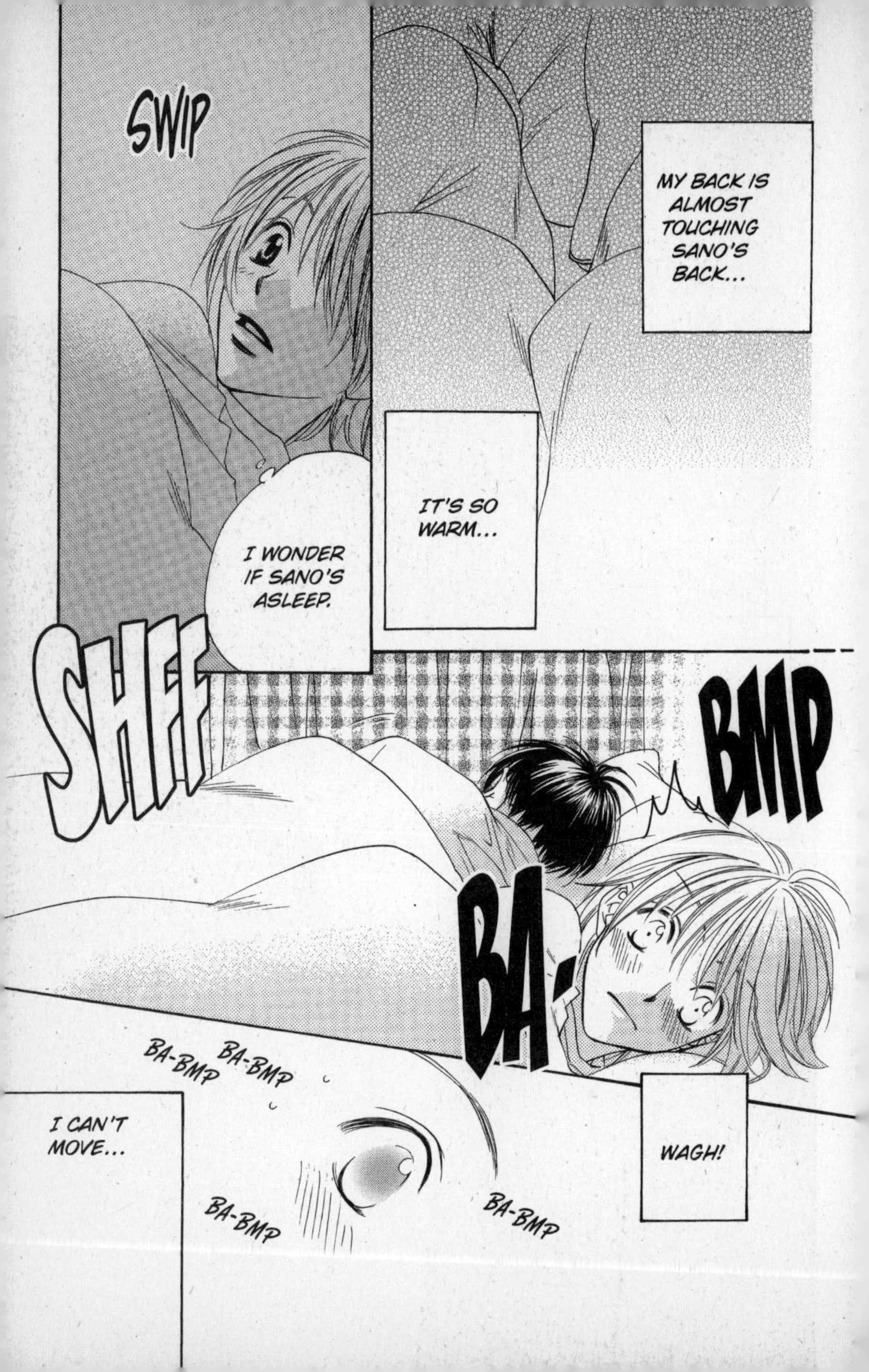
MY BACK IS ALMOST TOUCHING SANO'S BACK...
IT'S SO WARM...
SWIP
I WONDER IF SANO'S ASLEEP.
SHFF
BA-BMP
WAGH!
BA-BMP
BA-BMP
BA-BMP
BA-BMP
I CAN'T MOVE...

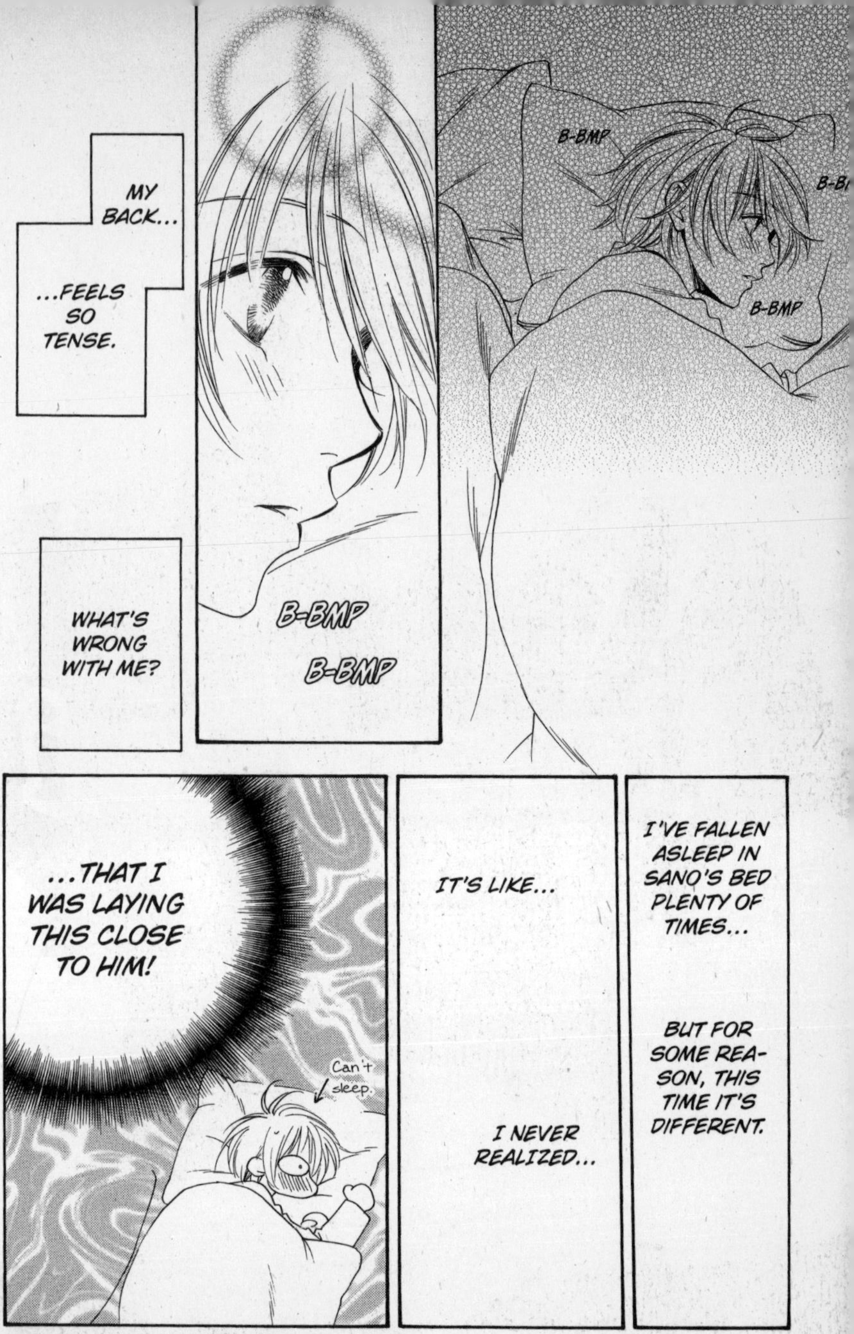
B-BMP
B-BMP
B-BMP
B-BMP
MY BACK...
...FEELS SO TENSE.
WHAT'S WRONG WITH ME?
I'VE FALLEN ASLEEP IN SANO'S BED PLENTY OF TIMES...
BUT FOR SOME REA-SON, THIS TIME IT'S DIFFERENT.
IT'S LIKE...
I NEVER REALIZED...
...THAT I WAS LAYING THIS CLOSE TO HIM!
Can't sleep.

HANA-KIMI CHAPTER 110/END

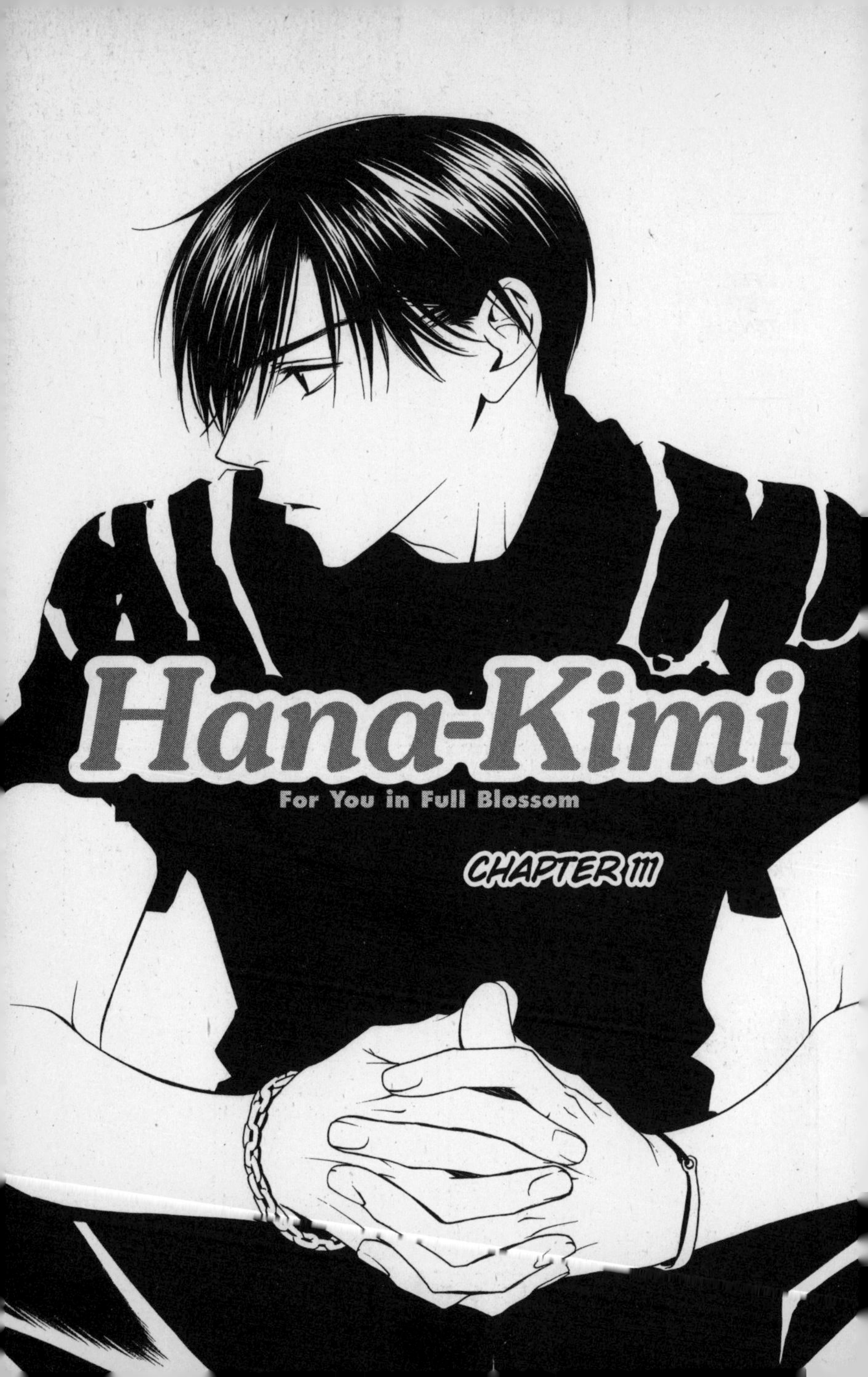
Hana-Kimi
For You in Full Blossom
CHAPTER 111

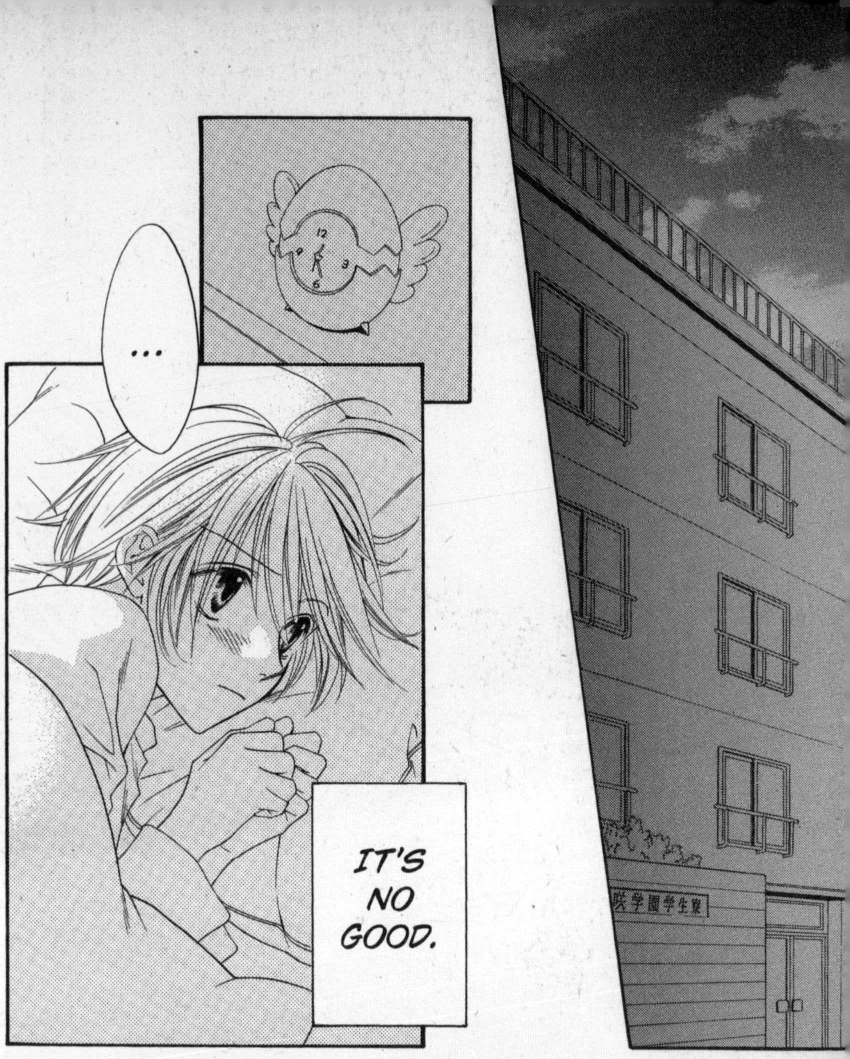
...
IT'S NO GOOD.

LORD OF THE RINGS Part 4

The series is going to be a trilogy. I've only seen the first movie so far, but I'm definitely gonna see them all!

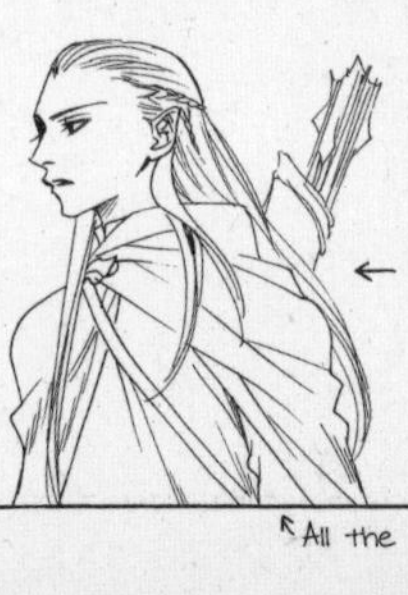

← Legolas the hot elf

↖ All the elves wear the same robe.

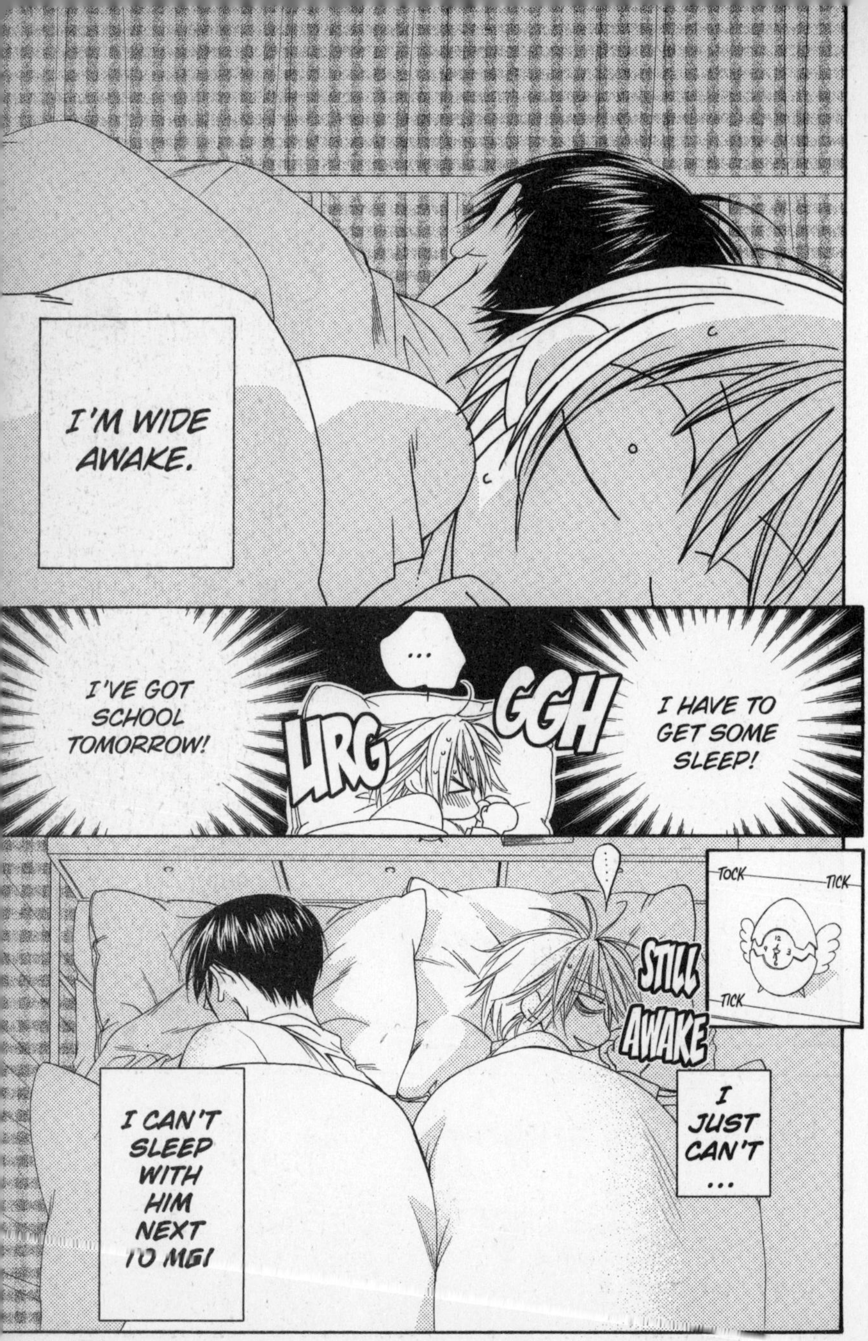
I'M WIDE AWAKE.
I HAVE TO GET SOME SLEEP!
URGGGH
...
I'VE GOT SCHOOL TOMORROW!
TOCK
TICK
TICK
STILL AWAKE
...
I JUST CAN'T ...
I CAN'T SLEEP WITH HIM NEXT TO ME!

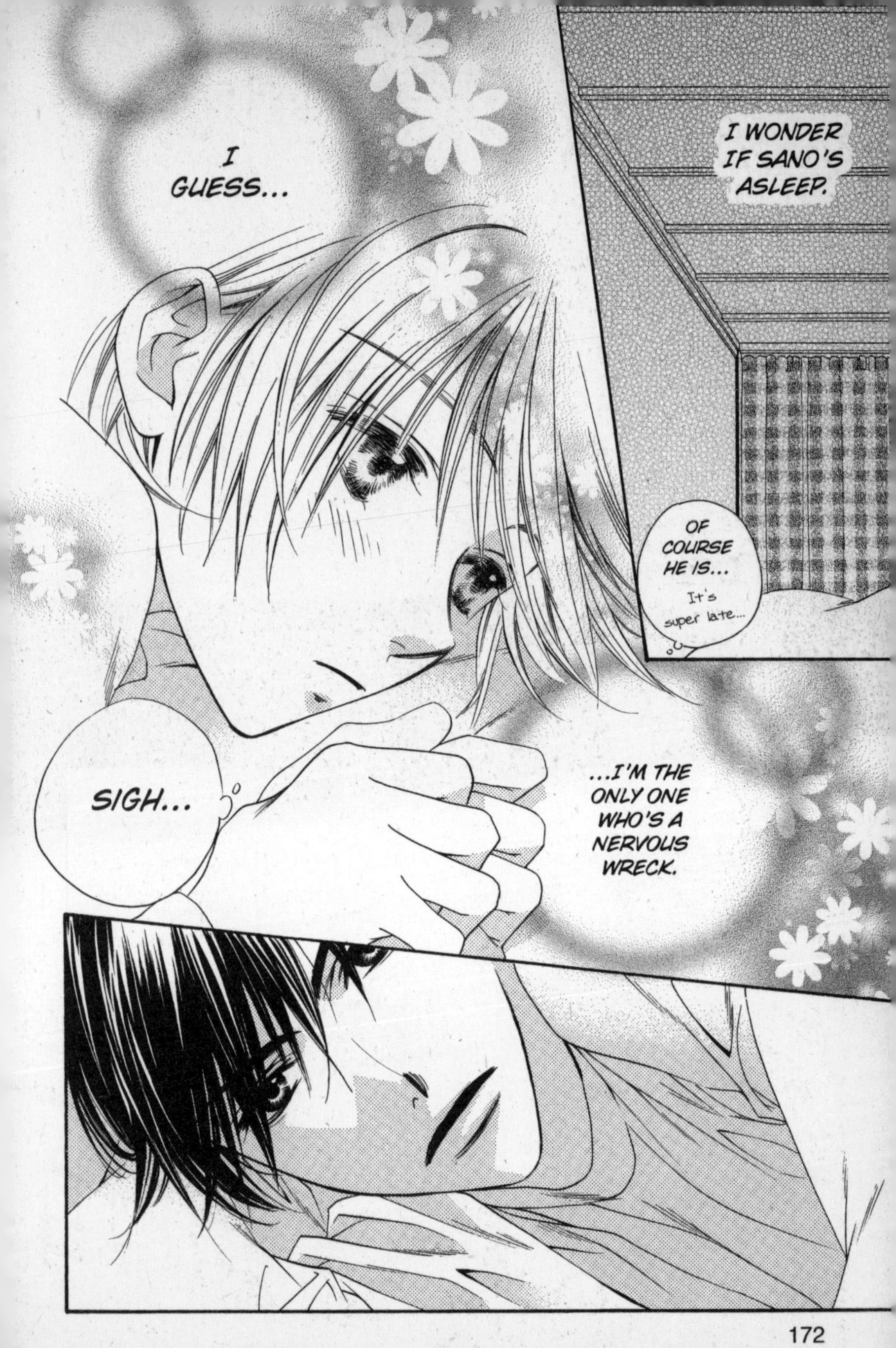
I WONDER IF SANO'S ASLEEP.
OF COURSE HE IS...
It's super late...
I GUESS...
...I'M THE ONLY ONE WHO'S A NERVOUS WRECK.
SIGH...

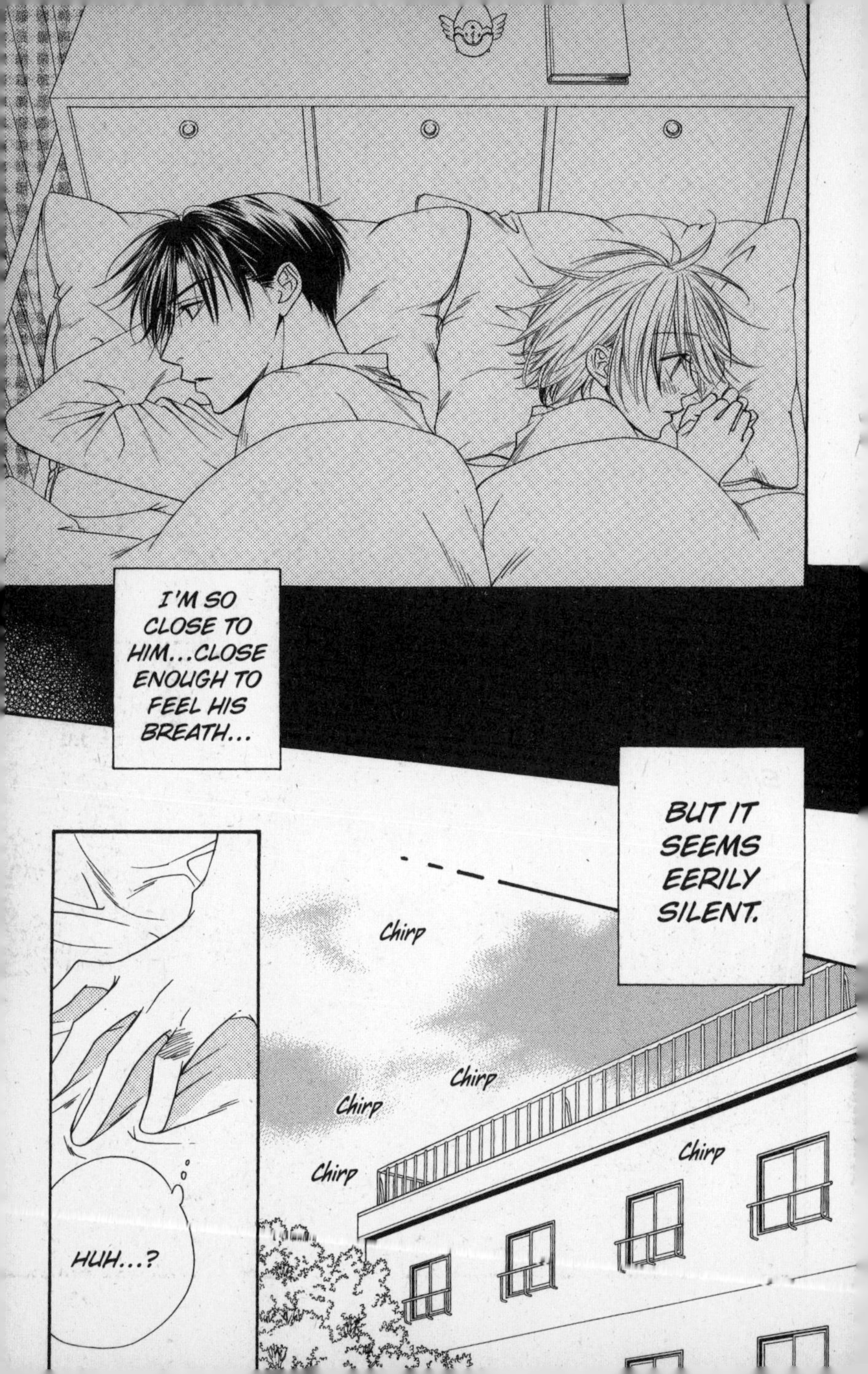
I'M SO CLOSE TO HIM...CLOSE ENOUGH TO FEEL HIS BREATH...
BUT IT SEEMS EERILY SILENT.
Chirp
Chirp
Chirp
Chirp
Chirp
HUH...?

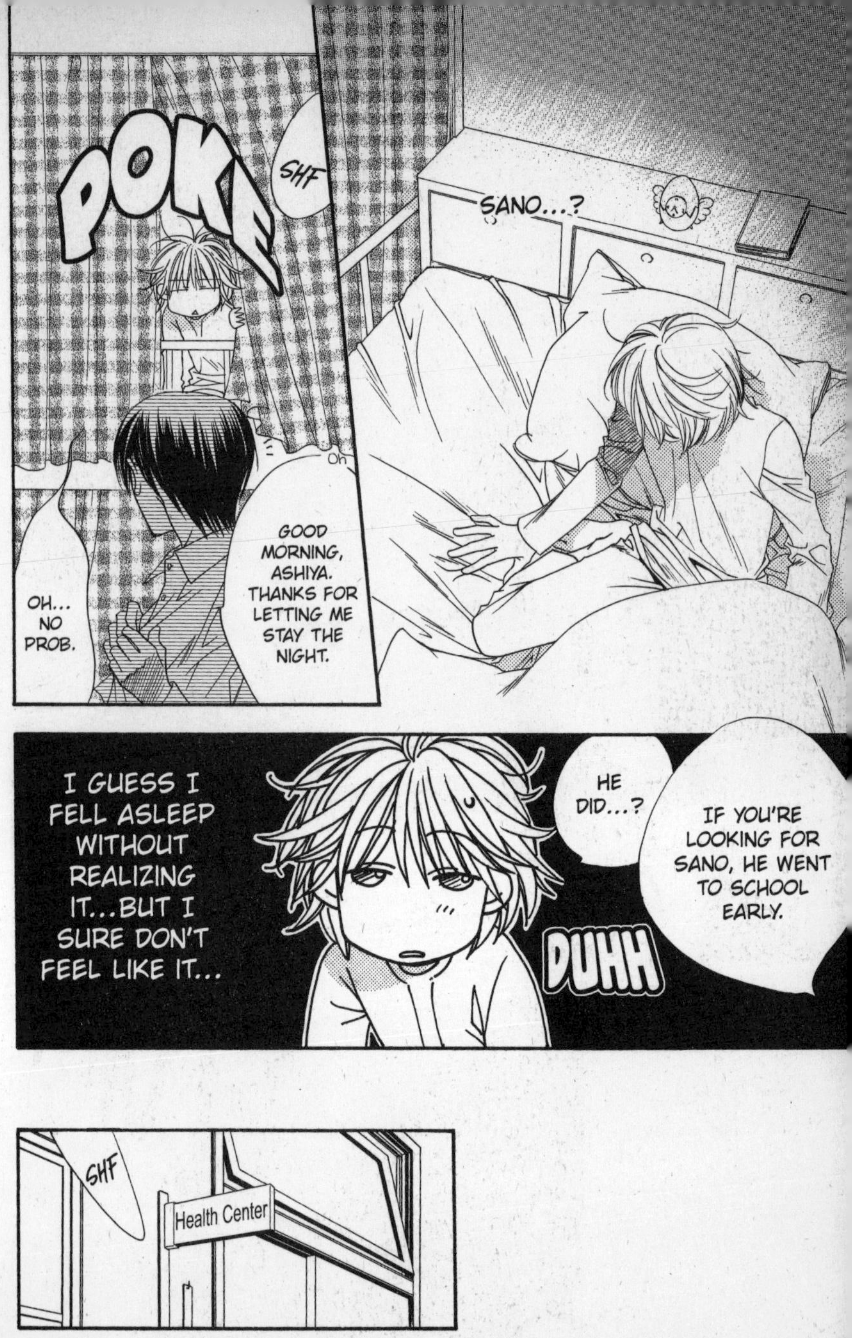

SANO...?
SHF
POKE
Oh
GOOD MORNING, ASHIYA. THANKS FOR LETTING ME STAY THE NIGHT.
OH... NO PROB.
IF YOU'RE LOOKING FOR SANO, HE WENT TO SCHOOL EARLY.
HE DID...?
DUHH
I GUESS I FELL ASLEEP WITHOUT REALIZING IT...BUT I SURE DON'T FEEL LIKE IT...
SHF
Health Center

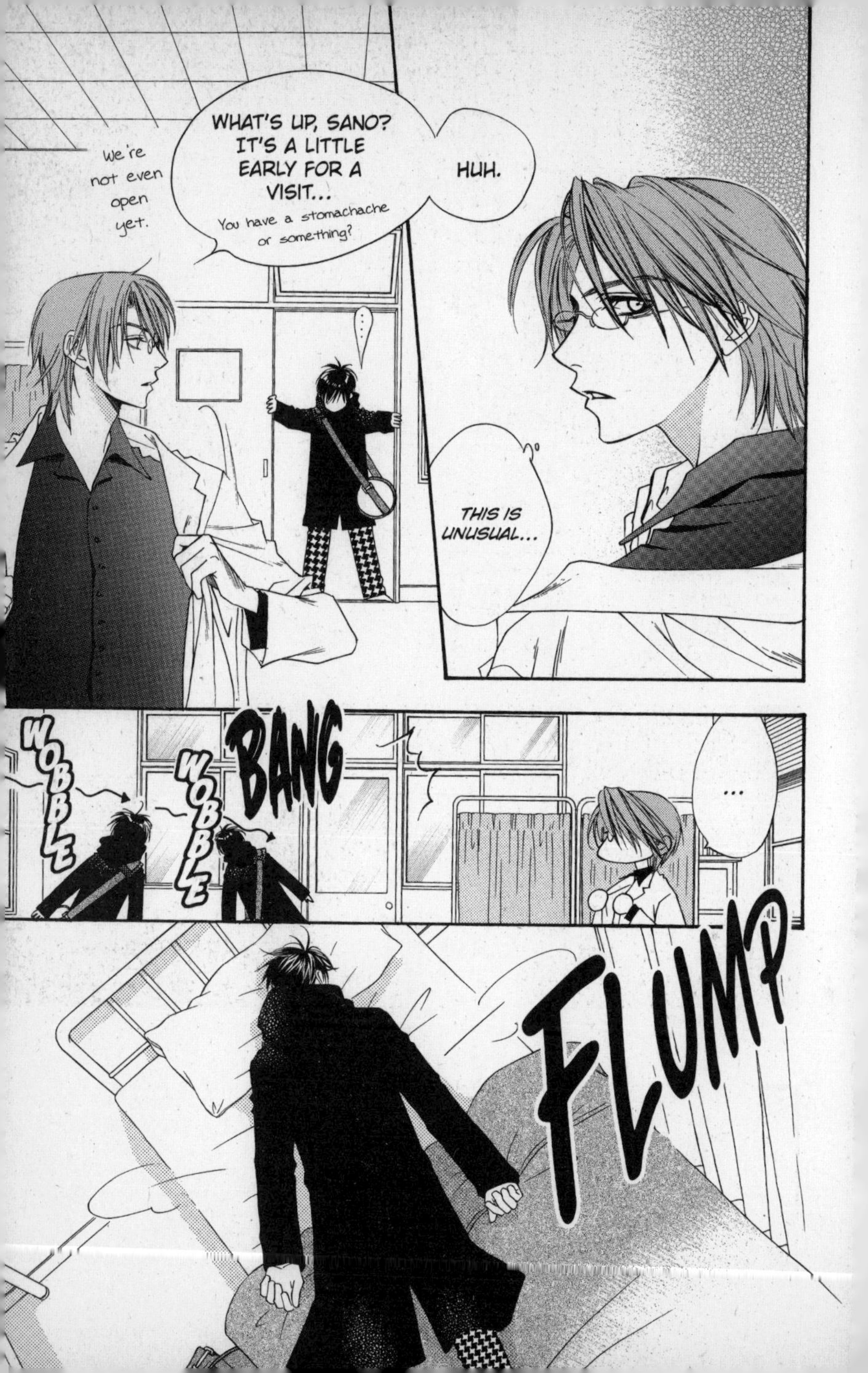
HUH.
THIS IS UNUSUAL...
WHAT'S UP, SANO? IT'S A LITTLE EARLY FOR A VISIT...
You have a stomachache or something?
We're not even open yet.
...
...
BANG
WOBBLE
WOBBLE
FLUMP

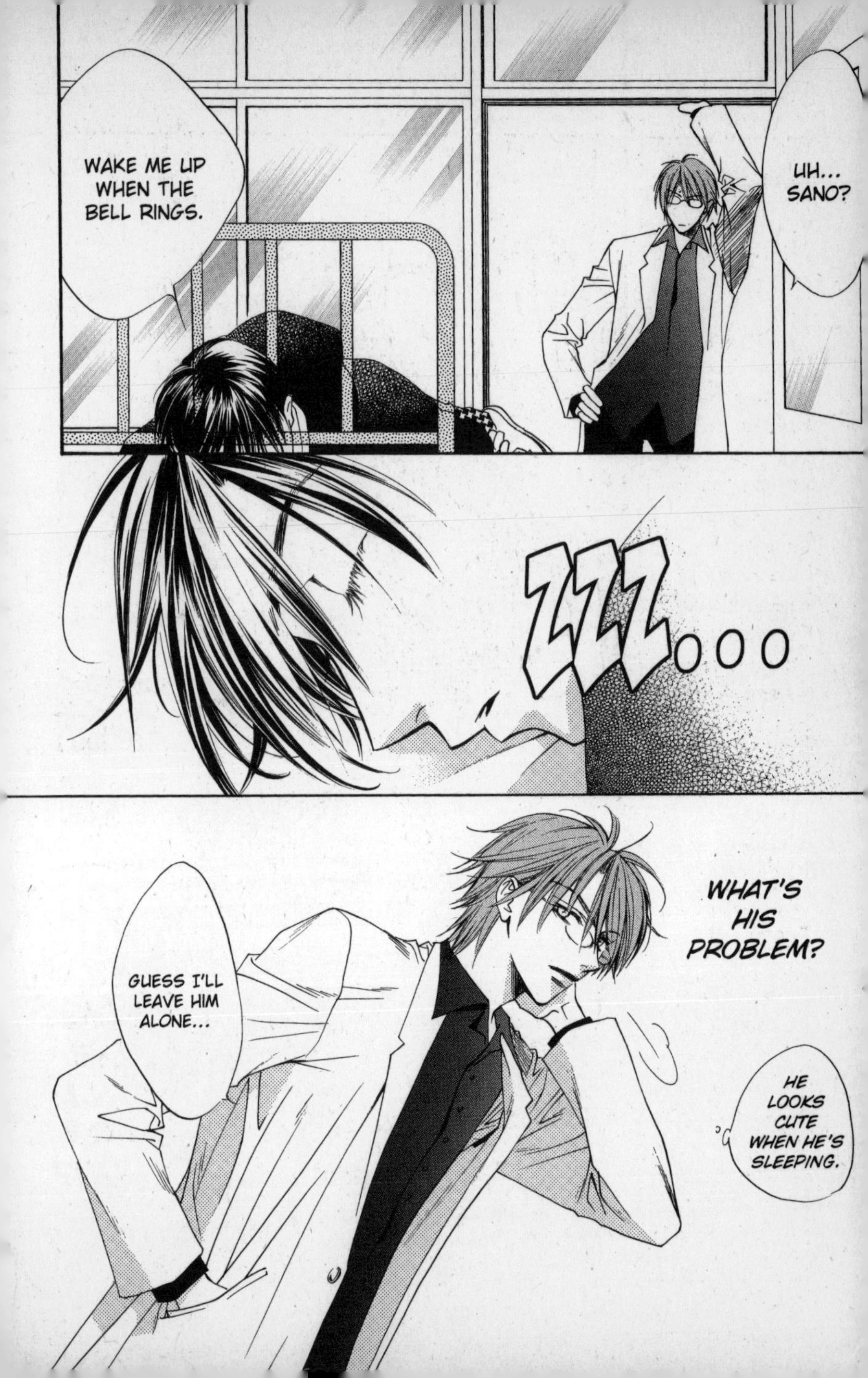
UH... SANO?
WAKE ME UP WHEN THE BELL RINGS.
ZZZ...
WHAT'S HIS PROBLEM?
GUESS I'LL LEAVE HIM ALONE...
HE LOOKS CUTE WHEN HE'S SLEEPING.

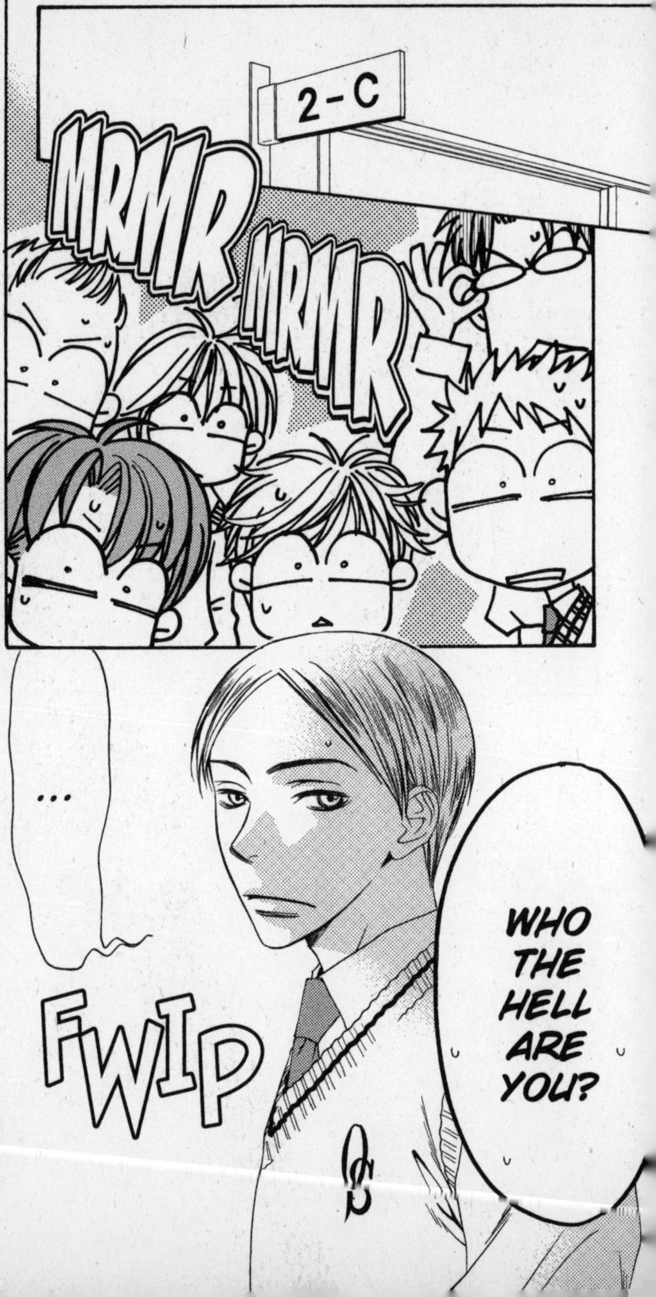
2-C
MRMR
MRMR
...
FWIP
WHO THE HELL ARE YOU?

HOWDY

Okay, this is the last quarter page in the book. I had so many of them this time, I was running out of things to write. Ahh?

The next book will be number 20 (waagh)! I'll try to make it a good one.

See you in volume 20!

10.2002

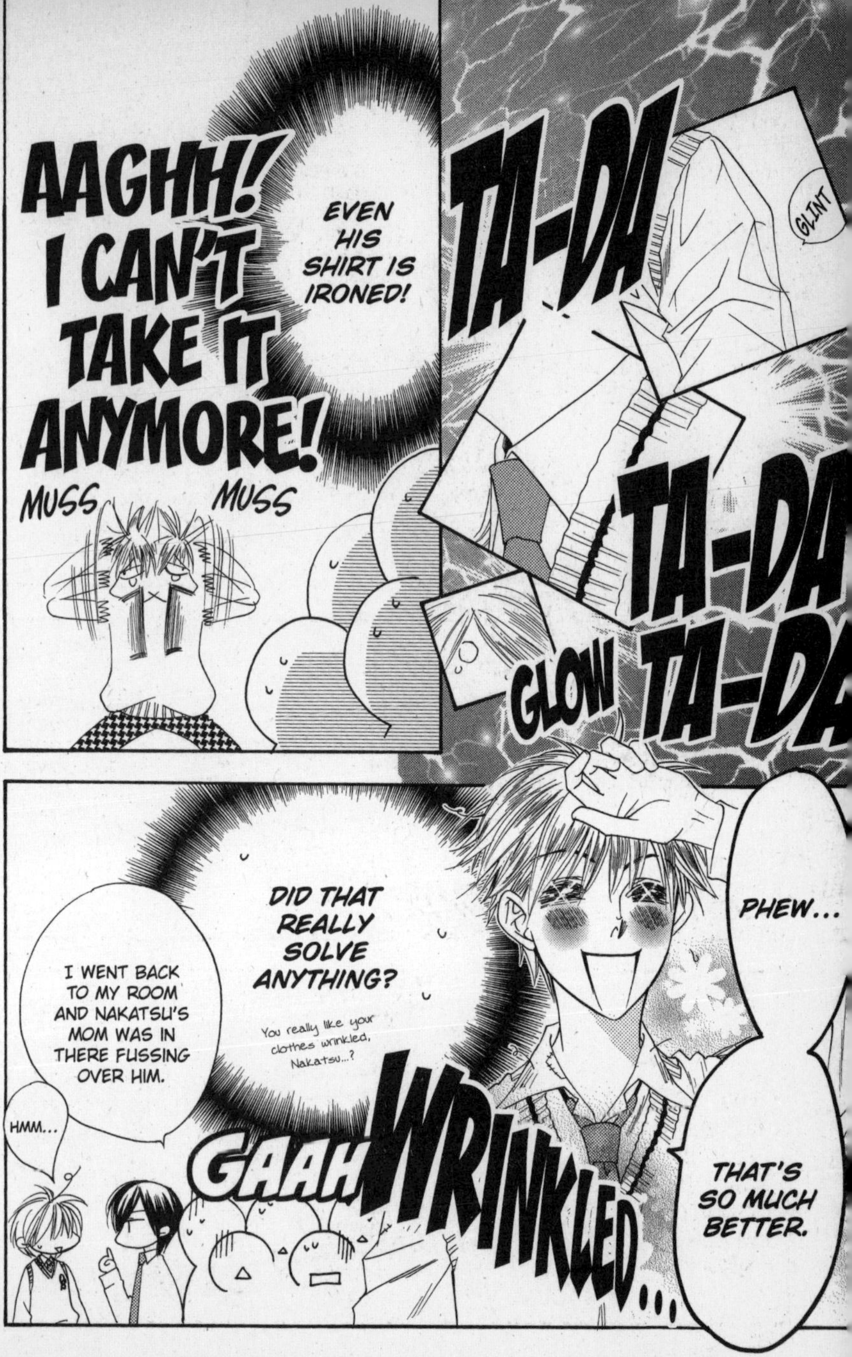
TA-DA
GLINT
TA-DA
TA-DA
GLOW
EVEN HIS SHIRT IS IRONED!
AAGHH! I CAN'T TAKE IT ANYMORE!
MUSS
MUSS
PHEW...
THAT'S SO MUCH BETTER.
WRINKLED...
GAAH
DID THAT REALLY SOLVE ANYTHING?
You really like your clothes wrinkled, Nakatsu...?
I WENT BACK TO MY ROOM AND NAKATSU'S MOM WAS IN THERE FUSSING OVER HIM.
HMM...

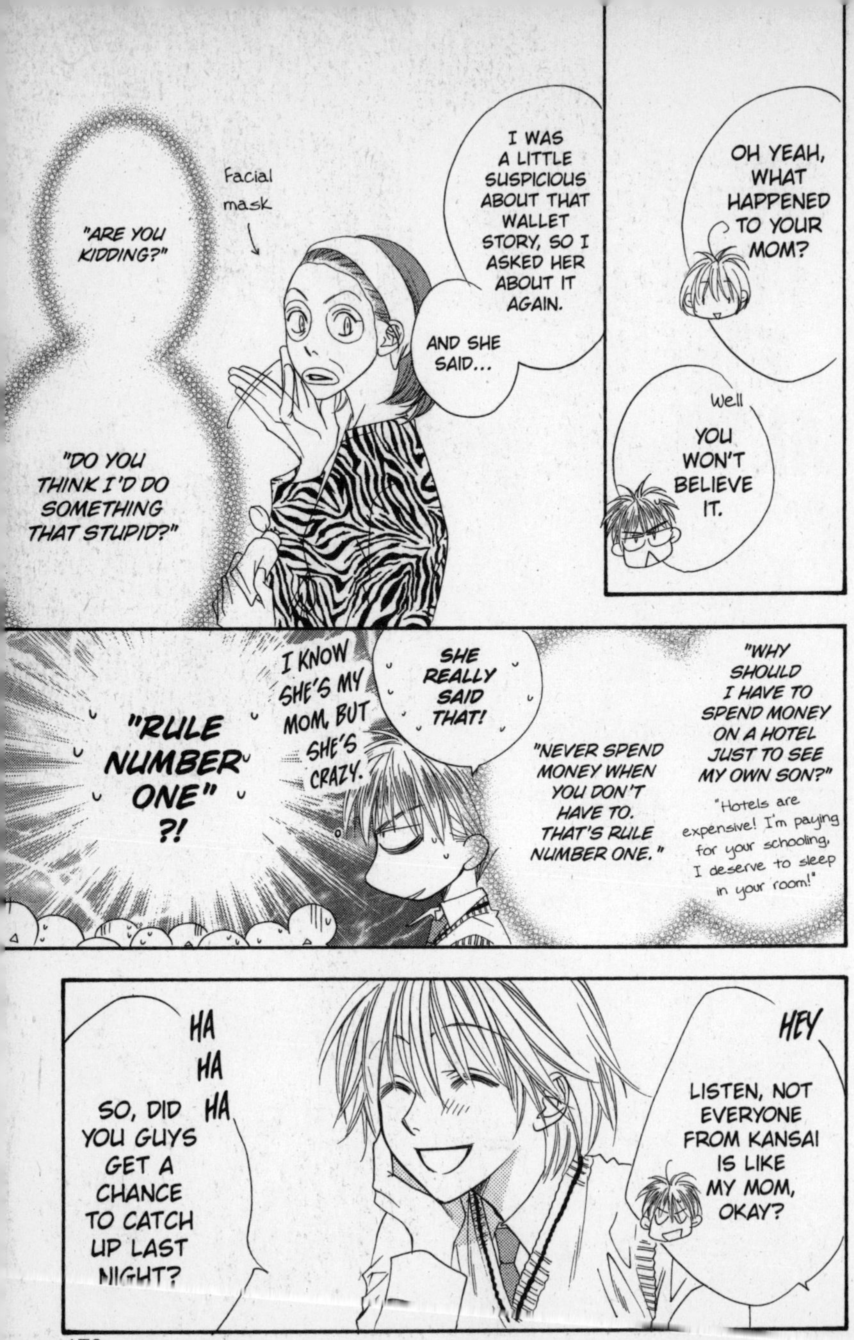
OH YEAH, WHAT HAPPENED TO YOUR MOM?
Well
YOU WON'T BELIEVE IT.
I WAS A LITTLE SUSPICIOUS ABOUT THAT WALLET STORY, SO I ASKED HER ABOUT IT AGAIN.
AND SHE SAID...
Facial mask
"ARE YOU KIDDING?"
"DO YOU THINK I'D DO SOMETHING THAT STUPID?"
"WHY SHOULD I HAVE TO SPEND MONEY ON A HOTEL JUST TO SEE MY OWN SON?"
"Hotels are expensive! I'm paying for your schooling, I deserve to sleep in your room!"
"NEVER SPEND MONEY WHEN YOU DON'T HAVE TO. THAT'S RULE NUMBER ONE."
SHE REALLY SAID THAT!
I KNOW SHE'S MY MOM, BUT SHE'S CRAZY.
"RULE NUMBER ONE" ?!
HEY
LISTEN, NOT EVERYONE FROM KANSAI IS LIKE MY MOM, OKAY?
HA HA HA
SO, DID YOU GUYS GET A CHANCE TO CATCH UP LAST NIGHT?

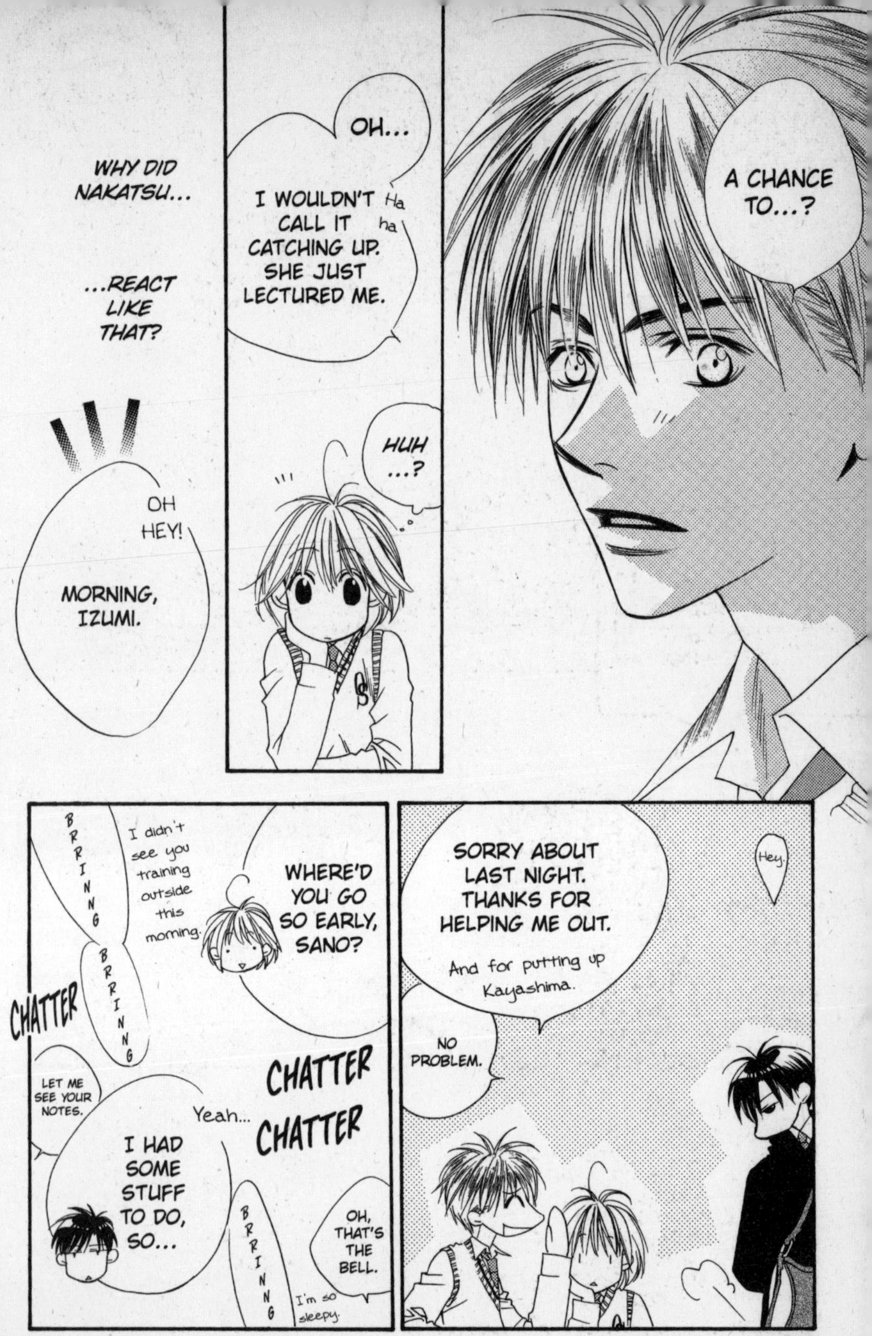
A CHANCE TO...?
OH...
I WOULDN'T CALL IT CATCHING UP. SHE JUST LECTURED ME.
Ha ha
HUH ...?
WHY DID NAKATSU...
...REACT LIKE THAT?
OH HEY!
MORNING, IZUMI.
Hey.
SORRY ABOUT LAST NIGHT. THANKS FOR HELPING ME OUT.
And for putting up Kayashima.
NO PROBLEM.
WHERE'D YOU GO SO EARLY, SANO?
I didn't see you training outside this morning.
BRRING
BRRING
CHATTER
CHATTER
CHATTER
LET ME SEE YOUR NOTES.
Yeah...
I HAD SOME STUFF TO DO, SO...
BRRING
OH, THAT'S THE BELL.
I'm so sleepy.

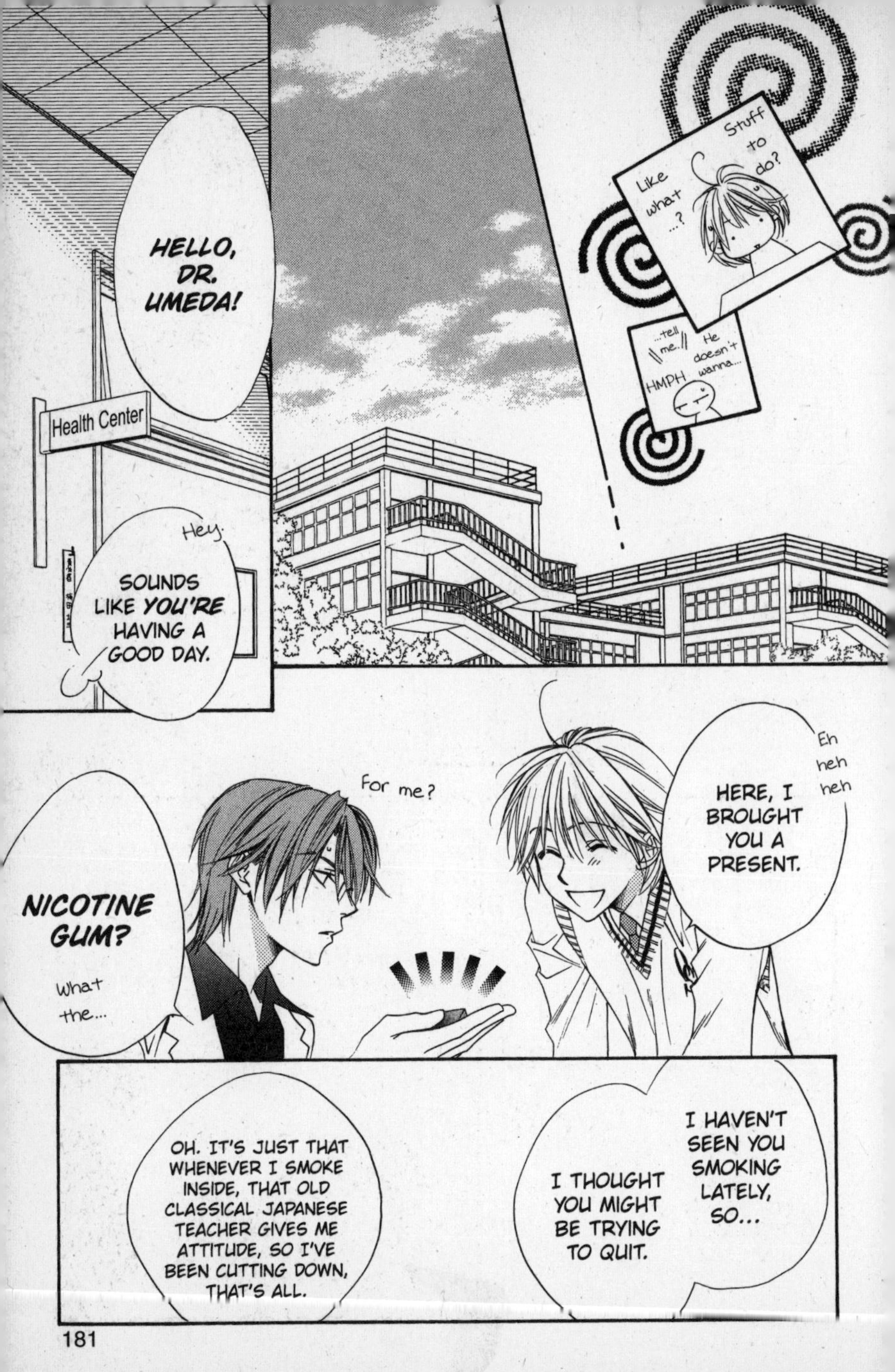
Stuff to do?
Like what ...?
He doesn't wanna... ...tell me..
HMPH
HELLO, DR. UMEDA!
Health Center
Hey.
SOUNDS LIKE YOU'RE HAVING A GOOD DAY.
Eh heh heh
HERE, I BROUGHT YOU A PRESENT.
For me?
NICOTINE GUM?
What the...
I HAVEN'T SEEN YOU SMOKING LATELY, SO...
I THOUGHT YOU MIGHT BE TRYING TO QUIT.
OH. IT'S JUST THAT WHENEVER I SMOKE INSIDE, THAT OLD CLASSICAL JAPANESE TEACHER GIVES ME ATTITUDE, SO I'VE BEEN CUTTING DOWN, THAT'S ALL.

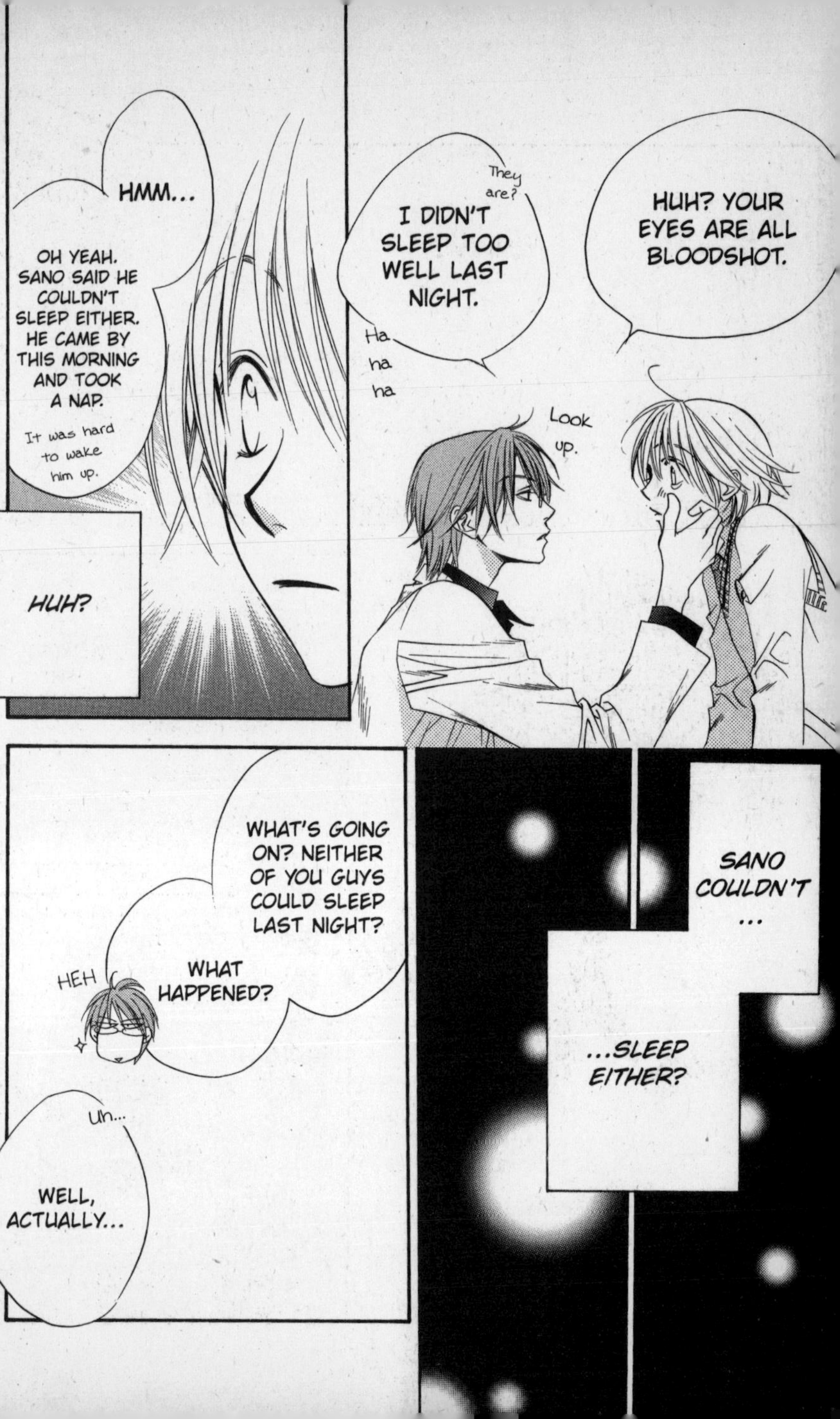
HUH? YOUR EYES ARE ALL BLOODSHOT.
They are?
I DIDN'T SLEEP TOO WELL LAST NIGHT.
Look up.
Ha ha ha
HMM...
OH YEAH. SANO SAID HE COULDN'T SLEEP EITHER. HE CAME BY THIS MORNING AND TOOK A NAP.
It was hard to wake him up.
HUH?
SANO COULDN'T ...
...SLEEP EITHER?
WHAT'S GOING ON? NEITHER OF YOU GUYS COULD SLEEP LAST NIGHT?
WHAT HAPPENED?
HEH
Uh...
WELL, ACTUALLY...

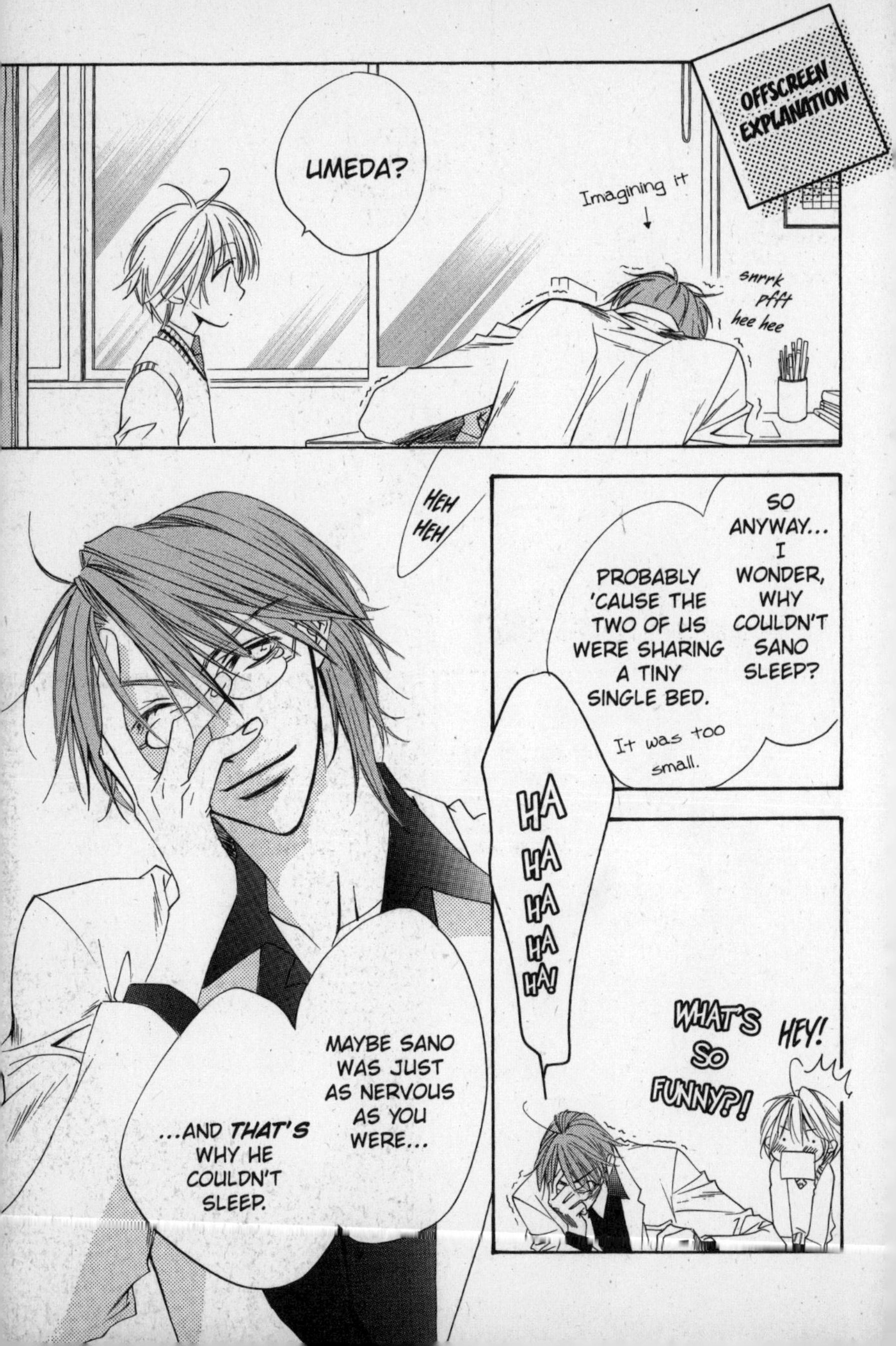
OFFSCREEN EXPLANATION
Imagining it
snrrk pfft hee hee
UMEDA?
SO ANYWAY... I WONDER, WHY COULDN'T SANO SLEEP?
PROBABLY 'CAUSE THE TWO OF US WERE SHARING A TINY SINGLE BED.
It was too small.
HEY!
WHAT'S SO FUNNY?!
HEH HEH
HA HA HA HA HA HA!
MAYBE SANO WAS JUST AS NERVOUS AS YOU WERE...
...AND THAT'S WHY HE COULDN'T SLEEP.

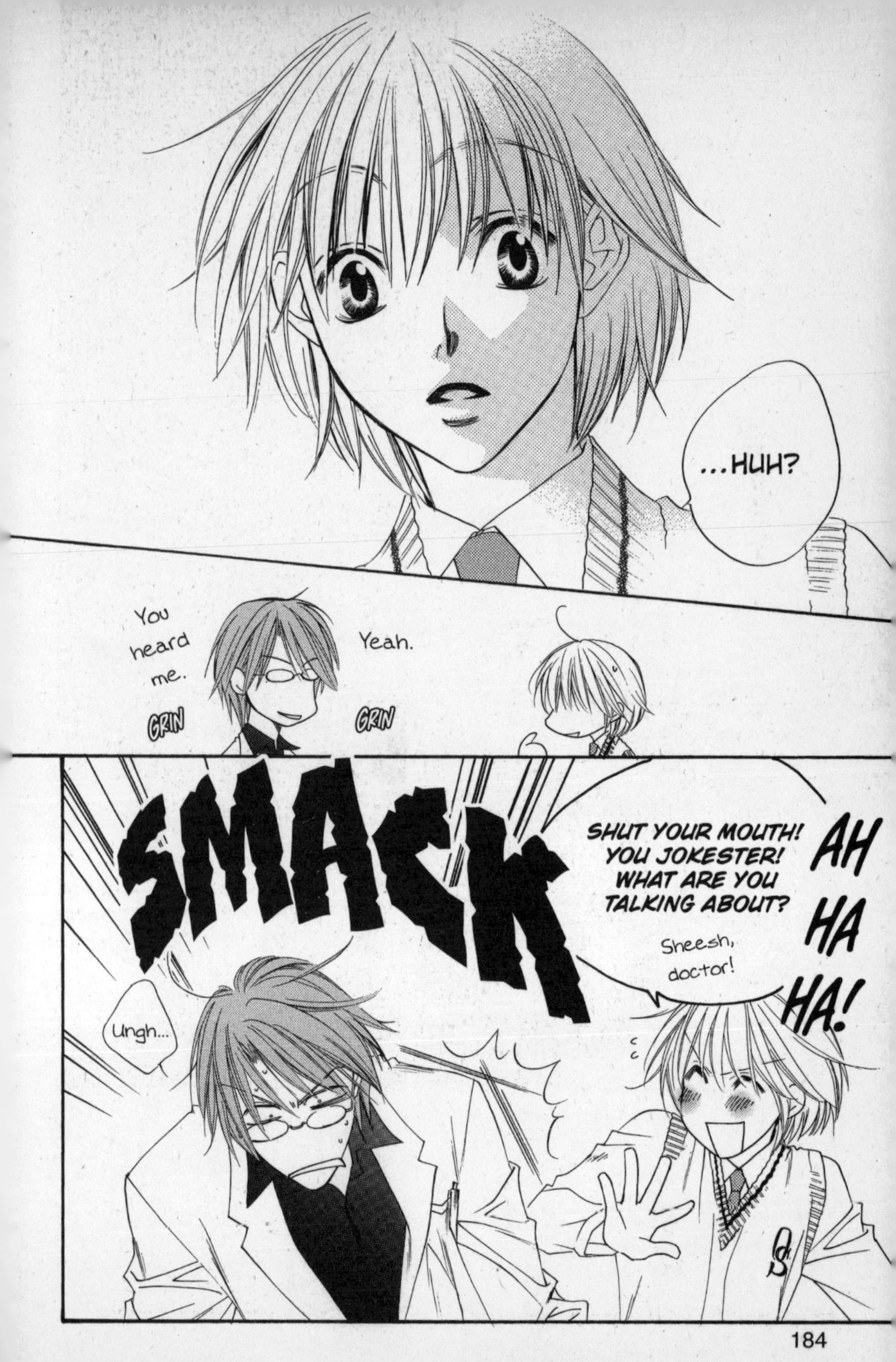

...HUH?
Yeah.
GRIN
You heard me.
GRIN
AH HA HA!
SHUT YOUR MOUTH! YOU JOKESTER! WHAT ARE YOU TALKING ABOUT?
Sheesh, doctor!
SMACK
Ungh...

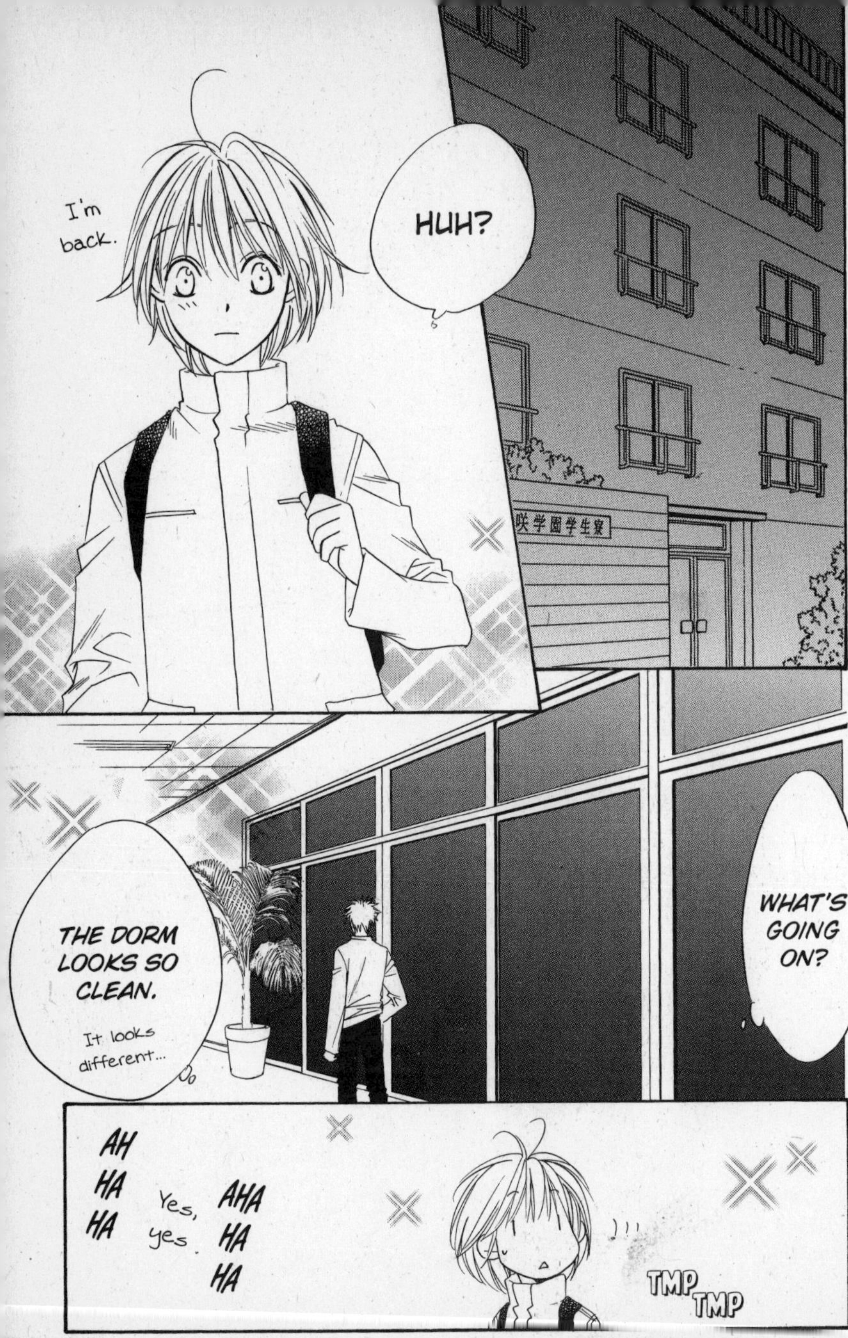

咲学園学生寮
HUH?
I'm back.
WHAT'S GOING ON?
THE DORM LOOKS SO CLEAN.
It looks different...
TMP TMP
AHA HA HA
Yes, yes.
AH HA HA

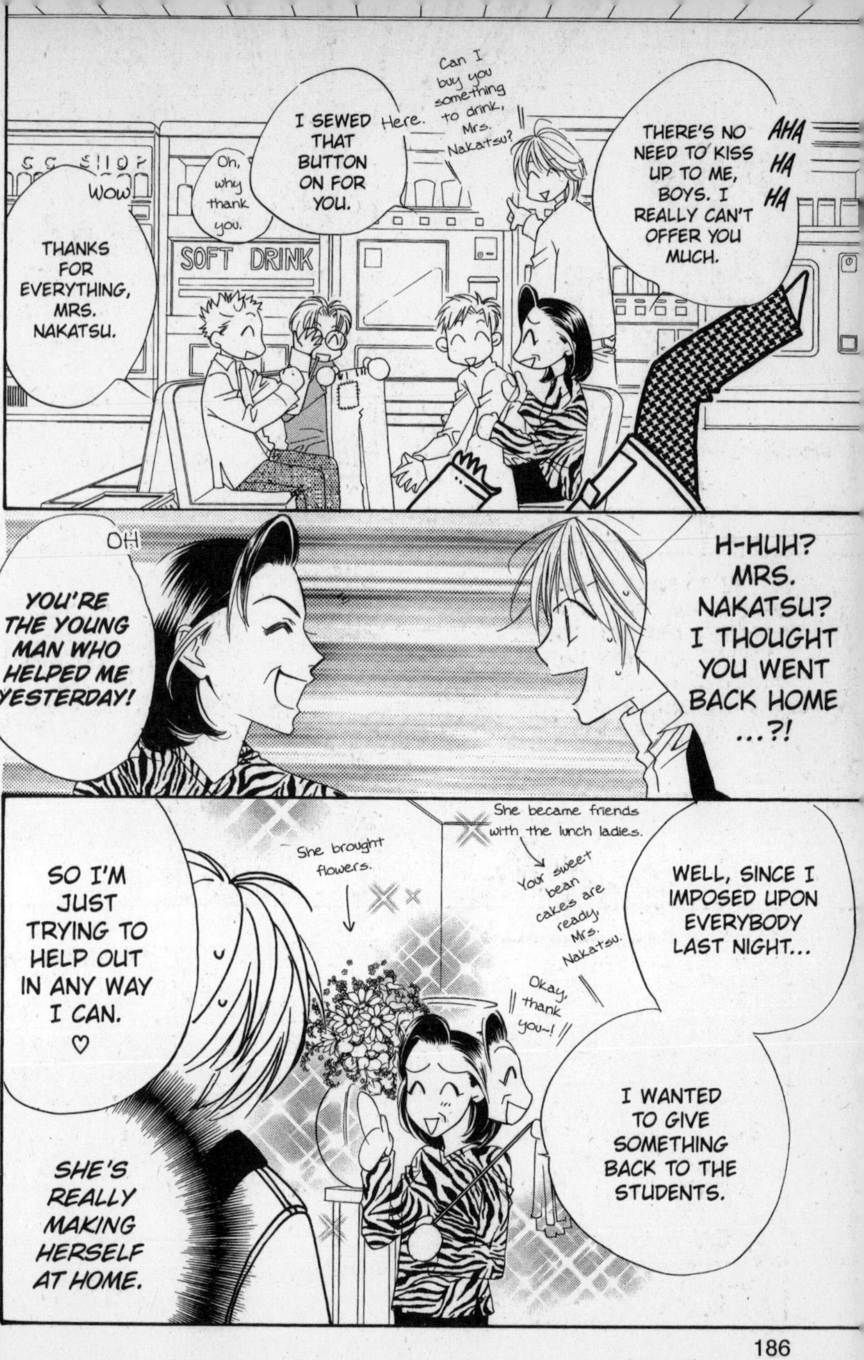
THERE'S NO NEED TO KISS UP TO ME, BOYS. I REALLY CAN'T OFFER YOU MUCH.
AHA HA HA
Can I buy you something to drink, Mrs. Nakatsu?
I SEWED THAT BUTTON ON FOR YOU.
Here.
Oh, why thank you.
SOFT DRINK
Wow
THANKS FOR EVERYTHING, MRS. NAKATSU.
H-HUH? MRS. NAKATSU? I THOUGHT YOU WENT BACK HOME ...?!
OH
YOU'RE THE YOUNG MAN WHO HELPED ME YESTERDAY!
WELL, SINCE I IMPOSED UPON EVERYBODY LAST NIGHT...
I WANTED TO GIVE SOMETHING BACK TO THE STUDENTS.
She became friends with the lunch ladies.
Your sweet bean cakes are ready, Mrs. Nakatsu.
Okay, thank you~!
She brought flowers.
SO I'M JUST TRYING TO HELP OUT IN ANY WAY I CAN. ♡
SHE'S REALLY MAKING HERSELF AT HOME.

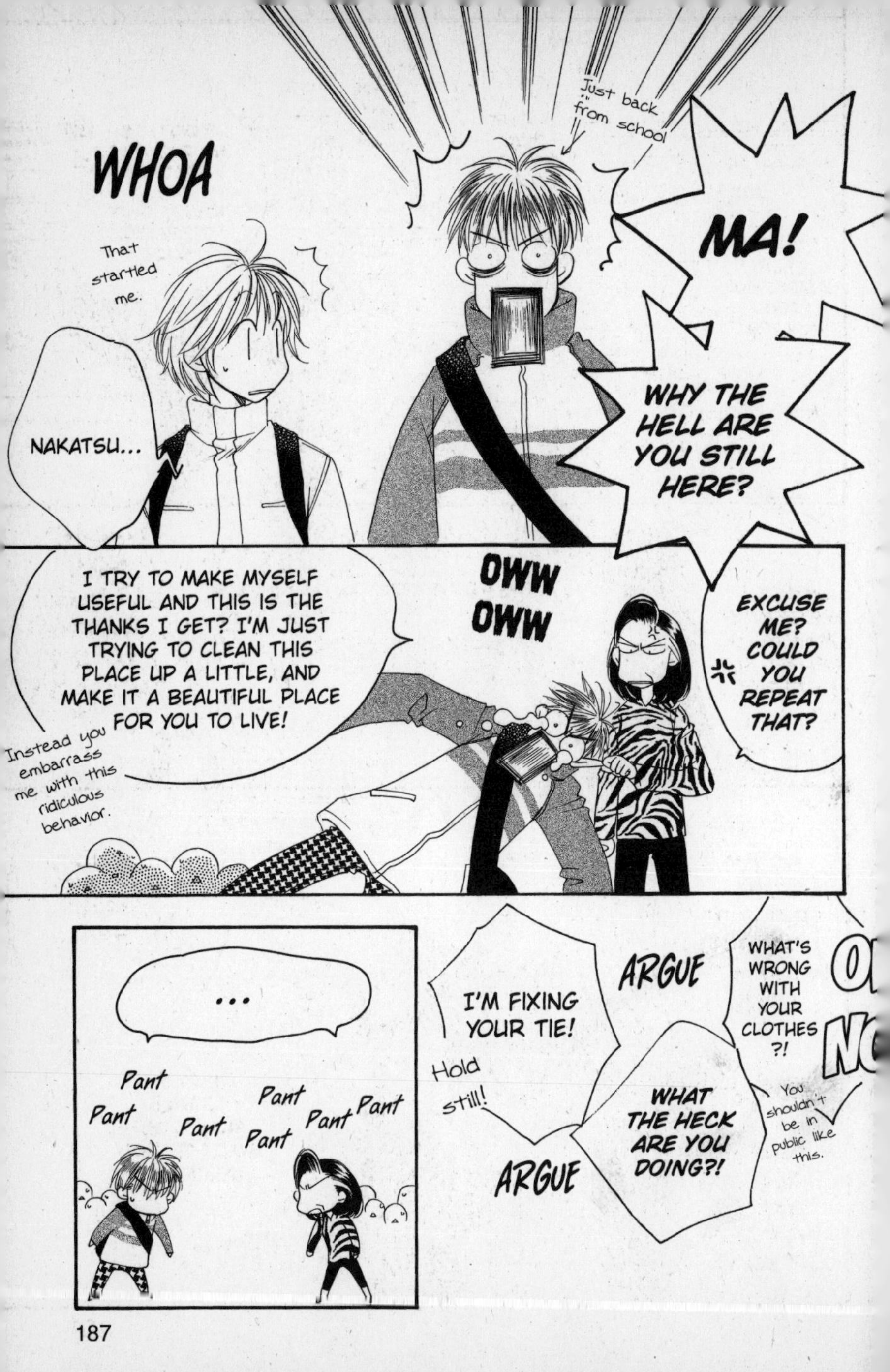
Just back from school
MA!
WHY THE HELL ARE YOU STILL HERE?
WHOA
That startled me.
NAKATSU...
EXCUSE ME? COULD YOU REPEAT THAT?
OWW OWW
I TRY TO MAKE MYSELF USEFUL AND THIS IS THE THANKS I GET? I'M JUST TRYING TO CLEAN THIS PLACE UP A LITTLE, AND MAKE IT A BEAUTIFUL PLACE FOR YOU TO LIVE!
Instead you embarrass me with this ridiculous behavior.
WHAT'S WRONG WITH YOUR CLOTHES?!
You shouldn't be in public like this.
ARGUE
I'M FIXING YOUR TIE!
WHAT THE HECK ARE YOU DOING?!
Hold still!
ARGUE
...
Pant
Pant
Pant
Pant
Pant
Pant
Pant

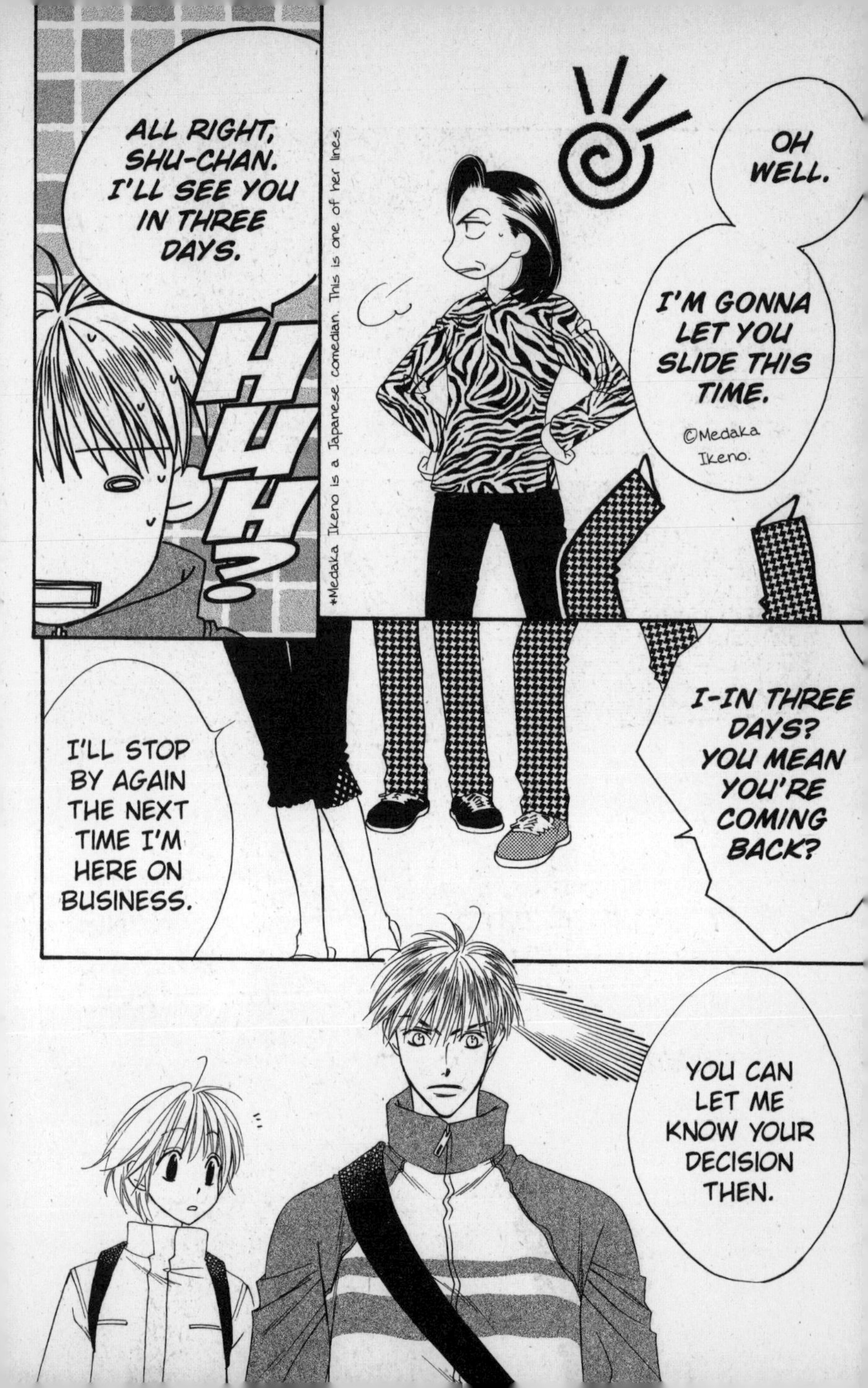
OH WELL.
I'M GONNA LET YOU SLIDE THIS TIME.
©Medaka Ikeno.
*Medaka Ikeno is a Japanese comedian. This is one of her lines.
ALL RIGHT, SHU-CHAN. I'LL SEE YOU IN THREE DAYS.
HUH?
I-IN THREE DAYS? YOU MEAN YOU'RE COMING BACK?
I'LL STOP BY AGAIN THE NEXT TIME I'M HERE ON BUSINESS.
YOU CAN LET ME KNOW YOUR DECISION THEN.

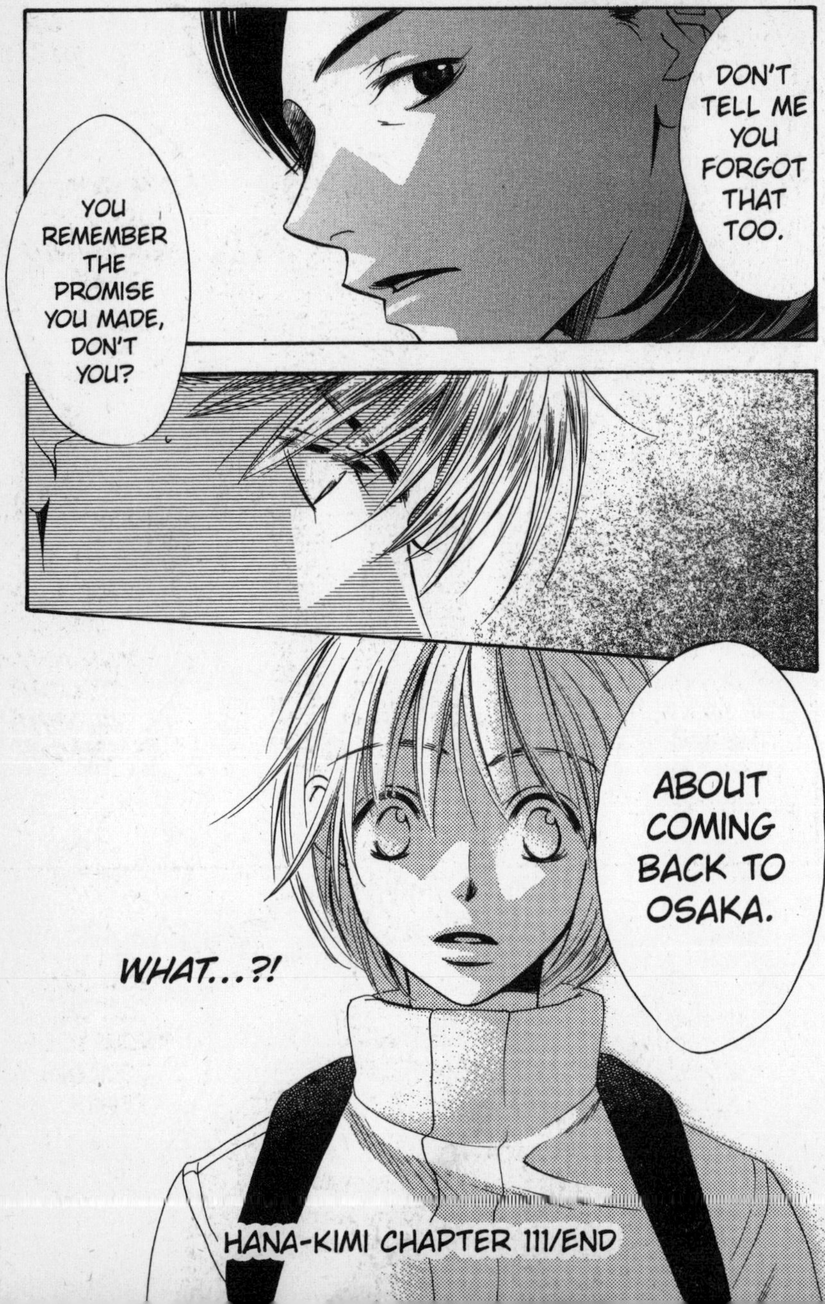
DON'T TELL ME YOU FORGOT THAT TOO.
YOU REMEMBER THE PROMISE YOU MADE, DON'T YOU?
ABOUT COMING BACK TO OSAKA.
WHAT...?!
HANA-KIMI CHAPTER 111/END

Now available!

HANA-KIMI DRAMA CD 2

On sale 8/23/2002

MAIN DRAMA:
HANA-KIMI
CHAPTERS 74-76
(THE "DORM
SWITCHING" STORY)

2,800¥
(TAX
INCLUDED)

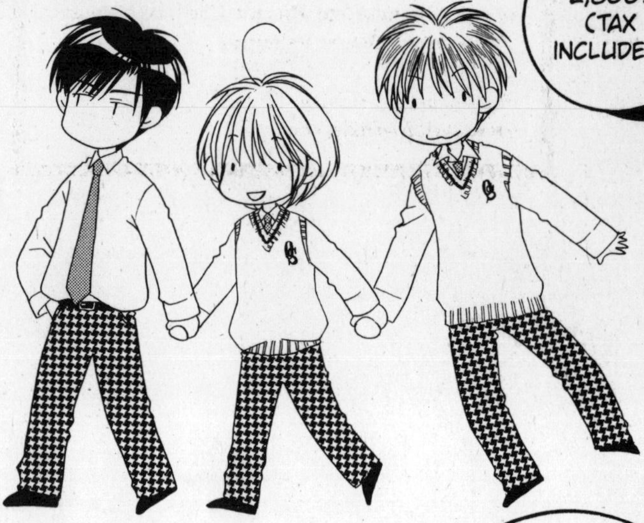

BONUS MINI DRAMA 1: "THE TRUTH ABOUT THE *KAÔKAI* (CHERRY BLOSSOM ALLIANCE)"

Cast

Mizuki Ashiya – Hoko Kuwashima
Izumi Sano – Atsushi Kisaichi
Shuichi Nakatsu – Shotaro Morikubo
Minami Nanba – Shinichiro Miki
Masao Himejima – Takehito Koyasu
Hokuto Umeda – Kazuya Ichijou
Megumi Tennoji – Toshiyuki Morikawa
Isuki Kujo - Ryotaro Okiayu
Shotaro Kadoma – Yuka Imai
Senri Nakao – Chiharu Tezuka
Taiki Kayashima – Kenichiro Ito
Shinji Noe – Hiroyuki Yoshino

BONUS MINI DRAMA 2: "KAYASHIMA'S SCARY STORIES"

(Unfortunately, this CD was only available in Japan and was never translated. Sorry, English speakers!) ♡

ABOUT THE AUTHOR

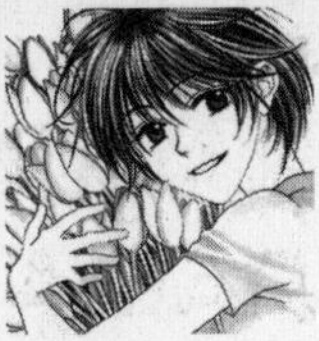

Hisaya Nakajo's manga series **Hanazakari no Kimitachi he** (For You in Full Blossom, casually known as **Hana-Kimi**) has been a hit since it first appeared in 1997 in the shôjo manga magazine **Hana to Yume** (Flowers and Dreams). In Japan, two **Hana-Kimi** art books and several "drama CDs" have been released. Her other manga series include **Missing Piece** (2 volumes), **Yumemiru Happa** (The Dreaming Leaf, 1 volume) and **Sugar Princess**.

Hisaya Nakajo's website:
www.wild-vanilla.com

IN THE NEXT VOLUME...

Will Nakatsu give up his dreams of soccer stardom to take care of the family business? Meanwhile, Nakao prepares to risk everything for his dreams...by confessing his love to Minami!

花ざかりの君たちへ

第115話

COMING OCTOBER 2007!